Building a New American State

The Expansion of National Administrative
Capacities, 1877–1920

D0874951

To my parents
Sidney and Esther Skowronek

Building a New American State

The Expansion of National Administrative Capacities, 1877–1920

STEPHEN SKOWRONEK

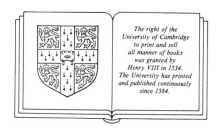

CAMBRIDGE UNIVERSITY PRESS

Cambridge

New York   Port Chester

Melbourne   Sydney

Published by the Press Syndicate of the University of Cambridge
The Pitt Building, Trumpington Street, Cambridge CB2 1RP
40 West 20th Street, New York, NY 10011, USA
10 Stamford Road, Oakleigh, Melbourne 3166, Australia

First published 1982
Reprinted 1984, 1987, 1988, 1990

Printed in the United States of America

Library of Congress Cataloging in Publication Data
Skowronek, Stephen
Building a new American state.
1. United States – Politics and government – 1865–1933.
I. Title.
JK231.S55   353'.0009   81-15225   AACR2

ISBN 0-521-23022-5 hardback
ISBN 0-521-28865-7 paperback

Contents

v

Contents

Preface

Professional social science has traditionally played the part of a protagonist in the expansion of American national government. Academics have been advocates of national administrative development in theory, and they have attached themselves to institution builders in practice. During the past decade, however, self-confident advocacy gave way to uncertainty and despair. The 1970s brought a set of governing problems that challenged the foundations of our politics and our institutional arrangements. As new directions in public policy appeared imperative, we were compelled to ask whether the government could be turned around or whether it had grown beyond control.

The answers offered little room for optimism. We were told that the burden on the modern presidency had become more than the office could bear, that the opportunities for effective leadership were few and fleeting. We were told that the resilience of Congress meant the eclipse of central direction and coordination in the affairs of state. We were told that the courts had lost all sense of their proper role, that our parties were impotent as instruments of government, that a headless bureaucracy had taken center stage in governmental operations, leaving constitutional authorities to jockey around it for positions of advantage.

As the structure of the modern American state clouded the future, it suggested new questions to ask about the past. Were there any parallels in American history to this situation? Had an established structure of political and institutional power ever before appeared so out of step with governing demands? Had the state itself ever before come under such severe attack as the greatest obstacle to effective government? If so, what happened then? How did it happen? What is the significance of what happened?

The first of these questions led me back to the late nineteenth century. There, more clearly than in any other period, I found another set of governing problems that challenged the established foundations of our national politics and institutions. In this book, I have tried to come to terms with the dynamics of the reconstruction of American national government that ensued. The title of the book is intended to focus attention on the systemic changes in long-established political and institutional arrangements that first had to be negotiated in order to begin to accommodate an expansion of national administrative capacities in American government. My purpose is twofold: first, to comprehend this change in government as a rather remarkable achievement in political reform claiming a special place in the comparative study of state development; second, to identify in this change the historical origins of modern institutional politics in America, a politics distinguished by incoherence and fragmentation in governmental operations and by the absence of clear lines of authoritative control.

Underlying the analysis of America's reform achievement and its limitations is a general perspective on the developmental process of state building. My research convinced me early on of the inadequacy of approaching state building as the natural and adaptive reaction of governments to changing conditions. It is my contention that American institutional development between 1877 and 1920 was not simply a gradual accretion of appropriate governmental responses to environmental problems. The functionalist formulation not only distorts the history of reform, it mistakes the achievement and ignores the limitations of modern American state building.

Of course, we are not lacking in alternative sources of insight into the problems and processes of American state development. The neo-Marxists have suggested that American state development is framed by an ongoing struggle to reconcile political democracy with support for the private economy.[1] Students of the crisis-sequence school of political development have called attention to America's peculiar state-building sequence: the development of a high level of popular participation in politics before the development of institutional penetration from and control at the center of government.[2] From the study of American electoral politics, we have evolved a general theory of American political development based upon periodic electoral realignments. The theory of critical elections posits that the process of development in America has not been uniform over time but sporadic, with a particular electoral configuration delimiting the makeup of the governing elite, the agenda of political issues, and the opportunities for institutional innovation.[3]

The reader will see that I have drawn a great deal from each of these sources. Ultimately, however, they turned out to be only the important points of departure. None of them directly addressed what I perceived to be the critical developmental problem at issue in Progressive state building: the regeneration of government through political reform. To highlight that problem, one additional consideration had to be brought to the fore: Short of revolutionary change, state building is most basically an exercise in reconstructing an already established organization of state power. Success hinges on recasting official power relationships within governmental institutions and on altering ongoing relations between state and society.

The premise of this book is that states change (or fail to change) through political struggles rooted in and mediated by preestablished institutional arrangements. From this starting point, the analysis focuses attention on the structure of the preestablished regime, the struggle for political power and institutional position that it frames, and the disjunction in time between environmental changes and new governing arrangements. Such factors do not simply complicate the notion of state building as functional adaptation; they ultimately confound that notion altogether. By demanding consideration of the organization of state power itself, this perspective alters our understanding of the state-building problem, the state-building process, and the state-building achievement.

Today we face the possibility of change once again. Students of American government are already looking beyond a tradition of advocacy and a decade of despair in search of new approaches to their subject. But, at present, the governmental problems that stood out so clearly in the 1970s are not easily dismissed, and the shape of a new order is by no means clear. The time is ripe to return to beginnings. In doing so, we may not only reassess the process of governmental change in America; we may also begin to consider how the governmental problems of the 1970s are linked to the governmental problems of the 1870s and how the reform challenge now before us is linked to the reform solutions of the past.

Many people have given generously of their time and energy for this project. They should share in the credit for whatever merit is to be found in it, and I am happy to acknowledge their contributions.

First and foremost, I am indebted to my teachers and advisors in the Government Department at Cornell University. Isaac Kramnick, Theodore Lowi, and Sidney Tarrow guided me through five years of graduate training. Working with them, I found the inspiration for this study. In the process of turning the idea into a dissertation, they offered more than is easily summarized. Perhaps most important of all, they did not push me to choose among political theory, American government, and comparative politics; instead they illuminated the research agendas that lie at the interfaces of these subfields.

Others at Cornell helped me fit the pieces together. Eldon Eisenach, now at the University of Arkansas, alerted me to the subtleties of Ameri-

can political thought. Peter Katzenstein gave me my first sense of the
state. Martin Shefter spent hours sharing with me his insight into American political development. Had I been able to match his support and
encouragement with more careful attention to his comments and criti-
cisms, the book would doubtlessly have been greatly improved.

Martha Derthick of the Brookings Institution was gracious enough to
find me a desk to come back to while I was roaming the libraries and
archives of Washington, D.C. It was through her shoebox of notes on the
National Guard that I developed my interest in army reform. Theda
Skocpol of the University of Chicago took an early interest in the manuscript and provided penetrating comments at several stages in its evolution. I also benefited from thorough reading by James Fesler of Yale
University, Karen Orren of UCLA, Louis Galambos of Johns Hopkins
University, and J. David Greenstone of the University of Chicago.

I am grateful to the Academic Senate of UCLA for much needed financial support and to my colleagues in the UCLA Political Science Department for the time and the encouragement that they gave me. Elizabeth
Skewes, John Queen, Cynthia Hody, David Anderson, and Monica Sena
provided critical readings and excellent research assistance. Claretta
Walker, Nancy Gusten, and Lila Merritt typed a seemingly endless series
of revisions with proficiency and care.

Finally, I would like to thank Susan Jacobs for her patience, her love,
and her sense of humor.

Los Angeles   S.S.
July 1981

PART I

The state-building problem in American political development

1

The new state and American political development

A "sense of the state" pervades contemporary American politics. It is the sense of an organization of coercive power operating beyond our immediate control and intruding into all aspects of our lives. We have labeled this organization an *administrative state,* a *bureaucratic state,* a *capitalist state,* a *corporate state,* a *postindustrial state,* a *regulatory state,* a *welfare state,* but we have yet to consider the grand historical irony that lingers behind these labels. After all, it is the absence of a sense of the state that has been the great hallmark of American political culture.

Our sense of the state mocks all that seemed to set the American system of government apart as something different. If we are finally to come to terms with the state in America, we will need more than a list of its generic characteristics; we will need a reassessment of the significance of our distinctive past. By defining the American state in terms of the traits it now shares with others, we have merely replaced the old image of "America, the exception" with an image of "America, the symptom." The American state itself remains a historical enigma.

This is a study of American state building. It attempts to illuminate the connection between our exceptional past and our present condition. It argues that the exceptional character of government in early America presented a knotty problem in American political development around the turn of the twentieth century and that this developmental problem shaped the character of the modern American state. Unraveling the state-building problem in modern American political development places the apparent statelessness of early America in a new light and makes the past a valuable source of insight into the ominous organization of power we are so conscious of today.

3

America's state-building problem will be traced through institutional innovations forged around the turn of the century. The innovations chosen for study encompass the reform of civil administration, the reorganization of the army, and the establishment of national railroad regulation. These were selected because any given state can be readily identified by its civil service, its army, and its regulation of the economy. The changes that can be observed concurrently across these three institutional realms reveal a systemic transformation of American state organization. Taken together, they mark the pivotal turn away from a state organization that presumed the absence of extensive institutional controls at the national level toward a state organized around national administrative capacities.

Generally speaking, the expansion of national administrative capacities in America around the turn of the century was a response to industrialism. The construction of a central bureaucratic apparatus was championed as the best way to maintain order during this period of upheaval in economic, social, and international affairs. Viewed at this level, the American experience fits a general pattern of institutional development and rationalization in public administration. Indeed, specific and contemporaneous parallels can be found throughout the rapidly industrializing Western states for each of the administrative innovations to be examined here.

At a deeper level, however, our administrative response to industrialism stands apart and deserves special attention. In America, the modernization of national administrative controls did not entail making the established state more efficient; it entailed building a qualitatively different kind of state. The path that had been traveled in the development of early American government did not anticipate the need for a strong national administrative arm. To embrace the cosmopolitan bureaucratic remedy in meeting new demands on government, America had to alter course and shed already well-articulated governing arrangements. The expansion of national administrative capacities in the age of industrialism became contingent on undermining the established structure of political and institutional power and on simultaneously forging an entirely new framework for governmental operations. The state that now supports so prominent a central bureaucracy is the product of this precarious politics of negotiating an internal governmental reconstruction.

Those who championed timely cosmopolitan departures in American administrative development around the turn of the century challenged the most basic political and institutional relationships defining powers and prerogatives within the established state apparatus. The analysis of state building presented here will focus on the struggles that ensued among government officials seeking to gain or maintain political power and institutional position as long-standing governmental arrangements were being thrown into question. These struggles were the critical factor intervening in and mediating our administrative response to industrialism. They kept the break with the old order suspended in institutional irresolution and political uncertainty at a time when unprecedented new demands for central control and direction were being pressed on the national government. Ultimately, the problems encountered in reconstructing American government internally affected the quality of the new relationships established between state and society in the industrial age.

Over the following pages, the modern American state will be traced to its origins in the unique developmental challenge that conditioned the rise of our modern bureaucratic apparatus. The distinguishing features of this state will be found in the specific forms new administrative institutions took, in the special place they claimed in the government as a whole, and in the peculiar problems officials faced in reestablishing a semblance of governmental order and political authority in their presence. The path taken in modern American institutional development has now fully eclipsed the sense of statelessness that so clearly marked our early politics, but that past was not without consequence for our present difficulties. Its impact is uncovered in the political and institutional struggles that attended the formation of the state in which we now live.

American exceptionalism and the study of state building

The problem of American state building in the industrial age was rooted in the exceptional character of the early American state. This preestablished governmental order was so peculiar that many have refused to consider it a state at all.[1] At base, however, early America maintained an integrated organization of institutions, procedures, and human talents whose specific purpose was to control the use of coercion within the national territory.[2] Rather than allowing the peculiarities of this organization to preempt consideration of early America as a state, it would seem more appropriate to treat these peculiarities as distinguishing marks of a particular state.

The exceptional character of the early American state is neatly summarized in the paradox that it failed to evoke any sense of a state. Implicit in this paradox is a set of comparisons between early American government and the European tradition. Indeed, the absence of a sense of the state in early America was carefully examined by European political theorists in the nineteenth century. From the key insights of three of these theorists – Tocqueville, Hegel, and Marx – we can construct a composite portrait of early America as the great anomaly among Western states. With this portrait, the significance of American exceptionalism for a study of state building can be brought into focus.

Tocqueville, of course, gave the most exhaustive account of the early American anomaly. Our most famous foreign visitor from the most renowned of European states observed that government in America functioned as an "invisible machine." A unified legal order was effectively maintained, but the distinction between state and society was blurred.[3] The official realm of government, so clearly demarcated in Europe, seemed to blend inconspicuously with American society.

Tocqueville traced this peculiarity directly to the early and full development of democracy in America. The absence of any readily apparent separation of the state from society at large was the result of America's "law of laws" – popular sovereignty.

> In some countries a power exists which, though it is in degree foreign to the social body, directs it, and forces it to pursue a certain tract. In others the ruling force is divided, being partly without the ranks of the people. But nothing of the kind is to be seen in the United States; there society governs itself for itself. All power centers in its bosom, and scarcely an individual is to be met with who would venture to conceive or, still less, to express the idea of seeking it elsewhere. The nation participates in the making of its laws by the choice of its legislators, and in the execution of them by the choice of agents of the executive government; it may also be said to govern itself, so feeble and so restricted is the share left to the administrators, so little do the authorities forget their popular origin and the power from which they emanate. The people reign in the American political world as the Deity does in the universe. They are the cause and the aim of all things; everything comes from them, and everything is absorbed in them.[4]

This relationship between the early development of democracy and the sense of statelessness characterizing our early government is nicely complemented by Hegel's perspective on America. Hegel refused to consider America a "Real State" because it had not developed the national governmental forms and orientations that distinguished the state realm in Europe. Specifically, there was no insulated bureaucratic class to give a distinct character to national administration and no hereditary monarchy to represent the permanent interest of the national community. There were no great national corporations or formal estates to sort out the major special interests in civil society and bring them to bear on these overarching institutions. There was also no national intellectual culture, rooted in a national church and attached to the state, that could raise individuals above their immediate concerns and express their cultural ideals. Lacking these, America was defined entirely by "the endeavor of the individual after acquisition, commercial profit, and gain; the preponderance of private interest devoting itself to that of the community only for its own advantage."[5]

The absence of the formal institutional arrangements that so clearly identified the European state was, for Hegel, directly related to the simplicity and isolation of early American society. There were no foreign enemies posing a threat to security, and internal social conflict could be diffused through movement to the frontier. In this remote nation, relations between society and government could remain direct, unmediated, and one-dimensional. The United States required no more than a "republican constitution" whose laws merely expressed the "subjective unity" of American social life. As far as Hegel was concerned, America was only a "land of the future." Until such time as the subjective unity of this society was threatened and the need for the higher form of unity offered by great national institutions became manifest, the United States would remain stateless.[6]

Although Hegel's institutional perspective provides a crucial element in a portrait of the early American anomaly, the absence of European state forms need not be equated with an undeveloped state. Indeed, Marx completely inverted this equation in the course of formulating his famous critique of Hegel. For Marx, the United States was "the most perfect example of the modern state."[7] It was the state of the most advanced class yet to come to political power. Early America presented, in purest form, the bourgeoisie's impulse to balance democracy and capitalism within a single legal order.[8]

Not unlike Tocqueville, Marx tied the peculiar appearance of statelessness in early America to its political democracy. The legitimacy of American government rested on the world's most fully developed principles of political equality. Here institutions were completely free from the fixed societal divisions that had anchored feudal remnants in European governments. American institutions were merely abstract forms, their content periodically determined by the people at large through an egalitarian electoral politics. In this, Marx saw a "fictive state"; American politics portrayed a state "trying to realize itself as pure society."[9]

Yet, Marx insisted that the way in which coercion is legitimized reveals only one side of the state. On the other side, America and Europe had much in common. The coercive apparatus in America, like that in the most clearly distinguishable states of the continent, was used rather effectively to support a particular economic system. America's "real state," its "material state," was revealed in its laws: "property, etc., in brief, the entire content of law and the state is, with small modification, the same in North America as in Prussia."[10] America's fully developed democratic politics, juxtaposed to its legal protections for private property, distilled an emergent pattern among Western states. The peculiar genius and modernity of early American government lay in its apparent, but ultimately illusory, statelessness.

Taken together, the comparative perspectives of Tocqueville, Hegel, and Marx go far in helping us come to terms with a nineteenth-century governmental order that failed to evoke the sense of a state. The basic insights of these three celebrated interpretations of the appearance of statelessness in early America can be combined into a single composite portrait of American exceptionalism. Early America exemplified an emergent pattern among Western states with its legal supports for democracy and capitalism, but its democracy was already highly developed, and it maintained a meager concentration of governmental controls at the national level. This combination of extremes – a highly developed democratic politics without a concentrated governing capacity – made early America the great anomaly among Western states. It also foreshadowed a developmental problem that was unique in the experience of Western states.

Returning to our original formulation of early America's claim to consideration as a state, we can now bring the problem of modern American state building into focus. After all the European comparisons have been made, the extreme features of American government in the nineteenth century are still best appreciated as distinguishing a particular organization of institutions, procedures, and human talents that asserted control within the national territory. In these terms, America remains an exceptional case; yet, it is exceptional not for the absence of a state but for the peculiar way state power was organized. Treating the great anomaly among Western states as a state organization with an integrity of its own allows us to move beyond assessments of its relative modernity or backwardness toward an examination of a structure of power that combined two extreme characteristics and an analysis of the way this structure of power conditioned subsequent development.

In this light, the study of modern American state building presents a striking variation on a classic developmental problem: that of negotiating a systemic change in relations between an established state and its society. This classic problem appeared in American political development when the bucolic environment in which the early American state had taken shape began to disappear. The close of the frontier, the rise of the city, the accentuation of class divisions, the end of isolation – these changes raised demands for national governmental capacities that were foreign to the existing state structure and that presupposed a very different mode of governmental operation.

To meet this challenge, American state organization had to be fundamentally altered. Governmental authority had to be concentrated at the national level and governmental offices insulated from the people at large. The institutional forms and procedures through which American government had been working for decades would not simply give way once their limitations became apparent. As America entered a new age, the seemingly innocuous governmental order that had been evolving over the nineteenth century was exposed for the tenacious organization of power that it was. It defined a tortuous course for the development of national institutional controls, and this course had to be negotiated through an already highly developed democratic politics.

The governmental forms and procedures necessary for securing order in industrial America emerged through a labored exercise in creative destruction. Our national bureaucratic apparatus clearly stands out as the major constructive achievement. Yet, this achievement was premised upon and delimited by an extended assault on the previously established governmental order. Modern American state building worked through this dilemma. To institutionalize a whole new range of governing capacities, the established state organization ultimately had to be thrown into internal disarray. The bureaucratic advance ultimately shattered the old governmental regimen, and this dynamic turned the reestablishment of internal governmental order into one of the most elusive problems of the twentieth century.

As the path linking past and present is studied, the question of America's contemporary status as a state appears in a new light. Did this break with the old order lead to "the end of American exceptionalism"?[11] Clearly, the United States is now one of several states that supports an electoral democracy, a private economy, and a powerful central bureaucracy. It shares similar problems with these states in maintaining political legitimacy, in planning for continued economic growth, and in overcoming bureaucratic intransigence. But simply treating America as a typical example of the "Western system of power" or a symptom of "the crisis of the modern Western state" can obscure as much as it clarifies.[12] The study of state building in America draws out the implications of the unique sequence and circumstances in which the modern American state developed the basic characteristics it now shares with others.

Democracy was firmly established in America before a concentration of national governmental controls was demanded. The development of the national government did not portend a "Europeanization" of America, nor, for that matter, did the democratization of Europe portend its "Americanization." In America, a new kind of state organization had to be fashioned through a highly developed electoral democracy to meet the governing challenges of the industrial age. The state-building problem was unique, and the state-building process inevitably pushed America off along another peculiar tangent. The modern American state, for all its cosmopolitan features, emerged as an institutional curiosity operating in a paradoxical but intimate relationship with the exceptional past it had to escape.

The state-building process: developmental imperatives and the struggle for institutional power

State building is a process basic to any nation's political development. Government officials seeking to maintain power and legitimacy try to mold institutional capacities in response to an ever-changing environment. Environmental stimuli, official responses, and new forms of government are the basic elements of the state-building process, and these can be compared cross-nationally to identify developmental patterns and contextual variations.

Students of political development have focused on three kinds of environmental changes that tend to stimulate efforts to expand governmental capacities. These are domestic or international crises, class conflicts, and the evolving complexity of routine social interactions. The combined impact of *crisis, class conflict,* and *complexity* was concentrated on a national scale for the first time in American history between 1877 and 1920. This complex of forces pressing simultaneously for an expansion of national governmental controls will be distinguished here to elaborate the notion of American administrative development as a response to "industrialism."

A *crisis* is a sporadic, disruptive event that suddenly challenges a state's capacity to maintain control and alters the boundaries defining the legitimate use of coercion. Crisis situations tend to become the watersheds in a state's institutional development. Actions taken to meet the challenge often lead to the establishment of new institutional forms, powers, and precedents. Students of political development have called attention to war, the most extreme environmental crisis, as "the mother of all states."[13]

The environmental crises encompassed in the years 1877–1920 are benchmarks in the emergence of modern America. The end of Reconstruction in 1877 saw a final dismantling of the institutional machinery that had supported the most costly war of the nineteenth century. The extraordinary demands of the Civil War had stimulated the growth of a powerful central government, but this rapid development had far outpaced routine demands for institutional control.[14] Ironically, the final reaction against the wartime state apparatus came in a year of unexpected domestic labor violence that placed new and more permanent demands on government. The international and domestic crisis situations created by the Spanish-American War and World War I posed additional challenges of a new era in world politics. The major environmental crises of this period punctuate America's abortive attempt to retreat to the provincial governmental style of its agrarian past and its emergence as a world power in the industrial age.

The state in a capitalist society is continually involved in controlling *class conflict*. Two basic stimuli for institutional development can be identified in the evolution of the private market economy. First is the interclass struggle between labor and capital; second is the intraclass conflict among factions of capitalists competing for market advantages.[15] If the state is to maintain order in the private economy, it must expand its institutional capacities for mediation and/or repression as these conflicts develop.

From a class perspective, the period chosen for study here reveals major institution-building stimuli. The years 1877–1920 are notable for the emergence of a nationally based market, the rise of organized labor to national prominence, the most violent struggles between capital and labor in American history, the growth of trusts and oligopolies with national orientations and national economic power, and the intrusion onto the national political scene of factional conflicts among merchant, finance, and industrial capital.[16] Such conditions radically altered the demands on the American state in its role as guarantor of the economic system as a whole.

The state also responds to a more general evolution in social *complexity*. This dynamic refers to the growth and concentration of the population, the division of labor, the specialization of functions, the differentiation of social sectors, and the advance of technology. These factors affect government internally as part of this evolving society, and they affect its functions in society as coordination and communication become more difficult. To use Durkheim's metaphor, the state is the society's "brain," which develops as the social organism becomes more complex and interdependent.[17]

In the eyes of contemporary historians, American history between 1877 and 1920 reveals a rapid movement from social simplicity to social complexity. Scholars have traced in these years the destruction of the isolated local community and its replacement with one interdependent nation tying together every group and section.[18] Provincial forms of social interaction gave way to the cosmopolitan as the dominant pattern in American life. By 1920, men were "separated more by skill and occupation than by community, they identified themselves more by their tasks in an urban–industrial society than by their reputation in a town or city neighborhood."[19] To accommodate this transformation in American life, early American government had to change dramatically.

The striking character of the combined forces of crisis, class conflict, and complexity in these years establishes the background to a pivotal episode in the development of American government. Each was a powerful catalyst for a nationalization of governmental controls. Yet, whether considered singly or in some combination, these environmental changes are only the stimuli for institutional development.[20] Government officials do not respond automatically with the appropriate institutional innovations. New institutional forms and new relations between state and society remain contingent on how these officials respond.

The intervention of government officials is the critical factor in the state-building process. As managers of the state apparatus, these officials assert the state's claim to control the use of coercion within the territory. Their most basic task is to vindicate this distinctive claim. It is a task that depends upon their collective action within the state apparatus from the determination of effective policies through their implementation.

The collective action of government officials in responding to environmental changes is mediated by the institutional and political arrangements that define their positions and support their prerogatives within the state apparatus. As an integrated organization of institutions, procedures, and human talents, an established state structures a set of power relationships among its discretionary officers, and it provides an operating framework through which these officers attempt to maintain order. This working organization of power routinizes and circumscribes the way government officials gain and maintain their positions, the way they relate to each other within and across institutions, and the way they relate back to social and economic groups.

An official's response to environmental disruptions will involve a distinctly political calculus of the impact of potential innovations on the particular arrangements that support him in office. Though any innovation can spark conflict among officials seeking to maintain or enhance their prerogatives, a given operating framework for concerted action is likely to facilitate a considerable amount of institutional adaptation. However, in the course of a nation's development, an impasse may be reached in relations between an established state and its society, an impasse in which the most basic political and institutional arrangements structuring state operations are no longer pertinent to the task of maintaining order.[21] The collective power calculations of officeholders can then do more to inhibit than to facilitate concerted state action. Vindicating the state's claims to control under such conditions would require a reconstruction of the foundations of official power within the state apparatus and a redefinition of the routine mode of governmental operations.

American state building around the turn of the century involved negotiating this kind of historical–structural impasse in relations between state and society. Industrialism, in all its dimensions, exposed severe limitations in the mode of governmental operations that had evolved over the nineteenth century and that supported the powers and prerogatives of those in office. An unprecedented concentration of environmental imperatives for a nationalization of governmental controls was met by a state whose working structure of political and institutional power presumed the absence of such controls. The arrangements established to facilitate the collective management of the state apparatus were now no longer appropriate for effective government. Providing the national institutional capacities commensurate with the demands of an industrial society required nothing less than building a different kind of state organization.

At this juncture, the political contingencies in the state-building process held sway. The reconstruction of institutional relationships and the establishment of a bureaucratic mode of governmental operations hinged on successful political challenges to the established foundations of official power. Reform efforts aimed at national administrative development became caught in an extended contest over the redefinition of power relationships and official prerogatives, the terms of the contest shifting with the changing shape of electoral politics. The leaders of America's administrative reform offensives held up European administrative models as their standard and argued the functional necessity of adopting them, but our governmental transformation followed a logic of its own. In the final analysis, the new American state was extorted from institutional struggles rooted in the peculiar structure of the old regime and mediated by shifts in electoral politics.

This perspective on the state-building process requires some further elaboration on two particulars. The first concerns the pressures for new state services and supports that were brought to bear on the government by specific social and economic groups. These pressures obviously played an important part in the power calculations of governmental elites. Focusing on institutional politics will not exclude these private interests from consideration, but it will concentrate our attention on the special difficulties presented to an ongoing organization of state power as it is being pressed to service groups in qualitatively new ways. In a situation in which long-established relationships between a state and its society are being thrown into question, the challenge of institutional development goes far beyond the efforts of private groups working to exploit governmental power on their own behalf. It becomes a matter of changing the working structure of governmental power itself. Indeed, the pressures exerted on government officials through established channels may, in these circumstances, actually intensify the problems of making an effective response. In analyzing a period in which environmental conditions and the nature of interest demands are changing radically, concern for whose interests outside government are served must be balanced with a concern for the way in which the collective power calculations of government officials determine the quality of the new services the private groups actually receive.

A second and final note concerns the obvious fact that American institutional development did not stop in 1920. Indeed, the institutions that have been added to the state apparatus and the functions that have been assumed by the national government since 1920 may seem to dwarf the significance of the state-building episode chosen for study here. The expansion of national administration accelerated dramatically in the 1930s and again in the 1960s. Yet, the course of institutional development during these more recent decades and the governmental problems encountered in these developments are rooted in this turn-of-the-century departure. The internal governmental changes negotiated between the end of Reconstruction and the end of World War I established a new institutional politics at the national level that has proven remarkably resistant to fundamental change. They also raised questions of political authority and the capacity for direction within government that have yet to be firmly resolved.

The analysis of state building in America

State building is usually identified with the development of new governmental institutions; that is, individual institutional innovations, in themselves, may be considered evidence of state building. This study presents a slightly different view. It looks at American state building as the systemic transformation of an entire mode of governmental operations that had to be negotiated in the process of establishing new institutions.

The development of a central bureaucratic apparatus in America entailed disrupting established institutional and political relationships as they had evolved over the nineteenth century among parties, courts, the presidency, Congress, and the individual states.[22] The great departure in American institutional development came between 1877 and 1920, when new national administrative institutions first emerged free from the clutches of party domination, direct court supervision, and localistic orientations. To comprehend this systemic change, an analysis had to be designed that would keep the centerpiece of American state building in the forefront without losing sight of the holistic nature of the developmental problem presented.

As noted above, this study focuses on three areas of national administrative innovation – the reform of civil administration, army reorganization, and the establishment of national railroad regulation. Scholars have already given considerable attention to innovations in each of these areas individually. Concern for the systemic changes that had to be negotiated in American government at this time suggested a different kind of treatment, that is, a comparison of concurrent developments across institutional realms. By identifying patterns of development over three distinct areas of administrative innovation, we can move beyond a history of each toward a cross-sectional view of a transformation in the integrated network of institutions, procedures, and human talents that constitutes the state as a working organization. In a comparative framework, the reform efforts complement each other in illuminating a single political process of reconstructing the American state around national administrative capacities in the industrial age.

The separate histories of reform in these three areas show governmental elites responding to very different kinds of problems presented by the crises, class conflicts, and complexity of the new industrial era. These histories also encompass the efforts of very different private groups as they pressed governmental elites for new institutional controls, and they address very different functions assumed by the state. A comparison of reform efforts in these three areas of state concern will bring to the fore the historical–structural problem of institutional development that they held in common. Attention will then be focused on the shared characteristics of the state-building politics that ensued to overcome this problem. Our approach will illuminate the politics of negotiating a fundamental change in the working structure of the early American state and allow us to observe the mediating effects of this politics on the consolidation of key institutional forms and political relationships in the new American state.

The next chapter will take a closer look at the early American state as a working organization of institutions, procedures, and human talents. The bulk of the text will trace political patterns of change in the operational dimensions of this preestablished state as they are observed across our three areas of study. Two patterns in the politics of building a new American state will be found. Each may be described briefly.

The first pattern, *state building as patchwork,* will be observed across our reform areas between 1877 and 1900. During these years, the early American state was stretched to the limits of its governing capacities. New institutions emerged to meet the most immediate new demands on government, but governmental elites could not sustain support for any effort that threatened to undermine long-established political and institutional relationships. They concentrated on perfecting the machinery of the early American state and held at bay an alternative governing cadre that attacked their regime head-on in the interest of building national administrative authority. The question of whether or not America's institutional response to industrialism would entail support for a powerful national administrative arm was first contested in these years but answered in the negative.

The second pattern, *state building as reconstitution,* will be observed across our reform areas between 1900 and 1920. During these years, the doors of power finally opened to the champions of national administrative development, and a new struggle ensued over the redistribution of official prerogatives and the reconstruction of constitutional relationships. The national administrative realm rose to prominence in this highly contentious and structurally amorphous institutional environment. The new American state emerged with a powerful administrative arm, but authoritative controls over this power were locked in a constitutional stalemate.

The state-building perspective and interpretation of the turn-of-the-century break with the past

Scholars have long recognized political reform around the turn of the century as a watershed in the development of American government. They have differed largely on interpretations of the nature of this break with the past. The period has been characterized in terms of the rise of a new democracy, the triumph of corporate conservatism, and the emergence of an administrative rationality based on principles of hierarchy and professionalism. At times, scholars find support for these different interpretations in the very same reform. For example, the reform of the party machines has been viewed alternatively as the repurification of a democracy grown corrupt, as a prerequisite to the rise of corporate capitalism, and as a concomitant element in the rise of modern bureaucratic forms of management.[23]

Whatever tension there is among the major interpretations of political reform in this era (and certainly some are written in direct opposition to others), their basic insights are not necessarily contradictory. It is difficult to imagine how corporate capitalism could have thrived in America without an alteration of the preestablished institutional supports for American democracy. Equally, it is difficult to imagine how the expansion of citizens' rights could have been balanced with support for the private economy without a recasting of national administrative organization. Evidence of building modern bureaucratic institutions and simultaneously restructuring the institutional supports for democracy and capitalism can be seen as the major systemic parts of a single process in the reconstruction of the American state. This period was pivotal in American political development precisely because the peculiar mode of governmental operations that had evolved over the nineteenth century was relegated to the provincial past, and a new governmental framework for maintaining democracy and the private economy in the industrial age took shape around administrative capacities.

Yet, if the only contribution of this work were in giving a synthetic new name to current interpretations of Progressive reform – if the goal were merely to sort out what others have said and call it "the triumph of a new cosmopolitan state" – the detailed reexamination of institutional developments that follows would hardly be necessary. The study of state building outlined above is designed to bring one of the less explored dimensions of America's approach to modernity into a general perspective.[24] Apart from their differences, the major interpretations of Progressive reform have tended to focus on the environmental disruptions and social interests that propelled American institutional development forward and to treat the state as an adaptive response mechanism providing the appropriate institutional instruments under the guiding light of timely reform principles. To concentrate on the external forces in the state-building process – on the implications of social interdependence, on the institutional demands of empire, on the political interests of corporations, on the reform impulse of a rising professional class – is to leave the emergence of a new state overdetermined but little understood. Treating institutional development as a focus for analysis rather than as a mere epiphenomenon will highlight the significance of form, timing, and governing potential in the state's responses to new conditions. It will permit consideration of the concentration of state power in an already highly developed electoral democracy as a significant developmental problem in its own right and facilitate an examination of the achievement on its own terms. Moreover, by approaching the early American state as an organization with its own operational integrity, we are forced to come to terms with the special task of negotiating a break with inherited governmental arrangements and to examine the distinctive process of institutional reconstruction through political reform.

As the state-building perspective highlights America's remarkable capacity to regenerate its government peacefully, it also shows how the promise of a new democracy, the embrace of corporate conservatism, the lure of professionalism, and the quest for administrative rationality all became caught up in an intense and extended struggle for power within the state apparatus. This struggle imparted new meaning and paradoxical effect to the reform principles of the day. The new structure of power that emerged in the end proved more serviceable for politically salient groups in society, and it preempted all radical alternatives in political and economic organization; but the institutional obstacles and political contingencies faced in the course of this maneuver left their marks upon the result. There were no unqualified triumphs in building the new American state. Today, the political uncertainty and dark historical irony that attended this break with the past are its most apparent legacy.

2

The early American state

No greater disservice has ever been rendered political science than the statement that the liberal state was a "weak" state. It was precisely as strong as it needed to be in the circumstances.

Franz Neumann, *Democratic and Authoritarian States*, 1957

An analysis of American state building around the turn of the century requires a closer look at the early American state. This state was not a directive force in social affairs, nor was it an ideal reified in American culture. To Tocqueville, Hegel, and Marx, it appeared as pure instrumentality, an innocuous reflection of the society it served. Yet, this organization of coercive power was no less indispensable for its unobtrusive character. The early American state maintained an integrated legal order on a continental scale; it fought wars, expropriated Indians, secured new territories, carried on relations with other states, and aided economic development. Despite the absence of a sense of the state, the state was essential to social order and social development in nineteenth-century America.

The early American state can be described much as one would describe any other state. Readily comparable determinants of a state's mode of operations will be used here to assess this great anomaly as a working complex of institutions and personnel. These determinants are: the *organizational orientations* of government, the *procedural routines* that tie institutions together within a given organizational scheme, and the *intellectual talents* employed in government. Identifying the early American state along these operational dimensions will capture the distinctive way it performed the basic tasks of government. The reconstruction of state power between 1877 and 1920 will be observed in qualitative changes along each of these dimensions.

The organizational dimension: the revolution, the Constitution, and the devolution of power

A state's mode of operations is most easily distinguished by its organizational orientations. Any given state may be described in terms of four basic organizational qualities. These are:

19

1. The *concentration* of authority at the national center of government
2. The *penetration* of institutional controls from the governmental center throughout the territory
3. The *centralization* of authority within the national government
4. The *specialization* of institutional tasks and individual roles within the government

Two points of caution are in order here. First, it should be noted that these qualities are not bound together in any a priori sense. They need not be fixed at the same level in any given state, nor need they all change simultaneously. Their utility is purely descriptive. A peculiar mixture of these qualities distinguishes one state organization from another. Second, one should not confuse a state's effectiveness with its relative location on these scales. The relationship between a government's organizational orientation and its effectiveness at any given point in time cannot be discerned without an examination of its operating procedures. With these caveats in mind, it may be observed that at the level of purely descriptive comparisons, the state that evolved in nineteenth-century America scored relatively low on all the basic measures of state organization.

The United States was born in a war that rejected the organizational qualities of the state as they had been evolving in Europe over the eighteenth century. Indeed, it has been argued that an underlying cause of the Revolution was the gradual development of a more concentrated, specialized, and penetrating state apparatus in Britain.[1] One may read in the Declaration of Independence a rejection of the substantive results of this organization. Standing armies, centralized taxing authorities, the denial of local prerogatives, burgeoning castes of administrators – these were the forces against which a new political culture found definition.

The radical republican regimes of 1776–83 clearly embodied the revolutionary thrust against the emergent European organization of state power. Sovereignty was fixed in thirteen separate state legislatures, in which strict majoritarian principles and frequent elections left government at the mercy of fast-changing popular sentiments. These arrangements prevented any effective concentration of governing power at the national center, made a mockery of executive prerogatives, and inhibited institutional specialization.[2] The effects were destabilizing. Yet, the problems in this radical republican prescription had to be overcome without appearing to betray the revolutionary ideals it represented. In this historical circumstance, there were no acceptable models for the construction of an effective state power.[3]

The political and intellectual achievement of the men who met in Philadelphia in 1787 was to formulate and legitimize an organizational framework for the state that bypassed both the European and revolutionary designs. They established the integrated legal order necessary for the control of the territory, but at the same time, they denied the institutions of American government the organizational orientations of a European state. Their Constitution, as it was "extorted from the grinding necessity of a reluctant nation," is fundamental to any assessment of the peculiarities of the early American state and later American state building.[4]

The Articles of Confederation had concentrated governing authority in the separate states, but the national authority it did provide had all been centralized in a single congressional assembly. As the Constitution concentrated authority in a new national government, it overturned the centralization of institutional authority in Congress. Three separate branches of government were to share national power equally. The powers of a bicameral legislature, an executive, and a judiciary were checked and balanced against each other so as to prevent domination by any single national institution. The founders legitimized this rather clumsy and conservative institutional arrangement with the most radically democratic and anti-institutional ideals of the age. They argued that, as the Constitution realized the benefits of an independent national authority, its complex institutional design would reaffirm the absolute power of the people over all institutions. Each institution of the new government would represent the whole people, but each would do so in a different way. The interchange among institutions of equal status would filter out distortions of the public will created by any particular form of representation and obtain an expression of popular sovereignty even purer than that possible under strict adherence to congressional supremacy.[5]

While Europe was moving toward simplicity in state design, America, in effect, established "the most complicated government on the face of the globe."[6] Specialized institutions continued to develop in nineteenth-century Europe within the general framework of concentrated and centralized political authority. As Samuel Huntington has noted, the European states began to act through "semi-autonomous but subordinate bodies in one way or another responsible to political bodies (monarch or parliament) which exercised sovereignty."[7] The American Constitution not only denied this framework for institutional development, it left the most practical questions of state operations shrouded in ambiguity.

Here sovereignty was to be shared between the new central government and the old regional units of government, which retained their revolutionary designation as "states." Constitutional federalism inhibited the penetration of central power throughout the nation by ensuring the integrity of these states, each with its own institutional organization, legal code, and law enforcement apparatus. The unity of the American legal order rested on the vaguely worded constitutional prerogatives of the national government, broadly or narrowly construed, to intervene as the final authority in the affairs of these regionally controlled governments. In contrast, the often acclaimed "stateness" of France was manifested by the legal unity consolidated in the Napoleonic Code and by the establishment of the prefectoral system, which brought direct and continuous institutional control from the nation's governmental center to each territorial unit.

The focal point of state activity was clouded further by the conflicts structured among the institutions of the new national government. The three coequal branches of national authority provided for a greater degree of institutional specialization than had the Articles of Confederation, but overlapping jurisdictions inhibited a clear demarcation of institutional responsibilities. Political control over military and civil administration stretched across separate authorities sharing power equally. After the bewildering interactions of legislative, executive, and juridical prerogatives – all claiming the absolute power of the people – only the law itself emerged as a substantive referent of state direction. In contrast, Great Britain – which like America also preserved much local autonomy – experienced a progressive centralization of authority in Parliament and, in particular, within the ministry.[8]

From the very beginning, there were those who sought to resolve the operational ambiguities in the American Constitution by superimposing more European-like organizational orientations on our basic institutional framework. Alexander Hamilton pursued a vigorous and wide-ranging program aimed at concentrating power in the national government and centralizing national powers in the executive branch. His efforts in the areas of internal taxation, finance, banking, public works, and military organization reflect a comprehensive vision of national and executive preeminence in governmental affairs.[9] Later, in the nineteenth century, statesmen following Henry Clay hoped to "thicken" the bonds of the union with an American System of great national institutions under congressional direction.[10] Yet, neither of these organizational designs rose far above the status of highly controversial party programs. Those who sought to build the central state apparatus in early America ended up building minority parties instead.[11] In this guise, their plans could bear little fruit.

Federalist and Whig party programs notwithstanding, the most striking operational characteristics of early American state organization were a radical devolution of power accompanied by a serviceable but unassuming national government. The national government throughout the nineteenth century routinely provided promotional and support services for the state governments and left the substantive tasks of governing to these regional units.[12] This broad diffusion of power among the localities was the organizational feature of early American government most clearly responsible for the distinctive sense of statelessness in our political culture.

The national institutions that penetrated the territory are one indication of the rather innocuous role played by central authority in the government of the nation. Land offices, post offices, and customhouses were the most important of these national institutions, and they illustrate the orientation toward basic services that routinely dominated federal concerns.[13] Except in war, the activities of these field offices could bring in more than enough revenue to keep the national government solvent. Another example of the radically decentralized organizational scheme is provided by the army. The early American state routinely relegated to its tiny regular army the tasks of securing the frontier and aiding economic development with the talents of its corps of engineers.[14] American national defense relied upon a militia system of citizen-soldiers organized and controlled by the several states. The role of the national government in the militia system consisted of providing a modest subsidy and offering perfunctory administrative guidelines.[15] Finally, the primary concern of the national government in providing support for regional centers of decision making is confirmed in a general overview of the corpus of nineteenth-century law. One finds the most fundamental social choices – from the organization of capitalism to the regulation of family life – firmly lodged in state legal codes.[16]

With regard to the national government itself, operations tended to center in Congress, where a logrolling politics could best service the states and localities.[17] Conflicts ensued between the Senate and the House, and battles were fought among all federal institutions over the definition of their respective constitutional prerogatives.[18] Yet, given the radical devolution of governmental activity, these contentious institutional relations at the national level could be suffered with relative impunity. The most pressing operational problems were how to integrate the support services of the national government with these widely scattered regional centers of action and how to maintain an overall coherence within this broad dispersion of governing power. An ingenious solution was found in the cohesive procedures of courts and parties.

The procedural dimension: early America as a state of courts and parties

A state is, to use John R. Commons's phrase, "officials-in-action."[19] A procedural view of the state looks at the way these actions are coordinated. Stable, valued, and recurring modes of behavior within and among institutions are needed to lend governmental operations coherence and effectiveness.[20] The governing potential within any given organizational scheme will be found in the working rules developed to guide the actions of those in office.

Working rules of behavior inform the everyday boundaries of what governmental officials must do, what they may do, and what they can expect others to do.[21] A description of the state as a procedural entity focuses on the sources of these rules. They may be informally rooted in loyalty to a particular leader, grounded in the authority of a particular institution, or formally explicated in a written code of conduct. Once the sources of standard operating procedures have been discovered, one can discern how they determine the character of the state and the nature of relations between state and society.

The success of the early American state came to depend on the working rules of behavior provided by courts and parties. These two nationally integrated institutional systems tied together this state's peculiar organizational determinants and established its effective mode of operations. They coordinated action from the bottom to the top of this radically deconcentrated governmental scheme. Under a Constitution designed to produce institutional conflicts and riddled with jurisdictional confusions, they came to lend order, predictability, and continuity to governmental activity.

The potential of parties to solve the knotty operational problems of governing under the Constitution was not realized right away. Indeed, the Federalists and Jeffersonians decried the very idea of partisan divisions in government and professed the need for unity among all elites. The early "parties" were largely collections of local notables, and their capacities to govern were limited by their patrician character. Federalists and Jeffersonians alike hoped for a consensus of enlightened leaders in a government designed to produce conflicts of interest and sought to institutionalize a politics of deference in a polity that was growing increasingly democratic. Their successes were precariously dependent on the exceptional man, the personal loyalties he could instill in others, and the high professional integrity of those he could appoint to office.[22] The failure of Federalist plans to orient government around executive–administrative initiatives and the passing of Jefferson's personal mediation of executive–congressional relations left the national government without means for concerted action.[23] The War of 1812 raised the specter of complete governmental collapse, and in its aftermath, the national government drifted aimlessly.[24] The administrations of the late Jeffersonian era exposed the worst features of America's disjointed constitutional framework.

But while an institutional breakdown was threatening from above, state and local party organizations were beginning to define a clear and irresistible discipline for gaining and manipulating political power. During the 1830s, this discipline gradually took hold of the national government. Electoral alliances, carefully negotiated among local political organizations, replaced the chaotic struggles of local notables as the foundation of Washington politics. These electoral machines did not require men of reputation and cultivation for their operation. Instead, they depended on cadres of professional politicians skilled in the techniques of mass mobilization and driven by a passion for organizational efficiency. The regimen of voter mobilization, party coalition building, and national two-party competition provided the extraconstitutional framework necessary for channeling the energies and ambitions of officials in government. The party machinery freed the Constitution from dependence on a patrician class, depersonalized power relationships, and focused activity within America's fragmented institutional structure.[25]

The dominant American parties have appropriately been labeled "constituent parties" because of the prominence of their role in facilitating state operations.[26] Party organizations bound the national government to each locale and linked the many discrete units of government horizontally across the territory. This brought a measure of cohesion to national politics and a measure of standardization to governmental forms and processes throughout the federal system. Moreover, parties organized governmental institutions internally. They facilitated working relationships within and among the branches and levels of the constitutional structure. They routinized administrative procedures with patronage recruitment, spoils rotation, and external controls over the widely scattered post offices, land offices, and customhouses. Local party organizations were tapped to staff these local federal offices and to oversee their operations.[27] National representatives of state party machines had a keen interest in the distribution of federal offices, and the federal patronage appointee became the embodiment of a series of concrete ties between President and Congress and between local and national governments.[28]

By 1850, the party machines had become "absolutely necessary to hold things . . . disconnected [by the Constitution] together and to give some coherence to the action of political forces."[29] It is curious, however, that in the world's first large-scale democracy, parties were less notable for their programs than for this procedural unity they lent the state. The organized forces of democracy in America came to represent only the most general policy preferences.[30] This curiosity must be explained by a party structure and a party system designed to integrate national governmental services into local centers of governing activity. These parties tended to be preoccupied with the "automatic aggregation of highly diverse and often antagonistic subgroupings to the near exclusion of concern for the development of 'modern', mass organization in the European sense."[31] Their loose electoral coalitions were forged with promises for a broad distribution of material prerequisites among their disparate elements. As the Whig party discovered in 1841, the imperatives of building a winning electoral coalition on a national scale substantially reduced the prospects for implementing a positive national program even when federal power was secured.[32]

Indeed, the idea of two parties competing on a continental scale – that is, the idea of a national two-party system – was first conceived in America as a way to circumvent not only factionalism within the national government but also comprehensive political programs for the nation. Holistic policy programs would only have exacerbated sectional cleavages and threatened national unity. In Martin Van Buren's master scheme, American government could be made to work only by two constituent parties competing across the major sectional divisions of the nation. In this way, the conflicting interests of all sections would be given an "equal opportunity" to gain national services and support within one governmental order.[33] Such parties would not articulate a clear policy linkage between citizens and government, but they would bind together a radically decentralized state and a faction-ridden nation.

American parties thus came to embody the ideals of popular sovereignty largely by their mere occupation and rotation in the governmental apparatus. The marriage of the American people to the Constitution was to be more physical than intellectual. Massive shifts in voter preferences were necessary to redirect the agenda set by the national electoral alignments of these coalitions of local machines, and such shifts invariably led to a renewal of their mechanical mediation of state–society relations. Between these electoral realignments, American parties indulged a remarkably diverse array of social interests with a broad distribution of the government's valuable goods and services.

The only institutions that could stand, at least partially, outside direct party domination and claim to complement the parties in the performance of such basic constituent tasks were the courts. Courts are procedural institutions par excellence. They need outside stimulation to set them in motion, their subject matter is defined by outside actors, and once their procedures have been completed, they depend on outside agencies to carry out their decision. Courts are naturally passive as instruments of government, and they are radically particularistic in decision making. But, despite their innocuous character as pillars of statism, American courts provided the essential counterpoise to the all-consuming electoral machines of America's party state.[34] As party procedures lent operational coherence to the disjointed institutions of the governmental apparatus, court proceedings determined the meaning and effect of the law itself.

Courts complemented parties in binding the legal apparatus of government. Ultimately, the Constitution and the prerogatives of governmental elites came to be what the Supreme Court said they were.[35] As the final arbiter in institutional and jurisdictional disputes, the Court shaped the boundaries of intergovernmental relations. It defined the legitimate forms of interaction between states, between state and national governments, and within the national government itself. In the evolution of the constitutional law, the fragmented system of governmental authority became malleable and responsive.[36]

The judiciary not only helped define the terms of internal governmental activity, it also helped define relations between state and society. It fell to the courts at each level of government to nurture, protect, interpret, and invoke the state's prerogatives over economy and society as expressed in law. Most notable in this regard was the way nineteenth-century courts filled a governmental vacuum left by abortive experiments in the administrative promotion of economic development. The generally inept supervision of public works projects and joint public–private ventures combined with a depression in 1837 to make state legislatures increasingly reluctant to invest in large and costly promotional activities.[37] By the late 1830s, an alternative means of fostering economic development had come to the fore – the widespread distribution of special corporate charters. These charters were designed to promote and channel private economic ventures, yet they left to the courts a fairly loose reign over the state's police powers. By interpreting the charters' reserve clauses for the protection of the public interest, the judiciary became the chief source of economic surveillance in the nineteenth century. Over time, courts molded the prerogatives of government into predictable but flexible patterns of policy toward capital accumulation.[38]

This system of control was well established by 1850, when the race for railroad access was becoming the centerpiece of national economic development. The courts had become the American surrogate for a more fully developed administrative apparatus.[39] The corporate law they articulated during the nineteenth century stands next to the party machinery as a distinctive and key element in America's effective mode of governmental operations.

American courts exhibit peculiarities as curious as those of American parties. Where the parties are less notable for their substantive policies than for the procedural unity they lent the state, the courts, though the most procedural of all institutions, are notable for their substantive definition of the law. On the side of the courts, this curiosity must first be rooted in a common law tradition that tends to turn judicial proceedings toward substantive law making. The subtle manipulation of judicial precedents suggests less government by law than government by gentlemen.[40] But the malleability of the common law alone cannot account for the exceptional governing role assumed by the early American judiciary. Legal historians have drawn attention to the distinctive path of American jurisprudence that established a peculiarly aggressive posture in the courts. Gradually, American judges embraced a pragmatic and positive view of themselves as policymakers. Adopting an instrumental outlook toward the judicial proceeding, the judges blurred the distinction between the law and the facts of their cases. Thinking in utilitarian terms, they slowly came to treat the common law "as equally responsible with legislation for governing society and promoting socially desirable conduct."[41]

If one might discover in this substantive law making by the courts some basis for the oft-noted antagonism between courts and parties in American politics, there is also discernible a complementary relationship between these two procedural systems in the early American state. Consider, for a moment, the characteristic judicial reform proposed by the radical Jeffersonians. Decrying the arbitrary qualities of judicial policy making as inconsistent with a democratic republic, they sought to secure the supremacy of the legislatures and reduce judges to agents of legislative will.[42] The problem with this prescription was that the locally based representative system of this democratic republic made it difficult for the legislatures to declare their will in any precise or lasting terms. With the rise of the constituent party machines, the thrust of the attack on the bench shifted. The nature of these machines as loose aggregations of disparate elements united in mutual self-interest militated against the Jeffersonian ideal of strict legislative supremacy. The characteristic demand for judicial reform now aimed at a democratization of the bar and the bench. The status distinctions of the lawyers were to be stripped away, and judges were to be made electorally accountable. Yet, through these reforms, it was possible to leave intact the courts' discretionary authority over specific cases and to relieve anxious legislators of the always difficult task of formulating a specific regulatory policy with wide application. Judicial activism was a natural complement to an electoral–representative system that had a natural impulse to distribute benefits widely through a logrolling politics (like the politics of granting special corporate charters) and to avoid, so far as possible, bold declarations of winners and losers in legislation.

Together, courts and parties formed the bulwark of the early American state. Their routines lent operational integrity and internal order to government, allowing it to service a sprawling and pluralistic nation. Moreover, by institutionalizing effective supports for mass democracy and the private economy, courts and parties also supported America's claim to consideration as the most modern of all states in the nineteenth century.

At the same time, however, courts and parties imparted an evanescent or elusive quality to the early American state that, at least until the 1870s, reinforced the characteristic sense of statelessness in early American political culture. In the first place, they paralleled the organizational orientation of government toward the state level of the federal system. The work of both institutional systems centered in these regional units, where the actual governing activity was concentrated and the essential services of the national government were deployed. Secondly, the operations of courts and parties made American government fluid and malleable. Parties alternated in control of the institutional apparatus at different times throughout the levels of government, and the powers of the state were constantly being molded by judicial decisions at various levels. Finally, and most importantly, continuity in this state remained contingent on continuity in the electoral system as a whole and on the perceived legitimacy of court decisions.[43]

The evanescent quality of a state tied together by the routines of courts and parties was well illustrated in the fateful years between 1856 and 1861. When the Supreme Court accepted the Dred Scott case, it faced a policy decision that proper procedures alone could not legitimize and that threatened to divide the nation along the sectional lines so carefully avoided by the organizational strategies and the compromise politics of Democrats and Whigs. Characteristically, party leaders had urged President Buchanan to shy away from any position on slave policy that might threaten the sectional balance, but leaving the slavery issue to the courts could not circumvent the perceived political dangers. The electoral divisiveness of the Dred Scott decision and the subsequent disintegration of the party system left the American state in a shambles.[44]

The state of courts and parties did not, however, pass away with the

Civil War. Indeed, the war experience testified to its regenerative capacities and its governing potential. The great northern war machine was first and foremost a new party machine.[45] Apt appraisal of America's Civil War state may be found in the rhetoric of one local party convention of 1862. The convention reminded Lincoln that he was "responsible" for the war,

> ... and yet he has no army, he has no navy, no resources of any kind except what the people give him. In a word, he is powerless unless the people stand at his side and uphold his hands... The Republican Organization, in all its principles, in all its practices, and by all its members, is committed to the preservation of the Union and the overthrow of the Rebellion. It is the power of the State and the power of the Nation.[46]

The national governing resources mobilized during the Civil War were enormous, but, as this local party convention well understood, the state's power was rooted in the new Republican organization and its capacity to channel the actions of governing elites.[47]

In these terms, we can make sense of a most remarkable episode in state development. The war had brought national military conscription, a military occupation of the South, a national welfare agency for former slaves, a national income tax, national monetary controls, and national citizenship. One historian reviewing this list writes: "In brief, the United States had become a state in the full meaning of the word."[48] Yet, this was a state grounded in only half the nation. As the South returned, national electoral politics changed, and these institutional achievements began to be undone. As if to prove that the great institutions of the war machine had no intrinsic value or independent power base, they were simply swept aside in the party politics of the 1870s. Here, then, was a state only in the sense of the word imputed to it by the interests and strategies of the mass electoral organizations controlling its offices. No institution stood beyond the reach of party concerns. Changing party strategies might effect sudden changes in the governmental apparatus. In the 1870s, national party politics dictated a return to localism, laissez-faire, and racism.[49]

After the wartime crisis, American government moved ahead within its effective mode of operations bounded by court decisions and national party competition. The fate of the wartime governmental apparatus suggests that a state is not transformed by merely creating new governing institutions under some extreme crisis. If new institutional forms are to constitute a new state, they must alter the procedural bonds that tie governmental institutions together and define their relationship to society. The Civil War did not do this. The constituent party machine reigned supreme in governmental operations before, during, and after the crisis. The onset of the war marks the great failure of the American party state; the victory, its greatest achievement. The postwar decades were to bring the rule of courts and parties to its fullest flower.

The intellectual dimension: lawyers in the state of courts and parties

The final dimension of a state viewed as a distinctive operational entity is to be found in the kinds of intellectual skills and human talents integrated into the government. The state is not only an arrangement of institutions and procedures; it is also an intellectual enterprise. The routine work of government is primarily a mental rather than a manual labor, and the intellectual talent available in government for problem solving and innovation is critical to the capacities of a state to maintain itself over time. Indeed, the significance of the intellectuals attached to an existing state (and those attached to associations championing alternatives to an existing state) is most clearly manifest in crisis situations when established routines falter and the reestablishment of control is essential.[50]

The distinctiveness of a state sphere may be described in terms of the kinds of intellectual talents employed within it. Associated with all highly institutionalized states is a special intellectual cadre that maintains an underlying continuity in governmental activity through social and political changes. These intellectuals may be recruited through an established church, an aristocracy of birth, or a university. Such institutions tend to confer legitimacy on the state as they generate the personnel to operate it. By their education and their social status, the intellectuals come to embody the special identity of the state. Clearly, there is a close connection between the state determined by its "status officialdom" and a state determined by its procedural bonds. The intellectual cadre cultivated to manage the state both manipulates and personifies its procedural characteristics.[51]

In pre-Jacksonian America, one finds the makings of a fairly traditional status officialdom at the national level. The Federalists and the Jeffersonians recruited officers into political and administrative posts from among the notables of the local communities. In administration, in particular, a stable patrician elite of high social status, eastern university education, and high professional self-consciousness began to emerge.[52] American administration in its earliest years was the envy of Great Britain as it labored under the burden of aristocratic property in office – an irony not lost on those who would later try to reform the American spoils system along British lines.[53] Yet, by the late Jeffersonian era, office was becoming a species of property for the American patricians as well.[54]

With the rise of the constituent party machines, this embryonic status officialdom was gradually pushed from office.[55] Spoils and rotation replaced local notables with local party workers. Although some always managed to escape rotation, the new organization men now defined the character of politics and administration. This transformation in the intellectual constitution of the American state may be traced through an examination of its most important intellectual resource – the lawyers.

No one was more attuned to the crucial place of lawyers in the early years of American government than Tocqueville. Tocqueville compared American lawyers with the aristocrats of Europe as the primary force of moderation and reflection in the affairs of state. He identified the lawyers as the preponderant majority in high offices. They dominated the elective branches at the state and national levels and held a monopoly in the judicial branch, where they controlled a vast repository of discretionary authority. Tocqueville also spoke of the lawyers as a distinct social group of high status and public prestige. This "aristocracy of the bar and the bench" represented "the most cultivated portion of society." In a land consumed by the democratic spirit, the lawyers were, of course, only a surrogate aristocracy. They belonged "to the aristocracy by taste and habit" but "to the people by birth and interest." Finally, Tocqueville pointed to characteristics inherent in the legally oriented mind and in legal processes themselves that made the lawyer a brake on popular passions. He noted that lawyers exerted an "invisible influence" merely by the inhibitive effect of their procedural mentality on impulsive actions.[56]

The model of the Tocquevillian lawyer finds impressive historical referents in figures such as Joseph Story, John Marshall, Chancellor Kent, and above all, Daniel Webster. Webster personified the lawyer as patrician–statesman in early America.[57] He wielded his legal talents for political causes of major significance and became the leading professional of his age. Before the Supreme Court, he argued the Dartmouth College case to vindicate the cause of economic nationalism. He routinely provided legal services for the National Bank and defended its existence on the Senate floor against the leveling attacks of Jacksonian Democrats. He countered John C. Calhoun in the nullification crisis to save the legal prerogatives of the national government from dismemberment under the banner of states' rights.

Ironically, however, the career of this Brahmin of American law is also suggestive of the limitations in the analogy between the early American lawyer and the European aristocracy. Fame did not make Webster any less a curiosity in the late 1820s and 1830s.[58] Here was a lawyer–politician of Federalist vintage in an age that was witnessing a division of labor between lawyers and politicians.[59] The new professional politician was an organizational manager first and a lawyer second, if at all. On the other hand, the professional lawyer had begun to narrow his intellectual concerns and concentrate his institutional activity. Rather than embracing a tradition of statesmanlike political leadership, the mid-century lawyer declared himself apolitical. He offered a technical mastery of the law and the specialized skills and talents necessary to represent clients in court. His self-justification was his instrumental value in a rapidly developing private economy.[60] Professional lawyers and professional politicians emerged as distinct types working within distinct spheres of the early American state. One held the reigns of political power, whereas the other subtly molded the means of capital accumulation.

The Tocquevillian image of a surrogate aristocracy in the early American bar must be qualified on other grounds as well. In the years following the establishment of the Constitution, tight-knit local bar organizations had functioned as corporate entities enjoying semiofficial status and exercising strict control over the recruitment, training, and conduct of their members. They produced men who guided their actions by the standards of the group, who looked to their peers for approbation, and who viewed public service as a duty and a credit to their professional reputation.[61] Yet the capacity of the professions generally to control and protect their membership began to deteriorate markedly in the 1820s. By the mid-nineteenth century, the corporate spirit and internal discipline of the American bar had succumbed to internal and external pressures.

On the one hand, the expansion and diffusion of the population placed severe internal strains on these early bonds of professionalism. Appropriate standards of conduct were becoming less obvious, controls less enforceable, and the informal and personalistic ties of the small group more difficult to maintain. On the other hand, the institutional insulation and status pretensions of the early American lawyers came under bitter attack from a people organized for a more democratic politics. The Jacksonian celebration of the common man rekindled America's revolutionary anti-institutionalism and its fabled anti-intellectualism.[62] The result was a Tocquevillian nightmare come true. State legislatures swept aside the protective bulwark of the early bar by establishing general criteria for recruitment into the professions. Barriers on entry to legal practice were relaxed, local controls were nullified, and recruitment into the professions was opened wide.[63]

By 1850 formal professional associations had virtually disappeared from the American scene. With them went the corporate character of the bar and the patrician character of the lawyers as a group. Rather than rising above the diffuse and pluralistic qualities of American society, the legal professional came to embody those qualities. The typical lawyer of midcentury America was a rather mundane fellow, content to let the public interest emerge from the private interests of his clients.[64] The Brahmins of Boston and New York found themselves isolated and out of place in a state structured to work without great principles or great men.

Of course, the internal breakdown of professional organization did not spell disaster for lawyers individually, nor did it detract from their significance as a group in early American development. The key position of the courts in economic affairs and the disposition to view the judicial proceeding as a positive policy-making instrument were enough to secure a crucial place for professional lawyers in mediating relations between state and society. Indeed, the attack on the corporate character of the legal profession did more than vent the leveling impulses of American democracy; it also provided a burgeoning middle class with inexpensive and readily accessible legal services.[65] In a sense, the very indispensability of legal aid in court preempted the reign of that insulated and high-minded intellectual aristocracy that Tocqueville so admired.[66]

The decline of the patrician statesman of the upper bar and the proliferation of politically neutral legal advocates mark a general movement toward greater rationality in the operations of the early American state. By midcentury, technical competence within a particular institutional sphere stood as the intellectual standard of the professional lawyer. Significantly, this standard applies with equal force to the state's other human resources. Like the lawyer, the professional politician and the army engineer concentrated on perfecting technical skills, skills that would make them effective conduits for channeling social energies.[67] Such men were not set apart from society by exclusive training, social cultivation, or an ethic of service to the state. Judged by European standards, these intellectual types again suggest America's relative statelessness.[68] In their own unobtrusive way, however, they stood steadfast against aimless drift and turned the state of courts and parties into a vital instrument for American development.

From the solution to the problem

The operational determinants of the early American state were all innocuous enough to make it seem as if there was no state in America at all. In combination, however, these determinants bound a mode of governmental operations that proved remarkably serviceable within the context of early American society. Clearly, the capacities of this state of courts and parties to direct social development were limited, but within those limits the great anomaly among Western states successfully met the challenges it faced during the nineteenth century.

It was not until the pressures of industrialism created irresistible demands for a permanent concentration of governmental controls that this rather ingenious resolution of the problems of governing in America became a serious problem in itself. The state of courts and parties had been organized to provide a regional focus for governmental action. Its working structure presumed a highly mobilized democratic polity and the absence of national administrative capacities. Its mode of operations was not geared for an interdependent industrial society.

To cope with categorically new demands for national control, the nature and status of the state in America had to be fundamentally altered. National administrative expansion called into question the entire network of political and institutional relationships that had been built up over the course of a century to facilitate governmental operations. In turn, it challenged all officials whose positions and prerogatives were supported by those relationships. The following chapters trace the political struggles through which the organizational, procedural, and intellectual dimensions of the American state were transformed for the new age.

PART II

State building as patchwork, 1877–1900

With a new country, in which there was room and remunerative employment for everybody, with liberal principles of government and unlimited skill in practical politics, we were long exempted from the need of being anxiously careful about plans and methods of administration. We have been naturally slow to see the use or significance of those many volumes of learned research and painstaking examination into the ways and means of conducting government which the presses of Europe have been sending to our libraries. Like a lusty child, government with us has expanded in nature and grown great in stature, but it has also become awkward in movement. The vigor and increase of its life has been altogether out of proportion to its skill in living. It has gained strength, but it has not acquired deportment. Great, therefore, as has been our advantage over the countries of Europe in point of ease and health of constitutional development, now that the time for careful administrative adjustments and larger administrative knowledge has come to us, we are at a signal disadvantage as compared with the transatlantic states.

Woodrow Wilson, "The Study of Administration," 1887

Introduction: The triumph of the state of courts and parties

The triumph and its limits

The state of courts and parties emerged triumphant from the politics of Reconstruction. As the extraordinary institutional machinery of the Civil War was swept aside, American government resumed its normal mode of operations.[1] This was not a retreat to antebellum solutions to the problems of governing in America but a further development of those solutions. The late nineteenth century saw the clearest articulation of the early American state as a distinctive organization. At the same time, however, major changes in the society and the economy cast serious doubt on the relevance of that organization.

The demise of the Radical Republican crusade and the resurgence of the Democrats in 1874 ushered in an extended period of intense electoral competition in American politics. The major parties organized the electorate into two highly mobilized and evenly divided political armies contending for the spoils of the federal government. Between 1874 and 1896, national campaigns were fought to virtual dead-heat conclusions, and the parties divided control of the national government in all but three separate two-year intervals. The nature of electoral competition in these years further extended the hegemony of party concerns over governmental operations. More than ever before, the calculations of those in power were wedded to the imperatives of maintaining efficiency in state and local political machines and of forging a national coalition from these machines for presidential elections.[2]

The full flowering of the American party state in this period of radical environmental change strained relations between state and society. Parties continued to operate the national government for the broad dispersion of particularistic benefits downward to the localities at a time in which social interactions and economic conflicts were becoming increasingly national in scope.[3] The creation of more centralized, stable, and functionally specific institutional connections between state and society was impeded by the tenacity of this highly mobilized, highly competitive, and locally oriented party democracy. No matter how intensely the party professionals supported the further development of the private economy, no matter how closely they were tied to particular private interests demanding new national services and supports, no matter how clearly they perceived the need for a nationalization of governmental authority, their responses were restricted by the structure of political and institutional power in which they acted. The political risks were too high and the margins of political support too narrow to sustain any concerted effort aimed at breaking with established institutional arrangements.

An impasse in the evolution of relations between state and society began to form out of the unintended consequences of an old governing formula. Institutions and procedures once created to serve socioeconomic development now appeared as self-perpetuating perversions of that purpose. Writing in 1891, Frederick Engels specifically pointed to America as the clearest contemporary example of this classic developmental dynamic.

> Nowhere do "politicians" form a more separate and powerful section of the nation than precisely in North America. There, each of the two major parties which alternately succeed each other in power is itself in turn controlled by people who make a business of politics, who speculate on seats in the legislative assemblies of the Union as well as of the separate states, or who make a living by carrying on agitation for their party and on its victory are rewarded with positions. It is well known how the Americans have been trying for thirty years to shake off this yoke, which has become intolerable, and how in spite of it all they continue to sink ever deeper in this swamp of corruption. It is precisely in America that we see best how there takes place this process of the state power making itself an instrument in relation to society, whose mere instrument it was intended to be. Here there exists no dynasty, no nobility, no standing army, beyond the few men keeping watch on the Indians, no bureaucracy with permanent posts or the right to pensions. And nevertheless we find here two great gangs of political speculators, who alternately take possession of the state power and exploit it by the most corrupt means and for the most corrupt ends – and the nation is powerless against those two great cartels of politicians, who are ostensibly its servants, but in reality dominate and plunder it.[4]

If late-century America was a classic example of maladjustment in relations between state and society, it remained a peculiar example with peculiar implications. The distinctive logic of institutional modernization in this context was bounded, on one side, by the fact that America had never developed a dynasty, a nobility, a standing army, or an insulated bureaucracy and, on the other, by the fact that it had far outpaced all other states in the development of organizations of mass democracy. Parties in this context were the cornerstone of an old order, an order that presumed the absence of strong national controls. The hold that the party machines had gained over American institutions would have to be broken before new centers of national institutional authority could be built. The expansion of national administrative capacities thus threatened to undermine party government in the nation that first gave it full expression. At the very time that parties were developing in Europe to challenge the hegemony of more traditional state institutions, state-building efforts in America aimed at the disintegration of party hegemony as it had developed over the course of a century.

It should come as no surprise that the power of the courts grew with the power of the party machines. The judiciary's governing capacities were stretched to their limits in the late nineteenth century to fill the "void in governance" left between party hegemony and rapid social change. As Congress tore down the Civil War institutional apparatus with one hand, it vastly expanded the jurisdiction of the federal courts with the other. The sweeping powers granted were an open invitation to the federal judiciary to assume the role of stern policeman for the new national economy.[5] In 1890, the federal judicial structure itself was reinforced with the establishment of a national appellate court system.[6] The expansion of federal judicial power in the late nineteenth century was the natural response of the early American state to demands for national authority in the industrial age.[7]

Gradually over the 1870s and 1880s, the federal judiciary molded its new powers into an aggressive discipline for ordering governmental affairs. By the 1890s, the Supreme Court had articulated principles of nationalism, substantive due process, and constitutional laissez-faire that both extended and consolidated its traditional hold over governmental operations.[8] With nationalism, the Court recognized the continental scale of the new economic order and facilitated a concentration of governing authority. With substantive due process, the Court asserted that the judiciary itself was the only reliable bastion of rational policy making in this volatile democracy. With constitutional laissez-faire, the Court sought to sharpen the boundaries between the public and private spheres, to provide clear and predictable standards for gauging the scope of acceptable state action, and to affirm with the certainty of fundamental law the prerogatives of property owners in the marketplace.[9]

This new science of jurisprudence fortified the early American state in the industrial age, but bolstering this structure of power could not hide its inherent limitations. No matter how authoritative and aggressive the courts were, they could not hope to supervise the new economy or manage the kinds of conflicts to which it gave rise. Given the nature of the judicial proceeding as a governing instrument, a surveillance posture was the most that this state could achieve. The consolidation of national judicial authority in the late nineteenth century formalized a system of economic control that economic developments themselves were proving restrictive and shallow. Moreover, building a qualitatively different system of economic controls, one with the capacities to deal with the new problems arising in the private economy, raised the specter of a major challenge to the preeminence of the judiciary in setting the standards of state action in this sphere.

In the late nineteenth century, courts and parties revealed the full extent of their capacities to control the internal operations of American government and to define the relations between state and society. Ironically, the more thoroughly courts and parties structured relations between state and society, the less appropriate that structure became; and the more thoroughly courts and parties controlled the internal operations of government, the less room remained for alternative kinds of institutional relations between state and society to take over. The hegemony of these highly developed but functionally limited supports for democracy and capitalism gave the illusion of statelessness in America an ironic twist. These once innocuous pillars of governmental order now appeared as imposing obstacles to any new departures in institutional development.

The new intellectuals: America's state-building vanguard

The challenge of building a new kind of state in America was taken up in the post-Civil War era by an emergent intelligentsia rooted in a revitalized professional sector and a burgeoning university sector. These intellectuals championed a fundamental reconstruction of the mode of governmental operations to be centered in an administrative realm possessing "finish, efficacy, and permanence."[10] If the discipline of courts and parties could be broken and replaced with the discipline of cosmopolitan bureaucratic routines, new capacities for national governmental control could be tapped in the maintenance of social order, and the influence of a new type of professional could be institutionalized in the high affairs of state.

The emergence of this interest in a reconstruction of American government was grounded in a general reorganization of American professional life. A more secure infrastructure for the professional classes began to evolve in the post-Civil War years. New communities of intellectual competence – socially differentiated and internally ordered – were heralded in broad-ranging movements to establish formal professional associations, to upgrade standards of professional recruitment and practice, and to build universities that would train specialists and define expertise. Often these efforts engaged the energies of an older class of gentlemen who had seen the social position, internal discipline, and political standing of the professions deteriorate in the antebellum period. At the base, however, were growing cadres of younger men with eyes on the future.[11]

The intellectuals most closely associated with government clearly manifested this newfound sense of professional identity and purpose. The best elements of the legal profession sought to reassert their leadership in these years through the formation of bar associations.[12] The most notable among the organizational drives by the upper bar at this time include the formation of the Bar Association of the City of New York in 1870, the Chicago Bar Association in 1874, and the American Bar Association in 1878. Gentlemen reformers joined a small group of "social scientists" in 1865 to establish the American Social Science Association (ASSA).[13] Over the following decades, the ASSA spawned professional academic associations in the various social science specialties.[14] Parallel developments are notable in the military profession. Naval officers formed the United States Naval Institute in 1873, and the officers of the army formed the Military Service Institution in 1878.[15] The intimate connections in leadership and support that would be forged between these professionalization movements and the various campaigns for structural reform in American government mark the efforts of an alternative governing class to remake the state in its own image.[16]

The political orientation of this new professional class is manifested in the late-century attack on the "despotism of party" and the "oligarchy of professional politicians." A new generation of publicists, editors, and political commentators proclaimed it "the duty of educated men" to reject the party machines and dedicate their political efforts to resurrecting morality in government. American parties were deemed inimical to "good government" because they thrived on the ignorance of the voters, because they were void of principle, and because they systematically excluded those of "the finest culture and highest intellectual power" from positions of influence.[17]

The self-serving and righteously indignant style of this critique reflected the decades of political frustration that American gentility had experienced under the party regimen.[18] Yet, the political posture of the intellectual–reformers of the late nineteenth century was significantly different from that of the patrician statesmen of earlier days. In the first place, those of the "finest culture and highest intellectual power" recognized that the imperatives of institution building were now on their side. They addressed themselves to a crisis of institutional authority that could persuasively be laid at the doorstep of party hegemony. They exposed American party government as "the machinery of a much earlier state of things" and blasted its incompetence in the face of new social and economic conditions.[19] In the second place, the journals that carried their political criticism – *Atlantic Monthly, Century, Forum, Harper's Weekly, Nation,* and *North American Review* – created a national intellectual community for the first time and provided a national forum where positive and concrete proposals for institutional reform could be aired and debated.[20] In these journals, the traditional interests of virtuous gentlemen in a politics of deference and high principle merged with the new policy interests of the social scientist and the expert. Together they formed a politically aggressive and professionally authoritative voice for a timely program of bureaucratic reforms. In the third place, the intellectuals of the late nineteenth century worked to establish the legitimacy of a new kind of politics. They cleared a place for "conscientious political activity outside of regular party organizations."[21] The Liberal–Republican debacle of 1872 was the last major effort of the "best men" to tie their political fortunes to the instrumentality of a party. Gradually, they discovered that nonpartisanship did not have to be synonymous with the apolitical. By adopting the position of independent policy advocates, the intellectuals assumed a political stance more in line with their interest in institutions that were insulated from partisan manipulation, and they openly acknowledged the basic antagonism between their reform proposals and the established structure of governmental power.

The new professionalism and the new political orientation alone cannot account for the position of the intellectuals in the vanguard of American state building. Their self-consciousness, their aggressive political posture, and even their interest in securing influence in the high affairs of state would have counted for little were it not for the substance of what they had to offer at this critical juncture in American development. These reformers perceived the structural problems of the American state in the industrial age. They cultivated an understanding of the alternative institutional designs found in the great states of Europe. They developed specific plans for a bureaucratic reconstruction of governmental operations, and they were ready to assume control of the new institutions they advocated. In a period in which the established mode of governmental operations was being stretched to the limits of its capacities to govern effectively, the new professionals were the dynamic and creative force on the side of building new systems of control. They could, in Woodrow Wilson's words, take "the cosmopolitan what-to-do" and provide an "American how-to-do-it."[22]

The governmental alternatives held out by the intellectual–reformers had obvious appeal to many politically salient groups in society. The potential this created for the formation of reform coalitions was an essential part of the politics of state building. These coalitions offered the intellectuals political strength beyond their meager numbers and promised the interest groups improved services through bureaucratic organization. It is worth emphasizing, however, that the intellectuals entered these state-building coalitions with special talents and specific interests. They were not merely the spokesmen for others. Their concerns centered on the state per se, that is, on the problems of reconstructing the established mode of governmental operations and on institutionalizing the place of the "bureaucratic and professional elements."[23] These creative concerns secured the position of the intellectuals in the vanguard of American state building and separated them from those who merely wanted a specific service from the state. Moreover, because each element in these reform coalitions had a slightly different stake in the outcome, results that satisfied one element might not satisfy the other.

State building as patchwork, 1877–1900

Interpretations of late-century politics in America have traditionally been dominated by the reformers' views of the "weakened springs of government." These interpretations emphasize the corruption of the parties, the freedom that the courts gave the corporations, and the absence of national centers of authority commensurate with the national scope of social interactions.[24] Recently, scholars have begun to provide a more sympathetic portrait of the period. They have shown an appreciation for the strong party organizations capable of achieving an unprecedented mobilization of citizens into electoral politics and for the tenacity of the judiciary in its efforts to articulate clear and authoritative standards of governmental conduct.[25] These portraits of governmental weakness and governmental vitality are not mutually exclusive; but there is a tension that runs between them, and it is this tension that takes us to the heart of the politics of state building at this time. The preestablished state organization was revealing the full extent of its particular strengths and capacities just as society was moving beyond the point at which those particular strengths and capacities were still pertinent to the maintenance of order and control.

Those holding positions of power in the state of courts and parties did not ignore new demands for government. They strove to provide controls and services sufficient to satisfy the immediate concerns of politically salient groups. When it came to substantive institutional innovation, however, their actions were constrained by the nature of their power. They could not sustain support for any effort that threatened to undermine the established political and institutional relationships that supported them as a collectivity in the state apparatus. They deflected all broadside challenges to the established mode of governmental operations, and they maintained their prerogatives by keeping innovations subordinate to preexisting political and institutional arrangements. State building was simply a patch-up operation.

An entrenched state organization that presumed the absence of national administrative capacities could, at best, accommodate only a bastardized version of the cosmopolitan reform program. Between 1877 and 1900, America's state-building vanguard waged a series of losing struggles to restructure American government around a national bureaucratic regimen. Their efforts were frustrated just at those critical junctures where a timely administrative innovation would have altered the foundations of power in the state apparatus and recast the boundaries of national institutional politics. They were employed in government only so far as they supplemented the arrangements they sought to supplant. They found themselves unwittingly implicated in the implementation of stopgap measures to defuse immediate governing problems without penetrating to the problem of American government itself.

America's institutional response to industrialism in the late nineteenth century was delimited at every turn by the consolidation of the state of courts and parties. State building in this period is marked by the appearance of a series of notable institutional adaptations, each of which was caught in the unresolved tension between the governing demands of a new age and the triumph of this old governmental order. Alternative governing arrangements designed to support national administrative capacities intruded into existing institutional relationships, only to be held in an awkward state of suspension. The question of whether or not America was going to build an independent arm of national administrative power was contested but answered in the negative. Turning to the political struggles behind this pattern of patchwork reforms, we see the inherent incompatibility of the highly institutionalized structure of late-century American government with the rise of national administrative power. Moreover, we see the special difficulties of reconstructing institutional power relationships so as to support insulated centers of national governmental control in a highly developed electoral democracy.

3

Patching civil administration: the limits of reform in the party state

This is a republican government; it is democratic in form, and you will have to change the nature of the Government and change human nature also before you will be able to adopt in practice here any utopian theories about civil service.

Senator Joseph E. Brown, *Congressional Record,* December 14, 1882

A civil service career system is one of the hallmarks of the modern state. Its chief characteristics are political neutrality, tenure in office, recruitment by criteria of special training or competitive examination, and uniform rules for the control of promotion, discipline, remuneration, and retirement.[1] While offering institutional insulation and job security to the employee, a career civil service promises stability, proficiency, and regularity in public administration.

A comparative survey of institutional development in the late nineteenth century reveals a pattern of concerted efforts to structure administrative careers along these lines. The merit principle of filling administrative vacancies through competitive examinations was instituted in Great Britain in 1870.[2] Canada passed its landmark Civil Service Act in 1882. Japan implemented an examination system for promotions in 1887. A comprehensive career system for Prussian bureaucrats was codified in 1873. The Third Republic in France witnessed continuous, though unsuccessful, attempts at this time for a comprehensive civil service statute to reform the old Napoleonic administrative system.[3]

The American expression of this international trend was the Pendleton Civil Service Act of 1883.[4] Indeed, from the very beginning of the American civil service reform campaign, the cosmopolitan character of the idea was impressed upon those who would adhere to the traditional ways of the spoilsmen. Thomas Jenckes, a genteel Rhode Island congressman, began advocating civil service legislation in the late 1860s with detailed reports on the progress of reform in England, France, and Prussia. These

47

reports portrayed the United States as the only "civilized nation" without a commitment to a professional public service.[5] In 1879, Dorman Eaton, the chief architect of the Pendleton Act, produced the single most important piece of civil service reform propaganda, *The Civil Service in Great Britain*. This book not only set a British standard for American legislation, it also fused the idea of a merit service with "irrefutable laws of progress" and linked the patronage system to provincialism and incompetence.[6]

The lessons of comparative political development are, however, never as simple as the march of the civilized world toward a professional civil service. The reform theme was orchestrated in national variations, each of which harmonized with a particular structure of governmental power. The German reform of 1873 followed on the heels of imperial unification. It reaffirmed the "rank, file, independence and permanence" of a guardian bureaucracy that had been the centerpiece of the governmental structure since 1810.[7] Reform in Great Britain closed the last vestiges of patronage to a declining aristocracy and consolidated the liberal order. It followed the establishment of central party leadership, and it linked the parliamentary party organization, the recently enfranchised commercial classes, and the Ox-bridge intellectuals in a new mode of governmental operations.[8] In America, there was neither the interest of an established administrative class nor the vision of a rising political party to carry the cause of a professional civil service. America's party state had grown hand in hand with the use of administrative offices as rewards for local party workers. Assessments on these patronage appointees had become an important resource in financing national electoral compaigns. By mid-century, administrative patronage had become a key element in supporting the prerogatives of party elites and in facilitating their collective action within America's fragmented institutional system.[9] Far from representing the consolidation of an evolving governmental order, the establishment of a professional civil service in America posed a direct challenge to the governmental order. For this reason, the leading proponents of civil service reform in America had to organize in opposition to the centerpiece of the established mode of governmental operations: the constituent party machine.

Herein lies the special interest of American civil service reform in the study of late-century state building. Though in the mainstream of an international trend, the reform movement appeared as a countercurrent in American state development. Without a doubt, the establishment of merit examinations for administrative appointments was the single most significant departure in American governmental procedure effected during this era. Between 1877 and 1900, almost 100,000 federal employees were placed under merit rules.[10] But on what terms could this benchmark in the emergence of the modern state be reconciled with the triumph of an ostensibly antagonistic governmental order? To answer this question is to call attention to the limits of central administrative reform in the American party state and to show how a reform initiative aimed at displacing this structure of power actually provided a timely support for its further development in an age of rapid expansion.

Developmental imperatives and reform interests

The growing complexity of governmental affairs in the late nineteenth century made some reform of civil administration imperative. In 1871, the civilian payroll of the federal government supported a mere 53,000 employees; by 1901, it had increased fivefold to 256,000. In 1871, federal expenditures amounted to a mere $292 million; 1891 was the year of the "billion-dollar Congress."[11] The mode of governmental operations that had taken shape in Jacksonian America began to strain under the pressures of this burgeoning federal establishment. Administrative procedures designed in an earlier era to facilitate the delivery of governmental services now seemed to impede efficiency. The reform of civil administration was, as its champions well knew, a logical response to the arrival of a new stage in national development.[12]

When Carl Schurz, the German-born American reformer, lectured to his supporters in the civil service reform movement, he rested his argument on this logic of increasing complexity in social and governmental affairs. "The bucolic stage has long since past," he declared. With the close of the frontier, the expansion of industry, and the specter of a political majority concentrated in the cities, Schurz saw America "approaching the social conditions of the Old World." Our early governmental arrangements were facing "new burdens which tax their working capacity as well as their wisdom."[13] In this situation, no reasonable man could deny the need for a thorough reform of civil administration. The problem, however, was that all reasonable men were not prepared to accept the kind of reform that Schurz and his supporters had in mind.

> There are certain propositions so self-evident and so easily understood that it would appear like discourtesy to argue them before persons of intelligence. Such a one it is, that as the functions of government grow in extent, importance and complexity, the necessity grows of their being administered not only with honesty, but also with trained ability and knowledge ... But while every sane man accepts this proposition as self-evident in theory, it may be said that every opponent of Civil Service Reform denies it in practice – and, I

regret to add, a good many men deny it in practice who would object
to being called opponents of Civil Service Reform.[14]

Speaking in 1895, Schurz had twenty-five years of experience in the
civil service reform movement and forty years' experience in the rough
and tumble of Republican party politics to back up his suspicion of many
who called themselves friends of reform. Between the environmental imperatives for institutional development and the development of a merit
civil service in American government lay a state-building politics that
frustrated the champions of professionalism even as it implemented their
reform. The key interests engaged in this state-building politics can be
reviewed under three heads: the interest in retrenchment, the interest in
reconstitution, and the interest in party maintenance.

The most widely held interest in central administrative reform in the
post-Civil War era was expressed in the idea of retrenchment. Retrenchment, broadly construed, meant disposing of the excess baggage of wartime government, strengthening the government within a clearly de-
lineated sphere of action, and imposing a strict regimen of economy and
efficiency on the administrative apparatus. These concerns culminated in
the late 1880s and early 1890s with the first comprehensive reviews of
the administrative methods of the federal government.

The Dockery–Cockrell Commission (1893–95) undertook the most
impressive of these reviews. This joint congressional commission hired
consultants and managers from the private sector to apply the latest
business techniques to public administration. Labor- and money-saving
devices occupied the commission's time to the exclusion of any systema-
tic reevaluation of the institutional power relationships that underlay the
established mode of governmental operations. Congress specifically prohibited the commission from investigating the field offices of the federal
government, where the bulk of the federal service worked and where
public administration was linked most closely to party concerns. Congress also excluded the administration of military pensions from the
investigation, thus protecting the intimate relationship established between the Grand Army of the Republic and the Republican party from
the retrenchment test of economy and efficiency. The commission's
achievements lay in reorganizing accounting procedures in the Treasury
Department, cutting some minor clerks from the departmental service in
Washington, and reducing paperwork in routine matters.[15] Here was the
retrenchment ideal in its pure form as an ideologically incontestable and
politically innocuous response to the expansion of governmental activity
in the industrial era.

The merit system for civil service appointment posed as another retrenchment reform. Its first aim was, in President Hayes's words, "to have the business of government done on business principles."[16] From the very beginning, advocates of the merit system drew heavily upon such retrenchment rhetoric.[17] As a member of the Joint Select Committee on Retrenchment, Thomas Jenckes reported the earliest civil service legislation with the following appeal:

> Let us seek to obtain skill, ability, fidelity, zeal and integrity in the public service, and we shall not be called upon to increase salaries or the number of offices. It is safe to assert that the number of offices may be diminished by one-third, and the efficiency of the whole force of the civil service increased by one-half, with a corresponding reduction of salaries for discontinued offices, if a healthy system of appointment and discipline be established for its government.[18]

The merit system was, however, a retrenchment reform with an inherent difference. It could not maintain the political innocence of a mere alteration in office procedures. When tampering with civil service appointment procedures, the values of economy and efficiency clashed directly with the value of administrative patronage in the operations of the American party state.

The natural constituency for the retrenchment rhetoric of the civil service reformers lay outside of government in the business community. Business associations came to Jenckes's support early and he, like all reformers after him, eagerly cultivated it.[19] This reform constituency was composed largely of urban merchants, with bankers and brokers adding a significant voice. At the height of the reform movement, businessmen from these sectors constituted about one-half of the membership of the civil service reform associations.[20]

This business interest in reform is not difficult to explain. Those engaged in banking and trade were most dependent upon the basic administrative services provided by the federal government. Local customhouses and post offices were vital to these businesses. As the workload and staff of the field offices expanded, urban businessmen developed a keen sense of the limitations of the spoils system in providing dependable services. Reformers harped on reports of post offices where bags of undelivered mail lay forgotten in locked rooms, and they lectured local chambers of commerce about customhouses in Prussia and Britain that were four and five times more cost efficient per volume of work done. They argued that "the primary needs of the merchants and the great interests of national commerce [have] been constantly surrendered to the demands of party."[21] A merit civil service promised merchants and bankers an administrative system that would "protect their interests and secure efficient services in the departments in which they were most directly affected."[22]

Two characteristics of the "business side of reform" are worthy of special note. First, the businessmen who swelled the ranks of reformers did not assume leadership positions in the movement. Although they were to be the immediate beneficiaries of a more stable and competent civil service, the merchants' role was basically supportive.[23] The specific terms upon which their services were to be improved were debated and ultimately determined by others with other interests in the outcome. Second, new industrial capital is notable for its absence from the reform campaign. In the very beginning, several manufacturers' associations openly endorsed Jenckes's proposals, but this support was not sustained over time.[24] Not only were industrialists less directly affected by spoils administration than were the urban merchants, but the reform movement itself took on a distinctly antimonopoly, if not anti-industrial, tone. Spoils and industrial combinations were linked by reformers and merchants in a single system of governmental corruption and collusion. E. L. Godkin argued that the spoils system kept the government weak in the face of the "new money power": "The system is utterly unfit for the exercise of any control over large capitalists, or if it does obtain the necessary ability, it does not obtain the character necessary to resist the temptations which capital, when it thinks itself harassed, is always ready to use for its deliverance."[25] The civil service reform movement was fed by fears of a partnership of party and industry that would exclude the "interests of the great middle classes" from government. An administrative realm insulated from party would prevent the state from becoming the hostage of the plutocrat.[26] Retrenchment through civil service reform meant more than economy and efficiency; it meant giving the government a new internal discipline and a capacity to resist pressures from industrial interests.

The dominant interest in the civil service reform movement looked far beyond retrenchment. For the reform leaders and agitators, improved efficiency, more businesslike administration, and a clear demarcation of the public and private spheres were all important by-products of reform but not its central purpose. Their main concern was to eliminate a resource vital to the survival of the American party state.[27] As George Curtis, the single most important spokesman for reform, explained, "The difficulty is not the abuse of patronage but the patronage itself."[28]

What has been vaguely called the "moral side of reform" was the political strategy of an alternative governing cadre to transform the foundations of power in the state apparatus.[29] Both spoilsmen and reform leaders saw the patronage as "intimately related to success in the maintenance of party organization."[30] Reform promised to neutralize this motor force of the established mode of governmental operations. Deprive the party bosses of control over administrative positions, and they would no longer be able to command armies of loyal party workers. Deprive the party bosses of assessments on administrative officeholders, and a major resource in campaign financing would dry up. The American party state itself was the target of the men who organized the reform movement, wrote the reform legislation, and oversaw its implementation.

The leading element in the reform movement was composed of lawyers, journalists, academics, and clergy. These professionals controlled the executive committees of the reform associations and made up the other half of the associations' membership.[31] As a group, they represent a key link between America's old patrician elite and its new professional sector. Their roots lay in established American families and high New England culture. They attended the old eastern universities, and they proclaimed themselves the rightful heirs of a lost tradition of enlightened statesmanship. Yet, during the Civil War they had turned the United States Sanitary Commission into a propaganda instrument for espousing new values of professionalism, self-discipline, and science.[32] After the war, they filled the ranks of the American Social Science Association and proclaimed civil service reform the social scientific solution to America's growing "crisis of institutional authority."[33] The formation of the Bar Association of the City of New York in 1870 also linked the old patrician style, the new professionalism, and civil service reform. The gentlemen of the upper bar in New York organized to defend the "honor," "integrity," and "independence" of their profession after one of them, Dorman Eaton, was physically assaulted by members of the Tweed Ring for his involvement in litigation against the machine. The peaceful coexistence of the professional lawyer and the professional party politician working within different spheres of the early American state had been broken. The Bar Association became a bastion of support for civil service reform, and in a traumatized Eaton, it produced one of the reform movement's great leaders.[34]

Though predominantly Republican in background, these resurgent professionals perceived more similarities than differences between Democrats and Republicans in the postwar era. They saw two great coalitions of local electoral machines controlling the entire federal apparatus and reflexively distributing material rewards and jobs to anyone who lent them support. Their own experiences in postwar government confirmed that under this regimen "decent private citizens must inevitably be driven out of politics."[35] There was no longer any room left for men of policy and principle. In George Curtis's words: "The great officers of government [are] constrained to become mere office-brokers." National politics was locked in "a desperate conflict to obtain all the offices, with all their salaries, and all their unlawful chances." The spoils were the all-consuming concern of those in power. "No one escape[s]."[36]

With the interests of the party machine controlling all aspects of governmental affairs, civil service reform became "the prerequisite to all other reforms, whether legislative or administrative . . ."[37] Of course, the idea of a merit civil service had an intrinsic appeal to this meritorious elite. James Parton, the great biographer of the nineteenth century, called civil service reform "the duty of all professionals of influence, independence and standing" to strengthen the other professions.[38] Yet, although the common cause of professionalism was voiced by reformers, we can rest assured that the leaders of the movement were not primarily interested in the careers of administrative clerks and postmen.[39] Their sights were much higher. A merit system for administrative appointment promised to break the hold of the party bosses over national institutions. It promised to reopen the government to America's "intellectual nobility" and to permit them to resume their rightful posts as the leaders of American institutions.[40] Civil service reform was the instrument that would restore to power "that class of men who had gradually been driven from politics."[41] Reformers aimed "to rid our country thoroughly and once and for all of [these] dangerous and noxious counterfeits of statesmen, and thus make room for the genuine article, which we produced in good measure a hundred years ago."[42] They had reason to believe that the demands of a new age had brought back the need for enlightened statesmanship and that civil service reform would prepare the way for them to provide it in a new and modern state.

Significantly, reformers did not dispense with the idea of party government altogether. Their new American state was to be built around a new kind of party democracy. Standing next to their permanent and professional administrative apparatus, they envisioned a "responsible" national party system. As Curtis explained, the goal of civil service reform was not "merely a system of examinations" for administrative appointments but "the restoration of political parties to their true function, which is the maintenance and enforcement of national policies."[43] Schurz spoke of a "legitimate party politics" that would appeal to the public on the basis of great issues and then set a professional public service to work on behalf of their policy commitments.[44] This was precisely the kind of politics that the hegemony of the patronage machines blocked, and it was the only kind of party politics in which these professionals could hope to excel. Remove the spoils from American government, and party as well as administration might be fundamentally altered. Men with skills in the formulation of great issues, in the leadership of national opinion, and in the implementation of policy objectives would be catapulted into the center of power and become the new motor force in governmental operations. A new politics "fired with enthusiasm for great principles" would produce a "government of public spirit in which the best men [will] be proud to take a part."[45]

The goal of the dominant segment of the civil service reform movement was, then, nothing less than a reconstitution of the American state in its organizational, procedural, and intellectual dimensions. As a catalyst for this transformation, they offered a simple and timely alteration in the methods of recruiting administrative personnel. They took their model for reform and for the new American state from Great Britain, where the civil service had been successfully restructured and where policy-oriented parties, commercial classes, and Ox-bridge intellectuals had recently consolidated their hold over the central government. The only thing that seemed to stand in the way of national direction, authoritative policy making, and intellectual leadership in American government was an outmoded civil service system that secured the reign of localism, log-rolling, and bossism.

The third key interest in the politics of civil service reform was rooted in the position of executive officers working within the party state. The leaders of the reform movement clearly understood the strategic importance of obtaining support from the men who officially held appointment prerogatives. With the status of the executive branch at an all-time low and with the assassination of President Garfield by a disappointed office seeker, the reformers had a good case with which to appeal to the institutional interests of federal executives. Civil service reform promised to rebuild the autonomy and prestige of their offices. By freeing the executive branch from the domination of party bosses in Congress, reform would give its leaders an opportunity to assert an independent control over government.[46] Reform would usher in a new era "when our Presidents and heads of the executive departments will no longer be almoners of party government in danger for their lives for the furious onset of the begging throng, but will be respected officers of state having high duties to fulfill which demand strength and ability."[47]

No President more clearly articulated this institutional interest in reform than Rutherford B. Hayes. Taking stock of his appointment policy, Hayes wrote:

> The end I have chiefly aimed at has been to break down Congressional patronage, especially Senatorial patronage . . . It seemed to me that as Executive I could advance the reform of the civil service in no way so effectively as by rescuing the power of appointing to office from Congressional leaders. I began with selecting a Cabinet in opposition to their wishes, and I have gone on in that path steadily until now I am filling the important places of collector of the port and postmaster at Philadelphia almost without a suggestion even from Senators or Representatives![48]

This bit of self-congratulation cannot, however, be taken at face value. Even those who find "courage and honor" in Hayes's actions recognize that his successes were largely the result of a factional struggle within the Republican party over control of patronage and that his personal assertions of executive independence from Congress and party did more to leave him politically isolated than to bolster his institutional position. Indeed, to the extent that Hayes actually did assert his independence, his term in office is a lesson in the severe political costs of insisting on the purity of the appointment prerogative during this era of intense interparty competition.[49] No doubt, all late-century Presidents and many executive officers felt burdened by the never-ending task of reviewing the appointment recommendations of partisan supporters.[50] But Hayes's actions and reform visions notwithstanding, a late-century executive officer was nothing if not an astute party politician, sensitive to the risks and obligations that informed his position in the party state.

Late-century Presidents did have a natural interest in civil service reform, but it was, as a practical matter, distinct from the lofty ideals to which the reformers appealed. It was an interest constrained, if not entirely defined, by the political imperatives of maintaining a winning coalition of electoral support.[51] The President sat atop a precarious party alliance that had barely held off the opposition in the last election. Whatever his personal inclinations, this was not a propitious time for a chief executive to present a broadside challenge to his party. Neither, however, was it advisable to allow the opposition to monopolize the reform constituency. Thus, Presidents, as a rule, tried to accommodate the reformers as far as possible within the boundaries of the inter- and intraparty struggle. On this score, the politically pragmatic Ulysses S. Grant proves a better guide to late-century executive support for civil service reform than the high-minded Rutherford B. Hayes.

In his second annual address to Congress, President Grant asked for legislative action on civil service reform. The response came on March 3,

1871, at the very end of the legislative session, in the form of a rider to a sundry appropriations bill. It declared:

> That the President of the United States be, and he is hereby, autho-rized to prescribe such rules and regulations for the admission of persons into the civil service of the United States as will best promote the efficiency thereof, and ascertain the fitness of each candidate in respect to age, health, character, knowledge, and ability for the branch of the service into which he seeks to enter; and for this purpose the President is authorized to employ suitable persons to conduct such inquiries, to prescribe their duties, and to establish regulations for the conduct of persons who may receive appoint-ments to the civil service.[52]

At first glance, this sweeping delegation of power over a political re-source as valuable as the executive civil service appears a bit startling. But, upon closer inspection, it becomes clear how concern for the success of the Republican party could join President and Congress behind reform and overshadow any fears of executive aggrandizement.

The Republicans had suffered significant losses in the election of 1870.[53] Moreover, that year had brought to a head the disillusionment of the liberal reform element in the party with the ascendance of the machine politicians. Jacob Cox, Grant's reform-minded Secretary of the Interior, had tried to institute an examination system for appointments in his department on his own authority but resigned in frustration just before the election. Ebenezer Rockwood Hoar, Grant's Attorney General and a representative of the "best New England school," was also forced out of the cabinet, and his replacement, Amos Akerman, was seen as an affront to those who had looked to Hoar as an island of ability in a sea of spoils.[54] Grant had moved into a coalition with machine senators – most importantly Roscoe Conkling of New York, Oliver P. Morton of Indi-ana, and Zachariah Chandler of Michigan. By delegating sweeping pow-ers over civil service reform to the President in 1871, the Republican Congress had little to lose and much to gain. Grant might be able to patch up the party breach with the reformers before the election of 1872, but he was not expected to threaten the vital center of his political sup-port.[55] There were no surprises forthcoming.

Grant appointed the most prominent Republican reformer, George Curtis, chairman of the first Civil Service Commission in June 1871. As this commission worked to formulate a set of rules for the civil service, both the reform-minded "stop Grant" faction of the party and those leaning toward a Liberal Republican third party movement were thrown off balance. In March 1872, Curtis presented the President with a com-prehensive set of civil service rules, and they were accepted with only minor changes. Grant's congressional supporters kept silent, and the urban press hailed the administration's support for civil service reform. The prestigious Curtis defended the President against charges of corruption and insincerity, and a number of independent-minded Republicans came back into the party fold. A Liberal Republican–Democratic coalition, now jointly supporting Horace Greeley for the presidency, had lost a major issue. Grant emerged triumphant from the election, with the patronage forces taking credit for a major administrative reform.[56]

After the election, Grant sought to rebuild his 1868 party coalition of reformers and state bosses. While encouraging those on the Civil Service Commission to continue the good work with his full support, he openly defied the rules by making his appointments in accordance with his party and congressional support. Curtis, wanting a consistent national policy, not a place in a coalition, tendered his resignation in March 1873. Grant then appointed another leading reformer, Dorman Eaton, to replace him as chairman, and the shaky experiment continued. The first merit examinations were administered in the Treasury Department offices in Washington late in 1873. Now, however, congressional hostility came into the open, and the position of a reform Civil Service Commission, totally dependent on presidential support, became completely untenable. Funds were cut off in 1874. Grant told Congress that he would end the experiment unless an appropriation was made. On March 9, 1875, the President officially abandoned the rules. Eaton, the nominal head of an inoperable agency, vented his rage at a meeting of the American Social Science Association: "The fair field of reform is deformed, obstructed and darkened by the sombre ruin of this disastrous, humiliating experiment."[57]

The experience of the first Civil Service Commission can be understood only by distinguishing Grant's interest in reform from that of the reformers themselves. The President's central concern was to hold together the diverse elements within his party as long as possible. On this basis, Congress supported the reform effort, and the President used his new discretion over the civil service much like patronage to maintain a winning party coalition. Grant's actions diluted the electoral impact of the reformers' unrest without sacrificing the center of his political support. When push came to shove, the President accepted the sacrifice of reform to congressional interests and moved to consolidate his political position as the balance wheel in the Stalwart wing of the Republican party.

As a rule, late-century Presidents followed Grant's lead in handling the civil service reform issue. To the extent that the reformers were important to the President's political support, their interests had to be balanced with others in the President's electoral coalition. Rather than treating civil service reform as the cornerstone of an alternative structure of institutional power, Presidents tried, so far as it was practicable, to fit it into the existing structure. It should come as no surprise that once a new chief executive took office, his relations with the reform element quickly degenerated into mutual suspicion and intolerance.[58] Presidential interest in civil service reform, bounded as it was by a primary concern with sustaining internal party support and an all too slim electoral majority, led to bitterness among reformers even as they were called upon to oversee the administration of the merit civil service in the federal government. As Curtis knew when he resigned from the Civil Service Commission in 1873, to the extent that the civil service issue was treated as an extension of regular inter- and intraparty politics, the reformers' true cause – that of building a new American state – was lost.

Confluence and accommodation: the politics of civil service reform, 1877–1883

The critical years for civil service reform in late-nineteenth-century America lay between the electoral compromise of 1877 and the heavy Republican losses in the congressional elections of 1882. During these years, reform progressed through two distinct phases. The first centered on the New York Customhouse. Here reform rode a confluence of interests among a faction of the Republican party, a reform-minded President, the merchants of New York, and reform leaders. The second phase may be dated from Garfield's assassination in 1881. It was characterized by the jockeying of the two major parties for political advantage in accommodating the policy goal of an independent reform movement within the boundaries of intense interparty competition.

The electoral compromise of 1877 set the political conditions for civil service reform's first major success in American government. The official end of Reconstruction and the rise of the Democratic South intensified a factional split within the Republican party between those tied to the old southern strategy (the Stalwarts) and those who sought to redefine Republican party strategy (labeled the "Half-Breeds" by their Stalwart opponents). The Stalwarts' strength in the late 1870s lay in their control of three key state machines – New York under Roscoe Conkling, Pennsylvania under Simon and James Cameron, and Illinois under John Logan. Beyond their control of the Republican party in these key states, the Stalwarts' adherence to the old Reconstruction plans for building the party in the South brought a natural alliance with the southern delegates to the national party convention. Their failure to hold the South for the party in the general election of 1876 and the specter of a Democratic victory in that year suggested that Stalwart convention strength and party strategy could not be easily translated into national electoral success. In 1880, the Stalwarts unsuccessfully joined ranks at the convention behind a third-term presidential bid for Grant. By 1882, each of the state machines that formed the backbone of Stalwart strength had experienced a major political defeat.[59]

The Half-Breeds perceived the need for change in the Republican party strategy. They would rather sacrifice the South to the Democrats than sacrifice the party nationally to the interests of a few state party chieftains. The Half-Breeds saw Stalwart party strategy as inherently defeatist and their convention strength as potentially disastrous. The Stalwarts seemed "desperate old men" whose hold on the party prevented it from adjusting to the post-Reconstruction electoral alignment. The Half-Breeds wanted to strengthen the party's position in the North, to consolidate a lucrative alliance with industrial capital, and to build a centralized and independent party organ that could coordinate and direct political activity at a national level. By 1896 they had reached the first two of these goals, but the third proved elusive.[60] Their failure to transform the loose, segmented structure of the constituent party organization from within, along with the failure of civil service reformers to catalyze a reconstruction of party government from without, did not bode well for the future of parties as instruments of national government in the twentieth century.

It is essential to keep in mind the fact that the leaders of the Half-Breed faction – most notably John Sherman of Ohio and James Blaine of Maine – were first and foremost men of the organization. Their foresight concerning electoral strategy and party reform made them no less sensitive than the Stalwarts to the value of spoils in securing party power, and they were, if anything, even more instrumental in their pursuit of expedient electoral alliances. Blaine viewed the liberal–reform element in the party as a pretentious group of "man-milliners" whose loyalty to ideas came before the cause of Republican victory.[61] In the bolt of the Mugwumps from Blaine to Grover Cleveland during the 1884 campaign, this disdain was appropriately reciprocated. Still, in their desire to undercut the Stalwart machines and to increase the independence of the national campaign from local control, the Half-Breeds found something of interest in Mugwump demands for administrative reform. Though the champions of a merit civil service intended to undercut their power, civil service reform could, if used selectively, become a handy tool for securing the position of the Half-Breeds and facilitating their plans for the party's development.

The nomination of Rutherford B. Hayes as a compromise candidate at the 1876 Republican convention was not a fatal blow to the Stalwarts, but his complicity in the postelection bargain to end Reconstruction and hand the South to the Democrats placed him, for all practical purposes, in league with the Half-Breeds. During the postelection dispute, prominent Stalwarts not so discreetly hoped for a Tilden victory.[62] When Hayes appointed John Sherman Secretary of the Treasury, the new President's personal inclination to move forward with civil service reform blended with Half-Breed interests in replacing Stalwarts with more agreeable party leaders at the state level. In April 1877, Hayes ordered Sherman to undertake an investigation of the administration of the nation's customhouses. Following this order, Sherman appointed John Jay, a noted advocate of civil service reform with a well-known contempt for Roscoe Conkling's New York machine, head of a special commission to report on the New York Customhouse.[63] The battle lines were drawn; the classic political struggle of the Gilded Age had begun.

The Port of New York was the lifeline of American government, accounting for well over 50 percent of all federal revenues. It was also the lifeline of Conkling's political power, employing upward of a thousand workers in nonelection periods.[64] More than any other single office, the New York Customhouse symbolized the fusion of party and state, and more than any other single office, it focused the interests of merchants and gentlemen reformers against spoils administration. When the Jay Commission made its preliminary recommendations in May, all interests except the Stalwarts had reason to be pleased. The report called for a 20 percent reduction in Customhouse personnel, an end to political assessments on employees, and the "emancipation of the service from partisan control." It documented its recommendations with extensive testimony taken at the New York Chamber of Commerce. Hayes accepted the report in full. Sherman, charged with acting upon the commission's recommendations, placed the emphasis on reducing the staff by 20 percent (or about 200 men). Chester Arthur, Conkling's lieutenant and Collector of the Port, complied with the reduction.[65]

Sherman hesitated in going further at this time, but Hayes advanced. He issued an executive order to end political activity on the part of all federal officeholders and to forbid political assessments on them. When evidence of defiance of this order at the Customhouse was presented, Hayes attempted to remove Arthur and two other officers at the port. Conkling drew upon senatorial courtesy to have the President's offensive defeated. Hayes, incensed at this insult to executive authority, waited until the Senate recessed and then removed Arthur and the Naval Officer of the Port, Alonzo Cornell.[66] The President's new appointees, Edwin

Merritt and Silas Burt, reflected his political position as part reformer, part Half-Breed. Merritt was closely tied to the Republican forces in New York led by Reuben Fenton. Fenton had suffered serious defeats at the hands of Conkling during the Grant administration and was a likely ally for the Half-Breed interests in New York. Burt was a longtime employee at the Customhouse and a well-respected supporter of a merit civil service.[67]

During the congressional recess in 1878 the political prospects for reform changed considerably. On the one hand, Merritt had replaced Arthur's head men at the Customhouse, and at Sherman's direction, he had reexpanded the Customhouse work force to its former level. On the other hand, the Republicans had lost control of the Senate. When the new Senate convened and faced action on Hayes's appointees, Sherman saw the opportunity to turn electoral losses into a Half-Breed victory. He took direct control of the confirmation proceedings on behalf of the administration. After convincing the indignant President to give cause for his removals, he was able to rally a coalition of southern Democrats and thirteen Republicans to defeat Conkling's second appeal to senatorial courtesy. Merritt and Burt were confirmed. Hayes then ordered the application of civil service rules, including open competitive examinations for all new appointments, to the Customhouse. Merritt put Burt in charge of the reforms.[68] In March 1879, the merit system gained a foothold in the most important field office in the land.

Hayes's victory over the spoilsmen had clear limits. Late in 1879, the President pushed the reform initiative further by extending the civil service rules in operation in New York to all the principal post offices and customhouses in the nation. (Principal offices were understood as those employing fifty or more officers.) Sherman and Postmaster General David Key (a southern Democrat) paid lip service to their chief's order but did not follow it up in any significant way. Lacking both political support and the machinery to oversee its implementation in the field, this sweeping order could be and was ignored with impunity.[69] The second limitation on reform was even more threatening. It was by no means certain that the reforms in New York City could survive the Hayes administration. Merritt, like Sherman, acquiesced to the exams, but neither displayed much interest in building the merit system for its own sake. Moreover, the Conkling machine had won the governorship in New York in 1879. This campaign in a highly contested state forced an embarrassed but loyal Hayes administration to close ranks behind the Republican machine candidate, Alonzo Cornell. The reform initiative was thrown off balance, caught in the vicissitudes of intra- and interparty politics. Conkling was again on the offensive, with every expectation of regaining the Customhouse under a new and more sympathetic administration.[70]

At the Republican convention of 1880, Stalwart plans were again thwarted. James Garfield emerged as a compromise candidate with close ties to James Blaine. Postnomination conciliation with the Stalwarts included placing Chester Arthur in the vice-presidential slot and assuring Conkling of a strong voice in the cabinet. Once elected, Garfield made good his promise by offering Conkling the choice of Postmaster General, Postmaster of New York, Minister to France, and various other minor spots. But the senator from New York was interested in the Customhouse, and here the new President had other obligations.

With Conkling's rejection of the Half-Breeds' best offer, Garfield and Secretary of State Blaine faced an intraparty struggle similar to that fought earlier by Hayes and Sherman. The difference was that Merritt, who had supported Sherman for the presidential nomination, was in place and nominally tied to civil service reform. Garfield pushed ahead, removing Merritt and appointing William Robertson, a New York state senator who had led a critical revolt against the Conkling forces in the New York delegation at the party convention. The reform press was outraged at the mockery this made of their efforts to remove the Customhouse from partisan manipulation. Conkling was outraged at this direct assault on his own partisan interests. To defeat this appointment, the senator now adopted the dubious position of a friend of reform. The old Stalwart went before the New York Chamber of Commerce to pledge his support for civil service reform and for Merritt's retention. Not to be outdone by this display of principle, Robertson was paraded in front of the Chamber of Commerce to pledge his support for reform and to portray Conkling as a desperate man with a long and sordid record on civil service matters. Conkling was indeed a desperate man; rather than face another Senate defeat, he resigned.[71]

In May 1881, Robertson was confirmed as Collector of the Port of New York. His pledge of support for reform was put to the test under most unusual circumstances. In July, Garfield was assassinated by a Stalwart who looked for better days with Arthur as President. Placed in a difficult position, Arthur wisely resolved not to remove Robertson; instead, he had appointments to the Customhouse screened by a close political friend, Colonel George Bliss. For what it was worth under these conditions, all new clerks still officially passed the open competitive exams designed by Silas Burt. Burt himself resigned his post at the Port when Arthur tried to demote him.[72] The battered reform hung on, surviving as a weapon of the party politics it was supposed to supersede.

The events of 1877–81 did not produce any strong commitments to reform on the part of government officials, but it did provide the impetus for the organization of an independent reform campaign. As the Customhouse controversy raged, civil service reform associations began to spring up across the Northeast. The first association appeared in New York and claimed George Curtis as its president. By the time of Robertson's appointment, "affiliated societies" could be found in Brooklyn, Boston, Cambridge, Cincinnati, Milwaukee, Philadelphia, Providence, West Newton (Mass.), and San Francisco. Within weeks of the Garfield assassination, a National Civil Service Reform League (NCSRL) was formed to join these local efforts and added those in Baltimore, Buffalo, Pittsburgh, St. Louis, and Springfield (Mass.). Reformers now proclaimed the beginning of a "new phase" in the civil service movement.[73]

The NCSRL was dedicated to the enactment of civil service legislation at all levels of government, to a publicity campaign for public education on the issue, and to the election of those candidates most amenable to their concerns. By withholding their allegiance from the two major parties and offering their votes to the candidates most firmly committed to their single issue, the reformers defied the discipline of American party politics. Their strategy was to stand apart from fixed allegiances so as to use the intense electoral competition of the day to their own advantage.[74]

The reformers had a substantive proposal already on hand. The New York Association had placed Dorman Eaton at the head of a legislative committee to draft model statutes for reform at all levels of government. Eaton based his efforts on his detailed study of reform in Great Britain and his keen understanding of American law. After George Pendleton, an Ohio Democrat, submitted his own reform bill in December 1880, Eaton paid him a visit. The reformer advised the senator that his bill was impractical and probably unconstitutional.[75] Assisted by Curtis, Schurz, Jay, Burt, and others, Eaton rewrote the Pendleton bill along the lines of the NCSRL's model, and after some further negotiation, Pendleton agreed to use it as a substitute. The new bill was presented in Congress on January 10, 1881, and within days Eaton was providing testimony before the Senate Committee on Retrenchment. The reformers had made their specific policy proposal the center of congressional debate on reform.

The Pendleton bill created personnel staff services for the President. A commission would recommend rules governing the executive civil service, supervise examinations, conduct investigations, and make an annual report. All enforcement powers rested with the chief executive and the department heads. The original bill called for a bipartisan five-man commission that would be appointed by the President and serve at his pleasure. A chief examiner and a secretary were also provided for by law. The primary function of the commission was to screen applicants for appointment. No power over removals was specified. Open competitive examinations were to be devised wherever practical, and noncompetitive examinations were to be provided in other cases. Original entrance was to be at the lowest grade within any given service, and promotion was to be based upon merit and competition. Notices of appointments and removals were to be filed at the commission. The actual appointment, however, was to be made by the legally constituted authority from among the highest exam scorers. Interference with examination procedures was punishable by a fine of up to $1,000 and imprisonment of ten days to one year. Merit examinations were to apply at the outset to the clerks in the departmental service in Washington and to those in post offices and customhouses employing fifty or more officers. Extensions in the classifications of merit positions were left to the discretion of the President. The remaining clauses outlawed political assessments, mandatory political activity by federal officeholders, nepotism, and drunkenness. These last provisions applied to the entire service, not just those subject to merit appointments.[76]

The proposed legislation was thorough, its implications were sweeping, and its prospects were dim. The Senate failed to act on the Pendleton bill after it was reported from committee in February 1881. A similar bill introduced by Albert Willis, also a Democrat, failed to receive action in the House. These initiatives were perceived as a thinly veiled attempt by the opposition party to impose restrictions on appointments and fund raising after the Republican sweep of both houses of Congress and the presidency in 1880. Indeed, Pendleton's original proposal would have undermined Garfield's appointment authority. Moreover, in negotiations with Eaton, Pendleton had insisted on including the antiassessment clause that the reformer himself wanted placed in a separate piece of legislation in order to facilitate passage of merit appointment under a Republican administration. To the Democrats, however, the antiassessment clause was the most important for it would deprive the Republicans of an advantage in campaign financing.[77]

Even after Garfield's assassination, little of the party politics changed. Arthur came out for reform in principle, but he criticized the Pendleton bill for establishing an officeholding class and for imposing a foreign invention on American institutions. Pendleton introduced his bill again in December 1881, but the Senate session ended without action. The party in power still had little interest in substantive reform.[78]

For reform leaders, however, Garfield's assassination provided the perfect symbol of what happens when party instrumentalities run wild. They exploited the propaganda value of the President's murder to the fullest extent of their means and skills. The NCSRL immediately launched a poster campaign portraying the martyred President, with selected quotations in support of reform principles. As Republicans prepared their usual circulars requesting contributions from federal employees, the political strategy of the NCSRL focused even further. In conjunction with the reform press, it targeted and published enemy lists of those most adamantly opposed to the merit system. Although it is difficult to discern the actual effect of this campaign, the November election routed Republicans in those states where reform organizations were strongest – in particular, New York, New Jersey, Massachusetts, Pennsylvania, Connecticut, and Ohio.[79] Republicans lost control of the House, with a drop from 147 to 127 members. Democratic strength rose from 135 to 197 members. In the Senate, the parties remained in a virtual tie. More importantly, perhaps, Grover Cleveland, a Democrat pledged to civil service reform, was elected governor of New York. In their pioneering effort to organize a nonpartisan, single-issue political campaign, the reformers had good reason for optimism. Success in a new kind of politics seemed to herald a new kind of government.

The lame duck session of Congress in 1882 saw a shift in party positions on civil service legislation. The Republicans, worried about 1884, now sought to take credit for a reform bill. Moreover, passage of a bill while Arthur was in office would mean that Republican appointees could be frozen in place if the Democrats actually came to power. Arthur endorsed the Pendleton bill early in December. The Democrats were now in a difficult position. They too looked toward 1884, but with a taste of victory rather than defeat. On the one hand, they still desired a strong antiassessment law to close the Republican advantage in campaign finance; on the other hand, they would now have preferred to delay the removal of offices from the spoils until after 1884. A committee of Democrats pressured Pendleton to withhold his comprehensive bill until after the national election. The senator refused, but this cost him dearly in party support and effectively ended his political career.[80] Senate debate opened on the Pendleton bill on December 12, 1882.

Interparty accommodation to reform now proceeded quickly. Republicans defeated Democrats on amendments to strengthen the antiassessment clause. The final clause outlawed only *compulsory* contributions and political services from federal officeholders and forbade solicitation by government officers only on government property. This kept the door open for campaign committee solicitations and "voluntary" contributions. The Republican majority also secured preference for veterans of the Grand Army of the Republic in merit appointments. The West and

South secured an amendment to make the service geographically representative by distributing appointments among the states on the basis of population. Democrats proposed and with the help of western Republicans succeeded in striking out the requirement of original appointment at the lowest grade. This may have undermined the reformers' vision of an insulated and hierarchical career structure for the public service, but it also promised a faster equalization of party and geographic representation in federal offices. Another significant alteration in Eaton's original plan prompted little debate. The Civil Service Commission was reduced from five to three members, and the President's appointment of the commissioners was made subject to the advice and consent of the Senate. This raised a thorny question that reformers had sought to foreclose: Was the new merit service ultimately an arm of the President or an arm of Congress?[81] After two weeks of writing the interests of Congress and party into the merit system, the Senate passed the bill with a weak bipartisan vote that contained a distinctly Republican bias. The bill was pushed through the House in fifteen minutes and signed by Arthur on January 16, 1883.[82]

Whatever reservations reformers may have felt about the way their bill had been handled by the party professionals, they could find both a victory for principle and their own concrete representation in government in Arthur's selection of commissioners. Dorman Eaton, still nominal head of the Grant commission, was appointed chairman. John Gregory, President of the new University of Illinois, was the other Republican. The Democrat was Leroy Thoman, a judge and reform advocate from Ohio. Moreover, activity at the NCSRL remained upbeat, scoring victories for the reform cause in New York and Massachusetts. The election of Grover Cleveland, the New York reformer, over Half-Breed Republican James Blaine in the presidential contest of 1884 was the crowning achievement of the new independent reform politics.

The passage of the Pendleton Act and the appointment of the commissioners brought the reformers' challenge to party into the formal apparatus of American government. With the merit system as its instrument, the Civil Service Commission set out on a task that amounted to nothing less than recasting the foundations of national institutional power. A professional, nonpartisan discipline might now take hold of governmental operations. An insulated administrative realm might now drive a wedge between party and government and force the parties themselves to adopt the responsible posture exemplified in the independent reform movement itself. Yet, from the confluence of interests opposing Conkling in the New York Customhouse controversy to the interparty accommodation to civil service legislation, there was scant evidence of support for this reform agenda. Established governmental elites had not sanctioned a governmental reconstruction. Neither the Half-Breed Republicans nor the Democrats rallying around Grover Cleveland gave any indication that they were now willing to blaze the path the reformers had charted. The merit system was born a bastard in the party state. The support it had gained among the party professionals was that of another weapon in the contest for party power. The status of a merit civil service in the heyday of American party government remained uncertain at best.

Politics and administration: nonpartisanship in the party state, 1883-1900

From the administration of Chester Arthur through that of William McKinley, the Civil Service Commission struggled for recognition at the periphery of power. It supervised examinations, made investigations, recommended rules to govern federal personnel, and requested disciplinary action; but enforcement depended entirely on the President and the department heads. The problems the commission faced in American government during these years reflected the contradictions of its creation. By its very nature, it challenged the power base of the party professionals; its raison d'être was to place administrative offices outside the sphere of party politics. Yet, its fate was in the hands of officials who were nothing if not good party men. To build a merit system in American government, government officers would have to move against resources and procedures vital to their power and position. If the President's own political position as a balance wheel among party factions was shaky in this period of intense electoral competition, so much more so was that of his antiparty personnel agency.

The new Civil Service Commission could not alter the structure of power in the American party state. Ironically, however, it could and did help to make that structure more efficient during the personnel expansion of the late nineteenth century. The most important function of the Civil Service Commission during the triumph of American party government was to dry up selected pockets of patronage so as to improve efficiency and, at the same time, serve strategic party goals. The development of the merit civil service in these years followed the development of party power rather than challenging it and supplemented the dominant patronage relationship rather than supplanting it. Kept within strict limits, the commission provided a patchwork support for the party state and yielded little more than symbolism for the bureaucratic reconstruction that lay at the heart of the reform leaders' concerns.

The course of merit civil service classifications lends support to this interpretation. In January 1884, there were 131,208 positions in the executive civil service. The Pendleton Act had placed 13,924 positions (or about 11 percent) under an examination system for future appointments. The 117,284 positions left open to patronage appointment represented a spoils pool far larger than the one that had been available under the Grant administration. In January 1900, there were 208,000 positions in the executive civil service; 94,839 (or about 46 percent) were subject to appointment by examination, but 113,161 were still left open to patronage appointment.[83] These figures begin to suggest that although the merit civil service grew large during these years, its impact on the patronage system was basically one of moderation.

There was, moreover, a great deal of flexibility built into the patronage pool. Congress could, at will, exempt specific employees or whole classes of employees from merit procedures. Indeed, the slight decline in the absolute number of patronage positions between 1884 and 1900 is more apparent that real because the 1900 figure does not include employees hired under the Spanish-American War emergency appropriations or those hired to canvass in the 1900 census. Both groups were exempted from the merit system by law. Further, whereas a "position" in the merit service represented one employee, a "position" not classified within the examination system represented only a salary expenditure. Spoils positions were often divided among several employees, each receiving a percentage of the annual salary.[84]

Under these conditions, a neutral civil service could grow large without threatening the vitality of a governmental order that depended on a vast repository of administrative patronage to support its basic machinery. One might add that given the growth in the overall size of the executive civil service as a whole, some relief from the burden of executive review of congressional appointment recommendations was surely timely in preventing the entire system from collapsing under its own weight. Merit appointment administered by a Civil Service Commission provided a stopgap solution to this immediate administrative problem without undermining the preestablished mode of governmental operations.

A more detailed look at the classifications made between 1883 and 1900 shows how the advantages of a merit system were tapped within boundaries set by party interests (see Table 1). The positions subject to examination were largely clerical and technical. By 1900, the merit service encompassed the bulk of the full-time clerical work force of the federal government. Patronage appointment was preserved in most field positions and, of course, in the upper reaches of administration in Washington.[85] In this way, a concern for administrative efficiency was

Table 1. *Civil Service Classifications, 1883–1901*

	Pendleton Act of 1883		
	Customs	2,573	
	Postal	5,699	
	Departmental	5,652	
	Total	13,924	

Arthur

By dept. head	1884	Interior	249
By exec. order	Feb. 6, 1885	Departmental	1,200
By growth of service		Postal	200
Total under Arthur			1,649
Total classified			15,573

Cleveland

By exec. order	Mar. 1, 1888	Civil Serv. Comm.	8
Rules revision	June 29, 1888	Departmental	1,931
By exec. order	Dec. 5, 1888	Railway mail	5,320
By growth of service		Postal	800
Misc. growth			3,698
Total under Cleveland			11,757
Total classified	Mar. 3, 1889		27,330

Harrison

By exec. order	Apr. 13, 1891	Indian Serv.	626
By exec. order	May 5, 1892	Fish Comm.	140
By exec. order	Jan. 5, 1893	Weather Bur.	314
By exec. order	Jan 5, 1893	Free delivery post	7,610
By growth of service		Postal	500
Misc. growth			1,345
Total under Harrison			10,535
Total classified	Mar. 3, 1893		37,865

Cleveland

By exec. order	1894–96	Indian Serv.; Dept. Agriculture; Dept. Interior; departmental messengers and watchmen; Customs Serv.; postal dept.; Internal Revenue Serv.; Census Bur.; Govt. Print. Off.; departmental firemen; pension agents; Indian agents; school employees	10,396

Table 1. (*Continued*)

Rules revision		All branches (approx. 8,600 Dept. Interior; 9,000 Treasury Dept.; 6,700 War Dept.)	27,052
Growth of service		Postal	119
Misc. growth			6,549
Exec. order	Nov. 2, 1896		5,063[a]
Total under Cleveland			49,179
Total classified	Mar. 3, 1897		87,044
McKinley			
By exec. order			1,715
By growth of service		Postal	1,931
Misc. growth			15,900
			19,546
Rollback and exemptions under McKinley			−9,185[b]
Total classified under McKinley			10,361
Total classified positions	Sept. 3, 1901		97,405

[a] This figure represents Naval Yard laborers, who were not classified but counted by the commission because Cleveland's Secretary of the Navy instituted his own rules for their appointment.

[b] This includes approximately 8,800 McKinley exceptions not subtracted from Sageser's totals. Sageser marks the 1901 total as 106,205.

Source: United States Civil Service Commission, "The Classified Executive Service of the United States Government" (Washington, D.C.: Form No. 2909, 1933); A. Bower Sageser, "The First Two Decades of the Pendleton Act: A Study of Civil Service Reform" *University of Nebraska Studies* 34–5 (Omaha: University of Nebraska Press, 1934–5).

balanced with a concern for the spoils most vital to the maintenance of the party leadership and the locally based party work force.

The Pendleton Act itself brought three categories of employees under the merit system. The departmental clerks in Washington (5,652 positions) were of comparatively little value as a party resource. More important were those clerks in the twenty-three post offices (5,699 positions) and eleven customhouses (2,573 positions) that employed more than fifty officers. The act provided for the automatic classification of new post offices and customhouses as they reached that level of employment. This was a direct response to the interests of urban merchants, and if the reports of the Civil Service Commission are to be believed, the merit system did improve cost, personnel, and service efficiency in the offices most directly affecting this politically important constituency.[86]

The classification of these large field offices is one area where civil service reform might have significantly altered established political power relationships. Here, a wedge was being driven between state and local politics on the one hand and the national government on the other. As the New York Customhouse struggle suggests, such a change could have claimed the support of many of the more progressive leaders within the Republican party. Other factors, however, weakened the reconstituting effect of this opening wedge during these years. First, other sources of federal patronage were also concentrated in the larger cities. Second, the bulk of the expansion in the federal service in these years came in the minor postal positions and the smaller post offices, both of which were carefully kept outside the reach of merit classification.

By 1896, there were 78,500 patronage positions in the postal service alone; 76,000 of these were fourth-class postmasters. The fourth-class postmasters were part-time employees earning less than $1,000 annually. They were not covered by the Pendleton Act regardless of the size of the post office, and they could be found in every village and city in the nation.[87] With resources of this magnitude in minor postal positions, party elites could well afford to appease the interests of urban businessmen by classifying the administrative clerks in the largest field offices. At this time, the average congressman of the President's party claimed more than 200 appointments from the postal service alone. Senators or other party elites claimed those positions in districts held by the opposing party.[88] Despite the pleas of the commission and the rantings of reformers, minor postal patronage remained untouched by the merit system until Theodore Roosevelt became President. In the late nineteenth century, Democrats and Republicans alternated in making clean sweeps of this mainstay of American party government.[89]

Extensions of the classified service by executive order during this period fell into two categories (see Table 1). The first reflects a willingness on the part of Presidents to recognize the importance of special training and skill where party interests were not especially vital. Education and medical officers on Indian reservations, scientists at the Weather Bureau and on the Fish Commission, and Civil Service Commission personnel all fall into this category. As with the departmental service in

Washington, governmental services in these offices could be taken out of party politics without significant impact on party interests.

The second category of executive extensions includes large numbers of offices and more directly affected party concerns. Arthur, Cleveland in his first term, and Harrison all made such extensions as lame duck Presidents awaiting the ascendance of the opposition party to control of the executive branch. Because examinations applied only to new appointees to classified positions and not to those already in place, these Presidents could "blanket in" their own partisans, deprive the opposition party of valuable patronage just as it came to power, and retire as great supporters of executive independence and civil service reform. Ironically, this partisan strategy backfired with both Cleveland's classification of the infamous railway mail service and Harrison's classification of 548 free-delivery post offices. Congressional hostility to the Civil Service Commission had led to repeated denials of requests for adequate staff support. This caused long delays in completing the large lame duck classifications and allowed incoming Presidents to halt the postelection extension ordered by their predecessor before they had been fully processed. The new President would then rotate the unprocessed portion of the officers covered in the order with his own supporters before completing the blanketing in.[90] The fruits of administrative neutrality were thus harvested as an extension of interparty politics.

The most telling expression of the limits placed on reform by party interests was revealed in the Cleveland classifications in 1894–96. The first wave of classifications, about 10,000 positions, came in the wake of the Republican sweep in the 1894 election. The bulk came in 1896, when the President was fast losing the support of his own party to southern and western insurgents. In the spring, just before the Democratic convention, Cleveland froze about 27,000 appointees in office. Politically, the most important of these lay in major field offices of the Interior, Treasury, and War departments, including the Internal Revenue Service and the Census Bureau.

At first, the *Nation* proclaimed this action "The Completion of the Work."[91] Indeed, it might well have seemed so. Cleveland had included 87,000 out of 179,000 offices in the merit system. Out of the 92,000 federal workers still outside the exam system, 78,500 were postal employees. But partisans on both sides were outraged by this vengeful act of a President whose party support had dissolved. Democrats were even more vehement in their protest than Republicans. William Jennings Bryan became the only presidential candidate to campaign actively against the merit system. McKinley, once elected, also acknowledged that things had gone too far. Despite the fact that he was, from a partisan perspective, far more secure than any other late-century President, McKinley became the first and only President actually to reverse a civil service classification. Bowing to the sentiments of congressional party leaders, he exempted more than 9,000 of Cleveland's newly classified positions from examination. The expansion of governmental personnel in 1898 relieved pressures for even further rollbacks.[92] Thus, after losing his party's support, a bitter and isolated Democrat hastened the growth of the merit service, but a triumphant Republican restored that sense of moderation necessary for an expedient coexistence of merit and patronage appointment in the party state.

The politics of civil service classification adapted an antiparty reform to the exigencies of intra- and interparty competition. Still, the "nonpartisan" space in the federal civil service grew large, and Presidents after 1900 would be subject to many of the same party pressures for office. To appreciate fully the limits of reform in these years, we must look beyond classifications to the way the Civil Service Commission was treated by governmental elites and to the internal administration of the merit system itself.

The course of reform between 1888 and 1892 neatly illustrates how national party development could open possibilities for the development of a neutral civil service while at the same time delimiting the scope of reform in ways that not only frustrated but directly countered the reformers' purposes. For example, in successive annual reports, the Civil Service Commission declared that political assessments on officeholders had virtually disappeared from the federal service. Despite a weak antiassessment clause in the Pendleton Act, compliance rather than evasion was becoming the norm.[93] Although one cannot deny the importance of the watchdog role played by the commission and the NCSRL over assessments, it would overstate their authority to account for the change in this way. It is more appropriate to observe that compliance with the antiassessment clause became more convenient as parties developed alternative means for financing national campaigns.

Changes in party financing are notable in the Republican campaign of 1888. With the Democrats in control of the federal patronage, Half-Breed efforts to modernize the national campaign organization were propelled forward. To prepare for the canvass, the patronage-starved Republicans formalized their relationship with industry and big business. Businessmen's "advisory committees" were formed to work with the Republican National Committee in raising funds. The most famous of these new committees was chaired by Philadelphia merchant John

Wanamaker.[94] Working closely with the Manufacturers' Club of Philadelphia, the Wanamaker committee raised funds in $10,000 lump sums. The exact amount raised by all these committees combined is unknown. Estimates have put the contribution of the Wanamaker drive alone at about $400,000.[95]

As these resources were developed, the importance of assessments on federal employees declined markedly. Maneuvering around the antiassessment clause became more trouble than it was worth. As Robert Marcus notes, assessments on loyal party workers came to be seen as "poor politics and unprofitable." Quoting from a leading party strategist at the time, Marcus writes: "Assessments were an 'old barbarism.' The party could not 'honorably accept, much less coerce subscriptions from clerks or officers whose salaries are all needed to support their families'."[96]

With the decline of federal assessments, the reformers achieved one of their strategic goals. But success came with the realization of one of their most basic fears. This separation of politics and administration did not provide a bulwark against the "money power" in government; rather, it followed the fusion of party and big business in American politics. Clearly, the reformers did not have a monopoly on the quest for efficiency. The Wanamaker committee reveals a modernizing party adapting to new conditions, adopting its own innovative techniques, and defying the designs of the civil service reformers.

Apt expression was given to the emerging new character of the Republican party when President Harrison chose Wanamaker to be his Postmaster General and placed James Clarkson, a prominent campaign strategist and spoils manager, in the number two slot as First Assistant Postmaster General. This combination of a merchant and a party manager represented more than just a repayment of Harrison's campaign debts. It brought the new alliance of spoilsmen and businessmen directly into government. The reform press clearly perceived this and looked with horror at the prospect of this team in charge of the bulk of federal patronage distribution.[97] The Civil Service Commission, now boasting Theodore Roosevelt as its junior member, joined the NCSRL in a not so inconspicuous four-year campaign to rid the government of Wanamaker by exposing corruption in his administration of personnel regulations.

Roosevelt and Wanamaker disliked each other intensely. But the conflict between the commission–reform movement and the Wanamaker–Clarkson team has a significance that goes beyond personal animosities. Wanamaker posed a counterchallenge to the reformers on their own terms, economy and efficiency. Interestingly enough, the new Postmaster General himself might have made a good candidate for the reform movement. He was a merchant who had no special interest in the protec-

tionist policies that attracted industrial capital to the Republican party
but who had a great interest in the businesslike delivery of governmental
services. He viewed the old state party machines as backward, incapable
of meeting the new demands of the day, and potentially dangerous for
their hold over national affairs. He had amassed a fortune through
pioneering efforts in department store organization and mass merchan-
dising and now wanted to put the government's house in order.[98]

Yet, Wanamaker did not turn to the civil service reform movement to
express his passion for economy and efficiency. He entered politics to
work with men who, like himself, already held power. Wanamaker came
as an amateur into high party circles and offered to refortify American
party government. Farsighted Republican leaders could embrace such a
man, whereas Roosevelt remained suspect in his search for a political
position somewhere between the independent reformers and the party
professionals. Wanamaker, not Roosevelt, held the late-century Republican solutions to the problems of improving government services. The
Wanamaker campaign committee had formally joined business and
party. The merchant minister now took control of the governmental
business most important to both interests to make it work to the mutual
advantage of each. A Wanamaker success threatened to taint the reform
movement and its definition of good government with the stigma of
irrelevance.

The Postmaster General handed Clarkson the job of making political
appointments and removals (a task that was performed with unprecedented speed and thoroughness) and turned his own talents toward a
modernization of postal services that was to produce more improvements
in this area than any other late-century administration. He planned the
parcel post system, expanded the free delivery service, integrated the U.S.
Post Office and the merchant marine, introduced steamship post offices
and a postal tugboat service for intercontinental delivery and, in the
process, increased the postal surplus. His success in balancing party
interests and postal services places him within the ranks of such great
nineteenth-century administrative politicians as Amos Kendall (Postmaster General under Jackson) and Montgomery Blair (Postmaster General
under Lincoln).[99]

Even in civil service reform, Wanamaker claimed distinction by planning a career structure for merit employees. Working exclusively within
the classified service of the post offices employing fifty or more officers,
he attempted to rationalize personnel positions so as to equalize salaries
for equal work done. He then instituted a Board of Promotions in
Washington to regulate passage upward through the grades.[100]

Wanamaker's Board of Promotions sparked the first in a long series of conflicts involving the Civil Service Commission, the department heads, and the President over the control of civil service personnel. The commission argued that the rules governing promotion should be controlled by the government's legally constituted personnel agency, and that giving control to the department heads would not only create inequalities across departments but inject political interests into a procedure that should be based solely on merit. Roosevelt countered Wanamaker's board with an alternative plan for centralizing control over promotions in the commission. The President, however, decided to leave discretion with the department heads, thus giving his Postmaster General the satisfaction of effecting a civil service innovation in spite of the reformers. The Civil Service Commission kept up its criticism of departmental controls, but for all practical purposes it had been shut out of the promotions process. Merit service personnel were to have their careers supervised by trusted party loyalists.[101]

The Civil Service Commission's clash with the Postmaster General over the control of promotions was minor compared to the battles that raged over the enforcement of already established civil service regulations. With the help of local reform associations, the commission launched a series of investigations into post office administration. Roosevelt combed the field, gathering ammunition to embarrass Wanamaker and force the President to switch the balance of his support from the spoilsmen to the reformers. These assaults prompted a vicious counterattack alleging corruption in the commission's own administration of the civil service rules. As the battles dragged on, it became clear that the Harrison–Wanamaker alliance was secure. The commission failed to make itself more than a thorn in the side of the President, whose support it desperately needed. It was left to press for the symbolic victory and vindicate its legitimacy by exposing corruption to the public.

The most bitter of these struggles began when members of the civil service reform association in Baltimore called upon Roosevelt to investigate political activity by postal clerks in a primary campaign. Such activity violated an executive order issued by Cleveland in 1887. Upon investigation, Roosevelt found that postal employees not only took their campaign activities for granted but violated the Pendleton Act directly by raising campaign funds within their office. In a report to the President, Roosevelt put the prestige of the commission on the line by recommending the removal of the head postmaster and twenty-one employees. The President turned the matter over to Wanamaker, who made his own investigation and declared the charges unfounded. An infuriated

Roosevelt publicly denounced Wanamaker at a meeting of the NCSRL, and, with league leaders, a decision was made to press for a House investigation.

Because the House had turned Democratic in 1891, the reformers had a strategic advantage in appealing to Congress over presidential indifference. Once again, the advocates of administrative reform exploited interparty rivalry to their own benefit. The Democratic majority on the House committee supported the Roosevelt report. Ironically, the man whose campaign activities had done so much to alleviate the pressure for political assessments was found to be covering up violations of the antiassessment clause in his administration of the post offices. Yet, if vindication by an opposition Congress helped the Civil Service Commission save face, it did not enhance its political position within the administration. Neither Harrison nor Wanamaker took any action with regard to the removal recommendations of the commission or the Congress.[102]

The Roosevelt–Wanamaker struggle is instructive in illuminating the path opened for reform in civil administration during late-nineteenth-century America. On the one hand, as Roosevelt gained the moral victory for the Civil Service Commission's cause, he exposed its severe weaknesses as a substantive challenge to party power. On the other hand, as Wanamaker bore the brunt of the reformers' outrage, he demonstrated substantively how economy and efficiency could still be attained within the evolving boundaries of the party state. Wanamaker's vision of good government stressed new services for business on a grand scale. His efforts to realize that vision bypassed the commission and left it in a position of noble isolation within the state apparatus. At times, as with the decline in political assessments, administrative reform might ride the back of party development. At times, as with the post office Board of Promotions, party elites might effect an innovation in administrative procedure within a carefully delimited and party-controlled sphere. There was, however, an inherent conflict of interest between those who championed the cause of professionalism in American government and those who held the reins of governmental power. The limits of reform became clear whenever these interests clashed.

Turning to a broader overview of the nonpartisan civil service in the party state, it becomes evident that the very concept of a merit *system* overstates the achievement of reform in these years. Between 1877 and 1900, the merit service as a whole failed to attain internal coherence or to establish its integrity within the federal government. Large as it was, it remained inchoate. The Civil Service Commission zealously advocated the reforms necessary to build a new personnel system. Its annual reports to Congress denounced "patronage-mongering methods of administration" and offered the remedy of a new professionalism. But political elites were not moved to act upon this counsel. For them, civil service reform was basically a holding action that permitted an alternative and antagonistic system of civil administration to continue to flourish.

The investigations undertaken during the Harrison administration suggest that reform may have been more restricted in the depth of compliance than in the scope of classification. As the Civil Service Commission noted time and again, no one really knew the extent of compliance with the civil service rules. Whereas the three commissioners themselves constituted the only official investigation force for the agency, four-fifths of the merit service lay scattered in field offices across the continent by 1900. Roosevelt, as we have seen, built a reputation by roaming these field offices and publicizing abuses. Still, with this kind of spot checking, with inadequate travel allowances, and with no independent sanctions to levy against violators, enforcement of the rules at the local level depended largely on good faith. Reform associations often adopted the role of surrogate investigative units for the commission, but the formal machinery and political support for such an extensive operation simply did not exist.[103]

A closely related problem is found in the meager institutional resources provided for the administration of merit examinations. The new civil service "system" grew from 38 examination boards in 1883 (4 in Washington and 34 in the field) to more than 1,000 local examining boards in 1900. Effective administration of the examinations presupposed an independent supervisory capacity in the field, but the permanent staff of the Civil Service Commission was all based in Washington. The local boards of examiners and much of the commission's Washington staff were made up of clerks detailed by the departments in which the examinations were taking place. The commission testified to the status of the examination system in the minds of department heads in its early complaints that the clerks chosen for detail were among the most incompetent in the federal service.[104]

Working under severe political and institutional handicaps, the Civil Service Commission made valiant efforts to improve the processes of examination and supervision. Gradually, it gained a voice in determining which clerks would be detailed by the departments to help with its examinations. In 1898, a pet project was realized with the establishment of an experimental district office. Located in the amicable Boston area, the office was to demonstrate the value of regional supervision and administration. Yet, such accomplishments did more to expose than to overcome the problems confronting the development of a merit system in American government. For this central personnel agency to develop a new personnel system, it needed a concentration of authority, a specialization of personnel, and a penetration of institutional controls – all of which were basically out of step with the interests and orientations of the state in which it operated.

Nowhere was the gap between the Civil Service Commission's aspirations for the merit system and its actual operations more apparent than in the area of position classification and salary standardization. Building a modern personnel system for the employees who had taken the merit examinations required a wholly new conception of the federal administrative position as an element in a career structure, and any serious consideration of establishing an administrative career structure raised issues with sweeping implications for the federal establishment as a whole. In reclassifying positions, the commission could do little more than expose the need for a holistic reconstruction of governmental operations.

The Pendleton Act applied to "classes" of offices that had been specified in law in 1853.[105] The federal service had at that time been divided into classes based on salaries received. The civil service legislation of 1883 was designed to apply to clerks within three specific service areas (post, customs, departmental) receiving salaries in the range of $1,200 to $1,800 per year. Extensions in the classes (or salary ranges) as well as in the service areas were left to presidential discretion. Both the Civil Service Commission and the House Committee on Retrenchment recognized the crudity of this approach.[106] There was, by this time, only the most general relationship between a salary class and the duties performed within it. For example, it was common for a clerk receiving $1,200 a year to be included in the merit service, whereas another receiving $840 a year was not included even though he did the same work in the same office. Moreover, spoilsmen could easily circumvent the merit system by hiring a partisan under an unclassified division, say as a manual laborer, and having him do the work of a clerk who would have been classified.[107] Without coherent and binding relationships among salaries, positions, qualifications, and duties performed, there could be no semblance of order among the employees in the new merit service. They were little more than a hodgepodge of officers in a number of services intruding almost indiscriminately into the patronage system.

The Civil Service Commission could not deal with this systemic problem in any comprehensive way. Besides the fact that it lacked the staff and institutional resources to take on such a task, a servicewide reclassification and standardization of administrative offices presented an enormous political challenge. The idea of imposing from above an abstract structure of positions, salaries, job qualifications, and duties on the administrative branch challenged the way Congress appropriated funds. It challenged the discretion of executive officers in controlling their departments. It challenged the prerogatives of congressmen to intervene in departmental affairs. It challenged the supremacy of the spoils system by threatening to close the back doors that had made circumvention of merit appointments so easy. Ultimately, the specter of reclassification under the direction of the Civil Service Commission raised even more knotty questions concerning the precise responsibilities of the commission to the President and Congress and of the respective prerogatives of the President and Congress in controlling the administrative branch.

As long as these challenges were skirted by those wielding power, the commission's work had to proceed in a piecemeal fashion. Each area of the service had to be given a new set of personnel rules to cover its merit appointees, and the rules had to be altered whenever extensions were made in the scope and depth of merit appointment. The commission was consumed by the details of this work, but the results yielded little satisfaction.[108] Maintaining the old classification system as the basic structure of federal administration kept the merit system weak and the spoilsmen strong. Reclassification did not become a serious political issue until the administration of Theodore Roosevelt, and then it dominated much of reform politics in civil administration through World War I.

The impact of merit appointment on the intellectual character of the federal service remains as the final aspect of late-century civil service reform to be considered. The Civil Service Commission's greatest achievements lay in the formulation of examinations, the popular dissemination of information regarding exam schedules and eligibility, and the creation of appointment rosters. The examinations were, of course, designed largely for a clerical staff. By legislative provision, they were to be practical and geared only to what the job required. The commission defended itself against charges of creating an intellectual aristocracy by proclaiming that a grammar school education was all that was needed to pass in most cases. Merit appointment eliminated the ignorant and the incompetent and left what Carl Russell Fish called the "steady going and unimaginative."[109] Examinations, by their very nature, attracted recruits with college training. About 12 percent of the examinees in this period had some college experience.[110] Yet, merit appointment working as an adjunct to party patronage appointment seemed to militate against the kind of university–government connection forged by reform in Britain. Merit service was restricted to technical and clerical workers, whereas those jobs holding the most interest for the new professionals remained securely in the hands of party elites. In these circumstances, promising young students were actually being advised by their mentors against planning careers in government.[111] For those who did come, clerical work provided merely short-term employment in preparation for a career in the private sphere. In 1895, Roosevelt noted that a new kind of self-rotation had replaced the spoils rotation among merit employees.

> ... the civil service is not looked to as a career by anyone. Very few young men come into the service at Washington with any idea of remaining more than a few years; often merely long enough to support themselves through a course at a professional evening school ... This feeling will continue until ... promotions are based upon merit, and a check put upon unjust removals.[112]

Merit appointment did, of course, undercut the major incentive for political removals. There was little partisan advantage for the appointing officer in choosing among the three unfamiliar names listed as qualified on the civil service rosters. In Cleveland's first sixteen months in office there was a 90 percent turnover in presidential officers, a 68 percent turnover in unclassified executive officers, and a 6.5 percent turnover in classified executive officers.[113] The stability of the classified service raised questions of its own. The position of this mass of officers within the government could not be kept inchoate indefinitely. Workers who previously might have expected removal for political reasons began to suspect political reasons for every removal. The issue of employee rights began to fester as the century closed.[114]

The merit civil service in late-century America reflected the paradox of its political position in the heyday of American party government. Established elites found it possible to use merit examination as a convenient supplement to spoils appointment in the task of filling administrative offices, but few had a political interest in developing a new system of civil administration or in supporting the new professionals who championed it. The merit service grew as an expedient response to new demands on government, but it operated as a contradiction within a state that relied upon very different talents and procedures.

Patching civil administration

In the final analysis, late-century America shared one element with Britain and Prussia in the reform of civil administration. In each case, the results served the interests of the governing class that had been gradually extending its hold over governmental operations for decades. What makes the American case peculiar is that here the champions of a career bureaucracy were seeking to reconstruct the nineteenth-century governmental order and were held at bay by the consolidation of that order. Paradoxically, to the extent that the underlying political dynamics of central administrative reform in America followed the cosmopolitan pattern of the consolidation of a governmental order, the substantive results were actually quite different, and to the extent that substantive results of central administrative reform in America resembled the cosmopolitan pattern of professionalism, the underlying political dynamics diverged dramatically.

By 1901, about 100,000 federal positions had been placed under merit appointment, but as E. L. Godkin recognized, this accomplishment masked a frustrating failure of the reformers' purposes. America "was still ruled by a small knot of 'bosses' of the mental calibre and education of Platt."[115] Civil service reform had been accepted in American government only so far as it patched up the state it was intended to displace. A reform designed to catalyze an organizational, procedural, and intellectual reconstitution of American government had been awkwardly forced into an ameliorative mold. Like the Wanamaker initiatives and the Dockery–Cockrell Commission's retrenchment campaign, civil service reform became a further support for party and business interests in an age of rapid expansion.

In its early years, the Civil Service Commission provided little more than a symbol of a new American state. Party power and patronage politics remained the central preoccupations of governmental elites and preempted the development of a merit *system* for civil administration. The commission took selected officers *out* of politics. It ruled a huge, dormant zone – a neutralized, nonpartisan space in the American party state. The issues that would create an alternative source of governing power out of an independent bureaucracy and establish a new orientation for governmental activity had been brought to light, but they had received little serious action. The rules of an earlier era still held sway.

To find the true significance of the reformers' efforts, we must look beyond their limited administrative accomplishment. In their appeal to a new professionalism, their independent political strategy, and their cosmopolitan bureaucratic vision, we find the portents of the state of the future. The alliance forged among their Reform League, the American Social Science Association, and the Civil Service Commission presents in embryonic form the outlines of a new governing coalition. Moreover, the reformers were basically correct in their assessment that increasing demands for a national center of authority could not ultimately be met within the confines of American party government.[116] The success of the more farsighted party leaders in tapping some of the immediate benefits of reform while holding the reformers at bay had only delayed a confrontation with this basic problem in modern American state building. It was left to this alternative governing cadre, excluded from positions of influence, to expose the structural tension between a governmental order organized around the constituent party machine and the rise of national administrative authority. Whereas the parties relied upon consuming the federal government, the reformers looked toward a system of national administration more attuned to the task of governing and insisted that the construction of this system involve a reconstitution of the most basic determinants of governmental operations.

4

Patching the army: the limits of provincial virtue

Of late no argument has been used more effectively to prevent military legislation than the assertion that the principles of military organization abroad are
designed to support monarchies, and that, if not dangerous, they are at least
incompatible with free institutions. No delusion could be greater. The student
of modern history cannot fail to discover that the principles of organization,
like those of strategy, are of universal application, and that no nation has ever
violated them, except at its peril.

Emory Upton, *The Military Policy of the United States* 1881

A professional army stands next to a professional civil service as an
institutional standard of the modern state. In the late nineteenth century,
the Prussian army emerged as the undisputed model of military professionalism. With lightning-fast victories over Denmark, Austria, and
France, the Prussians redefined the concept of warfare. The key to their
success was a mass citizen army that was rigorously trained in peacetime,
readied for immediate mobilization, and commanded by a highly educated and centrally coordinated cadre of staff and line officers. This form
of military organization made possible short, decisive wars, and it put a
premium on long-term peacetime preparation, comprehensive planning,
and professional leadership.

By the 1880s, the basic principles of the *Landwehr* had been adapted
to indigenous military traditions in France, Russia, Austria, Italy, and the
minor continental states. The Prussian model was also the standard for
professional army reformers in Great Britain and America, but in terms
of actual structural changes, these more isolated states lagged behind
those of the Continent. Britain and America both relied primarily on
naval power for defense and expansion, and each put off a major army
reorganization until after a turn-of-the-century war – the Boer Wars
(1899–1902) and the Spanish-American War (1898), respectively.[1]

One is tempted to pass over an analysis of American army reform in
the late nineteenth century with this neat British parallel. Our shared
lethargy may be explained by the fortunes of geography, which freed

both nations from any immediate threat from land forces. Yet to leave it at that, at least on this side of the Atlantic, would be to dismiss as insignificant the period of American army development that set the terms of reform politics in this institutional realm for decades to come.

The first factor to be considered in an analysis of American army development between 1877 and 1900 is the failure of efforts by professionals at the national level to reconstruct the army establishment along cosmopolitan lines. The second factor is that this era witnessed a major army renaissance, an intellectual and organizational revival that was constrained to keep pace with new military demands within the confines of the old provincial forms.[2] This twenty-three-year period of army renaissance without reform offers a second look at the political dynamics of institutional development that carried the early American state into the industrial age.

Maintaining an army organization of any integrity within the state of courts and parties had always been difficult. At all levels, the American army establishment had been molded to fit a radically decentralized governmental order where national authority was employed to provide support services to the localities. The political significance of the tiny band of regulars supported in peacetime rested largely on the pork barrel contracts and development projects its Washington staff could distribute to congressional constituencies. The professional concerns of regular line officers carried little political clout. Indeed, these concerns only added an intellectual dimension to their physical isolation on the western frontier. The backbone of the American army was a locally based militia system. In the grand republican tradition, a strong citizens' militia was considered an essential safeguard against the rise of an independent sovereign prerogative. It was "the property and independence of the people in arms," a military force that could not act against liberty without destroying itself.[3] In America, these traditional republican virtues had been adapted to the rise of mass democracy. The citizens' militia took the form of voluntary social clubs organized by various ethnic and status groups, subsidized by the federal government, and fused with state and local party politics through ties of patronage.[4]

The army that fought the Civil War proved only a temporary deviation from the rule. After the Radicals' victory over Johnson and the election of Grant, congressional support for the expanded force of regulars eroded quickly. In March 1868, Republicans authorized the Reconstruction governors of the South to organize state forces (the "black militia") for the maintenance of their unpopular regimes. At the same time, they carried on a massive military retrenchment. The Union army, which claimed over 1 million men and officers in 1865, was limited to 54,000 in

1866; 45,000 in 1869; 30,000 in 1870; and 25,000 enlisted men and 2,161 officers in 1874. When the Germans marched into Paris in 1870, America was firmly committed to a thorough demilitarization. Once again, international main currents in institutional development ran directly counter to the main currents of American political development. As the Prussian revolution in military organization swept Europe, the American army was being swept back into obscurity as an Indian patrol.[5]

There was, however, no going back. It soon became apparent that industrial America could not afford the military innocence of the bucolic age. As in the case of civil administration, the governing demands of a new era placed unforeseen burdens on America's old governing formulas. By rejuvenating the army for radically new tasks without supporting structural reform in army administration, established governmental elites met the most immediate military demands of the day while sidestepping the political challenges of institutional modernization. The provincial military virtues of the early republic quickly yielded to industrial realities, but the provincial forms of army organization were steadfastly maintained. The politics of army development in the late nineteenth century breathed new life into the old and inherently limited structure of army administration and made the task of reconstruction that much more complex when it was finally embraced in the Progressive era.

Developmental imperatives and reform interests

Despite the blessings of geography, late-century America was far from immune to environmental imperatives for army development. The demand for a military revival at this time was rooted in increasing class conflict and international capital expansion. The years between the nationwide railroad strike of 1877 and the Spanish-American War define an era of labor violence unparalleled in any other industrial nation and one in which the expansionist aims of James Blaine, Benjamin Harrison, and John Hay reshaped American foreign policy.[6]

The implications of the late-century environment for the army were clearly perceived at the time. General George McClellan gave a fairly typical assessment of the situation in 1886.[7] On the domestic scene, McClellan declared: "It is idle to close our eyes to the fact that there now exists in certain localities an element, mostly imported from abroad, fraught with danger to order and well being unless firmly and wisely controlled." The unfortunate thing about a high protective tariff, the Democratic general quipped, was that it "did not exclude anarchists, internationalists, and nihilists of strictly foreign production." The endless waves of industrial violence could not be tolerated. In McClellan's words, "it is absolutely necessary to meet force with overwhelming force and crush the outbreak at once and effectually." America, in short, needed a well-trained internal police.

Turning to the international arena, McClellan identified "one of our greatest needs" as "an outlet in foreign markets for the products of our soil and manufactures." Competition for markets had drawn America into "closer relations with other nations." An expanding commercial power, no matter how favored geographically, required an international military capacity to protect its worldwide economic interests. McClellan acknowledged that primary responsibility for protecting American commerce would rest with the navy. But as the navy assumed a more international role, the army would have to take over the task of coastal defense, and it would have to be prepared to back up the navy with troop support. This, incidentally, echoed the navy's own assessments of the changing military needs of the day.[8] Surveying problem areas where the army might soon be needed, the general specifically pointed to Cuba as a key to the Gulf and a future isthmian canal and to Mexico, where "trouble may grow out of questions arising from business relations so rapidly developing, the large investments of American capital in railways and other industrial enterprises, the great number of our people residing [in Mexico], and the often recurring border difficulties."

Of course, America's army needs still remained substantially below those of continental Europe. McClellan was not calling for large numbers of troops or burdensome expenditures. The situation demanded administrative modernization more than expansion. He called for reorganization, strategic planning, administrative coordination, technical retooling, and the retraining and redistribution of troops – all of which could be accommodated with only a small change in the actual size of the standing force. In this view, also, McClellan was not alone. Time and again, professional army reformers denied that they needed or wanted a cumbersome and expensive standing army. The standard plea was to bring the permanent force back up to about 30,000 men.[9] Emphasis was placed on reforming the organizational, procedural, and intellectual dimensions of the nineteenth-century military establishment.

On the surface, McClellan's logic seems persuasive enough. He provided a sober assessment of changing conditions and a conservative appraisal of their implications for the army. But McClellan left out the complex calculus of political power and institutional position that would mediate any movement toward meeting new military demands. The political interests that intervened between the dynamics of American capitalism and the development of the American army can be reviewed under three heads: the interests of the professionals in an administrative reconstitution, the interests of the amateurs in a revival of the militia system, and the interests of those supported by existing arrangements in thwarting structural reform.

The last chapter focused on a group of intellectual–reformers who moved from positions in the Civil War Sanitary Commission, to the American Social Science Association, to the civil service reform movement. A parallel can be found among professional army elites. Military officers who had been catapulted to positions of power and prestige during the Civil War found that their total dependence on party strategy and electoral circumstances had placed them in a precarious position with dismal career prospects in the postwar era. Many followed Grant's lead, using their military records to launch a new career in party politics. But a small group, following the example of William T. Sherman, made a determined effort to establish the autonomy and integrity of the military profession and to institutionalize a place for it at that center of a new American state. For these men, the government's retrenchment policies were nothing less than a political "war on the army" waged by an ignorant and ungrateful public and their unscrupulous representatives. They openly rejected arguments that America's small regular force posed a threat to the republic, asserting that it was less a standing army than a "standing contradiction" within the established governmental structure.[10] They set out to resolve this contradiction once and for all through thorough administrative reforms carried out in the name of professionalism.

The foremost theoretician for the new army professionalism was a West Point professor named Emory Upton. Distinguished as a Civil War tactician and favored by Sherman, Upton was sent on a world tour in 1875 to report on the state of the art. He used the opportunity well. In his *Armies of Asia and Europe* (1878) and *The Military Policy of the United States* (left incomplete at his death in 1881), Upton took up the Prussian standard and launched a comprehensive critique of American military backwardness. Upton did for the army what Dorman Eaton did for civil service reform. Both used a foreign administrative model to define the agenda for institutional reform in America. Moreover, in each case, their institutional vision entailed a reconstruction of the American state that would bring the new professional elements into the center of power.[11]

Upton railed against those for whom retrenchment meant the destruction of the army in peacetime and asserted that the Prussian example showed the only true path to long-term economy and efficiency. He detailed how a system of warfare that began preparation only after hostilities broke out consistently led to inordinate delays, extravagant costs, and an unpardonable waste of life in protracted and bungled campaigns. The message was simple: When at peace, prepare for war. From this position, Upton launched his plan for an integrated, centrally controlled, and professionally directed military organization.

At the center of the Uptonian program was the institutionalization of military control by the intellectual elite of the army. Upton proposed the creation of a General Staff to supervise army affairs and specified a revised system of military education through which this staff would be recruited. A basic education at West Point was to be supplemented by a complete set of army postgraduate schools for special education, technical training, and strategic and theoretical investigations. A merit system would select the men to be guided up the educational hierarchy to the General Staff. Duty on the General Staff, however, was to be temporary to ensure a constant interchange of ideas and experiences between the staff and the line. The staff would concern itself with long-range planning, peacetime preparation, coordination of field and supply operations, and intelligence.

The program moved from intellectual leadership to a series of important procedural reforms. The General Staff would consolidate professional control over both the administrative staff bureaus in Washington and the troops on the line. The President, as Commander in Chief, would bypass the Secretary of War, taking his military advice directly from, and issuing orders directly to, the Commanding General of the army, who would preside over the General Staff. Changes were also to be made in the procedures of recruitment to the administrative bureaus of the War Department. Again, Upton prescribed merit examinations for promotion and periodic rotation between the bureau and line positions. For the entire regular army, he proposed compulsory retirement at age sixty-two. Together, these reforms would internally integrate and externally insulate the army hierarchy; inhibit the establishment of long-term ties between politicians and officers; establish a multifaceted and dynamic military career; and constantly ensure the highest-caliber talent for army leadership. A final procedural alteration involved the relationship between Congress and the army. Legislation concerning the organizational and material needs of the War Department was to be prepared by the planning experts on the General Staff and presented in old Hamiltonian style to Congress for approval. Of course, civilian authorities might ultimately reject the army's requests, but the professionals would gain the initiative in formulating their own legislation.

To these procedural and intellectual changes at the top were added major organizational changes throughout the military establishment. Upton's program called for a concentration of power, a centralization of authority, an insulation of army administration from politics, and a penetration of central controls throughout the territory. Between this vision of the military establishment and the American army of the late 1870s lay the deeply rooted traditions of voluntarism, federalism, and republicanism embodied in the institution of the state militia. Upton had no use for the virtues of this locally based amateur organization. He called for the abolition of the militia system and its replacement with an "expansible" national organization.

Under the extant system, the small regular army was supposed to form a self-contained model for the organization of the administratively autonomous militia units at the state level. In an emergency, these state units, complete with their own officers, would be called into national service to join the regular force. In Upton's view, American military history showed that this system was administratively and tactically debilitating, and he appealed to authorities from George Washington to John Calhoun to support this position.[12] The Civil War debacle in army administration was reviewed in detail to argue that an expansible organization was long past due in America. Under this plan, the small regular army would not be a self-contained organization providing a model for autonomous state forces to imitate, but the skeletal organization for an integrated national force. All the units necessary for wartime would be organized by professional officers of the regular army and filled by regular enlisted men at less than full strength. Regular officers would be placed in charge of military depots located throughout the country at major rail junctions. These would become recruitment and training centers for a truly *national* reserve force that would fill out the ranks of the skeletal units in time of emergency. Upton thought that battalion officers working directly in the localities and training their own reserves might bring new social respect and prestige to the regulars. He hoped that securing national volunteers would not become a problem, but he did not hesitate to endorse the principle of universal male conscription. He insisted, however, that this plan did not call for a large standing army and even went so far as to claim that the existing army of 27,000 might be adequate.[13] This small regular force, if properly organized and given complete control of the nation's land forces, could keep America on an efficient military footing during periods of peacetime retrenchment.

The Uptonian program offered a coordinated leadership core, a uniform program of reserve training, a consistent administrative structure for all units, and a capacity for speedy and orderly mobilization. The vision was holistic, and it was politically naive. Because of this, Upton's work was destined to become more of a guide than a gospel. Although it

focused and directed the professionals' reform interests, most of its ad-
mirers saw the need to search for some common ground with extant
institutions. By the mid-1880s, even General Sherman, Upton's staunch-
est supporter, recognized that his protege's proposed remedies were simply "too radical to be received with much favor in Congress."[14]

Just as important as the Uptonian program itself, then, was the creation of a forum in which it could be criticized, modified, and
supplemented. Sherman, working with General Winfield Hancock, organized such a professional association in 1878. One of the central goals
of the Military Service Institution of the United States was to bring about
a unanimity of sentiment in military circles so as to provide a united front
of military opinion before Congress.[15] The institute began publishing a
journal in 1879. Along with the *United Service* journal, which began
publication in that same year, it provided the men most interested in
professional army reform the opportunity for a full airing of their ideas.

In the early years of the period under study, America's regular army
officers had at hand a comprehensive program for reform, professional
journals to elaborate their ideas, and a professional association to join
their efforts. Like the leaders of the civil service reform movement, the
army's new professionals sought to build national administrative authority so as to play a key role in the high affairs of state, and, like the civil
service reformers, their vision called into question the entire mode of
governmental operations. But the political position of the professional
army reformers differed from that of the civil service reformers in some
significant respects. The army reformers were outcasts within the government. Their official status attached them directly to the structure of
power that systematically thwarted their interests, and as they knew all
too well, they were completely dependent on and subordinate to the
politicians who controlled that structure. The independent, antiparty
political strategy of the civil service reform movement was simply beyond
the reach of the regular army. Moreover, army reform promised to evoke
resistance at every stage from within the ranks, and this would hamper
the emergence of a politically salient constituency clearly attached to one
particular version of reform. All in all, the political position of the new
army professionals posed the more difficult problems for defining and
prompting legislative action.

The citizen–soldiers of the state militia posed one of the most perplexing
strategic problems for the champions of military professionalism. Sensing
the professional challenge and recognizing their susceptibility to attack as
an incompetent military force, the natural rivals of the regular army

organized for political action. In 1878, the National Guard Association (NGA) was formed to "promote military efficiency throughout the active militia of the United States, and to secure united representation before Congress for such legislation ... necessary for this purpose."[16] The NGA tried to define a reform alternative somewhere between the weak military posture of the old militia system and the radical administrative reconstruction of the new professionals.[17] One could not have asked for an interest more in tune with the patchwork politics of late-nineteenth-century state building. Here was a political force already well integrated into the established structure of power, pressing for reforms that would revitalize an indigenous military tradition to meet the new demands of the day.[18]

Yet, if the NGA's position was timely, it was also symptomatic. The divisions and confusions that riddled the association reflected the tensions inherent in a patchwork solution. Did the NGA speak for a new kind of military force or merely the revival of the old system? Did it seek to reassert the traditional ideals of localism, voluntarism, and republicanism, or did it speak for new ideals of nationalism, expertise, and professionalism? Were its politics that of a new nonpartisan interest group or that of an old appendage to the party patronage system? The NGA could not answer these questions for itself, let alone for those who viewed it with skepticism.

To the extent that the NGA was truly an attempt to mold an old military form into something new, representatives of the northeastern units best represent what it had to offer.[19] Above all, these veteran state officers recognized that a thorough reform of the militia system was necessary if it was to continue as the backbone of the American army. They cautioned the NGA to take seriously the professionals' challenge that local units, trained and controlled by state officers, could never attain the standards demanded by modern warfare. Accepting this challenge meant returning to the original concept of self-contained, state-based units that organized themselves along the lines of the regular army. They proposed the establishment of military academies at the state level and the opening of West Point – traditionally the nemesis of the militia spirit in America – to state officers. Mandatory summer encampments were suggested to improve training and eliminate those units with no serious commitment to military service. Inspection by the regulars was presented as a way both to standardize unit quality and to lend legitimacy to the state-based system. Compensation for militia duty, disability benefits, and pensions were called for. Pushing party politics out of the militia by ending the practice of electing officers and replacing political appointment to staff positions with merit examinations was viewed as a necessary part of the effort to gain the respect of the regulars. Taken together, such reforms promised to infuse the militia with a new military discipline and to erase the stigma of a social and political club that tainted its ranks.[20]

In practice, however, it proved difficult to gain unity behind these ideas. State jealousies and sectional controversies were never far below the surface at NGA meetings. Officers were deeply divided over how to strike a balance among the expectations of the regulars, the social traditions of the volunteer units, and the pull of local politics.

The official NGA program outlined the actual area of agreement. It called for a distinction in federal and state laws between the "organized militia" of actually operating state units and the "unorganized militia" that encompassed all men between the ages of eighteen and forty-five. The organized militia was to be officially designated the "National Guard." The NGA then demanded official recognition of the National Guard as the first-line reserve to be called in any national emergency. The federal subsidy for the state militia was to be raised from the $200,000 set in 1808 to $1 million, and it was to be distributed by the states only to the officially designated units of the National Guard. Summer encampments, direct compensation for duties performed, and rifle contests with the regulars were also supported.

The telltale point of dispute in all this was how the federal and state governments were to distinguish a National Guard unit fit for a subsidy from a social or political club claiming guard status. If the NGA as a whole did in fact speak for more than a band of independent state organizations united to raid the federal treasury, one would expect to find support for some official national board that would set standards of training and organization for subsidized units. The NGA easily agreed that regulars might be invited at the state's discretion to give advice and consultation, but proposals for more substantive supervision met with cries of centralization. Even a moderate proposal for a five-member national militia review board, including two regulars and one militia officer from each section of the country, proved to be more than the NGA could support. The search for a compromise between state control and national supervision dominated the NGA's meetings throughout this era and reflected its own uncertainty as to its real intentions.[21]

Of course, there were still distinct political advantages to the ambiguities in the guard's official reform position. The NGA could claim some support from both southern states' righters, who would just as soon have replaced the regulars altogether with the militia system, and from nationalist professionals, who hoped ultimately to replace the state-based system with a national reserve under regular army control. It could ally itself with the regulars on general issues of military improvement and with state politicians on issues of local control. It appeared a force for modernization in its call for exclusive recognition of high-quality, active troops, and yet, it claimed to represent the traditional republican virtues against European-style professionalism. Added to the advantages of its temporizing reform position was the fact that the guard carried political clout. The men who spent their recreational hours in the militia at considerable personal expense were either thoroughly committed to the cause, advancing careers in local politics, or both. In any case, they controlled more than their share of votes on election day.[22] Whatever the NGA really represented in terms of army reform, it constituted a political force that national politicians could not afford to ignore.

The National Guard and the regular army both spoke for reform in the old military establishment. During much of the late nineteenth century, these traditional rivals tried to move closer together. Kept within limits, a national militia reform movement could become a boon for the regulars' own cause "because it would throw in favor of the military establishment of the nation as a whole a popular and political influence which the Army has never been able to command and which it sorely needs."[23] Militia reformers, in turn, looked to the regulars to bestow legitimacy on their efforts. Yet the common interests in this reform coalition were severely restricted in scope. Basically, the guard sought army reform from the bottom up in the name of federalism and the amateur, whereas the regulars sought army reform from the top down in the name of nationalism and professionalism. Put in more concrete terms, the regulars wanted a truly national reserve organized on the expansible model, whereas the guard insisted that their state units be designated the first-line reserve.[24] These fundamentally different approaches kept the two major interests for army reform at arm's length despite their acknowledged need for mutual support.

Those with a stake in reform may have found it difficult to join forces, but those with a stake in the status quo found many political allies. The state governors were one political power standing steadfast against any structural reforms. It should come as no surprise that the governors joined the guard in opposing the expansible army plan. The governors had been able to build substantial political empires early in the Civil War by appointing new sets of officers to new militia units with each call for troops. The expansible plan threatened to render the governors powerless in wartime by having regular officers organize all the units necessary at less than full strength and by merely filling and refilling these units under the same officers with each call for troops. The governors were, however, little more enthusiastic about the proposals of the NGA. Even though the guard declared itself opposed to central control, the governors were instinctively wary of a national political lobby that wanted to upgrade and standardize their militia for ready use as a national reserve. The party machines had packed the states' adjutant generals' offices with patronage appointees, leaving the militia top-heavy with political generals, disorganized at the line, and vulnerable to federal meddling. Regardless of the sincerity of the militia reformers themselves, guardsmen were severely constrained in any effective pursuit of their national goals by the determination of state political elites to maintain complete administrative control.[25]

The governors were, of course, not the only ones threatened by proposals to modernize the army. The challenge of the professionals' reform program reached into all areas of the integrated structure of political and institutional power that governed late-century America. No proposal cut through more established arrangements than the call for a General Staff. The unparalleled confusion over the meaning of General Staff reform in America and the interminable struggle over its role in the army hierarchy followed directly from its reconstructive implications.

In the first place, the General Staff idea appeared in America as a thinly veiled attack on the Secretary of War and the tradition of civilian control over military affairs. Under the established structure of command, the Secretary of War directed the administrative staff bureaus of the War Department. Through these bureaus, he controlled the distribution of War Department patronage and had some access to the troops of the line. In theory, however, actual command over the line rested in the office of the Commanding General, usually held by the senior top-ranking officer in the regular army. This division of control over the staff and the line was obviously flawed from the point of view of military efficiency, and it sparked some of the most bitter bureaucratic conflicts of the nineteenth century. The call for a General Staff to consolidate the army establishment under professional leadership merely restated the long-standing conflict between the Secretary of War and the Commanding General in terms of a timely need for comprehensive and long-range military planning. In the Uptonian scheme, a Secretary of War was a superfluous figure standing completely outside the chain of command.[26]

The political implications of the General Staff proposal extended downward through the army and outward to relations between the army and Congress. The political resources of the Secretary of War usually gave him the advantage in fending off a challenge from a Commanding General, but short tenure and lack of expertise confined the secretary largely to legal, financial, and patronage matters. While two weak officials clashed over the command question, de facto control of the War Department became lodged in the administrative bureaus and consolidated in close political and social ties between bureau chiefs and Congress. In peacetime, even the President's authority over the armed forces took second place to these horizontal relationships.[27]

The technical and supply bureaus of the War Department were composed of regular army officers who held their staff appointments for life.[28] Original appointments to the staff were, more often than not, political in nature, and movement through the ranks was determined by seniority. Staff duty was the plum of the army. It meant escape from the drudgery of the fort and the frontier, a life in the nation's most desirable cities, and direct contact with those holding the reins of political power.

Though the chiefs of the bureaus were generals, they were not *generalists* and did not perform the functions of a General Staff. They maintained their bureaus as separate and independent fiefdoms. They were able technical experts in their specific fields, but they did not provide a central planning unit for army operations, nor did they press for an exalted role for their profession in the high councils of government. Like the lawyer–technicians and the party managers, they were professionals of the old school, and they embodied the political mores of the nineteenth century.[29] They had built the administrative autonomy and political power of their bureaus as an extension of the structure of the early American state. Congress was less interested in an integrated national army organization than in the perquisites that the War Department had to distribute to the separate states in the form of engineering projects and contracts. The staff handled all such matters and cultivated a role as the servants of congressmen. Over the years, Congress gave the bureaus independent statutory authority, effectively removing them from direct military supervision. Congressmen became the political defenders of the staff, and the bureaus secured a position outside the regular army hierarchy, operating as intermediaries among the army, the Secretary of War, and Congress.[30]

The regulars on the staff and line could unite behind several elements of the professional reform program – maintaining or slightly increasing the size of the regular force, adopting an expansible army organization, and limiting the role of the militia to state duty. But when it came to the centerpiece of the plan – the proposal for a General Staff to consolidate and coordinate army operations – the ranks of the professionals split wide open. A General Staff threatened to break bureau power as it had been nurtured through personal, pork barrel, and legal connections with Congress. In this light, it is significant that those, like Upton and Sher-

man, who spearheaded the professional reform program were officers of
the line. Along with the Commanding General, the line officers were the
ones most systematically disadvantaged by the established structure of
army administration and the ones who stood to gain the most by displacing the Secretary of War with General Staff controls over the administrative bureaus.[31] It is also significant in this regard that the linesmen insisted
on a rationalization of the military career structure as part of their plan.
In this era of retrenchment, the linesmen, not the staffers, bore the brunt
of frustration in severely restricted career opportunities. Through proposals for periodic rotation between the staff and the line and merit
examinations for promotion, they aimed to brighten their prospects.

One final set of interests must be added to the political maze mediating
army reform – that of the national parties. On the Democratic side, there
was a strong tradition of antiprofessional, pro-militia sentiment rooted in
Jacksonian doctrines of states' rights, frugal government, and the virtues
of the common man. The return of the South over the 1870s suggested
that the regulars had yet to feel the worst from this quarter. Democrats
returned to a position of strength in the national government with an
unveiled hatred for troops that had not only occupied the South but
openly colluded with the Radicals to impose the Republican party and
the Negro on southern politics. On the Republican side, traditions were
more favorable to the regulars, but the exigencies of electoral politics
were not. The Half-Breed electoral compromise to remove the occupation troops and return the army to a meager force on the Indian frontier
was a treaty for peaceful coexistence between racists and industrialists
premised on the absence of a national military capacity. Until the summer
of 1877, there was little reason to doubt that a thorough dismantling of
the regular army was a policy consistent with rising Republican interest
in industrial expansion.[32]

Domestic crisis and army fragmentation: revival without reform, 1877–1898

Within months of Hayes's inauguration, the critical weakness in the
Half-Breed formula for reconciling political and economic interests in the
antebellum years was dramatically brought to light. In July 1877, a railroad strike spread across the nation, immobilizing the transportation
network of the industrial North. The Half-Breed Republicans, resurgent
Democrats, and influential railroad magnates who had so recently joined
to end the military occupation of the South suddenly found that they had
very different interests in the army. Somehow, the southern reaction

against the army had to be balanced with a new northern reaction in favor of the army.

In this situation, a politically feasible path for army development was difficult to discern. National policy progressed on two opposing levels simultaneously. One was dictated by the demands of the southern compromise, the other by the demands of the northern strike. One was based on an old states' rights politics, the other on a new national economy. This juxtaposition of political and economic developments set the boundaries for the revival of the army during the strike and its aftermath.

Even before Hayes's inauguration, the Democratic House had moved to secure the terms of the electoral compromise by reducing the ranks of the regulars from 27,000 to 17,000 and by forbidding in statute the use of federal troops at the polls. The appropriate clauses were included in a House appropriation bill for the army in February 1877, but the Republican Senate refused to concur. The Democrats stood their ground, and no appropriation was made. When pulling the troops out of the South, President Hayes defended himself against criticism by calling attention to the fact that he really had no army to keep there. Indeed, when the Great Strike began, the regulars found themselves without pay or provisions, surviving only on leftover rations and government loans.[33]

Then, for a moment, the political fortunes of the army took a radical turn. Between July and November, support swelled for reforms that would strengthen the position of the regulars in both society and government. During the early days of the strike, the old republican faith in citizen–soldiers appeared to threaten capitulation to the mob. Militia units faltered badly in actions at Baltimore, Philadelphia, and Pittsburgh. There were no organized militia units on hand when the strike reached Indiana and Missouri. Most fearful of all were reports of fraternization between militia men and strikers in West Virginia, New York, and Ohio. The specter of a militia collapse drew anxious appeals for federal troops.[34]

The crisis placed Hayes in a difficult position. His embryonic presidency was a concrete expression of the Republican bargain struck the previous fall with railroad interests and southern Democrats. The Democrats had just cut off all funds for the army; the railroads were now demanding immediate army mobilization. Added to this political dilemma were certain strategic problems. There were only 3,000 regular troops on hand in the entire Atlantic Division. The President could nationalize militia units for deployment across state lines; but at this time, only southern units were both available and accessible, and the prospect of using southern boys to fight in northern cities was both politically and tactically undesirable.[35]

The President's response was necessarily conservative. By sending regulars only at the formal request of a governor, he precluded charges of federal interference and federal responsibility. By directing troops to protect United States property and *by their presence* to promote law and order, he attempted to limit the necessarily small federal detachments to a show of force and to avoid major clashes with strikers. In practice, however, when the regulars arrived on the scene, these restrained presidential orders were countered by pressures from governors, federal marshals, and railroad men. Confusion over who actually commanded the federal troops in the localities during a strike led to a more active role for the regulars.[36]

As the summer wore on, militia units were reinforced by local businessmen's associations with personnel and material support.[37] By the end of August, they had become considerably more effective in restoring order.[38] Yet, the memories of the early militia debacle remained strong, and public admiration for the regulars soared. In the northern cities in particular, the strike left traditional comparisons between the citizen–soldier and the professional completely inverted. The *Chicago Tribune* praised the regulars, criticized the constitutional formalities that hampered their immediate employment in industrial disputes, and called for stationing regulars in the major cities, where they would become instant rallying points for state and local forces. The paper favored the development of the regulars into a "national police force," because the citizen–soldiers had proven too much a part of the society that now had to be controlled. Unlike the amateur, the regular "has no politics, no affiliations, no connections with trade unions or corporations." The regulars were the independent strong arm of the state. "Every federal regiment is a devil fish – one body with fifty arms. The men have no sympathy with any class. They are colorless in sentiment. They are police armed with muskets."[39]

So much for the old republican virtues in the industrial age. The rationale for depending upon militia over regulars to suppress insurrection seemed to have outlived its usefulness in a society torn by class conflict. Those who still had an interest in upholding the old virtues were to be exposed and condemned. As the *New York Times* put it:

> The Democratic majority in Congress are responsible for a reduction [in the Army] which has rendered the Government incapable of meeting satisfactorily the ordinary difficulties to which it is now exposed ... [State] military organizations are supposed to be admirably adapted for all probable domestic emergencies and furnish the favorite Democratic protest for a crusade against the standing army.

Under the first serious trial they have endured apart from the Civil War, they have ignominiously broken down ... Just as the Democratic theory in the matter of states' rights was incompatible with the integrity of the Union, so Democratic policy in regard to the military power of the Federal Government would make it incompatible with performing its most urgent duties. It needs above all things an increase in the regular Army as the force upon which the country must depend in such conflicts as that now in progress. The days are over in which this country could rejoice in its freedom from the elements of social strife which have long abounded in the old countries ... We cannot too soon face the unwelcome fact that we have dangerous social elements to contend with, and that they are rendered all the more dangerous by the peculiarities of our political system. There should be no delay in the adoption of measures required to impart to the Federal Government sufficient physical force for the maintenance of domestic order in any conceivable emergency.[40]

Respect for the regulars went beyond the editorial pages of the northern press. In cabinet meetings, Interior Secretary (and civil service reform leader) Carl Schurz vigorously supported the development of the army over the militia.[41] Tom Scott, president of the Pennsylvania Railroad and mastermind of the compromise that had put Hayes in office, demanded legislative assurances that troops stationed in the cities could be called directly and immediately by federal marshals.[42] The heavily Democratic city of Baltimore made a special splash when its Board of Trade and the board of directors of the Merchants' Exchange called upon the President to take any action necessary to prevent further uprisings.[43] When Secretary of War McCrary finally presented the War Department's annual report to Congress, his call for an expanded role for the army over the militia came as no surprise:

The Army is to the United States what a well-disciplined and trained police force is to a city, and the one is quite as necessary as the other. As our country increases in population and wealth, and as great cities become numerous it must be clearly seen that there may be great danger of uprisings of large masses of people for the redress of grievances, real or fancied; and it is a well known fact that such uprisings enlist in greater or lesser degree the sympathies of the communities in which they occur. This fact alone renders the militia unreliable in such an emergency. Besides, it is known that few of the States have any permanent or well drilled soldiery, and the recent troubles have strongly illustrated the value, in such an emergency, of the discipline, steadiness and coolness which raw levies never possess and which characterize only the trained and experienced soldiery. Coolness, steadiness and implicit obedience to orders are the qualifications most needed in soldiers who are to deal with an excited and exasperated mob; and they are the qualities acquired only by training and are seldom found in inexperienced militia.[44]

Generals Sherman and Sheridan were elated by the new interest the summer's events had brought to the regulars.[45] Upton latched on to domestic violence on the very last pages of *The Armies of Asia and Europe* (completed in 1877) as if he had finally found the compelling justification for his professional, antimilitia reform program.[46] When Hayes called a special session of Congress in November to provide the long overdue army appropriation, public support for the regulars was at a high point, and an expansion and reorganization of the army were widely anticipated.[47] But when the issue reached the floor of Congress, the summer's drama closed in a tremendous anticlimax. The Democratic House stood firm against the army on grounds of state sovereignty and retrenchment. They defined the issue in the same terms in which it had been argued the previous February, that is, noninterference in local elections. Whereas northern Republicans were considering how much larger the standing force should be, the House Appropriations Committee, chaired by the New York Democrat and Tilden advocate Abram Hewitt, proposed a reduction in the number of enlisted men to 20,000 and a corresponding reduction in the number of officers. The committee then called for strict limitations on the use of regular troops in domestic affairs. The old Reconstruction tactic of allowing sheriffs and marshals to call troops directly as a *posse comitatus* was to be forbidden. In the November debate over the use of the army as a *posse,* Democrats pointed out the summer's abuses in the North, with marshals and sheriffs unlawfully leading federal troops to suppress the strike.[48] The committee's report shattered the professionals' dream of using labor violence to catalyze constructive army reforms. American government refused to recognize the indispensability of the professional. In an embittered note to his brother in the Senate, General Sherman wrote, "Last week Congress took open ground that the Army must not be used to suppress labor riots. You had better overhaul all the muskets and pistols in the attic, for a time will soon come when every householder must defend with firearms his own castle. This may seem absurd, but to such an end we are drifting."[49]

The House passed the appropriation bill with the *posse* restrictions and troop reductions, but the Republican Senate again refused to concur. Under pressure for an appropriation before the end of the special session, a conference committee merely restored the old troop level and struck out the *posse* clause.[50] Thus, just after the first nationwide industrial crisis, the best the army could do was to maintain the status quo. In 1878, they would not even be this fortunate. Hewitt had served warning that the status quo was unacceptable and that the Democrats would move for retrenchment and legal restrictions on the use of the army in the spring.

In the next appropriation debate, the issue of the army's new role in the industrial North was largely determined by its recent history in the South. Democrats again proposed an army reduction to 20,000 men and the *posse* restrictions. The Republicans held the line on the size of the standing force, but a *posse* clause passed. This rider restricted the use of federal troops to those conditions expressly authorized in the Constitution or in an act of Congress. It effectively restrained federal marshals from using their discretion to order troops in civil disturbances. The rider had been specifically designed to meet southern demands for local control of the polls, but its language extended to the use of regulars in labor riots in subtle ways. Because the clause ruled out discretionary troop orders from local officials or federal marshals, it prevented an immediate, on-the-scene response by regulars in a labor dispute. The President's constitutional authority to employ troops on such occasions remained intact, as did the states' option to request federal troops, but as Tom Scott and the *Chicago Tribune* had pointed out, these constitutional procedures used up the crucial time that made the difference between a major strike and a minor disturbance. The *posse* restriction controversy relegated federal troops to a backup and supportive role for local and state forces and foreclosed the designs of those who wanted to concentrate federal troops in urban garrisons for immediate employment by authorities on the scene.[51]

The *posse* controversy turned Hayes's conservative policy into a general rule for using federal troops to control labor riots.[52] Calls for federal assistance were not infrequent after 1877, and even as the militia improved, Presidents consistently chose to use regulars rather than nationalize state units to meet such calls.[53] But the army's strike duty ultimately became a source of frustration for the professionals. Without being able to turn this functional revival toward substantive reform, they were left with an unpleasant and unrewarding task carried out as a patchwork service for the captains of industry.[54] As one regular officer put it in 1895: "In reality, the army is now a gendarmery – a national police – in its civil relations. But the fact lacks acknowledgment; and in the lack of sanction by bold laws to this effect, its action is uncertain, doubtful and naturally curtailed in its power."[55]

The southern and Democratic reaction against the army had effectively checked the northern and Republican reaction for the army. Reform from the top down was impossible; reform from the bottom up was the only alternative. Hewitt clearly recognized this when pressing the strict states' rights position in the appropriations debate of May 1878. As a practical matter, he cautioned his northern colleagues that fears of communist revolution might be more likely to be borne out if Congress supported an army of regulars to function as a national police. He claimed further that it was "intended by the framers of the Constitution that the states should not only be sovereign within their own limits, but, that they should maintain order within their own limits, and if they failed to do so, that they should and must take the consequences." Yet, this New Yorker could not sanction violence and disorder. To protect the interests of the South and maintain order in the North, he called for a revitalization of the state militia, perhaps even a "national militia system." He concluded with a plea to shun European military models and maintain American traditions: "If we cannot trust our citizen-soldiers . . . if it has come to this, that you cannot trust the people, then republican institutions are a failure . . . For one, I protest that the time has not yet been reached for making such a humiliating confession."[56]

Thus, late-century America still found advantages in directing institutional development away from Washington. Reviving the state militia was the only feasible way to secure both northern industrialism and southern racism. If Hewitt's appeal to traditional republican virtues appears a bit misplaced in this context, his political logic was impeccable. Given new content and new functions, the old governmental forms might yet patch over the tension between America's political and economic development.

The states themselves did not need a formal invitation from the national government to begin the task of militia revival. Even before the NGA was formed, politicians in every state that had been forced to call for federal troops had begun to transform their paper militia into effective police for riot control. In Pennsylvania, where the strike was most violent and widespread, reform came earliest and was most thorough. Reforms spread outward from the industrial North during the 1880s. States such as Iowa and Nebraska, which were largely spared the violence of the Great Strike, followed suit with reform after local labor riots in the early 1880s.[57] Between 1878 and 1892, every state in the Union revised its military code. Virtually all of them formally divided the militia into two classes, recognizing in law the active and organized units as the National Guard and all other able-bodied men as the inactive militia. Thirty-three states established annual encampments, and thirty provided a small compensation for the men who attended.[58]

Though this militia revival at the state level encompassed the entire nation, its substance varied greatly according to each state's internal politics and its need for an internal police. A few southern states made no independent appropriation for their state troops, relying entirely on their share of the small federal subsidy. No southern state did more than match its federal share for militia support.[59] State troops in the South at this time were being revived primarily to replace federal troops in the control of racial disturbances, lynchings, and vigilantism.[60] In contrast, states with large working-class populations took the lead in the militia revival. Taken together, Massachusetts, Connecticut, New York, New Jersey, and Pennsylvania spent about thirteen times their combined federal allowances on their units. New York alone more than matched the entire federal appropriation for all the states for troop support. Over and above this expenditure, New York led a general movement in building armories in major towns and cities. The armory became a military center for training, supply, and operations at the local level. States in the Old Northwest followed the Atlantic states, appropriating about five times their federal allowance. The far western states appropriated about three times their federal allowance.[61]

The strength of the organized militia in this period grew to over 100,000 men. About 70,000 of these guardsmen were located east of the Missouri River and north of the Mason–Dixon Line. There were 21,000 troops available in New York and Pennsylvania alone. Their primary function in the North was that of a state police employed in the control of labor disturbances.[62] The guard normally proved itself adequate to this task and had the added advantages of being inexpensive relative to regulars and of dissolving back into society after riot duty.[63] The guardsmen themselves still incurred much of the cost of their equipment and time, and in returning to their jobs and homes they left, at most, an empty armory as the only institutional referent of state control.[64] Labor leaders were left with the difficult problem of labeling the volunteer militia a statist instrument of class repression. Here was an institution that had traditionally symbolized the blending of state and society and that maintained strong ethnic identifications among the working class. Yet, by 1892, even the cautious Samuel Gompers denounced the new wine in the old bottle. He formally denied the militia to be an "organization of the masses" and declared "that membership in a labor organization and the militia at one and the same time is inconsistent and incompatible."[65]

The revival of the militia as a state police for riot control did little to further the higher aspirations of the NGA. Instead, it tended to reinforce the nineteenth-century tradition of state-centered government. In the first place, each state was left to its own devices to reconcile the need for military quality with the traditional integration of the militia and local politics. Whereas the NGA supported merit appointments for staff and the elimination of local unit elections for officers, staff appointments remained firmly within the patronage system in all states, and the election of officers remained in all states except Pennsylvania, Connecticut, Illinois, Michigan, Vermont, and New Hampshire. A compromise between politics and military quality was struck in many states by having political appointees and elected officers pass an examination before assuming their posts. This system secured both local political interests and a minimum standard of quality control.[66] Second, the state police function brought an interest into the guard that was concerned solely with the preservation of law and order in the localities. The business community provided many units with substantial monetary support and often dominated the ranks of the guard officers after 1877. These new arrivals had less desire than the old Civil War militiamen to excel in the military arts for their own sake or to spend time and effort on militia development beyond that needed for the protection of local property.[67] Third, the state governors with the best and largest units became increasingly adamant in declaring their autonomy from federal interference. Officials in New York, Pennsylvania, Massachusetts, and New Jersey actually opposed the federal legislation proposed by the NGA.[68] The governor of New Jersey declared in 1880 that he would rather see the entire federal subsidy taken away "than accept very large aid coupled with any conditions which would tend to weaken the present absolute control of the state authorities over the National Guard and the militia in time of peace."[69] State political elites were not interested in the guard's dreams of national reserve status or its plans for a national militia system. They provided only for their immediate needs and did so in a way that minimized interference in local politics.

The efforts of the NGA to secure its more prestigious national goals began at its first meeting in 1879. General George Wingate of New York, head of the association, tried to mobilize his new lobby behind a comprehensive reform package for a militia system that would be integrated into the national military establishment. But he was limited by the membership to do this without "any change in relations between the federal government and the militia which have now become well established by long custom."[70] After five years of legislative frustration and internal bickering over a comprehensive reform bill that would increase the federal subsidy and impose centralized quality controls, the NGA decided to divide its demands into two bills. The first, known as the Sewell bill, requested an annual appropriation of $600,000 for federal military equipment to be distributed to the states in proportion to their population. To receive funds, a state had to maintain 100 militiamen for each of its senators and congressmen. The second, known as the Slocum bill, looked toward the development of a national militia system. It proposed a national review board to recommend uniform standards for militia units, required annual reports from the states to the War Department, and stipulated mobilization procedures to call the guard as the first line of reserve in national emergencies. The Slocum bill was delicately and somewhat ambiguously worded to maintain guard support and allay fears of federal control. The national review board was to be composed solely of militia representatives from the states, and its inspectors were to have no substantive power over state guard units. In this way, the guard promised to gain uniformity, quality, and national stature without losing the autonomy of state-controlled administration.[71]

The War Department joined the NGA in promoting both of these bills in Congress.[72] The results, however, were disappointing. In 1887, the House and Senate agreed to the Sewell bill, but after some haggling they reduced the appropriation from the requested $600,000 to $400,000.[73] This doubled the federal support level set in 1808 and was hailed by the guard as a major legislative victory. Yet, the sum was still pitifully meager. The first significant piece of national militia legislation in seventy years was a feeble recognition of delinquency in keeping up a traditional federal commitment to subsidize state services rather than a substantive commitment to a new national militia system. In effect, the federal government had made a token gesture of support for the guard's state-centered police functions. The most that can be said of the 1887 legislation is that it held the NGA together after years of frustration. Yet, more frustration lay ahead. Efforts to increase further the national subsidy and to move ahead on the Slocum bill met with no success.

Paradoxically, the twenty years following 1877 witnessed a major military transformation in America with few corresponding changes in political or institutional relationships. The militia had come back from a virtual collapse in July 1877 to constitute a formidable internal police of over 100,000 men. But this dramatic change in the content and function of America's military establishment had been contained within the old forms. Would-be reformers within the NGA, like those within the regular army, were held in suspension between the revival of political support for their performance of an undesirable task and the imposing political obstacles to their national aspirations. The NGA's dreams of reforming the military establishment from the bottom up had stalled in midstream.

The cause of professionalism in the regular army had not been abandoned in the aftermath of the Great Strike. Pushing wherever possible, the regulars continued to express the whole range of their new concerns. No sooner had Congress preempted the dominance of the regulars in strikebreaking than another opportunity for reform presented itself. Seeking to forestall further partisan confrontation on the fate of the army, Congress relegated the entire issue to a joint bipartisan committee in the summer of 1878. This committee, chaired by Republican Senator and former General Ambrose Burnside, is notable for the first full public airing of the new professional view on modernization.[74] The nation's most eminent military figures came before the committee to discuss problems of internal army administration, and the long-simmering conflict between the staff and the line finally boiled over.

Burnside's reorganization bill emerged from committee in December 1878. It presented an odd combination of the sentiments of the line officers and the Democrats. One part of the plan reduced enlisted personnel to 20,000, closed several army bases, and drastically reduced staff personnel. This drew opposition from all segments of the army, most Republicans, and commercial groups in the larger cities who still remembered 1877. The second part of the plan included a major administrative reorganization along professional lines. It permanently reorganized the reduced standing force on an expansible model. It combined the Adjutant General's Department and the Inspector General's Department into a new General Staff, much as Upton had suggested in his *Armies of Asia and Europe*. It abolished the existing staff corps as a distinct administrative entity outside the military hierarchy and made staff personnel report directly to a new "General in Chief." It also introduced rotation between line and staff positions.[75] These sections of the bill split the army establishment in two and instigated an unprecedented staff lobby campaign in Congress for rejection of the entire package.

Linesmen were encouraged by the administrative provisions of the bill.[76] Sherman wrote in support of the measure that "the Army ought to be a unit, with different parts arranged like the human body, thus a head, generals; body, Army; hands and legs, staff."[77] But it soon became clear which part of the army establishment wielded political influence on such matters. One line officer, observing the "undo advantage" of the staff in debates on the bill, complained that the press gave the impression "that 'the Army opposes the bill' because the staff, about the only representatives of the Army seen or known, oppose it." He observed:

> They [the staff] are able and cultivated men, have seen this contest coming for years, and have prepared for it; while all their stations being in Washington, the seat of legislation, or in cities, the centers of the press, they have facilities for finding both ... while the Army itself, the members of which are friends of the reform, are stationed in the remote and frozen Territories, and cannot be heard ... Even if they could be heard, the gentlemen of the staff by long acquaintance, contact and friendship can impress their views and wishes upon

Congress and the press with a facility and a power which the Army cannot hope to do.[78]

The Democratic House actually passed a shortened version of Burnside's recommendations for reorganization and reduction in the name of retrenchment and economy. Ironically, the Republican Senate took out virtually all the controversial reorganization provisions. Burnside himself pointed to staff pressures as the cause of the Senate's action. Joint committees failed to agree on a compromise, and the Forty-fifth Congress adjourned without an army appropriation and without resolving the issue of the army's status in post-Reconstruction America.[79] For the second time in two years, the cause of professionalism dissolved before interests with a stake in the status quo. Legislative support for any comprehensive legislation along the lines of the professional program had now been checked on all sides. Hopes for enhancing the army's presence downward through American society had been thwarted by the revival of the militia from below. Hopes for internal reorganization in the name of professional insulation from politics and administrative coordination had been thwarted by lateral bureau–staff ties to Congress.

Failing to break established political and institutional relationships, regular army reformers made a determined effort to establish a shadow presence for their new army within the confines of the old forms. Sherman moved ahead with plans to reorient the army intellectually. He took West Point out of direct control by the Corps of Engineers and broadened its curriculum to provide a basic liberal arts education. He then established a series of specialized graduate schools. The most important of these was the School of Application for Cavalry and Infantry at Fort Leavenworth, founded in 1881, the year of Upton's death. Under the guidance of Colonel Arthur Wagner, a young Uptonian and an admirer of Prussian military education, the school institutionalized advanced officer training in the sciences of high command. In a letter to Sheridan, Sherman emphasized the need to keep the school's affairs out of the political arena. "I don't want to meddle with the new school or have it the subject of legislation, because if this is done, like West Point, it will be made political and taken out of our control."[80] By the 1890s, the top graduates from Leavenworth were directing military education programs in several of the nation's colleges and universities.[81]

Procedural and organizational reforms were also made in the name of professionalism. The army consolidated its frontier garrisons at major rail junctions to facilitate transportation and training and to upgrade the quality of life on the line.[82] In 1882, the War Department obtained legislation for the mandatory retirement of regular officers at age sixty-four. This speeded promotions up the ranks. In 1890, professional exam-

inations were instituted for promotions to all ranks below lieutenant
colonel, although preference still went to the senior officer who passed.[83]
To make available to all linesmen the advanced education needed for
these examinations, an officer's lyceum was established at every field
outpost. The War Department also began keeping internal records on
special talents demonstrated by those within the officer corps.[84]

Reforms were also attempted at the top of the army hierarchy. After
successive failures by Commanding Generals to wrest control of the staff
from the Secretary of War, General John Schofield came up with an
alternative that was more compatible with the American tradition of
civilian authority. Schofield was a scholar and teacher with an influence
that rivaled Upton's. Assuming the post of Commanding General in 1880,
he openly avowed his subordination to the Secretary of War. After
acknowledging his civilian superior, he attempted to extend his control
over both staff and line. He tried to redefine the position of Commanding
General as that of a "Chief of Staff" sitting atop the entire professional
army hierarchy but reporting directly to the civilian secretary.[85] This
design did not survive Schofield's retirement in 1895; but the general
continued to agitate for it in later years, and the basic idea reappeared
during the Roosevelt administration in Elihu Root's plan for a General
Staff.

Another effort to respond to the need for central planning is notable in
these years. In 1888, the Adjutant General created the first peacetime
intelligence unit in his offices for the collection of information from
abroad. In 1892, Secretary of War Elkins reorganized this Military Information Division (MID) so as to be more directly responsible to him
and to perform some of the basic tasks of a General Staff. Elkins's hopes
for a complete division to develop war strategy and mobilization plans
were, however, thwarted by meager congressional appropriations. The
MID remained confined to the task of gathering and filing information of
general interest to the army and maintaining a system of military attaches
in foreign capitals. In 1898, the MID could do little more for the army
than predict the strength of the Spanish army and supply maps of Cuba.[86]

International commercial expansion and a favorable turn of opinion
toward naval development provided the army its best opportunity to
press its interests in the 1880s. In 1883, Congress authorized an Army–
Navy Gun Foundry Board to study the status of American iron and steel
capabilities in comparison to modern ordinance manufacture in Europe.
The board gave special attention to the dismal state of America's seacoast
defenses. Its report concluded that the best way to Americanize European
advances in this field was to give generous contracts to private steel
manufacturers for new forgings and to have the actual assembly of the

new guns controlled by new army and navy factories. With the steel industry as an ally in production, the board's recommendations were favorably received.[87]

The War Department seized this new angle for the army's revival. Seacoast refortification promised to bring the linesmen back from the frontier to the nation's great urban centers. The professionals elaborated the idea that an international navy demanded an army capable of defending the coastal cities. They played upon popular fears of American defenselessness with 1812-like images of European fleets sailing into our major harbors and holding our cities hostage.[88] They nurtured the support of the steel industry and the urban commercial sector. And, last but not least, they enlisted the political influence of the Army Corps of Engineers, with its reputation for delivering the pork to congressmen. With something for many and very few threats to anyone, the seacoast fortification project became the army's main focus of attention between 1883 and 1898.[89]

In 1885, the Cleveland administration established an army board to plan the rebuilding of America's seacoast defenses. Under the direction of Secretary of War William Endicott, this board proceeded as if the enemy were at the gates and the nation was desperate for drastic action. A comprehensive plan emerged that would turn the Gun Foundry Board's joint public–private venture into a massive project for approximately 2,000 heavy guns and mortars fixed in newly constructed emplacements surrounding twenty-seven city harbors. The board went so far as to call for a fortification of the Great Lakes to meet the little known threat of invasion from Canada.[90] As with most of the proposed reforms of this period, the Endicott board's report produced more grist for the growing band of army literati than guns in the cities. But in 1888, Congress did manage to provide funds for a modest refortification program along the lines indicated.[91] Commanding General Schofield was appointed head of a new Board of Ordinance and Fortification to supervise the work.

The program brought the army's business back East but left it without the resources for actual operations. The projected fortifications would have required an artillery reserve force of over 80,000 men. With no hope for expansion or reorganization, the army made overtures to the National Guard. For guardsmen to take on the task of manning the seacoast guns, direct training and supervision by the regulars would be necessary. The seacoast project fed the guard's national ambitions, but it also promised to tie the militia more closely to the regulars. It was at this time that the War Department became a staunch supporter of the legislation being championed by the guard at the national level. Eastern guard units, in turn, began to request regular inspection and advice from the regulars.[92]

The frustration of reform from the top down and the bottom up ended with the courtship of these traditional rivals in the military establishment.

Seacoast fortification could move forward and leave suspended all the structural tensions growing in the army establishment – tensions between the staff and the line, between the Commanding General and the Secretary of War, between political controls and professional autonomy, between states' rights and national supervision. The fragmentation of army interests that characterized this era of military renaissance was never more than patched over. The coalition of outcasts interested in military modernization shattered each time the basic issues of reorganization were raised. In the international crisis of 1898, it became apparent that these years of constrained revival had done more to develop divisions within the army establishment than to pave the way toward its reconstruction.

International crisis and army reform: imperialism, old republican style

In the war with Spain, the previous twenty-year sequence of fragmentation in army politics was replayed as farce. Even the combined impact of war and colonial responsibilities failed to carry the day for structural reform. In 1900, as in 1877, the old forms were stretched to perform new functions. The legislation that framed America's imperial army between 1898 and 1900 testified to the strength of the political interest in maintaining the basic forms of the old military establishment.

Through the 1880s and 1890s, the War Department had warned of the possibility of a conflict involving Cuba, but the government made little effort to prepare for this new kind of military action. As a result, War Department opinion was decidedly mixed about the prospects for success in 1898. Commanding General Nelson Miles was adamantly opposed to any rash test of American forces on foreign soil. On the other side, Secretary of War Russell Alger, a lumber millionaire and a prominent figure in Republican politics in Michigan, was eager for war and added his voice to those around McKinley who believed that failure to act would prove disastrous for the party. The differences between these two men stemmed from their different positions in the military establishment and were exacerbated by the fact that each had further political ambitions. Conflict at the top of the military hierarchy accelerated to the point where the officials in control of the staff and the line were hardly speaking to each other at the opening of hostilities.[93]

After the sinking of the *Maine* in mid-February 1898, McKinley decided on a policy designed to intimidate Spain with a massive show of strength. On March 8, Congress unanimously appropriated $50 million for national defense.[94] But a show of strength strategy needed more than money; it needed an army. On this score, the regulars pressed the reorganization scheme that traditionally united most of its factions – the expansible army plan. Miles, Alger, and Adjutant General Corbin all backed a proposal for a standing force of 27,000 that was organized to expand at short notice to 104,000, all under the command of regular army officers. This was not a stopgap measure but a comprehensive and permanent new structure. It included the Uptonian three-battalion regiment organization for larger and fewer units. It skeletonized certain companies and divided the nation into recruiting districts with a skeletal unit attached to each. Here the regulars would find and train the volunteers who would flesh out its ranks in an emergency. The War Department convinced the President that this compact, professionally directed fighting force was the most efficient and economical way to meet the emergency. John Hull, chairman of the House Military Affairs Committee and an advocate of the professional army cause, became spokesman for the administration bill in Congress.[95] At long last, a coalition of imperialist Republicans and War Department professionals had formed around a concrete plan for the army's reconstruction.

The inevitable counterpart of the coalition behind the Hull bill was, of course, opposition from the National Guard and the state governors. The bill had been designed to prevent the organized guard from entering offensive action as a national reserve with its own units intact. Not only was the constitutionality of sending the guard outside the country in doubt, but the War Department feared incompetent state officers leading troops in an offensive campaign. The bill was also designed to preempt the governors' appointment power and the proliferation of new units led by political hacks that traditionally followed a call for troops. It fixed the number of units and the entire command structure. The regulars hoped that the already trained citizen–soldiers would enlist as *individuals* serving under regular command in the national volunteer force. There was also an expectation that trained guard units might secure the seacoast fortifications to relieve regular army artillery units. But the army plan dashed both the guard's hopes of having their units, complete with existing officers and men, serve as the organized reserve of the national army and the governors' hopes of using their appointment powers to reward friends with commissions and opportunities for glory.[96]

With the governors' patronage and the guard's claim to national status at stake, the Hull bill was overwhelmingly defeated twelve days before war was declared. Hull summed up the politics of his defeat as follows:

> ... the National Guard became violently excited ... Members [of Congress] would state that they knew nothing about the merits of the Bill, but they had a telegram from a general or a colonel of their Guard urging them to defeat it, and no amendment or concession on my part would avail. The opinions of Grant, Sherman, Schofield and Miles did not have the slightest weight when put in the balance against an officer of the state militia. The great generals had no votes, the militia officer had votes back of him with which to enforce his demands.[97]

The core of the guard's support in Congress came from the South and the West. Broad-based pressure from local officials turned enough additional votes to provide the guard its first major legislative victory at the national level. Republican majorities and imperialist plans notwithstanding, a final celebration of the virtues of a citizens' militia defeated the budding coalition of support for a professional reconstruction of the army.[98]

A compromise worked out among Hull, the guard leaders of the strongest opposition states, and the War Department also met with protests from the governors. Under this plan, guard units would serve as national reserves under their own officers and would dominate the volunteer force, but federal regulations and organizational structure would be imposed from above. Moreover, the President would appoint the generals and staff officers of the volunteers, and all other officers would have to pass before a board of review or pass an examination to ensure fitness for command. Further, new guard units were not to be created unless all extant units were already operating at full strength. In this way, the regulars were to get assurances of quality control and continuity, and the guard was to get concrete recognition of its national reserve status. The governors still faced restricted appointment opportunities, and in addition they would have to submit to federal regulations.[99]

The Volunteer Act as passed paid lip service to these federal controls. Throughout the war, War Department officials attempted to give them some teeth. But in basic structure, the wartime army was, in Hull's words, "substantially on the line of the entire organization of the volunteer force during our Civil War."[100] State control over officers up to the regiment level was secured, and the removal of unfit state officers was left to presidential discretion. Governors were given an option of having one regular officer serve with their field units. Whatever the potential for central and professional control may have been at this point, McKinley's first discretionary order under the act sealed the victory for the forces of localism and patronage. The bill had called for 60,000 state volunteers, but this figure was so small as to create a problem of choosing which state units the governors were to favor with national service. When McKinley made the call, he asked for 125,000 state volunteers, guaranteeing that more than all the extant state units could be accommodated.[101] The President, in effect, gave the governors all the appointments they could possibly want and, at the same time, created an administrative nightmare for the War Department.

Having ensured the position of the guard and the governors in the war effort, Congress turned attention to the regular army. The regular army bill called for a maximum strength of 61,000 men and endorsed the expansible three-battalion regiment form. This measure would have been a landmark reorganization had it not been carefully couched as a temporary emergency measure. The regular force was to return to its prewar status at the end of hostilities, at which time the issue of army organization was to be reopened.[102] Leaving no interest unattended, Congress also created special supplementary forces of National Volunteers. These units, which included Roosevelt's Rough Riders, provided the President with an enlarged pool of commissions for his own distribution. On May 25, McKinley called for an additional 75,000 volunteers, creating an imperial army of about 270,000 men.

The legislation of these weeks all too clearly fit the nineteenth-century pattern of military policy that Upton had so bitterly denounced in the name of professionalism, nationalism, and peacetime preparation. The early weeks of the war were a grim vindication of the Uptonian warnings. Problems were first encountered in filling the ranks with troops. Mature guardsmen who were accustomed to short, sporadic calls were reluctant to leave home and business for a two-year span of duty. The ranks of the organized National Guard shrank when the call for national service went out. States were forced to make up almost half of their unit quotas with eager but inexperienced new recruits. This produced a long-familiar recruitment competition between regulars and guardsmen for men at the local level and undermined the guard's claim to be a ready-for-service reserve force.[103] Second, the command structure grew increasingly obscure. The conflict between Alger and Miles intensified over the advisability of a summer land offensive against Cuba and over who was to have the glory of field command.[104] A disgusted McKinley increasingly bypassed both men, directing the war effort himself so far as it was practicable.[105] In effect, however, the war effort was run by the improvisations of the staff, led by the able Adjutant General Henry Corbin.[106] Third, the absence of preparation and coordination took a heavy toll on domestic mobilization. Existing storages in the Ordinance Department were sufficient for only about 30,000 troops.[107] The bureau chiefs were left to their own devices to find provisions. The debacle of debarkation at Tampa received complete press coverage. With no notion of rail capacities or priorities, the army spent much of the spring stalled in a train caravan stretching back as far as Columbia, South Carolina.[108] Lack of experience with overseas army transport and the absence of a transport fleet also took their toll. Guns went on one ship and ammunition on another. Doctors went to sea and found their supplies still on the mainland.[109] The Dodge Commission, appointed by McKinley after the war to investigate the conduct of the War Department, described the situation with a masterful bit of understatement: "there was lacking in the general administration of the War Department during the continuance of the War that complete grasp of the situation which was essential to the highest efficiency and discipline of the Army."[110]

Victory proved quick and sweet, but the peace was rancorous and vindictive. Not the least of the problems was that America had become an imperial power but maintained a provincial army. The legislation for army expansion in April 1898 had been a hodgepodge of temporary expedients. The state units began to disband immediately, and the national troops faced immediate reversion to prewar size. Moreover, the fragmented War Department, having barely held together under the pressures of the conflict, virtually fell apart in the fall of 1898. Maladministration and incompetence in the army were headline news, and everyone implicated sought to place the blame on someone else. General Miles, basking in the glory of his Puerto Rico campaign and dreaming of the presidency, began implicating the staff departments in the scandals that swept through the press.[111] The staff, however, had both a short victory on its side and General Corbin's prestige to stem the attack. Over the winter and spring, blame for the administrative debacle came to focus on Secretary of War Alger. Alger held his tongue but refused to resign until an opportunity came to run for the Senate.[112]

In the midst of bitter public recriminations, departmental disintegration, and impending army reductions, America faced the new responsibilities of colonial power. The army would have primary responsibility for establishing law and order in the new dependencies, for supporting transition governments, and, most immediately, for suppressing the Philippine insurrection. New army legislation was needed immediately. Under circumstances in which the need for a permanent military reorganization seemed self-evident, the professionals again went to Congress with their reforms.

Tensions between the guard and the regulars had subsided by the time the reorganization issue was reopened in the fall of 1898. The militiamen were busy with demobilization and a bit sobered by their war experiences. Moreover, the very fruits of victory seemed to exclude the part-time soldier from further consideration. An overseas occupation force had to be a regular force. Yet, as militia opposition to professional designs was alleviated, divisions within the professional ranks came to the fore. Three reorganization proposals competed for Hull's attention in this final reform effort of the nineteenth century. Each envisioned an army with a maximum troop strength of 100,000 men organized on the expansible model. Each represented a permanent structural reform. Differences centered on questions of creating a General Staff and altering relations between the staff and the line.[113]

Hoping to avoid conflicts that might again endanger the prospects for action, Hull took up a proposal from Secretary Alger and Adjutant General Corbin that bypassed the staff–line controversy and the General Staff idea altogether. A minimalist plan for an expansible army of 100,000, coupled with the prospects of scores of new positions in both the staff bureaus and officer corps, secured army unity before Congress. The new Hull bill escaped the House with minor reductions in the size of the standing force. The Senate Military Affairs Committee split, five Republicans for and five Democrats against. A compromise was reported that kept much of the professional view intact. The bill called for a smaller permanent force of 39,000 but organized it for rapid expansion to 65,000 and added 35,000 volunteers to continue until postwar problems were settled. The army was still ensured 100,000 men until 1901 and, more importantly, an expansible structure was retained as a permanent feature.[114]

The opponents made their stand on the Senate floor. A Democratic–Populist filibuster destroyed the professional reform design once again. A final compromise improvised a temporary emergency force of 100,000 that would disband in 1901. The army would then return to a size of 29,000. This bill, which passed in late February 1899, was bitterly denounced by Hull as "the worst kind of patchwork." Its units were designed for parades rather than combat.

> Regiments organized with such companies would be too absurd for China to adopt. The bill gives to each regiment a full band, and to each company two musicians. With respectably organized regiments, this would be all right, but with no men to speak of on the fighting line, it suggests the idea that this Government, hereafter, will make war with wind and attempt to gain victories with noise.[115]

Disillusionment was no less strong among the regulars. To them, the bill represented "nothing but malicious hostility to the Army on the part of a minority in Congress."[116]

A temporary and ill-organized army did not, of course, alter McKinley's determination to secure the new territories. When Alger finally resigned as Secretary of War in August 1899, the President turned to a faithful Republican lawyer, Elihu Root, to assume the tasks of formulating an American colonial policy and establishing colonial governments. Root had been closely tied to machine politics in New York, but he had no military expertise, and he controlled no political organization. Theodore Roosevelt, now governor of New York, feared that the choice of a machine lawyer would inhibit the "sweeping reforms" so desperately needed in the War Department.[117] Root would prove Roosevelt wrong, but not right away. He spent his first eighteen months in office working on the legal problems of colonial policy and administration. New initiatives on behalf of army reorganization were strategically put off until after the imperial designs of the Republican party were affirmed at the polls in 1900.[118]

Thus, so far as army structure was concerned, the nineteenth century closed with an ironic vindication of the old republican forms in a force employed for new Republican purposes. The imperial mission pressed forward, but the troops serving the new empire were a makeshift and marked time until their ranks were again scheduled to revert to that of an Indian-fighting cavalry. As in the summer of 1877, America in 1900 stood at a crossroads in military development. Being pulled in two directions at once, it opted once again to meet new demands for government in the old provincial style.

Patching the army

A few years after the war with Spain, the Military Service Institution awarded its annual essay prize to one regular's analysis of the "affect of democracy on the organization and discipline of the Army."[119] Taking his cues from "General Upton's remarkable and valuable work," Lieutenant Colonel James Pettit argued that the structure of American democracy made it "impossible to organize and discipline an effective Army from the point of view of military experts." He observed that "our entire system of government, from the township to the White House, [is] based on partisan politics." The army was, at every turn, subject to "the will of millions of people expressed through devious and changing channels." The first principle of military organization – "one man power, the strong commander" – was continually sacrificed to the exigencies of party politics. Presidents took every "opportunity to award political adherents with commissions in the army . . . without regard to the fitness of the recipient." The Secretary of War was "usually a civilian without military training and devoid of knowledge of the laws and customs governing armies in war and peace." Army legislation in Congress came "out of the hopper greased with the slimy oil of political spoils and party expediency, unredeemed by the salt of honest, manly independence and belief as to the right and justice of the causes and needs of the country." The governors of the "Sovereign states" exercised a power over the army that was "even greater than that of the President." To Pettit, a politics based in the states constituted the greatest of all obstacles to establishing an American army based on cosmopolitan principles of military organization. "What can discipline be when enlisted men elect their officers . . . when the soldier understands that his vote at home is more important than his presence at the front?"

From a turn-of-the-century professional's point of view, the most basic operating standards of the early American state – patronage appointment, pork barrel politics, and a radical devolution of authority – posed insuperable obstacles to national administrative modernization. The army could be made palatable to political elites only by destroying its organizational integrity and turning it into an extension of inimical political arrangements. Paradoxically, however, although the provincial forms of the American military establishment were steadfastly maintained, the military posture of the old republic had been thoroughly transformed. The most frustrating thing of all for the regular officer was that political elites had revolutionized the functions of the American army without acknowledging that fact in substantive institutional reforms.

As Pettit's essay implied, restructuring the army establishment was a sprawling, multifaceted task involving virtually every aspect of the established governmental order. Professional reformers of the new school simply could not carry an effective political coalition through the maze of interests attached to extant institutional arrangements. Failing to break through any of the structural barriers to reorganization, they were left to nurture a few faint symbols of their new military vision.

The political patchwork of late-century army development had for its centerpiece a revitalized National Guard. Yet, rather than posing as a solution to the problems of institutional modernization at this time, the guard merely epitomized these problems. It promised everything to everyone. It would provide a disciplined internal police for industrial violence without the threat or burden of a professional force. It would meet the military standards of the regulars and still maintain the republican virtues of the citizen-soldier. It would form a first-line national reserve, ensure noninterference by the national government in the southern states, and secure the governors' political prerogatives in the military affairs of the states and the nation. Balancing these pretensions proved difficult at best. The guard failed in these years to create a new position for itself between the national and state levels of the federal system. In effect, its accomplishments – enlarging the federal subsidy to the states and destroying the professional army plan for wartime mobilization – sustained the old operating standards of patronage privilege, pork barrel politics, and radically decentralized authority. In local strikebreaking and national wartime service, the guard was a political expedient for those in power.

If the army renaissance of the late nineteenth century failed to yield a structural breakthrough in the army establishment, it did vent all the interests and conflicts that would determine a distinctive course for such reforms over the following decades. Aggressive linesmen had served notice to the staff bureaus of the War Department that they were not willing to accept existing institutional arrangements. The rise of the National Guard as a convenient way to meet new military demands within the confines of the old state structure had brought to the fore a formidable interest group that would have to be reckoned with in any new strategy for reconstruction. The cauldron of interests that simmered on the issue of army reform in these years did not suggest any simple formula for building national institutions of authority and integrity. Some very peculiar political wizardry was needed to break with America's old military tradition and blaze a new path in institutional development.

5

Patching business regulation: the failure of administered capitalism

The inclination of the German mind, especially the North German, is bureaucratic... With us, in America, it is just the opposite. The commission is our bureau. We are constantly driven to recourse to it, but we always accept the necessity with reluctance, and the machine does not work well. We get from it no such results as are obtained by the Germans. The reason, if we choose to seek it, is obvious enough. The bureau is a natural outgrowth of the German polity; it is the regular and appropriate form in which that polity effects its work. With us it is a necessity, but nonetheless an excrescence. Our political system has come in contact, through the complex development of civilization, with a class of problems in the presence of which it has broken down.

Charles Francis Adams, Jr., *The Railroads: Their Origin and Problems*, 1887

With the consolidation of their national railway networks in the second half of the nineteenth century, the Western states shared their first common experience of the new demands for business regulation raised by an industrial economy. By the time America joined the national regulatory effort, the responses of the European states were already in full view. On the eve of passage of the Interstate Commerce Act, Charles Francis Adams, Jr., America's foremost authority on railroad regulation, could point to an "inherent and irresistible tendency" for the maturing railroad systems of all nations to assume closer relations with their governments. Yet, Adams despaired at the prospects for regulation in America. Although he saw that unrestrained railway competition had to give way here, as it had everywhere else, to some form of national administrative supervision, he also saw that this new imperative for institutional control threw into question "the very principles upon which the government was established."[1]

This third look at the dynamics of institutional development in late-century America reveals a state-building problem parallel to those found in reforming civil administration and army organization. International main currents in governmental regulation of business ran counter to the main currents of American state development. A regulatory posture that had helped make America the proud exception, the extreme example of the liberal state, the self-proclaimed anomaly among Western states, now began to haunt its efforts to meet the generally shared governmental problems of the advancing industrial societies. Once again, entrenched governing formulas stymied bold departures in institutional development.

The mode of business regulation which had been established during the nineteenth century in America was unique in several respects. In the first place, it lodged control in the separate states rather than in the national government. Second, it had moved steadily away from direct governmental supervision, progressing from public works and joint public–private ventures, to restrictive corporate charters, to general incorporation laws that overthrew charter limitations and abolished law-created monopolies.[2] Third, it depended to an unprecedented degree on courts and judge-made law to invoke the police powers reserved by the states and thus ensure some public surveillance over economic affairs. The demand for national railroad regulation posed the challenge of reversing all this. The prerequisite to effective governmental action at this juncture was agreement on rules that could relate a wholly new kind of national administrative authority to an arrangement of institutions and procedures that presupposed the absence of any strong national administrative arm.

As in the state-building efforts already reviewed, the champions of national administrative regulation faced the problem of forging an entirely new mode of governmental operations at a time when the political and institutional arrangements underlying the established mode were being reinforced. The highly mobilized, intensely competitive, and extremely volatile character of electoral politics in congressional districts throughout the North and West magnified the pluralism of legislative politics. The localistic orientations of national representatives were reinforced, and the traditional difficulties of formulating a consistent and generally applicable regulatory policy at the national level were accentuated. Moreover, as Congress fumbled with the regulatory issue, the courts were busy formulating their own response to the challenges of industrialism, a response that vigorously asserted and jealously guarded the prerogatives of the judiciary in regulating economic affairs. There was little room in this state of courts and parties for an administrative form of regulation to take root. Indeed, the early Interstate Commerce Commission (ICC) found itself thoroughly dominated and ultimately incapacitated by a mode of governmental operations basically at odds with the new regulatory functions it was ostensibly created to perform.

A state-building perspective on the early regulatory debacle in America is particularly timely in light of the attention that has been given to the role of private interests in prompting federal regulatory action. By tracing the influences of various economic factions in determining the nation's railway policy, scholars have challenged the notion that the government was acting to promote the "public interest."[3] Yet, it is difficult to come to terms with the first great national regulatory effort in this way. After all the interests have been specified and their influence evaluated, the most striking thing about this early regulatory effort remains the inability of the federal government to sustain concerted action in any interest at all. The pressures for national railroad regulation brought American government to a developmental impasse in which the established mode of responding to interests no longer fit the kind of issue the interests were raising. The structure of political and institutional power in late-century America thwarted the development of an effective regulatory response by the very way it had evolved to represent and serve private interests. By not attending to the problems confronting an established state in a changing society, both the celebratory public interest view and the muckraking private interest view of the early regulatory effort miss the mark. The ICC was the feeble "excrescence" of a governmental order no longer able to meet the very real needs of the economic interests as they entered the industrial age.

Developmental imperatives and reform interests

The transition from infancy to maturity in the American railroad industry sent a series of shock waves across the nation. The rise of a truly national railway network locked geographic regions and property interests together in a new system of economic interdependence. At once, this exposed the inadequacies of state-based regulation and defied the laws of the free market to restore order and confidence at the national level. Conflicts among factions of capital each seeking its own immediate interests in a national market and competition among localities hitherto separated by enormous distances made a reversal of the federal government's long-established tradition of noninterference imperative.[4]

Rail mileage in America doubled between 1870 and 1876. Merchants, farmers, and railroad entrepreneurs had supported this rapid construction of roads, but they found themselves at odds once the lines were pieced together. The completion of trunk lines connecting western agricultural regions, midwestern trade centers, and eastern manufacturing and port cities transformed the railway industry. Suspicion, resentment, and instability fed on two factors working in tandem: fierce railway competition in the interstate trunk line territory and extensive railway monopolies in localities served by branch and feeder lines. The five great trunk line corporations and their affiliates – the Grand Trunk, the New York Central, the Erie, the Pennsylvania, and the Baltimore and Ohio – operated on a national economic calculus based on these two factors and, in so doing, they ran roughshod over state and local concerns.

Trunk line competition was self-defeating for the railroads. Experience had shown that a line pushed into bankruptcy could disrupt the entire industry. Bankrupt railroads represented a massive investment in fixed capital that could not be converted to alternative uses but could still be operated in receivership. A road in receivership, without stock obligations and exonerated from interest payments, was said to "run wild" over solvent roads with rates that had to meet only the basic costs of operation. There was, then, an industry incentive to keep existing roads solvent. Added to this was an incentive to bar the construction of new competitive lines. A proliferation of new roads would lead to the underutilization of the carrying capacity of each and result in mutual starvation. The long-term interest of the railroads lay in cooperation in fixing rates or dividing traffic so as to ensure stability and predictability for each.

Yet, railroad attempts to escape competition through voluntary pooling agreements proved a failure time and again. In the first place, the short-term temptations to gain new traffic above the quotas agreed upon by the pool proved stronger than the long-term rationale for cooperation. Each deviation from a pooling agreement threatened one of the massive rate wars that became characteristic of the era. Moreover, different groups and locales served by the railroads benefited or lost depending on the state of railroad cooperation or competition. Merchants in the terminal cities, for example, continually pressed their respective trunk lines for lower rates and larger shares of the national traffic so as to improve their position vis-à-vis competing terminals. Pressures from shippers and localities increased the tension on any given railroad's commitment to a pooling agreement.

Oligopolistic competition among the railroads translated not only into destabilizing rate wars but also into irritating and somewhat arbitrary rate discriminations among localities and shippers. Long haulers were generally favored over short haulers. Collusion between railroads and big shippers for rebates and drawbacks on large freights antagonized smaller shippers. Branch and feeder lines were believed to bear the burden of losses incurred in low-rate competitive areas with higher rates for themselves. Localities with access to alternative water transportation were given lower rates and, thus, a dual advantage over localities not so favored.

Thus, whereas the railroads sought to escape competition, others sought more competition, and still others sought relief from some particular effect of competition. With everyone pursuing his own immediate interests, no one could maintain control of his situation. Chaos threatened for all. Each aggrieved party appealed to the national government to make good through legislation the deficiencies it perceived in the workings of the natural laws.[5]

In this archetypical regulatory situation, the federal government could not embrace any one economic interest without threatening the immediate interests of the others.[6] A governmental order geared to a distributive politics, in which access was opened wide and all comers were served in a rather reflexive fashion, promised only to transfer the regulatory conflicts in the economy to the state. Effective regulation presupposed a governmental capacity to resist the immediate interests of groups in conflict and to transform these conflicts, through mediation and authoritative direction, into a new order that would facilitate the further development of the private economy as a whole.

As noted above, scholars have done much to specify the political interests of the various economic factions engaged in the regulatory debate. Indeed, a classic scholarly debate has raged over which economic faction was most influential in prompting federal action. All the possibilities have now been argued, evaluated, and criticized. What emerges from a review of this literature is not only a rich composite portrait of the contending interests but also a clear sense of the limits of the pressure group perspective in the analysis of the regulatory problem.

As far back as 1913, Solon Buck traced federal railroad regulation to the agitation of western dirt farmers in the early 1870s.[7] The Granger campaign for railroad regulation, he argued, was largely rooted in the farmers' demand for cheap transportation to the East, a demand exacerbated by economic depression and the beginning of national railroad combinations. This movement had its greatest impact in the upper Mississippi Valley, where state Granger laws were aimed at securing lower rates, preventing rate discrimination, and ensuring intense railroad competition. At this time, Grangers also began to support federal regulatory action in a similar vein. The impact of the movement on the federal level is visible in several particulars. First, the Illinois Railroad and Warehouse Commission established in 1873 became an important legislative model for the ICC.[8] Second, when Granger agitation was at its height, the United States Senate undertook the first major federal investigation of the railroad problem. The Windom Committee was specifically concerned with the transport of goods from the West and South to the Atlantic ports and addressed itself directly to the Grangers' primary demand for cheap transportation.[9] Third, John Reagan (a Democrat from Texas) held back his long and ultimately successful campaign for federal railroad regulation until the Supreme Court upheld the state Granger laws and vindicated the principle of legislative regulation of the railroads in March 1877. With the farmers vindicated, Reagan vigorously pursued the agrarian antipathy to the transportation monopoly at the national level.[10]

Buck's claim that regulation was the product of radical agrarian discontent with railroad monopolies has been subjected to considerable modification on several counts. George Miller has demonstrated that Granger advocacy of regulation was dominated by merchants and shippers in the cities along the upper Mississippi River rather than by the dirt farmers themselves.[11] Further, he has pointed out that the more radical Granger laws of 1871 had been abandoned by the midwestern states long before their constitutionality was sustained by the Supreme Court in 1877. Finally, he has shown that the Illinois Commission of 1873, which Congress used as a model for the 1887 law, was a conservative reaction to these more radical Granger laws. This later Illinois system (not at issue in the famous *Munn v Illinois* case) shifted regulatory responsibility from the legislature to a joint effort by an administrative body and the courts. Moreover, it accommodated the demands of moderate merchants and railroads to the detriment of radicals and antimonopolists. For the railroads, the Illinois statute recognized the impracticality of rigid legislative direction of a complex and constantly changing industry and the need for a flexible and responsive stance toward regulation. It also openly acknowledged that the reasonableness of a railroad rate was ultimately a judicial decision, thereby securing a major point of Granger contention for the railroads, despite the *Munn* decision. For the merchants, a strong administrative commission was established "to assist individual shippers in their judicial struggles with giant corporations."[12] The commission was given the authority to fix and alter schedules of maximum rates, and these could be presented in court as prima facie evidence of what "reasonable" was in each instance. The railroad could refuse to comply with the commission's schedule, but the burden of proof of an unreasonable rate was then placed on the carrier in court. The act gave the commission power to initiate court proceedings and thus also recognized the burden of time, expense, and risk to a merchant challenging a corporation "whose favor he could not afford to lose."[13] The Illinois precedent was, then, an effort to get the legislature out of the business of regulation and to arbitrate the conflicts between the shippers and railroads through an administrative instrument.

More striking are the claims that the major interests behind federal railroad regulation were neither agrarian nor western. The Granger demand for lower throughrates to the East was largely satisfied in the mid-1870s by trunk line competition, favorable long-haul shipping arrangements, and periodic railroad rate wars. By 1877, the fundamental railroad problem was not high rates but rate discrimination and rate instability. Not only was this problem nationwide in scope, but action to rectify it would actually threaten those long-haul western merchants and farmers now favored by depressed throughrates.

In this vein, Gerald Nash has argued for the central role of eastern producers, in particular the independent oil producers and refiners of Pennsylvania, in the campaign for national railroad regulation. "It was their direct influence which led in 1878 to the introduction of the Reagan Bill in the House of Representatives. And it was the Reagan Bill from which the Interstate Commerce Act of 1887 was finally written."[14] Throughout the 1870s, the independents of Pennsylvania were threatened by the consolidation efforts of John D. Rockefeller. These efforts included rebate bargains on transportation between Standard Oil and the Erie and Pennsylvania Railroads. The independents decried this discrimination between large and small shippers, and they formed a Producers' Union to fight Rockefeller and promote regulation. Their representative, James Hopkins, obtained a formal House investigation in 1875.

In 1876, Hopkins introduced an interstate commerce bill based on the demands of the independents and the Reading Railroad, which also opposed the rebate deal in which it was not included. Failing reelection, Hopkins appealed to Reagan, the new Democratic chairman of the House Commerce Committee, to take over his bill. Reagan was hesitant, awaiting the Granger decision from the Supreme Court. Meanwhile, the Producers' Union amended the Hopkins proposal. When Reagan picked up the bill in 1878, he amended it again. The bill now included Hopkins's clause outlawing rebates (which favored small shippers), a Producers' Union clause prohibiting discrimination between long- and short-haul fares (which favored more eastern shippers), and a Reagan antimonopoly clause prohibiting pooling (which attacked the railroads head-on in the name of agrarian radicalism).

Nash's analysis significantly broadens the scope of the special interests contending for federal action, and his review of the development of the Reagan bill suggests that many economic and regional interests were involved. Lee Benson agrees with Nash that federal action was not in the Granger tradition but points out that the Pennsylvania oilmen capitulated to Rockefeller in 1880. Benson picks up the argument to show that federal action was spearheaded not by Pennsylvanians but by the merchants of New York, who began to give support to the Reagan bill in 1879. Indeed, Benson builds a strong case that the New York merchants "constituted the single most important group behind the passage of the Interstate Commerce Act."[15] Put more forcefully, he proposes that the 1887 act is best understood as New York's answer to the great trunk line pooling experiment organized by Albert Fink in 1877.[16]

Since 1873, New York's unquestioned dominance as the center of transport to the East and from Europe to the West seemed endangered by the alternative trunk line rail connections to rival eastern ports. Clearly, New York's decline was relative, at best, but its jealous merchants demanded that the Erie and the New York Central railroads serve the competitive interests of their terminal city over their own interest in pooling with the other trunks and dividing the West-to-East freight. When the great trunk line pooling experiment was organized in 1877, the New York Cheap Transportation Association (later renamed the New York Board of Trade and Transportation) joined with the farmers of the New York Grange in an alliance to break the pool. The alliance was shaky because the groups opposed the pool for conflicting reasons. The New York farmers sought to block western goods from eastern markets by strict pro-rata laws that would end the pool's long-haul advantages. The merchants, however, sought to increase New York's share of the western market at the expense of rival wholesalers in other terminal cities. This conflict in the reform coalition might have been more of a problem had the railroads' own position been more consistent. Their pooling agreement charged relatively more for a western shipment to New York (defended on the basis of longer distance), whereas New York farmers were charged relatively more than western farmers (defended on the basis of the short-haul, higher-rate principle). Merchants and farmers were thus able to overlook their own differences in general outrage long enough to instigate and control the single most significant public exposé of the railroad problem, the New York legislature's Hepburn Committee investigation of 1879. This committee defined the railroad problem in terms of excessively high rates, place discrimination, personal discrimination, and railroad corruption.[17]

New York's interests dovetailed with Reagan's strict antidiscrimination bill at the national level and immediately each began to feed on the support of the other. In Benson's view, New York sustained support for Reagan until federal action became irresistible. In 1881, merchant pressure on the New York Central caused that railroad to break its pooling agreement. A rate war ensued. In 1882, Benson admits that the predominant influence of the New York merchants had peaked. After that, "the near anarchy characterizing the American railroad system 'carried the Congress to inevitable action.' "[18]

Gabriel Kolko takes issue with Benson on this last point, showing that the railroads themselves began pushing their own interests in regulation around 1880. When a recession in 1884 led to the collapse of several overcapitalized roads and the widespread failure of pools, the railroads became "the most important single advocates of federal regulation."[19] The prime railroad interest in regulation was "uniformity, stability and impartiality among railways, their patrons and the States."[20] More specifically, the railroads wanted to use federal authority to guarantee their pooling agreements and thus free them from the disrupting pressures and temptations of the market. Concern over their own inability to maintain these agreements and fear of the antipooling clause in the Reagan bill prompted the railroads to enter the legislative struggle with their own reform proposal. Railroad interests in regulation checked the Reagan bill, despite its merchant–farmer support. With the failure of the pools and the onset of near chaos in the railroad industry, the railroads' legislative "quest for stability" began to gain support from erstwhile opponents. By 1884, New York merchants, among other mercantile groups, had noticeably shifted their antimonopoly, procompetition, farmer alliance toward the railroad position and could no longer be counted among the chief supporters of the Reagan bill. The new moderate railroad–merchant position was expressed in the Senate's Cullom Committee investigation (1885–86) and embodied in the Cullom railroad bill.

The novelty and value of Kolko's argument rest on a general observation. His "crucial point" is that "railroads, for the most part, consistently accepted the basic premise of federal regulation since only through the positive intervention of the national political structure could the destabilizing, costly effects of cutthroat competition, predatory speculation, and greedy shippers be overcome."[21] In this, Kolko must be credited with illuminating the changing relationship between business and government in the evolution of the private economy. However, in Kolko's treatment, the basic proposition that the railroads needed and actively sought regulation tends to wander onto the more dubious ground that the federal government served railroad interests in particular, above others, or more consistently than others. In the first place, any movement on the part of the government away from the procompetition Reagan position toward the cooperative railroad position would have been no more representative of a movement toward the railroad interest than a movement toward a more enlightened governmental disposition toward railroad regulation. The fact is that the immediate interests of the more progressive railroad entrepreneurs coincided most closely with a more broad-based, long-term interest in market stability and predictability. Kolko's own evidence of a noticeable merchant shift in the mid-1880s suggests that the railroads were only the first to proclaim the more enlightened policy. As we shall see, the American Economic Association, the ICC, and in the 1890s even John Reagan himself argued for legalized pooling not because they were the pawns of the railroads but simply because this was the more sophisticated regulatory posture. Only by holding the untenable position that the railroad industry is "inherently competitive" can Kolko claim that the government sought to elevate railroad interests above others. As Robert Harbeson writes: "Kolko is logically impelled to the view that federal railway legislation represented, in effect, a kind of conspiracy to enforce the cartelization of an inherently competitive industry to the detriment of shippers and consumers, despite the fact that the railroad industry is demonstrably not 'inherently competitive' and despite the fact that unrestricted price competition had been and would be demonstrably impervious to the long-run interests of shippers as a whole no less than railroads."[22]

Of more immediate concern in an evaluation of the early regulatory effort are the uncomfortable facts that despite the pressures of the railroads, the government did not secure an enlightened pooling policy in the legislation of 1887, and despite continuing efforts, pooling was not sanctioned by the government until World War I. Whatever other concessions the railroads may have won from Congress, it is beyond dispute that they failed to obtain their most basic legislative demand until the winter crisis of 1917, and that the only clear policy position staked out in the 1887 act was the radical antipooling position of the original Reagan bill. At once, Kolko seems to pass this off to the expediency of getting a bill through Congress and to suggest that it "imposed havoc" on the railroads.[23] In either case, it is just such details that cast most serious doubt on the adequacy of an interpretation of government action that rests on the political influence of big business. Not only were other interests secured; the interests most antithetical to the railroads were secured. The pertinent question seems to be why the United States, alone among Western states and against the pressures of a vital industry, persisted for thirty years (1887–1917) with a regulatory policy that was demonstrably irrational.[24]

The inevitable anticlimax that emerges from a review of the interest literature is the vindication of a mundane pluralism. Such a view lingers in the background qualifications of all the works cited so far and is brought to the fore by Edward Purcell's analysis of businessmen and the Commerce Act.[25] Purcell revels in the multiplicity of ideas and interests that were aired in the regulation debate. He concludes with the only possible interest argument left. Widespread business support for regulation "was more important in forcing federal action than was the endorsement by any one group." Purcell notes that the interests disagreed widely on the precise regulatory policy the government should adopt, and that even within groups there was a wide range of opinion. But there was "near unanimity" that some federal regulation was needed. Thus, "it was neither, 'the people,' nor 'the farmers' nor even 'the businessmen' who were responsible for the government's regulation of the railroads. Rather it was many diverse economic groups in combination throughout the nation which felt threatened by the new national economy and sought to protect their interests through the federal government."[26]

The truth of Purcell's position is ultimately unsatisfying. No single interest can account for the first national regulatory initiative, and all the interests together can only account for the fact that there was an initiative. Add to this the fact that the initiative lay in complete collapse by 1900, and the limits of the pressure group perspective become inescapable. A different order of analysis is needed to understand this turning point in relations between state and society. The group perspective offers a map of the economic factions engaged in political action on behalf of what each perceived to be its immediate interests in the new national railway network, but in the end, this only clarifies a more basic problem – how to formulate a coherent regulatory policy in a government that was open to all contending factions.

The key to understanding the early regulatory effort is not to be found in the interests themselves but in the structure of the institutions they sought to influence. In an archetypical case of the pluralist paradigm, each of the interests contesting the railroad issue found representation in American national government, and each was able to make its mark on the blank slate of national regulatory policy. Yet, in this new regulatory situation, the sum of the interests could not possibly serve any one of them, let alone some "public interest" standing apart from each; it only promised an incoherent, unworkable policy from which no one stood to benefit. A state that promoted pluralism promoted a formula for failure in regulation.

To the extent that the politics of national railroad regulation directly engaged the energies of a variety of economic factions, none of which agreed on the appropriate governmental response, there is an unmistakable distance separating it from both the civil service and the army cases. But the question at the heart of the railroad regulation issue was not which of these interests the government sought to serve, but whether the government could be changed so as to serve interests in a new way. The railroad regulation case emerges as congruent with the others in this state-building challenge. The men who rose to meet that challenge dealt with the question of regulation in the same terms as those who championed civil service reform and army reorganization, and they attempted to push the national regulatory effort along a similar path.

In 1885, a small band of economists established the American Economic Association (AEA) and proclaimed the legitimacy of a "progressive theory of regulation." No longer willing to suffer the strict laissez-faire orientation of the American Social Science Association, the AEA spoke for a thorough reevaluation of relations between the state and the economy.[27] The association was too late in forming and too controversial in its opinions to rally professional economists under its umbrella for the railroad debates in Congress, but it did give theoretical grounding to the interest in regulation that the Interstate Commerce Commission tried to adopt for the government after its formation in 1887. Indeed, one of the cofounders of the AEA, Henry Carter Adams, was appointed chief economist of the new commission and became its leading light in the 1890s.[28]

Adams expressed the association's point of view in a premier essay, "The Relation of the State to Industrial Action," published in 1886.[29] A nation floundering at a crossroads in economic and political development gave his topic its "special pertinence."

> ... the collapse of faith in the sufficiency of the philosophy of laissez faire, has left the present generation without principles adequate for the guidance of public affairs. We are now passing through a period of interregnum in the authoritative control of economic and governmental principles. This is indeed cause for grave solicitude, for never were there more difficult problems demanding solution than at the present time, and never were men so poorly equipped for the accomplishment of such a task as are those upon whom these questions are being forced ... Principles of action we must have, for nothing is so mischievous as the attempted solution of great questions on the basis of immediate interests alone.[30]

Adams offered two principles to "guide legislation" away from the confusion and conflict of immediate interests toward a clear and constructive purpose. First, he argued that the government should raise the "plane of competitive action" in the marketplace. By defining basic rules of business conduct, the government could reverse the natural tendency of businessmen to sink to the morality of the worst of their members and allow the best to "set the fashion." Second, he argued that the government should realize the benefits of inherently monopolistic industries (in which he included the railroads as the prime example) for society. Adams observed that in an enterprise like railroading, which exhibits proportionately increasing returns per increment of capital and labor, enforced competition is ruthless, self-defeating, and wasteful. Yet, when left free to pursue their incentive for cooperation or combination, these industries escaped the financial controls inherent in a competitive market. Thus, the state must openly recognize the monopolistic character of these industries, allow them to associate, and then subject them to the rule of "public financiering." By developing the administrative capacities for public accounting and public valuation of corporate properties, the government would be in a position to make informed judgments in disputes concerning rates and prices. The rule of public financiers would secure the lowest price consistent with the maintenance of efficient services.[31]

These were, this University of Michigan professor declared, the principles of the "economic mugwump." Like those of the political Mugwump, they represented an enlightened conservatism. They looked toward the preservation of order from a position above the conflict of immediate interests. Yet, unlike the political Mugwumps, who, on economic issues, tended to cling dogmatically to laissez-faire doctrines, Adams saw himself clearing an independent ground between the political traditions of Anglo-American liberalism and the governmental capacities of German statism.[32] He would use the state in a positive way to compensate for the market's most manifest deficiencies. In a characteristically progressive style, he looked forward to a day when the power of the state and the energies of the entrepreneur would be joined in harmony on behalf of their mutual interest in the further development of the private economy as a whole. Before this new harmony could be attained, however, the American state had to gain a measure of autonomy from the private sphere – a capacity to stand apart from the private interests and to assume a supervisory role on the basis of disciplined and principled action.

Over the 1880s, a number of men coming from a variety of interests in the railroad regulation controversy arrived at positions generally in line with Adams's economic mugwumpery.[33] Among the most prominent were Charles Francis Adams, Jr. – son of America's first family of patrician statesmen, pioneer of the nation's first state railway commission, president of the Union-Pacific Railroad, and leading spokesman for the railroads in Congress;[34] Simon Sterne – attorney for the New York Board of Trade and Transportation, member of Governor Samuel Tilden's blue ribbon commission on governmental reform, chief prosecutor in New York's Hepburn Committee investigation of the railroad problem, and leading spokesman for the merchants in Congress;[35] Arthur Twining Hadley – the nation's leading economist, advisor to Congress and the commission, first choice for Henry Carter Adams's position as commission economist, and later, president of Yale University.[36]

These men did not form a political organ to promote their enlightened consensus concerning regulation. They advocated the general principles of the progressive theory of regulation from within their disparate affiliations. Yet, what they lacked in common association they made up for in a common intellectual predisposition to seek the reestablishment of order in building authoritative institutions controlled by experts. Viewed together, their credentials bear a striking resemblance to those of the leaders of the civil service reform movement. In fact, each gave active support to civil service reform and linked it to success in railroad regulation. Moreover, as they moved toward a consensus on an appropriate regulatory posture for the government, they increasingly focused their attention on a structure of governmental power that showed "little genius or faculty" for making the appropriate response.[37] Indeed, the closer the federal government came to taking concrete action, the more circumspect the economic mugwumps became in their advocacy. They perceived that railroad regulation without a more basic reconstruction of American government was likely to prove counterproductive.

Sterne, Hadley, and Charles Adams each turned to the study of past American developments and current administrative practices in Europe to gain some perspective on the problems at hand. They most admired the continental methods of regulation but dwelt upon the British example because of our shared experience with the common law, a small central bureaucracy, and the use of the commission form of administration. Doubts were raised, however, as to whether America could imitate the British without a radical reversal of the present course of American political development. Assessing our respective histories, it became clear that over the first half of the nineteenth century, America had taken British theories of laissez-faire more seriously than the British themselves. Sterne, sent by President Cleveland on that familiar tour of Europe to study the relationship between Western governments and their railroads, opened his report by contrasting the continuity in the British tradition of governmental supervision to the disjunction that would have to be negotiated between past American policies and current demands.

... in the United States even more than in England there was an entire absence of all control as to railway building; and as to control of traffic charges this abdication of rightful authority was carried far beyond anything that had been known in England ... Besides, the English Government carefully guarded at all times the grant of the right of eminent domain. No general railway act under which railways could incorporate themselves without special permission of Parliament was ever enacted by England, and every railway enterprise was compelled to come to Parliament for all its original powers to construct the line, to obtain Parliamentary consent for all leases of other railway enterprises of which they took control, and for all amalgamations or consolidations which in the progress of events took place, and for all further powers of any nature attempted to be exercised by the railway beyond the limits of its original charter.

The enactment of general railway laws in the United States throwing open the power of constructing railroads at every and any point, and ... granting by wholesale the power of eminent domain to any thirteen or more persons who might see fit to incorporate themselves as a railway company was a condition utterly unknown and remains unknown to the English people.[38]

The economic mugwumps continually returned to the revolution in economic policy that attended the rise of general incorporation laws between 1837 and 1850 as the source of the unique institutional constraints on administrative regulation in America in the 1880s. The idea behind general incorporation was to purge thoroughly "the corrupting influences which were exercised upon our law-making bodies by the authority to grant and withhold concessions" and to free private energies to accumulate capital.[39] The railway acts of the 1850s were extreme examples of this impulse to relinquish governmental controls in favor of the laws of the marketplace.[40] These acts proved quite successful in promoting railway construction, but they had the effect of leaving the government unchallenged and undeveloped for decades. When the operations of the national railway network shook the nation, it became all too apparent that the government was dangerously lacking in the institutional resources necessary for dealing on a more or less equal footing with the great industry it had spawned.

From the point of view of the economic mugwump, the American railroad industry of the late nineteenth century was something of a Frankenstein monster. Unintentionally but inevitably it had overpowered its sponsors at the state level, and finding no higher authority capable of providing supervision, it had become unruly and disruptive. Although it was easy to blame the railroads, enlightened opinion turned its critical eye to the problems of reconstructing governmental authority. Before attempting to regulate the railroads, the government would somehow have to bridge the gap that had developed in the evolution of public and private power. Charles Adams spoke from personal experience in observing that the nation's economic and administrative talents had been so thoroughly absorbed into industry that the government was forced to deal with the regulatory issue from a pathetically underskilled and unprepared position. He believed that a government with "a weak and unstable civil service" could not possibly meet the challenge of regulating the railroads.[41] For Arthur Hadley, "the worst evil which could possibly befall us would be to apply a great deal of regulation somewhere to an agency which was not strong enough to enforce such regulation everywhere."[42] Henry Carter Adams pointed out that no national regulatory policy would work unless the federal government first established an executive bureau of railway statistics capable of corroborating information obtained from the private interests.[43]

The governmental problem was not merely the relative weakness of the American state vis-à-vis the private sphere but the paradoxical strength of the governing arrangements which maintained that weak posture. Before national authority could hope to catch up with private power, the established structure of public power would have to be undermined or circumvented. As the economic mugwumps well knew, the American state was not undeveloped; it was highly developed but functionally irrelevant. The challenge was to reconstruct an already clearly articulated organization of state power.

The economic mugwumps pointed to America's system of local representation – operated, controlled, and reinforced as it was by a "vicious party system" – as a primary obstacle to formulating a clear and consistent regulatory response. They saw the abdication of governmental supervision over economic development manifested in the indulgent general incorporation strategy as running hand in hand with the development of a locally based, highly competitive party government that oiled the representative machinery to serve all interests but naturally shunned making responsible choices among them. Moreover, they saw electoral instability at the local level tying the representative inextricably to the sentiments of his district and precluding a reasoned and detached response now that a regulatory decision was imperative. Unless this highly mobilized and highly competitive electoral democracy was significantly defused, governmental elites would never be able to sustain support for the kind of insulated institutional machinery needed to develop a coherent regulatory posture. The bankruptcy of a government run by "unscrupulous politicians banded together in party machines" was fully exposed in the legislative debate on an issue that required a degree of detachment from local interests.[44] The challenge of building national institutional capacities commensurate with the scope and power of the interests to be regulated seemed to require a basic overhaul of the electoral–representative system. In Sterne's view it was essential

> as a necessary part of the solution before us, that the people of the United States should awaken to the fact that their methods of legislation and their methods of selecting legislators, their political organizations and their political administration must be reformed as well as the railway administration, and that the amenability of the railways to the public is largely dependent upon such reforms in political administration.[45]

There was, of course, another dimension to the problems of extricating American government from the decisions of the 1850s and building a national regulatory capacity. To those who advocated the "progressive theory of regulation," the courts posed no less of a challenge than Congress. Corporation lawyers were appealing to the federal courts in these years to turn the de facto freedoms granted in midcentury corporate charters into de jure rights. If the railroads wanted regulation, it was also clear that they, like other corporations, not only feared the wrong kind of regulation but desired to maintain as much of their charter liberties as possible. Federal judges disgusted by the incompetence of democratic legislatures and attracted to the social science of Herbert Spencer gradually became more receptive to the corporate point of view and set a course that would impart the authority of fundamental law to laissez-faire ideology.[46]

This prospect sparked Henry Carter Adams to plead the case for a "new jurisprudence" that would be compatible with his new economics and consonant with the development of administrative decision making. True, the judiciary was asserting principles of action to guide the government in dealing with the new economy, but Adams argued, the principles it had chosen merely perpetuated the basic problem of weakness in the legislative and executive branches. The courts' strong stand in favor of laissez-faire kept the government feeble in the face of rising corporate power. General incorporation was, in Adams's view, "fast becoming the fundamental defect of our legal frame." A judiciary intent on securing that defect against the progressive remedy posed more of a threat to, than a support for, the further development of the private economy. The subtleties of legal theory did not impress this new-school economist. "In a simple society," Adams declared, "the laws of property may be simple; in a complex society, they must be complex. Only in recognition of this principle can our marvelous national development be saved from anarchy and decay."[47] He despaired for the absence of "great lawyers and judges who shall by their arguments and decisions evolve new legal principles fitted to modern commercial and social conditions, rather than in a spirit of pedantry confess themselves bound in the fetters of precedent."[48]

Adams did not seem to appreciate how many precedents had to be overturned in order to bring laissez-faire to the bench. His frustration underscores an important point: The economic mugwumps did not have a monopoly on principled leadership, intellectual creativity, or professional opinion. National railroad regulation split the professional community, counterposing the advocates of administrative management with the supporters of strict judicial surveillance. The professionals offered two different solutions to the challenge of regulation and two different visions of the state. One vision implied an administrative reconstruction of power; the other, a judicial consolidation of power.

Charles Adams's progressive railway point of view, Simon Sterne's progressive merchant point of view, and Henry Adams's progressive academic point of view converged on the issue of national railroad regulation in the mid-1880s.[49] These economic mugwumps each looked to experts working as administrative authorities in government for a solution to the railway problem. National administrative regulation under the guidance of enlightened professionals promised to mediate economic conflicts, to stabilize a vital industry, and, in the process, to circumvent the unfettered plutocracy and the chaotic market competition emerging out of our past economic policy. Yet, the economic mugwumps observed a system of local representation, a system of court surveillance, and the instrument of general incorporation, all reaching their fullest flower in the mid-1880s, and because of these, they held out faint hope for their new governmental vision. There were to be no pleasant surprises.

Genesis of an administrative experiment: courts and Congress in pursuit of regulation, 1877–1887

The Interstate Commerce Act of 1887 embodied neither the interests of a dominant economic faction nor the progressive theory of regulation advocated by the economic mugwumps. Nine years and a hundred legislative proposals after a serious effort to obtain national regulation had begun, Congress found itself stymied by the task and finally opted for the largest possible coalition of support with the most ambiguous of measures. Unable to agree on its own distinct purposes in regulation, Congress capitulated to all concerned. In the end, this first national regulatory policy partook of the old distributive principle that the best measure was the one that every legislator could take back to his district with some evidence of dutiful service. The result was, as one legislator put it, "a bill that practically no one wants and yet everyone will vote for; that practically no one is satisfied with and yet they are ready to accept it; a bill that no one knows what it means and yet all propose to try the remedy provided therein."[50]

The legislation of 1887 may be traced through three interacting chains of events set in motion in 1877–78. The first was the Supreme Court decisions in the Granger cases. The second was the introduction of John Reagan's railroad bill in the House. The third was the great trunk line pooling experiment organized by Albert Fink.

The federal government's first authoritative statement on the subject of railroad regulation came as something of an anticlimax. In the Granger cases, of which Munn *v* Illinois was the most significant, the Supreme Court affirmed on all counts the authority of state legislatures to regulate railroads and warehouses as an exercise of police power and declared that "if the right to regulate exists at all it implies the right to fix maximum charges." In this view, the reasonableness of transportation charges was a judicial decision only to the extent that a legislature failed to assert its own prerogatives to control them. Once legislative action was taken, "the people must resort to the polls, not to the courts."[51] Further, in the absence of federal regulation of interstate commerce, the states were deemed to have the right to regulate all commerce within their borders. The Court thus rejected railroad pleas that state law could not extend to interstate traffic, that fixing rates by a legislature was a deprivation of property without due process of law, and that judicial control was the only proper and necessary form of regulation. Also unheeded were railroad admonitions that the Court proceed empirically and recognize the special need of expanding industries for freedom from rigid legislative restrictions and the impulses of democracy.

The state Granger laws had countered nineteenth-century trends away from strict legislative controls over business and toward judicial surveillance. In the Granger cases, the Court rejected pleas to formalize these trends. It refused both to interpret past legislative neglect as an abdication of legislative prerogatives and to use its enhanced jurisdiction under the Fourteenth Amendment to assert judicial supremacy. The Court accepted the notion that judicial authority in economic affairs was reserved for those matters on which the legislature did not make its will clearly known. Yet, in reaffirming the powers of the state legislatures, the Court was sanctioning a regulatory posture that had not worked in the past and could not possibly work in the future. The Granger states themselves had already abandoned strict legislative controls in favor of judicial and administrative solutions.[52] More importantly, the Granger decisions sanctioned state-based control over what was now a national railway network. By condoning state regulation of interstate commerce, the Court refused to acknowledge the adverse effects that a system of local controls could have on a national economy.

Still, the railroads had not amassed the most impressive array of legal talent in the land in vain. They had exposed the Court's position as both too radical (in capitulating to an increasingly volatile democracy) and too reactionary (in capitulating to localism). Moreover, the Court had, in fact, recognized the central principle raised by the railroads. In his majority opinion, Chief Justice Morrison Waite had upheld legislative interference in business "affected with a public interest." This was a delimitation of a standard for judging the validity of governmental interference in business. Railroad attorneys had succeeded in focusing attention on where and how to draw a line between the public and private spheres. As a first cut into this problem, the broad public interest doctrine was particularly susceptible to future attack for failing on the most basic measures of a good standard of action. It was vague, unpredictable, and open to dispute. The Granger decisions brought the government to a legal crossroads in which debate was to center on the development of new standards for gauging appropriate regulatory activity. Battle lines were drawn not only on the question of where to set limits on the government but also on who should set them. Those arguing for judicial restraint appealed to the *Munn* decision for support; those arguing for judicial activism used *Munn* as a foil.[53]

The first indication of the direction in which the Court would go in resolving this controversy came in Justice Stephen Field's bold dissent from Waite's opinion in *Munn*. In Field's view, the Court had passed up a tremendous opportunity to assert its new national authority and provide rules of action relevant to the new national economy. The judiciary had to assume the responsibility for imposing clear, predictable, and strict limits on governmental interference with the rights of propertyholders. Field wanted to place the federal courts above the convulsions of democratic legislatures, where they would stand as a fortress of discipline for the government and security for the entrepreneur. Fusing an assertion of judicial supremacy and a laissez-faire bias into a "new constitutionalism," he gradually moved the Court toward formalizing nineteenth-century trends in the liberation of the corporation from legislative control.[54]

If the railroads could find hope for the future in Field's dissent, the immediate effect of the *Munn* decision in Congress must have made them shudder. John Reagan, the Democrat from Texas, took the Court's vindication of legislative powers as a signal to move ahead with a national regulatory bill that attacked the railroads at every turn.

As former Postmaster General of the Confederacy, Reagan had landed in Congress in 1875 with all the political problems and prospects of a reconstructed southerner. His two overriding concerns in this period were to consolidate the position of the Texas Democratic party in post-Reconstruction politics and to reestablish his national political reputation. He had supported the compromise to elect Hayes in 1877 and in so doing had helped ensure Texas access to a continental railroad. When he assumed the chairmanship of the House Interstate Commerce Committee in 1877, he began work on two major projects: a rivers and harbors bill designed to bring the federal pork back to the South and national railroad regulation. Railroad regulation was Reagan's ticket to national acclaim, but his political calculations for using this opportunity were informed at every step by his position in local party politics. As a southern conservative, he faced an ever-present threat from the waves of agrarian radicalism that were sweeping the Southwest at this time. Two things were never far from his mind in championing regulation: the Greenback challenge to his power in the state party organization and the widespread outrage in the South against the control wielded by the Southern Railway and Steamship Association over transportation resources.[55]

Reagan's legislative strategy was to build a broad coalition of support in Congress by compiling a composite bill that addressed virtually every grievance leveled against the railroads by farmers and small shippers. His bill outlawed rebates, drawbacks, and any other discrimination between persons. It required equal treatment in the facilities used for carrying like goods and in the expedition of their transport. It outlawed unnecessary interruption of a continuous carriage and made it illegal to charge more per carload of similar property for a continuous short haul than a continuous long haul. It outlawed pooling, and it required the public posting of all rates. Beyond this, Reagan was content to let competition set railway rates subject only to judicial review of their reasonableness. The controls specified in the bill applied to full-carload rail freight (not partial loads or passengers) traveling between states and territories or between the United States and adjacent countries.[56] Overall, Reagan claimed that by outlawing all forms of discrimination and prohibiting pools, his bill would secure the most noble standards of competition, end rate wars, and reestablish the natural harmony of the marketplace.

From an economic point of view, there was much to recommend an effort to "raise the plane of competition" by restricting the use of certain business practices. But by simply compiling a list of grievances, the Reagan bill slipped into an ill-conceived and contradictory attack on a basic industry. The heart of the problem lay in the juxtaposition of a prohibition on pooling and a prohibition on long- and short-haul discrimination. Not only was each of these clauses suspect in itself, but together they worked at cross purposes. Nine years of legislative debate examining the implications of these clauses in detail and pointing out the contradictions between them produced few improvements. No wonder, then, that many who studied this proposal over the 1880s began to suggest that no regulation at all would be preferable to the product of the United States Congress.

In a nutshell, to prohibit pooling was to try to enforce competition in the railroad industry, whereas to prohibit long- and short-haul discrimination was to destroy the essence of competition among existing railroads. The bill moved in opposing directions on the most basic regulatory issue, and its likely effects were not at all what its author intended. The railroads could be expected to resist enforced competition one way or another. To forbid governmentally supervised pools was, in effect, to promote railroad combinations or rate agreements (technically not the pooling of freight). On the other hand, by charging relatively less for goods to take a more circuitous route, a railroad was able to add freight to that which was naturally dependent on its services and thus to make better use of its carrying capacity. Some regulation of long- and short-haul discrimination was probably desirable to control the severe hardships it worked on certain localities, but a strict prohibition would have created a de facto pool at higher overall rates and/or stimulated the construction of unnecessary roads to reduce distances between terminals. Neither the antipooling clause nor the long- and short-haul clause recognized the basic economics of railroad transportation: large initial fixed-cost investments that could not be put to alternative use but that could yield increasing returns per increment of capital and labor. Ignoring these facts would produce waste and inefficiency through an underutilization of capacities and artificially high rates. Accounting for them would lead to governmentally supervised pools.[57]

Economics aside, the bill stood on its political support. In demanding a strict prohibition of pooling in the first year of Albert Fink's great trunk line pooling experiment, Reagan posed as the nation's most prominent antimonopolist. He met the radical agrarian challenge at home, he could count on support throughout the South and West, and he found the jealous New York merchants receptive. In insisting on a rigid long- and short-haul clause, Reagan did not fare as well. There was a radical agrarian notion that cheap long-haul rates added to the growth and power of the cities at the expense of the agrarian way of life.[58] In the main, however, this clause proved politically divisive. Support or opposition became a rough calculus of geographic advantages. The West and the eastern ports had a natural alliance in favor of cheap long-haul rates. New Englanders especially feared that rate equalization would make them dependent on Canadian railroads. Abram Hewitt of New York supported Reagan's stand against pools but opposed the long- and short-haul clause. Railway competition was seen to help New York City, whereas higher long-haul rates threatened to exclude western wheat from eastern ports and European markets.[59] William Philips of Kansas spoke for many in viewing the long- and short-haul clause as evidence of blatant hostility to the West.[60] Taking this clause from the Pennsylvania oil men, Reagan found that besides western Pennsylvania, only a few intermediate localities such as upstate New York and West Virginia could claim consistent losses due to relatively high short-haul rates. For others, it was a matter of costs and benefits weighed in terms of who was farther west than they.

After a brief floor debate on his bill in May 1878, Reagan realized that he was unprepared to deal with the subtle and complex issues raised by his seemingly simple list of restrictions.[61] When he introduced the bill again in December, his skill at parliamentary maneuvering made up for the still unresolved questions, and it passed by a vote of 139 to 104. The South and West provided the Texan with 100 votes. The Middle Atlantic states and California split. New England was in solid opposition. The long- and short-haul clause took a heavy toll on Reagan's support and made the vote a bit shakier than it might have been without it. Ninety-three representatives from the South and West opposed the measure or failed to vote at all. The Granger states and the Midwest (excluding Indiana) were either strongly divided or opposed. Wisconsin cast only one vote for the measure, allying with New England in fear of total dependence on the Canadian trunk line.[62]

In the Senate, where railroad pressures were stronger, the political pressure of agrarian radicalism less intense, and the dominant Republican sentiment less sympathetic, the Reagan bill died. The Senate's intransigence brought a deluge of petitions for federal regulation from the Grange, local chambers of commerce, and state legislatures. Several bills were introduced, none of which made much headway. When it was learned that Reagan was about to report his bill again early in 1880, railroad magnates William Vanderbilt and Tom Scott demanded to have their views heard before the House committee. From this point, one may mark a continuous effort to disengage Congress from the restrictive and inconsistent form of regulation specified in the Reagan bill and to move toward a more enlightened regulatory posture.

Albert Fink and Charles Francis Adams (at this time an official for Fink's pool) testified at length before Reagan's committee. From their experience in organizing and supervising the largest experiment yet in voluntary railroad cooperation, they were able to articulate the most advanced railroad thinking about regulation. So successful were they that the committee revolted against its chairman and voted to support a measure written by Adams over Reagan's own. Adams's proposal, known as the Henderson bill, followed Reagan's in raising the plane of competitive action. It required equal facilities and equal treatment and outlawed rebates, drawbacks, and other personal discrimination. Beyond this, however, it set up a commission modeled after the one Adams had pioneered in Massachusetts. This commission would be able to advise Congress on railroad policy, investigate and mediate conflicts among businessmen, and publicize abuses of the law. The bill was silent on the long- and short-haul issue and referred pooling to the experts on the commission for a report on any "expedient legislation."[63]

Reagan had opposed the creation of a commission from the beginning. Throughout the debate, he and his more adamant supporters would denounce commissions as an unnecessary bureaucratic burden on the people, as an illegitimate delegation of judicial and legislative power, as a hindrance to speedy and effective redress, and most especially, as a concentration of authority in an agency too easily controlled by the railroads. If the commission idea was suspect on the surface, the weak form outlined in the Henderson bill seemed to confirm the worst of Reagan's fears. It was given no power at all to enforce regulations that might actually restrict railroad activity, and thus it appeared to Reagan an instrument designed to impress the railroad point of view on Congress and the people.[64] To the end, Reagan called for direct recourse from the law to the courts. Suspicion of placing an intermediary body between the legislature and the judiciary caused him to place complete faith in clear legislative restrictions and court surveillance.

It would have been interesting to see how a Supreme Court, slowly moving toward a conservative and aggressive position in the post-*Munn* period, would have dealt with Reagan's protestation of complete confidence in judicial surveillance of his blatantly antirailroad bill. The capture of Reagan's committee by the Adams proposal seemed to preclude this possibility, at least for the moment. In the fall of 1880, the Republicans swept both houses of Congress. Reagan lost his chairmanship, and a relative lull fell over the regulatory debate in the House.

The House became Democratic again in 1883, and Reagan regained the initiative in regulation. Although his committee still opposed him, the

Texan won two decisive victories on the floor. Late in 1884, he secured exclusive consideration of his proposal, and early in 1885 he secured its passage for a second time. The latter vote, 161 to 75, reveals less vocal opposition to his measure than in 1878, but it also shows a doubling of those not voting. The South and the West remained the core of Reagan's support. The vote suggested two things: first, many in the House who might have recognized the value of a more moderate form of regulation or a commission form could not vote against the Reagan bill; second, an antipooling clause and a long- and short-haul clause were now essential to the passage of legislation in this chamber.[65]

Reagan's success combined with a recession in 1884 to push the Senate into taking positive action. Railroad bankruptcies, the failure of voluntary pools, and the resumption of destabilizing rate wars set the stage for the introduction of a moderate proposal from the junior Republican senator from Illinois, Shelby Cullom. The keynotes of the Cullom bill were an assertion of the inadequacy of both legislators and judges to deal with the subtleties of regulation in any specific terms and a determination to seek a remedy in a commission of "five wise, able, experienced men of reputation, commanding general confidence and clothed with a limited discretion."[66]

This proposal for the building of a national administrative authority was conceived, first and foremost, as a way to remove all politically divisive and potentially dangerous policy decisions from the legislative arena. The Reagan strategy of building political support by compiling a list of absolute restrictions on railroad activity was countered by the Cullom strategy of avoiding all hard-and-fast rules. As his biographer explains, Cullom wanted "legislation which could not possibly harm the railroads or other business interests of the nation."[67] His bill endorsed the principles of equal treatment, just and reasonable rates, and the continuous movement of traffic along connecting lines. It prohibited "undue and unreasonable preference or advantage" to any person, concern, locality, or type of traffic. It neither condoned nor outlawed pooling, and it contained a vague prohibition on long- and short-haul discrimination that allowed the commission to make exceptions. The bill had a wider application than Reagan's, encompassing passenger traffic and less than full carload shipments. Overall, it called for disallowing "unjust discriminations" without defining them and for a commission "to examine each case on its merits and decide, more or less on a general idea of fair dealing, whether or not the carrier complained of was acting unfairly."[68]

Cullom feared direct recourse to the courts in regulatory disputes almost as much as he feared a restrictive specification of controls by the legislature. He saw the creation of an administrative authority as a way to compensate for the biases that had come to adhere to the adjudication of business grievances in court as well as a way to compensate for the deficiencies of a representative body in formulating a regulatory policy. As a midwestern Republican, Cullom was concerned with countering Reagan's strict pro-court–anticommission stand on the Texan's own ground. To the assertion that a commission would always represent the railroad's point of view, Cullom countercharged that in direct appeals for judicial redress the natural advantage always lay with the railroads and that a strong commission held out the only real hope for the interests of the average shipper.

> Leaving out of consideration the natural disinclination of the average shipper to engage in litigation with a corporation which may have the power to determine his success or failure in business, and to enter the lists against an adversary with ample resources and the best legal talent at its command and able to wear out an opponent by the tedious delays of the law, it is plain that the average shipper is still at a great disadvantage in seeking redress for grievances under the common law, which places upon the complainant the burden of proof and requires him to affirmatively establish the unreasonableness of a given rate or the fact of an alleged discrimination.[69]

To remedy this problem, Cullom modeled his proposal after the strong Illinois commission of 1873. Unlike the weak Massachusetts commission that informed Charles Adams's proposal, Cullom's tribunal appeared to have more at its disposal than moral persuasion.[70] He claimed that it would be able to arbitrate disputes quickly and at low cost; that if the railroad refused to honor a commission ruling, the findings of the commission would become "*prima-facie* evidence as to each and every fact in all judicial proceedings." The prosecution would be taken over by the government, and the burden of proof would be passed to the intransigent party.[71]

Cullom saw other benefits in the administrative remedy as well. The more outrageous charges of merchants and farmers would quickly disappear in the face of a powerful complaint bureau committed to an informed view of railroading. The bitter resentment of corporate power would be diffused and absorbed by a commission dedicated to the promotion of business confidence, industrial efficiency, and fair dealing in its reconciliation of disputes. In the capacity of a commission to supervise railway accounts, Cullom saw a potential to secure stability and uniformity in the industry. In the commission's annual reports to Congress, he saw the potential for keeping regulatory legislation in tune with expert opinion.[72]

When the Reagan bill passed the House in 1885, the Senate grasped Cullom's alternative as a substitute. The Senate bill passed by a vote of 43 to 12.[73] Both houses were now committed to national regulatory legislation, but the Senate insisted on a commission, opposed the prohibition of pooling, and backed away from a strong statement on the long- and short-haul issue. The House refused to consider the Senate substitute. In the midst of the deadlock, a select Senate committee was established to investigate the matter. The famous Cullom Committee opened its hearings in March 1885.

A train of enlightened experts from a variety of interests testified before the committee.[74] As a rule, they blasted the concept underlying the Reagan proposal and encouraged Cullom to legalize pools under governmental supervision and to delete the long- and short-haul clause altogether. Beyond providing a forum for the expression of the emerging consensus among economic mugwumps, the committee had little actual effect on the course of the regulatory battle. Cullom resubmitted his bill along with the committee report in January 1886. The only significant change he had made in the original bill was to modify the long- and short-haul clause in a way that introduced even more ambiguity into an already muddied issue.

By now, the New York merchants had given up trying to modify the Reagan bill and moved to formal support of the Cullom bill. The National Board of Trade also came into the senator's camp.[75] Reagan was left with southern and radical agrarian support, to which was added that of the few localities that sought a strict long- and short-haul clause. This did not, however, improve the prospects for Cullom's bill in the House. Greenbackers had produced an electoral volatility in the West that made it dangerous for any Republican or Democrat to stray from Reagan's strict antimonopoly line. No one failed to notice that Iowa Republican William Hepburn, Cullom's most vociferous western supporter in the House, had been turned out of office in November by a Democrat–Greenback coalition.[76] Predictably enough, the Senate passed the Cullom bill by a vote of 47 to 4; the vocal opposition came exclusively from the South. The House substituted the Reagan bill and passed it 192 to 41. The South and West held for Reagan; 92 members preferred to abstain rather than vote against him.[77] In August 1886, a conference committee was called.

The work of the conference was decided in favor of expediency by the Supreme Court's first major step away from the regulatory posture outlined in the Granger cases. Wabash, St. Louis and Pacific Railway Co. *v* Illinois, handed down in October 1886, declared: "Notwithstanding what was said in Munn *v* Illinois and other cases, this court holds that a statute of a state intended to regulate or tax or to impose any other restrictions on the transportation of persons, property or telegraph messages from one state to another is not within that class of legislation which a state may enact in the absence of legislation by Congress."[78] Interstate commerce was suddenly subject to no regulation at all. State laws that had covered such traffic within their own borders were invalid. The Court now openly recognized the irrationality of controlling a national economy at the state level. Moreover, by creating a twilight zone of corporate freedom in interstate commerce, it forced Congress to assume its responsibilities and declare its will immediately. Time had run out on the legislative search for regulatory principles; accommodation was the rule of the day.

The Act to Regulate Interstate Commerce emerged from the conference with each side having secured the clause that was essential to its claim of victory. Reagan got his absolute prohibition of pooling. Cullom got his commission. Thus, the southern and agrarian interest in antimonopoly legislation was vindicated, and the merchants received a board of experts able to act as a judicial advocate on its behalf. Only the railroads had clearly lost their central legislative goal – to legalize or at least not prohibit pooling.[79] Yet, even they could gain solace in having replaced some of the other rigid Reagan clauses with an ambiguous commission mandate that would need clarification by the courts. Indeed, the compromise was a bargain in which no one interest predominated except perhaps the legislators' interest in finally getting the conflict of interests off their backs and shifting it to a commission and the courts. There were two crucial questions left open in the Reagan–Cullom compromise. First, what specific powers were being granted to the commission over railroad rates and national railroad policy? Second, what precisely was the relationship between the authority granted the commission and the prerogatives traditionally exercised by the judiciary in this field? These questions were dismissed in the final debate by characterizing the entire enterprise as "exploratory" and "experimental."[80]

The Senate's version of the long- and short-haul clause, which at this point could be interpreted to mean anything one wanted, had been accepted, as was the wider coverage of the Senate bill. Beyond this, the measure followed a standard format. All charges were to be "reasonable"; personal discrimination was prohibited; schedules of rates were to be posted and filed with the commission; no rate increases were to be made without ten days' notice; carriers were forbidden to combine to prevent continuous transport.

The new Interstate Commerce Commission (ICC) was to be composed of five members appointed by the President with the advice and consent of the Senate. The members served staggered terms at the pleasure of the President for a maximum of six years. Not more than three commissioners could come from the same political party, thus defusing the fear of partisanship that had figured prominently in the debates. None could have a pecuniary interest in common carriers subject to the act or sit in any proceeding involving a business in which he had an interest. As an investigating agency, the commission could inquire into the management and business of all common carriers and keep itself informed as to the manner and method in which they were conducted. It could subpoena witnesses for testimony as well as books and papers, and it could prescribe a uniform system of accounting for the railroads to be filed in annual reports to the commission. The commission could initiate proceedings or act upon a grievance. When a grievance was brought, the agency was required to inform the carrier of the charges against it and request reparation or a written response. If the complaint was contested, the commission would make a special investigation. If the aggrieved party was sustained, the commission would order the carrier to make reparation and cease and desist. Further noncompliance would require the commission to apply to a circuit court of the United States sitting in equity to enjoin obedience. It could appeal a circuit court ruling in all cases involving $2,000 or more, at which time prosecution became the responsibility of the United States attorney in the appropriate district. The commission was required to make an annual report to Congress, including recommendations for further legislation.

The conference bill passed by large majorities: 50 to 20 in the Senate and 231 to 48 in the House.[81] Opposition was heavily weighted toward the Republicans in both houses, but this seemed to reflect a more fundamental regional division. The bulk of the opposition came from New England, New York, and Pennsylvania, whose eastern cities would be adversely affected by a strict interpretation of the ambiguous long- and short-haul clause. On the other hand, upstate New York voted for the bill, hoping for a strict interpretation of that same clause. In the order of most solid support in both houses, the South, the Midwest, and the West could claim to have pushed the bill through. The order here reflects the extent to which a strict interpretation of the long- and short-haul clause might affect the region. The South, having easier access to alternative and competitive water transport, had fewer misgivings than the railroad-dependent West.

The problem with the Interstate Commerce Act was not that it served any one interest but that it ventured into inconsistency and ambiguity in failing to choose among the interests. Congress had not transformed the conflicts within society into a coherent regulatory policy but had merely translated those conflicts into governmental policy and shifted them to other institutions. The fact that after nine years of debate, congressmen, experts, and interest groups could not remove the contradiction between an antipooling clause and a long- and short-haul clause in the same bill, let alone strike the antipooling clause altogether on the basis of economic irrationality, was a testament to both the vitality of America's locally based electoral–representative system and the problems this system posed as a foundation for national government in an industrial society.

The immediate challenge facing the ICC in interpreting the Commerce Act was that of superseding pluralism with principle. This would entail systematically reducing the susceptibility of government to conflicting private interests, defining consistent standards of governmental action, and asserting the authority of an administrative instrument in providing national direction to the railroads. The challenge was, in other words, to replace one mode of governmental operations with another.

The struggle for institutional authority: the commission, the Court, and the failure of administrative regulation, 1887–1900

The Interstate Commerce Act was not completely lacking in potential. As Cullom knew, under extant political conditions ambiguity in legislation might be the only way to serve the purpose of enlightened policy making. "Five wise men" unbeholden to any local constituency were given the discretion to determine the appropriate regulatory posture for the government. Much still depended on the meaning the ICC would give the law and on the cooperation of the courts in upholding the commission's interpretation.

Moving cautiously at first and then with increasing confidence, the commission sought to mold its ambiguous legislative mandate into an aggressive and consistent instrument for regulation. In its first two annual reports, the commission reviewed the act and its potential effects on all parties. It began with a broad conception of legislative intent; Congress's basic purpose was "to bring the railroads of the country under the control of law representing an enlightened public opinion."[82] In surveying the law, the commission questioned the wisdom of some of its provisions, mollified the fears of those involved with declarations of its own more sophisticated understanding, and determined to explore the limits of the possibilities for administrative control under the act before calling for new legislation. Over the years, the agency proceeded to elaborate a constructive rather than a restrictive interpretation of the law, one as fully in line with the expert opinions expressed before the Cullom Committee as could be expected under the statute. The commission's annual reports reveal the first notion of positive government in America emerging simultaneously in theory and practice. By the mid-1890s, the commission had turned an obviously weak and inconsistent law into a public policy aimed at a progressive theory of regulation. It rejected the negative – to police, destroy, or cut and slash; rather, it sought to build administrative authority in order to conserve, protect, reconcile, guide, and educate.

Of course, this regulatory posture stood on the most tenuous legal foundations. It is hardly difficult to take issue with the commission's interpretation of the Commerce Act. If the ICC did not emerge stillborn from the congressional womb, it surely emerged a bastard and soon found itself in an inhospitable judicial environment with inadequate provisions for survival.[83] The Supreme Court, now firmly dedicated to saving the private economy from the impulsiveness of American democracy in a very different way, accepted this stepchild of legislative expedience as another indication of irresponsible and undisciplined policy making by a legislature. The Court rejected virtually every aspect of the commission's broad construction of the law and reduced the ICC to a mere statistics-gathering agency. There was to be no redistribution of institutional power to the administrative realm, no progressive reconstruction, no new relationship established between the state and the industrial economy.

Although the Court's refusal to sanction a wholly new kind of governmental authority based on an administrative agency's interpretation of an ambiguous, ill-conceived piece of legislation may be understandable, even admirable, on its face, the relationship between the Court and the commission is curious enough to warrant a look beneath the surface. The Court had, after all, played a prominent role in prompting congressional action through its *Munn* and *Wabash* decisions. By the 1890s, both the commission and the Court were rapidly moving away from the affirmation of decentralized authority and legislative supremacy articulated in the *Munn* decision. Both the commission and the Court posed as bastions of intellectual and professional leadership insulated from the unstable and threatening forces of democratic politics. Both the commission and the Court sought to develop principles of regulation that would protect the railroad industry and promote further industrial development. Sharing this much in interest and orientation, the Court's emasculation of the ICC takes on the added dimension of an institutional conflict between two ideologically charged instruments of economic control.

The Court had been struggling long and hard to develop principles that would fulfill its traditional responsibilities as the state's lone counterpoise to the indulgences of democratic legislatures in the economic affairs of the nation. The seeds of a judicial discipline for the industrial economy, sown in Justice Field's famous dissent in 1877, finally blossomed into majority opinions in the closing decade of the century. The doctrines of substantive due process, vested rights, and constitutional limitations on legislative powers not only kept the government's role in the economy limited to a night watchman's surveillance, they asserted that "the idea of justice goes hand in hand with that of the judge." To maintain the sanctity of property against the "pressures of the multitude," Justice David Brewer, for one, called upon the legal community to battle the "mischief makers who ever strive to get away from courts and judges." He opposed in principle "the demand for arbitrators to settle all disputes between employees and employers and for commissions to fix all tariffs for common carriers." He rejected out of hand the arguments "that judges are not adapted by their education and training to settle these matters, that procedures in the Courts are too slow, and that no action could be taken until long after the need for action has passed."[84]

The fusion of ideology and institutional imperialism that took hold of the Court in the 1890s worked against the ICC every bit as much as its weak legislative mandate. One indication of this is that the decisions that crippled the commission were split decisions that invariably pitted Justice Brewer against Justice Harlan, the increasingly isolated spokesman for moderation.[85] The meaning of the law was open to question; the commission's assertions of authority were not unsupportable. The decision to destroy rather than nurture administrative regulation was made by a majority holding an opposing view of the proper relationship between the state and the industrial economy and an alternative view of the institutional mechanism best suited to cope with new economic problems. In his ringing defense of the ICC in the face of judicial emasculation, Henry Carter Adams insisted that the act had openly recognized the limitations of the courts as well as those of the legislatures in the control of economic affairs, and he placed the blame for the commission's failure squarely on the institutional "jealousies" of the judges.[86]

> Had it been possible for the courts to accept the *spirit* of the act, and to render assistance heartily and without reserve, there is reason to believe that the pernicious discrimination in railway services and unjust charges for transportation would now be in large measure things of the past. As it is, the most significant chapter in the history of the commission pertains to its persistent endeavors to work out some *modus vivendi* without disturbing the dignity of the judiciary.[87]

As an instrument of government, the ICC was as inherently opposed to the new legal formalism, with its fusion of judicial supremacy and laissez-faire, as it was to the rigid legislative restrictions associated with the impulses of agrarian radicalism. No one was more acutely aware of the problems created by an assertion of administrative authority in the heyday of judicial supremacy than Thomas McIntyre Cooley, the first chairman of the commission. Cooley's book, *Constitutional Limitations Which Rest upon the Legislatures of the Several States* (1868), schooled the generation of judges who were now securing the loosest reigns of governmental control with the tight fist of judicial review. Cooley's background as a Michigan Supreme Court Justice, as the first dean of the law school at the University of Michigan, and as a receiver for Jay Gould's bankrupt Wabash Railroad certainly did not presage a radical or anticourt commission.[88] Yet, Cooley's career and his thinking took a turn in the 1880s. Like the other economic mugwumps, he was growing discontent with existing institutional solutions to the complex problems of the day. His appointment as chairman by President Cleveland stemmed as much from his failure to retain his position on the Michigan Supreme Court after leading the Mugwump bolt of Michigan Republicans in the election of 1884 as from his respectability in legal and railroad circles. Moreover, his writings in these years systematized a view of economic regulation quite at odds with the one that was emerging in his name on the bench. He retained a positive role for the state in the economy. He described the value of administrative mediation in upholding reason in the antagonism of the public to large corporations and in imposing good manners on the "arrogant, overbearing, and reckless" actions of the entrepreneurs.[89] The distance that Cooley was willing to move on these new ideas was foreshadowed in his appointment of Henry Carter Adams as the economist of the commission.

Cooley moved slowly at first, establishing a judicious case-by-case approach to administrative regulation. Yet, by 1888, he had already recognized that unless the commission could make itself "master of the situation," its office would be "rendered ridiculous."[90] He embraced the enormous challenge of establishing "a new body of administrative law for inland transportation" by developing uniform rules of conduct from several individual cases. It is a testament to his stature as an institution builder and to the inherent conflict between the judicial and administrative forms of regulation that Cooley also took up the challenge of lecturing the Court on the need to make way for administrative authority. The father of laissez-faire constitutionalism now attacked the equation of due process with judge-made law. He asserted that the proceedings and determinations of an administrative tribunal must be respected as a legitimate part of the due process doctrine. In the fourth annual report of the ICC, he set apart administrative rule making and administrative findings of fact from the normal compass of judicial review. Courts and administrative commissions each had their respective domains of authority. Judicial questions of "law" must not encroach upon administrative rulings based on "discretion and sound judgment" in technical matters.[91] Before he retired from the commission in January 1892, Cooley had articulated the tenets of a new theory of law to fit an alternative mode of regulation in a new American state.[92]

Cooperation between the Court and the ICC was necessary to the success of Congress's experiment in administrative regulation, but cooperation was precluded by a conflict of ideology and organization. The intellectual and procedural gap that separated the Court and the commission in the late nineteenth century caused each to view the other with suspicion. An institutional relationship that would be the key to the structure and operation of a new American state began with an administrative tribunal locked in a struggle for survival with a vigilant judiciary. The Court ultimately asserted the hegemony of its more limited solution to the problems of controlling an advancing industrial economy over an alternative originally conceived as a way of circumventing those limits. The first light of a Progressive reconstruction of economic controls was thus snuffed out.

Reviewing the most significant cases in the ICC's struggle with the Supreme Court, certain general dynamics become clear. Where the Commerce Act was vague, the commission moved to assert administrative authority. Where the act was specific but contrary to a progressive view of regulation, the commission chose to ignore its provisions. The Court countered by asserting judicial supremacy wherever the law was unclear and by demanding strict adherence to the clauses that were specific.[93] It is important to add that, although the Court's rejection of commission authority usually worked to the immediate advantage of the railroads and against that of the shippers, the commission can hardly be accused of following an antirailroad line. Indeed, when it came to the antipooling clause, it was the Court that rejected the enlightened policy of benign neglect worked out between the railroads and the commission. The consistent line running through these cases is the commission's struggle for authority over national railroad regulation. The end result of this struggle was to leave the government with nothing new to offer any of the interested parties.

From the very beginning, the Court insisted on hearing appeals from the commission's rulings de novo and considered them original proceedings. By 1896–97, the Court was openly declaring that it was not bound by the conclusions of the commission, that it could admit additional evidence, and that it could set aside the commission's findings altogether.[94] Refusing to accept the commission's presentation as prima facie evidence of all the facts, the Court effectively nullified the commission's value both as a board of experts able to gather and evaluate the relevant material and as a public advocate for aggrieved parties in court. Ignoring Cooley's early entreaties to separate considerations of law and procedure from administrative findings of fact, the Court reduced the commission's activities to the status of meaningless preliminaries. Parties to an ICC hearing began to withhold information until they reached the courtroom. The commission found itself making a decision on the reasonableness of a rate or the fairness of a business practice only to discover, to its great embarrassment, the irrationality of its position when new evidence was presented in court. Moreover, by insisting that the commission hear all grievances first, the judiciary mocked the supposed economy and efficiency of the administrative remedy. The average case coming before the ICC as a formal complaint took four years to receive a final judgment.[95]

Undercutting the commission's quest for authority went beyond questions of respect for its investigations and its findings. The Court also rejected the commission's pretensions to function as a policymaking, a rule-setting, and a supervisory institution. Each of these points is worthy of individual attention.

First, in the Import Rate case (162 U.S. 197 [1896]) the Court took issue with the commission's interpretation of an "unjust discrimination" under an ambiguous clause of the act, and in doing so, it rejected the commission's first major attempt at setting a national policy.[96] The issue concerned the validity of charging less for continuous shipments from Europe to points in the interior than for domestic shipments originating in the same port where the European goods were transferred to rails and destined for the same final point. Thus freight from Liverpool to San Francisco shipped through New Orleans went cheaper than domestic goods shipped from New Orleans to San Francisco. This discrimination more than balanced the protection of domestic goods afforded by the tariff. The commission held such discrimination unreasonable, in effect declaring a national policy of protecting American products. The railroads appealed to the Supreme Court. The commission argued that in ruling on discrimination, it only had to consider conditions within the United States; the railroads argued that the world commercial market must be considered. Deciding this ambiguous point in the law, the Court accepted the railroad view and, in effect, substituted another national policy, to increase foreign competition with domestic goods, for the commission's protectionist policy.[97]

Second, the Court overturned the commission's efforts at administrative rule making under the ambiguous clause prohibiting long- and short-haul discriminations. In the commission's first annual report, Cooley had attempted to meet the flood of petitions for relief from the prohibition by adopting an administrative rule interpreting the act's confused language. The clause prohibited charging more for a long haul than a short haul "under substantially similar circumstances and conditions." Cooley declared that the similarity of conditions should be judged in the first instance by the railroads themselves, subject to a review on appeals first to the commission and then to the courts. He then set forth guidelines of the conditions under which the commission would uphold a carrier for charging less per mile for a longer haul. These were: the existence of water competition; the existence of rail competition from roads not subject to the statute; and other "rare and peculiar" cases of competition from roads that were subject to the statute.[98] Cooley clearly rejected the strict interpretation of the clause, which implied an end to competition through the equalization of rates. But he also clearly indicated that the existence of competition alone was not an adequate criterion for judging circumstances and conditions dissimilar, and that except under rare and peculiar circumstances, competition between railroads would not be upheld as a justification for discriminating between localities. The commission thus determined to set general standards by which the fate of railroads and localities would be judged and to use its discretion in particular cases to modify its criteria or make exceptions to them.

The Court overturned this pathbreaking exercise of administrative rule making by declaring that the existence of competition itself, whether between trade centers or railroads, must be considered a factor in determining the similarity of circumstances and conditions.[99] Because long- and short-haul discriminations were the direct result of railroad competition, the Court's declaration meant, in effect, that there was no prohibition at all and no need for an administrative body to determine rules and exceptions for deviating from equal rates because all conditions were exceptional. Cooley's guidelines were an open invitation to the railroads to participate in refining an interpretation of the clause that would balance the concerns of all interested parties. The Court's ruling made the commission's offer irrelevant and short-circuited the potential benefits to railroads of using a government tribunal to make exceptions to a rule concerning a politically divisive practice.

Third, the commission's effort to supervise and direct the railroad industry was frustrated by Court rulings that refused to uphold its prescription of specific railway rates in response to a complaint. The commission recognized that the law did not give it the power to set rates in the first instance. Carriers were free to set their own rates, subject to a review of their reasonableness, which was in the final analysis a judicial decision. Yet, the commission assumed from the outset that it could correct a rate found to be unjust or unreasonable upon appeal from a shipper with a more reasonable rate that would be binding in the future. The new rate would, of course, be subject to judicial review of reasonableness, but, the commission argued, this would only refer to the reasonableness of the procedures by which it was determined, not to the rate itself. To this extent, the commission claimed that its authority to ensure just and reasonable rates necessarily implied the power to fix rates.

This authority was fully in line with the practice of the stronger commissions in the states that the ICC took as the models for its own powers. For nine years the commission exercised this limited rate-making power, and its authority was not questioned by the railroads or the courts. Then, in an *orbiter dictum* to the Social Circle case (162 U.S. 184 [1896]), the Court raised a doubt that the act "expressly or by necessity conferred such power." In the Maximum Freight Rate case (167 U.S. 479 [1897]), the Court declared that prescribing a rate for the future was a legislative act nowhere expressly delegated by Congress, and that it could not be presumed by the commission. The commission was, in effect, held to be exclusively a ward of the Court rather than an arm of the legislature, and like a court, it could only pass on the reasonableness of a past action. A carrier and a shipper would have to appear again and again before the commission and the Court until a rate, once found unreasonable, was voluntarily corrected and affirmed. The ruling inhibited shippers from bringing complaints and, the commission claimed, it ultimately hurt the consumer who bore the burden of unreasonably high charges that went unchallenged. More to the point was Justice Harlan's interpretation of the impact of this ruling:

> Taken in connection with the other decisions defining the powers of the Interstate Commerce Commission, the present decision, it seems to me, goes far to make that commission a useless body for all practical purposes, and to defeat many of the important objects designed to be accomplished by the various enactments of Congress relating to interstate commerce. The Commission was established to protect the public against improper practices of transportation companies engaged in commerce among the several states. It has been left, it is true, with power to make reports, and to issue protests. But it has been shorn, by judicial interpretation, of authority to do anything of an effective character.[100]

By denying the commission all its pretensions to the exercise of substantive power, the Court reduced the agency to something resembling the weak commission model embodied in the legislative proposals of Charles Francis Adams. Every potential administrative challenge to the hegemony of the Court in economic affairs had been put down through judicial interpretation of the act. But even the Adams's weak model proved too progressive for the law or the Court to sustain. Mere publicity, oversight, and enlightened judgment led the commission into an untenable legal position that the Court ultimately exposed and condemned.

In its second annual report the commission addressed itself to the railroad's chief objection to the Commerce Act, the antipooling clause. Recognizing the clause to be of dubious merit, the commission assured railroad officials that as long as their management was "conspicuously just and accommodating," the "enlightened opinion" of the government would "directly tend to the advancement of their best interest."[101] This was, in the commission's view, the basic intention of the law, and it justified neglect of the spirit, if not the letter, of an ill-conceived clause. The commission did not object to railroad associations or traffic agreements that avoided the technical definition of pooling as long as the railroads met the requirements for publicizing rates and keeping them within the bounds of reasonableness. In 1892 they received an endorsement of this policy from none other than John Reagan. Since leaving elective office and assuming a post as a railroad commissioner in Texas, Reagan was no longer willing to cater to radical agrarian sentiments. He completely reversed his former position and now advocated governmentally supervised pools coupled with administrative supervision of railway charges.[102]

But the law had already been written, and it had been followed in 1890 by the Sherman Anti-Trust Act. In two cases, United States *v* Trans Missouri Freight Association (166 U.S. 290 [1897]) and United States *v* Joint Traffic Association (171 U.S. 505 [1898]), the Court held railroad agreements in violation of the antipooling clause of the Commerce Act and an illegal restraint of trade under the Sherman Act. However well the railroads fared in using the Court to sustain their interests in other sections of the Commerce Act, they failed to gain a judicial sanction for their most basic interest in regulation. Moreover, the commission had been informed that its efforts to impute consistency to the purposes of the act through the neglect of certain of its provisions could not be sanctioned. The commission had argued that the provisions requiring that all rates be published in advance, that they be filed with the commission, and that they not be changed without ten days' notice not only invited the cooperation of the railroads in arriving at their rates but also implicated the commission in such cooperation. Merely to provide publicity and oversight was to facilitate a closer association of the railroads. The law spoke to uniformity and stability in railway charges and asked the commission to ensure both, but the law and now the Court precluded the most reasonable means to that end.[103]

In its annual report for 1898, the commission took stock of the situation. Traffic agreements that restrained competition were deemed rational, inevitable, and desirable from the point of view of a stable and orderly system of railroad transportation. The problem with such agreements was the lack of adequate recourse for an aggrieved shipper to keep a check on the rates charged by these associations. The Court had rendered the commission impotent as an advocate of shipper interests, and pools remained illegal. Under these conditions, the railways were being encouraged to indulge in practices that had been unambiguously forbidden and that lowered the plane of competition to the most unscrupulous level. The commission had been placed in a legal straitjacket in which no action to remedy this situation could be supported. The annual report called for congressional recognition of the railroad industry as a natural monopoly and for a law that would permit railroad associations under the supervision of the commission. It pointed out that a governmentally supervised monopoly in railroading was accepted "in every civilized country today"; only the United States insisted on enforced competition.[104] By 1901, the commission had become even more bold in its protestations. Although it was unable to act on its own authority, it was certainly not going to sanction other laws that countered its perceptions of appropriate governmental action.

> It is not the business of this Commission to enforce the anti-trust act and we express no opinion as to the legality of the measures adopted by [these] railway associations. We simply call attention to the fact that the decision of the United States Supreme Court in the Trans Missouri Case and the Joint Traffic Association Case has produced no practical effect on the railway operations of the country. Such associations, in fact, exist now as they did before those decisions, and with the same general effect. In justice to all parties, we ought probably to add that it is difficult to see how our interstate railways could be operated, with due regard to the interests of the shipper and railway, without concerted action of the kind afforded through these associations.[105]

Unable to gain mastery of the situation, the commission had indeed been rendered ridiculous. In 1887, the ICC seemed an unpredictable institutional anomaly in the state of courts and parties; by 1900 it had become a mere irrelevance. In 1892, thirty-nine formal complaints were filed with the commission. After a small rise in 1896, the number fell off again in the wake of the most damaging court decisions. In 1900, only nineteen formal complaints were filed. Of the sixteen cases of unreasonable rates sustained by the commission over this period, fifteen had been overturned by the courts.[106] For all practical purposes, the commission had effected no change in the established mode of governmental operations or in the business conditions of the country. The ICC's existence was more a patchwork symbol of the government's concern for a problem than a constructive contribution to its solution.

Patching business regulation

In his presidential address to the American Economic Association in 1898, Arthur Hadley reflected upon "The Relation between Politics and Economics."[107] He expressed a fear that American government was on a course set for "national disgrace, if not national ruin," and he implored professional economists to take up the cause of political reform as their central concern. "Their immediate future lies not in theories but in practice, not with students but with statesmen, not in the education of individual citizens, however widespread and salutary, but in the leadership of an organized body politic."

The problem, as Hadley reiterated it, was that "the judiciary, the legislature, and the administration were subject each of them to separate influences which made them less ready to rely on the political economist for advice and guidance." Hadley identified the judiciary as the branch of government most naturally identified with the economist through a mutual search for principles of governmental action in the marketplace. These natural partners had, however, recently parted company, creating two separate "sciences" whose conflict was as inevitable as it was destructive. The economist's concern for the multiplicity of facts had found expression in the government's new administrative commissions, but "the attempt to supplement courts by commissions, involving as it does a separation of the progressive from the conservative, of the theoretically instructed from the legally instructed, is questionable in theory and likely to produce conflicts in practice." The situation was even worse in Congress.

> Under the current system of political ethics there is in fact a direct antagonism between the theory of economics and the practical workings of representative government. The economist shows how the largely independent action of the parts may be made to conduce to the collective good of the whole. The practical workings of represen-

tative government, making each member primarily responsible to his district – or one might better say the members of his own party in his district – means that the collective action of the whole is made to fulfill the separate wants of the parts – even though the satisfaction of those wants may antagonize the general interests of the nation. In the face of hostility from the courts and incompetence in Congress, Hadley turned to the chief executive to find some hope for the future. Yet, at present, America denied its Presidents the independence they needed to make use of the trained economist. The President was, first and foremost, a party politician, consulting with the representatives of the local districts and paying the price they exacted for their political support.

> However much he may desire the advice of economists and even avail himself of their services, he is often divested of the power to utilize them, and it too frequently happens that economists in their encouragement of independent voting on each national issue as it arises deprive themselves of that influence within the party councils which is necessary for carrying any issue whatsoever to its logical test and conclusion.

So it was that American government as constituted in the late nineteenth century stood impervious to a new cadre of professional economists with new responses to the demands for governmental supervision of the new industrial economy. It is surely no coincidence that when Hadley outlined these political and institutional obstacles to the rise of these experts to a position of authority, the first national institution to assert this authority lay in complete collapse. In its organization, its procedures, and its intellectual orientation, the ICC marked an effort to break with the structure of the early American state and, in so doing, to secure the new professional viewpoint in the government's regulation of business. The early fears of the economic mugwumps were, however, fully vindicated. It was indeed impossible to bring the experts into the high affairs of state without first making the state safe for the kinds of institutions that could translate their new vision into effective action.

Like the patchwork reforms worked out in the fields of civil and army administration, late-century innovations in business regulation failed to serve the aspirations of the new professionals for wielding governmental authority within a new administrative sphere. In the other two cases, however, established governmental elites had been able to meet the most immediate demands for new services and supports without suffering the professionals' challenge of a wholesale reconstruction of political and institutional power. In the case of national railroad regulation, they did not. Despite the pressures of farmers, merchants, and railroad entrepreneurs for some form of railroad regulation, none could claim satisfaction from the actions the government took. Congress had refused to condone pools for the railroads, but the commission had refused to move against railroad combinations for the farmers. The Court had refused to sanction commission efforts either to aid shippers in their dealings with the railroads or to support the railroads in their efforts to escape competition. If the federal government did, in effect, serve any of the interests pressing for railroad regulation, it was only by default of support for any concerted action at all.[108]

The early American state had never worked so well to produce so unwelcome a result. Its very strengths had become its most serious liabilities; its mode of operations had become a threat to further economic development. The conflict of interests and institutions structured by the Madisonian Constitution, the distributive politics structured by the constituent party machines, and the surveillance posture in regulation structured by the judiciary all worked hand in hand to block concerted action in railroad regulation. The ICC's aborted experiment with administrative controls left economic interests and American institutions at an impasse.

PART III

State building as reconstitution, 1900–1920

The ideal of a constructive relation between American nationality and American democracy is in truth equivalent to a new Declaration of Independence ... At the present time there is a strong, almost a dominant, tendency to regard the existing Constitution with superstitious awe, and to shrink with horror from modifying it even in the smallest detail; and it is this superstitious fear of changing the most trivial parts of the fundamental legal fabric which brings to pass the great bondage of the American spirit ... There comes a time in the history of every nation when its independence of spirit vanishes, unless it emancipates itself in some measure from its traditional illusions; and that time is fast approaching the American people. They must either seize the chance for a better future, or else become a nation which is satisfied in spirit merely to repeat indefinitely the monotonous measures of its own past.

Herbert Croly, *The Promise of American Life,* 1909

Introduction: From patchwork to reconstitution

The rise of administrative power and the disintegration of governmental order

At the dawn of the twentieth century, opposition to party bosses and imperious judges was being voiced by a number of reform movements that otherwise had little in common. Populists, socialists, and corporate liberals railed against the way capitalism and democracy had developed under the aegis of courts and party machines and called for placing relations between the American economy and the American polity on a new foundation. With the legitimacy of the early American state under attack from all sides, government officials finally made the pivotal turn down the bureaucratic road. After 1900, the doors of power opened to those who saw a national administrative apparatus as the centerpiece of a new governmental order. The central question in institutional development was correspondingly altered. It was no longer a question of whether or not America was going to build a state that could support administrative power but of who was going to control administrative power in the new state that was to be built.

Considered against the alternatives, the special appeal of the bureaucratic remedy is not difficult to discern. It alone offered both a measure of moderation and a measure of continuity. Government officials had, after all, given their ears, if not their votes, to the bureaucratic reform agenda for over twenty years. The proponents of administrative expansion spoke to all who were fearful of socialists and agrarian radicals but were, at the same time, uncomfortable with making stark choices between support for industrial capitalism and support for democracy. Constructing a national administrative apparatus held a dual potential for promoting the further development of the private economy and providing new rights and guarantees to the average citizen. Packaged in the rhetoric of "good government", the rise of the professional public servant in America merged hopes for a responsible new democracy with hopes for a responsive new political economy. The bureaucratic remedy represented at once a narrowing of the political alternatives and an obfuscation of the distinctions among them. By transforming ideological conflicts into matters of expertise and efficiency, bureaucrats promised to reconcile the polity with the economy and to stem the tide of social disintegration.

Yet, the appeal of the bureaucratic remedy and the politics of bureaucratic development were two very different things. The shape of the new order remained an open and perplexing question. The frustrated administrative reform efforts of the late nineteenth century had exposed a critical state-building problem still to be resolved.

The challenge of constructing the political and institutional supports for the exercise of administrative power had been deflected by governmental elites in favor of preserving and further developing the basic structure of the state of courts and parties. The expansion of national administrative capacities had been stopped just at those junctures where a patchwork support for the old governmental order threatened the construction of a new order. No agreement had been reached on the forms and procedures that would restructure relations between state and society, and those who championed the rise of administrative power still posed a challenge to the established foundations of institutional authority and internal governmental control. Reform ideals notwithstanding, a bureaucratic reintegration of state and society in America still hinged on an internal disintegration of the early American state.

The expansion of national administrative capacities after the turn of the century worked through this dilemma. Administrative reformers were catapulted from their position as institutional outcasts struggling for recognition at the periphery of power into coalitions with major institutional actors willing to alter the basic determinants of governmental operations. As these new state-building coalitions broke through long-established political and institutional arrangements, they instigated a scramble for power and position throughout the governmental apparatus. The bureaucratic realm was instantly repoliticized. Administrative power rose to a prominent position in American government as the centerpiece of this broader struggle over the reconstitution of institutional power relationships.

America's clearly articulated but functionally limited state of courts and parties had thwarted the rise of national administrative power in the late nineteenth century. In the early twentieth century, this preestablished order gave way to expanding administrative power and internal governmental confusion. The result was the halting development of a new state that institutionalized governmental disarray as it spawned new kinds of services and supports for a burgeoning industrial society.

The fundamentals of structural change: electoral realignment and the changing shape of institutional politics

Environmental imperatives for institutional development continued to mount after the turn of the century. Functional strains on the old state structure continued to intensify.[1] Attacks on the legitimacy of the established order grew more pervasive. But these factors cannot explain why or how the politics of state building changed after 1900, nor can they account for the new institutional arrangements that evolved. After 1900, as before, governmental responses to pressures for new institutional services and supports were mediated by the strategic calculations of government officials as they pursued political power and institutional position within the existing state structure. Making the transition from state building as patchwork to state building as reconstitution required more than intense pressures for change; it required an alteration in the strategic universe of political and institutional action facing those in control of the state apparatus. A series of such alterations notable after 1896 formed the foundation for America's state building break with the past.

The universe of institutional opportunities, incentives, risks, and constraints informing the actions of government officials changed dramatically in the wake of the electoral realignment of the 1890s. As the electoral alignment of the 1850s had threatened the survival of the early American state and the alignment of the 1870s had brought that state to its fullest flower, so the new alignment of the 1890s opened the possibility of its supersession. The national electoral configuration of the late nineteenth century in which Democrats and Republicans could mobilize majorities in districts and states across the North and West gave way in 1896 to a sectional alignment pitting a solid Republican North against a solid Democratic South. With the precipitous decline of Democratic strength in the North, the competitiveness of national electoral politics fell off dramatically. After the results of 1896 were confirmed in 1898 and 1900, the Republicans seemed to be secure in their control of the entire national government. Until 1911, when the Democrats regained control of the House, the volatility and uncertainty of national electoral politics were markedly reduced, and even after 1911 there was no return to the level of partisan division and rotation in governing institutions that had characterized the late nineteenth century. Between 1875 and 1896, parties either exchanged control in one of the houses of Congress every two years or maintained divided control. Between 1896 and 1920, the parties divided control of Congress in only one two-year interval

(1911–13) and exchanged control only two other times (1913 and 1919). The President's party matched the majority party in both houses of Congress in only three separate two-year intervals between 1875 and 1896, whereas the parties matched in all but two separate two-year intervals between 1896 and 1920.

Much has been made of the impact of the electoral realignment of the 1890s in altering the course of American development. Scholars have pointed out that the realignment ushered in an era of intensified political reform that undermined the institutional autonomy and resources of the local party machines. They have pointed out that the position of northern industrial interests in the national government was greatly enhanced between 1896 and 1911 and that agrarian and southern interests were severely disadvantaged.[2] It would also appear that the very political interests that had played so large a part in thwarting the professional bureaucratic reform agendas in the areas of army organization and national railroad regulation were the ones now relegated to the minority position in national politics and that the systemic electoral pressures that had kept politicians so wary of the Civil Service Commission in the late nineteenth century were eased for a time.

Yet, the impact of the realignment on the state-building process must not be overstated. It was more permissive than determinative. It did not resolve the problem of reconstituting institutional power relationships; rather, it allowed that problem to be addressed directly. The new alignment ushered in an extended period of Republican hegemony (1896–1910) and suggested a general direction for reform, but it did not carry with it a consensus on the forms and procedures that would define the shape of a new state structure. The significance of parties did not simply fade away, and their structure as loose coalitions of disparate local interests remained basically at odds with the rise of national administrative authority. There was to be no leap to a bureaucratic–industrial order.

There were, however, new opportunities and incentives opened to certain officials in pursuing institutional innovation. Newfound electoral strength and stability released institutional innovation from the political constraints of the previous era. As the opportunities were exploited, a new kind of struggle for power and position began to take shape within the federal government. Before that struggle could be resolved, electoral politics began to fluctuate again (1910–20), and the terms of the institutional contest were correspondingly transformed.

The intensely competitive, highly mobilized, and extremely volatile electoral politics of the late nineteenth century had sustained a consistent, clearly articulated, and narrowly restricted institutional politics. The all-consuming electoral struggle imposed a strict regimen on elected officials, making it difficult and costly to stray from established arrangements in their collective responses to pressures to expand governmental services and supports. After 1896, the old rules of institutional politics no longer compelled such respect. Government officials seeking to maintain or enhance their positions faced an uncharted universe of political and institutional action. Exploring the new possibilities in responding to the continuing pressures to expand governmental services and supports caused a redrawing of the lines of conflict over institutional development. Structural reform no longer pitted institutional outsiders against a firmly entrenched structure of political and institutional power; it now pitted institutional insiders against each other in a struggle to redefine political and institutional prerogatives. Each time the strategic universe of official action shifted – most notably in 1911 with Republican party divisions and the resurgence of the Democrats, in 1913 with the Democratic sweep of the entire national government, and in 1919 with the return of Republican party control in Congress – institutional politics took on a new shape, and the rise of administrative power was molded by a different set of possibilities, a different set of limitations, and a different set of conflicts.

A state under continuing pressures for new institutional services and supports, no longer tied to the old rules of governmental order, and moving through a series of dramatic alterations in the strategic universe of official action – these were the conditions that delimited America's pivotal state-building break with the past and its turn down the bureaucratic road. In these circumstances, administrative power grew as part of an extended and shifting scramble over the reconstitution of political and institutional power relationships. The foundations of the modern American state were forged in the vicissitudes of this scramble.

Political strategy and political vision: three elusive models for a new governmental order

The dimensions of the politics of reconstitution may be elaborated a bit further by focusing on the changing position of one of its principal actors, the President. The President had never risen far above the status of a clerk during the heyday of party competition. The only truly national officer in American government and the ostensible head of the national administrative apparatus found his political and institutional resources hostaged to local party bosses in Congress. As America's state-building vanguard well knew, the presidency, above all other positions within the old order, stood to gain from a real opportunity to reconstitute institutional power relationships so as to support an expansion of national administrative capacities. The bureaucratic remedy promised the chief executive his own national political constituency, independent institutional resources, and an escape from the limitations that a locally based party state imposed on national leadership.

In the late nineteenth century, however, Presidents were well advised to adopt a party maintenance strategy in dealing with questions of institutional reform and to forego bold state-building initiatives. Partisan attachments in the electorate were strong and evenly divided. There were few new votes to be won by any particular reform, and there was much to be lost by challenging any part of the precarious majority coalition that had carried the last election. Significantly, Grover Cleveland's great assertion of executive authority in his first term – securing the repeal of the Tenure of Office Act – did not challenge his own party but a Republican Senate defiant of Democratic control of federal patronage. The difference in political strategy between Cleveland, the Democratic reformer, and Harrison, the Republican organization man, had proven insignificant insofar as institutional innovation was concerned. Intent on maintaining their positions, each demanded that reformers recognize the primacy of the electoral struggle and accept a place in his governing coalition subordinate to congressional party concerns.[3] When Hayes and Cleveland (in his second term) defied their respective parties with bold assertions of executive authority, they virtually committed political suicide. Whether the chief executive was a Democrat, a Republican, a reformer, or an organization man, he found himself locked in the same narrowly circumscribed strategic universe, with few opportunities and severe risks attached to any plans for change. So far as institutional politics was concerned, the particular incumbent in the office of the chief executive seemed to matter little.

The situation was quite different in the post-1896 period. Theodore Roosevelt, for example, faced a unique set of opportunities, incentives, risks, and constraints in formulating his institutional strategy, especially after a landslide election in 1904 gave him a second term with a solid Republican Congress. Security in office opened new possibilities for asserting executive prerogatives long preempted by Congress, for forging distinctly executive political alliances outside established party channels, and for pursuing institutional innovations that would rebuild the governmental resources of the executive branch. With the opportunities for action greatly enhanced and the risks correspondingly reduced, who the President was took on a new significance.

This raises a point of considerable importance in analyzing the politics of reconstitution. One might well wonder whether Benjamin Harrison, who proved so adept at playing by the rules of nineteenth-century party politics and who stood by John Wanamaker and James Clarkson against the Civil Service Commission, would have proven himself so able or avid a state builder as Roosevelt merely by being placed in a different strategic environment. One might also wonder whether McKinley, who played the faithful friend to party boss Mark Hanna in his first term, would have emerged as a great institutional reformer in his second term. Roosevelt always stood outside regular party circles. In the late nineteenth century, he had made himself a thorn in Harrison's side as a civil service commissioner. In his first term, he outmaneuvered Mark Hanna in order to maintain his leadership position. In 1912, he undertook a campaign to destroy the Republican party. As President, Roosevelt not only had a great opportunity to negotiate a break with the past, he had the personal determination to exploit such opportunities to their limits with a view toward some reconstructive purpose.[4]

Without creative political leadership, new strategic opportunities for action do not bear fruit. The creative dimension in state-building politics – carried largely by new cadres of professionals standing outside established centers of institutional power in the late nineteenth century – was taken up in the executive office by three consecutive Presidents in the early twentieth century. These three Presidents – a reform politican, a scholarly judge, and a political science professor – each stood a bit outside the regular party organizations. When in office, each entered the struggle for power and position on the side of administrative reform.

Significantly, the sets of institutional opportunities and risks confronting Roosevelt, Taft, and Wilson were as different from each other as they were from the set that Hayes, Cleveland, and Harrison shared. Each of the Presidents of the Progressive era faced a distinct challenge in pursuing reform. Each came to terms with his respective position vis-à-vis party and Congress and combined this understanding with a particular vision of a governmental order that would support the development of a strong national administrative arm. Thus, although these Presidents each promoted administrative expansion, they pushed the necessary reconstitution of institutional power relationships in different directions. A sequence of reform strategies and their ultimate frustrations can be outlined to mark the twisted, halting course taken by the reconstitution of American national government.

The strategic environment for state building was more favorable during the Roosevelt administration than at any other time in the entire scope of this study. From a position of party strength and electoral stability,

Roosevelt pushed executive prerogatives to their limits. Nurturing the development of substantive administrative powers, he drove a wedge into the institutional relationships established among parties, courts, Congress, and the states. Roosevelt championed a view of the President as steward of the nation, leading public opinion on reform and protecting the public interest within the government.

Significantly, Roosevelt's state-building offensive was free of the fears of imperialism and industrialization that had marked many of his cohorts in the civil service reform movement.[5] He was able to join the moral fervor of a reformer with these constituent Republican interests. In his neo-Hamiltonian scheme, the position of the President as a nationally elected officer was to be coupled with the professional discipline of the bureaucrat to ensure that special interests would be kept at arm's length and that the national interest would be raised above private power. If the power of the President and his top administrators could only be freed from past restraints, nationalism, imperialism, and industrialism could be properly joined, controlled, and legitimized in a strong bureaucratic state.

Although this vision of the American state posed a bold departure from established political and institutional arrangements, Roosevelt was not naive when it came to institutional strategy. His chief obstacle was a Republican Congress with a conservative leadership already secure in office. Understandably, he looked toward extending his control over the executive branch rather than gaining control over Congress. He forged an executive–professional reform coalition through support for a small cadre of ambitious young bureaucrats. When necessary, the President was willing to press the institutional interests of this coalition against those of party leaders in Congress, but he did not seek out such confrontations. He preferred to rely on an expansive interpretation of executive authority, to move ahead with the professionals' reform agenda on his own initiative, and to bypass Congress as much as possible. Maintaining that sensitivity to power politics so clearly lacking in Rutherford Hayes, Roosevelt was also careful to court the party leadership in Congress when he needed their support, and he did not shirk from using his patronage aggressively to try to pull his party along with his designs.[6]

The institutional initiatives that secure Roosevelt's reputation as the premier state builder of his age were concentrated in the period between his landslide election of 1904 and the congressional elections of 1906.[7] From a position of electoral strength and political security, the executive–professional reform coalition pursued a course of redistributing institutional powers and prerogatives away from Congress and the courts toward the President and the bureaucracy. By 1907, however,

Congress had clearly had enough. The executive–professional offensive became mired in bitter opposition from congressional leaders no longer fearful of presidential reprisals. Thus, as the interparty struggle for power and position eased, a constitutional struggle for power and position was accentuated. Rather than introducing harmony into institutional politics, party stability and electoral strength redefined the axis of institutional conflict. The Republican ranks splintered in the wake of the executive–professional advance, and the President and Congress faced off in a new contest over the distribution of institutional prerogatives.

A pattern of executive advance and congressional reaction will be notable across the three areas of administrative reform under investigation here. In each case, Roosevelt and his allies in the executive branch took the state-building challenge beyond the old political and institutional relationships that had bound late-century state building in a patchwork mode. He gained substantive powers for the new national administrative machinery, and he jolted loose the organizational, procedural, and intellectual determinants of governmental operations. Yet, although Roosevelt pushed America beyond the state of courts and parties, he could not consolidate his new order. The challenge of building a strong bureaucratic state was duly met at every turn before its steward left office.

To dismiss William Howard Taft as an incompetent politician who retreated from Roosevelt's bold reform initiatives is to obscure rather than clarify the dynamics of state-building politics. Taft came into office as Roosevelt's personal choice for protecting and furthering his executive–professional reform program. The new President was, however, well aware that opposition from Old Guard Republicans in Congress had stalled this program in its tracks. Taft found himself in a difficult position. He could neither advance nor retreat without antagonizing some part of his party. At the very least, new reforms would require a different institutional strategy.

Personally, the former judge was skeptical of Roosevelt's vision of executive stewardship. The idea that a President could do anything not expressly forbidden was, from the new President's point of view, not only inappropriate institutional strategy but also unsound political theory. Taft believed that a strict interpretation of the Constitution provided the only legitimate guide for rearticulating lines of authority and reestablishing governmental order while expanding national administrative capacities. This neo-Madisonian model for reconstitution implied trimming the abrasive edges off the stewardship theory, but it did not imply a return to the governmental order of the late nineteenth century. As separate and equal institutional authorities, the prerogatives of the Congress,

judiciary, and presidency each had to be respected, protected, and promoted "within their proper sphere." Administrative expansion was to be
carried on with an eye toward separating new bureaucratic powers and
reconciling them with the original constitutional design.[8]

Was there an institutional strategy capable of realizing such a vision in
the wake of the Roosevelt challenge? Taft surely chose a reasonable
course in reestablishing cordial relations with Old Guard Republicans in
Congress. With due deference to their interests and prerogatives, he was
able by 1910 to gain their explicit endorsement for his own institutional
reform initiatives. But the President's respect for the Old Guard tended to
leave moderate Republicans and Progressives isolated. Tensions mounted
as the interests of Roosevelt purists in the bureaucracy were compromised
and moderates in Congress were presented with the choice between subordination or insurgency.

When the Democrats gained control of Congress in 1911, Taft's institutional reform program became tangled in the very constitutional
conflicts it had been designed to avoid. What in 1909 had seemed a
reasonable strategy for moving institutional reform toward a Madisonian
reconstitution was now a serious liability. Insurgent Republicans joined
resurgent Democrats in open revolt against the administration. The shifting sands of electoral politics and institutional coalition building pushed
the President into a series of watershed constitutional confrontations
with Congress, each of which focused on the authority to control new
national administrative powers. By 1912, the executive–professional reform coalition had been placed in jeopardy, the President had been
placed on the defensive, and Congress had seized the initiative in controlling the administrative machinery.

The political position of Wilson's administration was as different from
that of Roosevelt as it was from that of Cleveland. The Republican party
split in 1912 gave Woodrow Wilson a landslide victory with a solid
Democratic Congress. However, Wilson could not afford to circumvent
party and Congress, as Roosevelt had, nor could he afford to rest his
hopes on a party maintenance strategy, as Cleveland had in 1884. His
opportunities and incentives to exert executive leadership were much
greater than Cleveland's, but they militated against Roosevelt's executive-
centered strategy.

During Wilson's first term, the strategic balance of opportunities, incentives, risks, and constraints was weighted heavily on the side of
broadening the Democratic party coalition. To rest content with the
party's electoral base was to court defeat in the face of a reunited Republican party. However, current Republican divisions and a new Democratic Congress suggested that the President might take control of the

legislative process, make a substantive appeal for the allegiance of Progressive voters, and give his party a new claim to majority status in national politics. In the old Jeffersonian style, he used his party to forge a cooperative partnership between Congress and the President. Working through regular party channels, the President personally bridged the constitutional separation of powers and realized the entire policy program upon which he had run for office. The New Freedom achievement represents one of the rare examples of responsible party government in modern America.[9]

Under the Wilson strategy, national administrative development became an extension of party development and was worked through the President's cooperative partnership with fellow partisans in Congress. In this way, the Labor Department, a newly fortified Agriculture Department, and the Federal Trade Commission emerged to welcome a number of different constituencies into a new national Democratic coalition. Yet, what Wilson presented as a cooperative partnership was received in Congress as a set of limited bargains and tradeoffs. Not only was the President ultimately forced to recognize that his policy leadership in Congress was limited in scope; he was also forced to retreat from the claims to control over the administrative apparatus that had been asserted by the Republican Presidents and to oversee a comprehensive counteroffensive aimed at securing congressional control.[10] Inverting the Roosevelt formula, Wilson traded administrative leadership for congressional leadership. The difference between the two hinged largely on the position of their party in Congress and in the electorate. In neither case would party power sustain a combination of these two types of leadership.

The outbreak of war in Europe undermined Wilson's efforts to forge a national electoral coalition of Democrats and Progressives and left him an increasingly uneasy partner in his new system of party government. By 1916, the executive retreat and congressional counteroffensive in the control of administrative affairs were proving incompatible with the administrative burdens of war preparedness. As the national administrative machinery faltered, it became evident that the cooperative party strategy was a luxury America could no longer afford. Wilson had to reverse course and attempt to gain control over the bureaucracy.

By the time the President obtained emergency authority to reorganize the executive branch at will, it was too late to begin reviving the Roosevelt model of the bureaucratic state. Makeshift arrangements were improvised for the duration of the war. Afterward, the return of Republican control to Congress and the newfound interest of the President in executive prerogatives opened an undirected scramble for the control of administrative power. The postwar consolidation of the administrative advances of the Progressive era forged a new institutional politics in American national government, a politics organized around administrative power and a stalemate of constitutional controls.

The underlying themes of institutional reform in the Progressive era were the regeneration of government and the redefinition of relations between state and society. But there were no simple or self-evident solutions. A state-building sequence that began with Roosevelt's determination to forge "a more orderly system of control" ended with the consolidation of a new governmental order defiant of all attempts at control. Roosevelt, Taft, and Wilson each facilitated the growth of national administrative power, but their neo-Hamiltonian, neo-Madisonian, and neo-Jeffersonian answers to the problem of rearticulating lines of internal governmental authority each fell short of the mark. The politics of reconstitution follows the same pattern across our three areas of administrative reform: a *challenge* under Roosevelt, a *confrontation* under Taft, a *congressional counteroffensive* in Wilson's first term, a *crisis of governmental authority* in wartime, and the *consolidation* of a constitutional stalemate in the postwar years.

6

Reconstituting civil administration: economy, efficiency, and the repoliticization of American bureaucracy

... greater efficiency on a far higher plane is necessary if we are to democratize our industrial and political life. Our political machinery – national, State and local; legislative, executive, administrative, and judicial; constitutional and extraconstitutional – our whole political machinery in all its parts must be adapted to all the changing purposes of government. It is of small advantage that our legislators are democratically nominated, elected and controlled; it is of small advantage that each separate government wheel turns with noiseless ease, if the system *as a whole* is ill-geared. If in a government there is a lack of proper co-ordination among the parts, if certain parts are weak which should be strong, and certain parts are strong which might be weak; if between State and nation there are jurisdictional disputes; and if there are jurisdictional disputes between legislative and judiciary; if there is fluctuation where there should be stability, and a stiff unchangeability where there should be elasticity and change – if there are these or any of these, then no true efficiency can be maintained.

Walter E. Weyl, *The New Democracy*, 1912

The Progressive era is celebrated as the age of economy and efficiency, the period in which business principles and scientific management techniques turned the tide in the battle against profligacy and waste in government. The list of official bodies formed in the early twentieth century to deal with questions of efficiency in civil administration lends credence to this characterization: The Commission on Department Methods, the Commission on Economy and Efficiency, the Bureau of Efficiency, the Central Bureau of Planning and Statistics, the Bureau of the Budget, the General Accounting Office, the Personnel Classification Board. The titles alone suggest something of an obsession with the rationalization of governmental forms and procedures.[1]

This burst of interest in the reform of civil administration represents more than an extension or intensification of late-nineteenth-century reform efforts. Over the preceding decades, the quest for economy and efficiency had yielded little more than a holding action. The Civil Service Commission was restricted to taking selected offices out of the spoils system, and special congressional commissions concentrated on cutting unneeded clerks from the departments in Washington. Reform after the turn of the century focused on the positive – the construction and control of new administrative systems. It entailed a basic reevaluation of the role and significance of civil administration in governmental operations as a whole. The issues that had been stifled by the patchwork politics of the earlier era now defined the reform agenda, and the champions of reform in civil administration were now directly engaged in the organizational, procedural, and intellectual reconstitution that had eluded their predecessors.

Yet, the reconstruction of civil administration defied in practice what everyone preached as gospel. Although the ideals of economy and efficiency evoked tremendous enthusiasm, the process of breaking with the old rules of governmental order and defining new rules followed a logic of its own. A shifting struggle over the reconstitution of institutional power relationships mediated the quest for administrative rationality in the early twentieth century. The result was not a depoliticization but a repoliticization of American bureaucracy. By 1920, the old administrative system organized around party had given way to a new system organized around a constitutional stalemate.

The challenge

Theodore Roosevelt understood his party's new position in the electorate and its bearing on the position of the chief executive in government. This was clearly illustrated in the last weeks of his administration, when he turned to the traditional lame-duck extensions in merit civil service classifications. Like his predecessors, Roosevelt left about 100,000 executive positions open to patronage appointments. But the classification of December 1908 stands apart on two counts. First, it was made while a President of the same party (indeed, of Roosevelt's own choosing) was awaiting office. Second, it moved against the motor force of the federal patronage system. Roosevelt placed all fourth-class postmasters north of the Ohio River and east of the Mississippi River under the merit rules.[2] This extension dried up the most valued and extensive federal patronage network in the states that had consistently voted Republican in the national contests of 1896, 1900, 1904, and 1908. Taft would still have a free hand with postal patronage in those areas where the Republican cause was doubtful or weak, but where the party appeared secure, the President moved to make the merit system the dominant system in federal administration.[3]

No one could accuse Roosevelt of failing to perceive the importance of administrative spoils to the vitality of his party. But the President also perceived how his party's strength opened new opportunities to replace party controls over civil administration with independent executive controls. The classification of selected fourth-class postmasters was one of the final acts in a seven-year administrative reform initiative calculated to exploit these opportunities. As in the postal classification, Roosevelt throughout his term relied heavily upon wielding discretionary authority to break the bonds that tied civil administration to local politics and to forge an executive-centered reconstitution of civil administration in its place.

Roosevelt's attention was first focused on gaining control over the merit civil service. In 1901 and 1902, he worked closely with the Civil Service Commission to rewrite the rules that were to regulate the nonpartisan realm of civil administration. In the new scheme, the Civil Service Commission was to be fortified with substantive supervisory authority in dealing with merit employees. Political ties between merit employees and officials outside the executive branch were to be severed. The neutral civil service was to be transformed into a separate class of citizens, a state caste insulated from party and Congress and dependent in all its interests on executive officers and the President's commission.

In 1901, Roosevelt moved to close the back door on spoils intrusions into the merit service by ordering the Comptroller of the Treasury to withhold the salary of any merit employee whose appointment violated the civil service rules. He then ordered all employees to testify upon request before the Civil Service Commission as to the conditions of their appointment. Refusal to testify was to result in dismissal from the service. In 1902, the President redefined "neutrality" for the civil service. This rule, further strengthened in 1907, stated that neutrality for nonmerit employees meant not using administrative *office* for political purposes or to cause public scandal. For merit employees, however, neutrality entailed a strict prohibition on all political activity, including *personal* participation in political management and political campaigns. Merit civil servants retained only the rights to vote and to express opinions privately. Also in 1902, the President stipulated that an appointing officer could remove a merit employee for any cause – other than political or religious affiliation – that would "promote the efficiency of the service," and that the removal procedure did not include the right of a hearing for the employee before the Civil Service Commission. Appeals to the commission were to be referred at the discretion of the appointing officer. Finally, in 1902 and again in 1906, Roosevelt imposed gag orders on public employees. These orders forbade employees "either directly or indirectly, individually or through associations, to solicit an increase of pay or to influence or attempt to influence in their own interest any legislation whatever, either before Congress or its committees, or in any way save through the heads of the Departments or independent agencies under which they serve, on penalty of dismissal from governmental service."[4] With these orders, Roosevelt took support for civil service reform and the Civil Service Commission beyond a moralistic statement against the spoils system toward the construction of an entirely new system of civil administration and a reconstitution of institutional power relationships. Giving teeth to the authority granted the President under the Pendleton Act, the President molded the merit civil service into an instrument of executive-centered government.

The new rules would have counted for little had Roosevelt not been able to back them up with a more effective personnel agency. In 1903 and 1904, the President concentrated on fortifying the Civil Service Commission with the institutional capacities to act as the supervisory arm of the new administrative system. His greatest achievement in this regard was to gain an increase in the commission's appropriation sufficient to permit the agency to control its own personnel and to oversee the administration of the rules at the local level.[5] The commission finally began to free itself from its crippling dependence on officers detailed from other federal agencies and responsible to other superiors. It also acquired a permanent field staff. Thirteen federal civil service districts were established, each with a supervisor responsible to the commission alone. As Chief Examiner Kiggins observed, these district offices not only made independent administrative supervision feasible, it also provided a political link between local civil service reform associations and the federal civil service system.[6] The new civil service supervisor had a local constituency already prepared to support his work, and he could provide the local associations with technical advice. As the President's personnel agency began to extend its supervision to the local level and to provide a workable alternative to local party controls over federal administration, an executive–professional reform coalition was also being knit together across the nation.

Dramatic as Roosevelt's first-term initiatives in the reform of civil administration were, the potential challenge they posed to the interests of party and Congress was overshadowed for a time by the rise of a new political phenomenon – congressional lobbying by the merit civil service.

In 1901, newly organized postal unions had begun to lobby Congress for a reclassification of positions and salaries. In response, Eugene Loud, chairman of the House Post Office Committee, appealed to the President to limit the political activities of the public employees and, in particular, to put an end to this civil service lobby. In these circumstances, imposing strict executive controls appeared as a sign of respect for Congress. At the same time, it infuriated the organized public workers. In 1902, the American Federation of Labor (AFL) demonstrated its support for the employees by spearheading a political campaign against Loud and securing the election of a friendly trade unionist in his place. The Civil Service Commission protested to the President that this political campaign was incompatible with the neutrality principle.[7]

The politics of the chief executive's early civil service initiatives thus seemed to be tying together party, Congress, President, and commission against the merit employees. Soon, however, the issue became more complex. Roosevelt promised the public service much more than controls and restrictions. In the first place, merit employees were fundamentally opposed to the spoils system. They welcomed the President's efforts to extend merit appointments and to close the back door on spoils intrusions into already classified positions. The unions had no better allies against partisan manipulation of the rules than Roosevelt and his commission.[8] Moreover, the Civil Service Commission had long advocated and the President had long supported the very things the postal employees were lobbying for – a reclassification of positions and salaries and an end to political controls over promotions.[9] After the election of 1904, Roosevelt launched his more comprehensive administrative reform initiative, which further developed plans for the professionalization of the merit service and the provision of substantive career supports.

For his part, the President looked toward the creation of a stable career service directly attached to and exclusively managed by executive officers. His approach to federal workers included a carrot as well as a stick. In Congress, on the other hand, efficiency still largely meant economy, and economy did not bode well for labor interests. Public employees would ultimately, if not immediately, find the chief executive an indispensable ally in their quest for bread-and-butter programs.

Roosevelt had always supported the right of federal employees to organize, and after imposing the gag order, he attempted to delimit its impact on the unionization movement.[10] In 1902, he wrote the president of the National Association of Letter Carriers, stating that his order was intended only to require public employees to present their demands to the appropriate department heads, who would then present them to Congress. The chief executive was not opposing the substantive concerns of the public workers; he was only insisting on the procedures that would ensure executive control. The union, however, remained unimpressed. From its point of view, the Postmaster General had his own interests to promote and protect in Congress and could never be trusted as an ally charged with making the case for employee demands. The union resolved to fight first for procedures that would ensure its political autonomy.[11]

The immediate effect of Roosevelt's bid for executive control over civil service employees was to spur the AFL to take up the cause of all federal workers.[12] The AFL offered to help eliminate the gag order, to regain political rights for merit employees, and to turn Congress into the agent of the federal workers in their struggle against executive aggrandizement. With the defeat of Loud as a demonstration of labor's political clout and the specter of further encroachments into the administrative sphere by the executive, the prospects for a favorable response from Congress, on this score at least, were promising.

The alliance of party, Congress, President, and commission against the merit employee was never much more than an appearance. Indeed, a new institutional politics was beginning to take shape around the now irrepressible problems of labor–management relations in the permanent bureaucracy. This politics was bounded by labor's efforts to manipulate Congress and the President to gain autonomy for itself, by the benefits championed by the President to build the merit service into a centrally controlled career service, by the inescapable question of whether Congress or the President was the proper locus of personnel development and administrative oversight, and by the constitutional limitations on the prerogatives of any one branch to gain control over the merit employees. By the end of Roosevelt's first term, the civil service, which had recently been taken out of party politics, was moving into the center of a new institutional politics in which party ties between President and Congress were largely irrelevant.

The scope of Roosevelt's designs for civil administration was not fully revealed until after the election of 1904. Bolstering the authority of the Civil Service Commission, fortifying it with new institutional resources, and restricting the activities of federal employees could take the necessary reconstitution of institutional power relationships only so far. At the beginning of his second term, Roosevelt accepted a proposal from Gifford Pinchot and James R. Garfield that promised to raise the executive–professional reform offensive to a new level.

Gifford Pinchot was the head of the Forest Service, an adjunct professor at the Yale Forestry School, and the leading light of the federal government's scientific conservation program. James Garfield was the son of the martyred President, a civil service commissioner in the early years of Roosevelt's administration, and, in 1905, head of the new Bureau of Corporations. Their proposal called for an in-house commission to look into ways of coordinating administrative activities and improving the performance of the executive branch. Such a commission would reverse the late-nineteenth-century precedent holding that comprehensive review of department methods was a congressional responsibility. Moreover, such a commission promised to expand the definition of economy and efficiency. It looked beyond saving money and cutting personnel toward clearing the way for the President and his most trusted agents in administration to secure positions and prerogatives commensurate with their interests in national leadership.

Roosevelt formed the Commission on Department Methods on his own authority and chose its personnel from among the young administrator–politicians at the subcabinet level.[13] Pinchot and Garfield dominated the work. Charles Keep (Assistant Secretary of the Treasury) was the chairman. Also included were Lawrence Murray (Assistant Secretary of the recently formed Department of Commerce and Labor) and Frank Hitchcock (First Assistant Postmaster General). The commission's work was bound in secrecy, with all reports and recommendations to be cleared directly with the President. From the beginning, congressional reaction to this executive-controlled administrative survey was tepid. Roosevelt requested $25,000 from Congress in 1906 to expand the commission's activities and the number of in-house personnel attached to it. Congress provided $5,000 and restricted its use to the hiring of accountants from the private sector.[14] It gave no sanction to the kind of administrative challenge that Roosevelt and his small cadre of bureaucratic entrepreneurs had in mind.

The major ongoing projects that occupied the commission's time reflected the President's interest in building a strong, stable, and professional arm of civil administration under executive control. The commission developed comprehensive plans for a reclassification of civil service positions that would not only provide equal pay for equal work but also upgrade salaries so as to compete with the private sphere and regulate promotions upward through the ranks. It developed a retirement plan for civil servants that included government contributions to a pension fund. It proposed a General Supply Committee to centralize federal purchasing under executive order, an Interdepartmental Statistics Committee to coordinate and control information, and a National Archives to accumulate and classify governmental documents. Each of these proposals would require congressional action if its implementation was to have any long-term prospects for success, but Roosevelt was willing to do what he could on his own initiative. In 1908, for example, he set up an Interdepartmental Statistics Committee by executive order.[15]

Soon after its creation, the Keep Commission took on an additional role as the President's special task force for administrative investigations.[16] Most telling in this regard was its investigation of the Department of the Interior. Through the concerted efforts of Roosevelt and Pinchot, the Forest Service had been transferred in 1905 from the General Land Office in the Department of the Interior to the Department of Agriculture. This transfer signaled an intensification of the Roosevelt–Pinchot program for conservation and resource management, a program that challenged virtually all aspects of the General Land Office's operations. The conflict between the Forest Service and the Land Office had an intellectual dimension, for the Land Office was dominated by lawyers trained in facilitating transactions between the government and private interests, whereas Pinchot had imbued his new office with the spirit of professional forestry and the bureaucratic discipline he had come to admire while studying in Europe. The conflict had an organizational dimension, for the Land Office was tied to local interests and decentralized decision making, whereas the Forest Service was dedicated to coordinated resource management and national planning. The conflict had a procedural dimension, for the distributive politics of the Land Office were thoroughly enmeshed in lateral ties to Congress, which Roosevelt and Pinchot aimed to replace with executive discretion and scientific management.[17]

With the support of the Secretary of the Interior, the Keep Commission delved into that department's methods of operation. The investigation assailed the semiautonomous status of the department's divisions for creating paralysis at the top. It recommended freeing the department secretary from routine business so as to facilitate his involvement in substantive operations, rotating personnel between Washington and the field offices so as to break local political ties, and consolidating the four divisions of the department directly under the department secretary.[18] The President implemented these recommendations by executive order. They were followed by a proposal to abolish the Office of Receiver of Public Monies for the United States Land Offices and to further investigate corruption and fraud in the regional offices of the General Land Office. Meanwhile, Garfield personally supervised an investigation into Pinchot's Forest Service and held it up as an administrative model worthy of emulation. He recommended a further centralization of financial and accounting controls in the office of the Chief Forester.[19]

In 1907, Garfield was appointed Secretary of the Interior. With Pinchot the dominant figure in the Agriculture Department and Garfield overseeing the reform of Interior, Roosevelt's conservation program appeared secure. The executive–professional reform coalition moved into a position to displace the old mode of governmental operations with a new structure of administrative power.

But it was just this kind of administrative reconstruction by investigation, public exposé, and executive fiat that Congress found insufferable. The administrative challenge that had been carried on so vigorously in the wake of the landslide election of 1904 met with increasing resistance after 1907. Tensions reached a breaking point when Roosevelt, Garfield, and Pinchot continued to withhold federal lands from public sale by the General Land Office after Congress had presented the President with legislation specifically restricting executive discretion in such matters.[20] Republican leaders in Congress resolved to halt the executive offensive and to vindicate their own institutional prerogatives. Led by Joseph Cannon in the House and Nelson Aldrich in the Senate, Congress rejected every one of the Keep Commission's long-term projects for administrative reform. So vehement was the opposition that Congress even refused a public printing of the commission's final reports. Republican Senator Thomas Carter proclaimed the arrival of a new era in institutional politics by openly denouncing the Keep Commission as an "executive encroachment on the sphere of Congressional action" that threatened to make Congress the "victim of a bureaucratic advance to power." In March 1909, on the eve of Taft's inauguration, Congress passed an appropriation bill explicitly forbidding any expenditure of funds by any body for administrative investigations unless that body had first been officially authorized by Congress.[21]

Roosevelt's quest for executive control ended in scandal and dirty tricks.[22] The final degeneration began when Congress discovered that the President had been using the Secret Service to aid in his administrative investigations and exposés. Joe Cannon personally supervised the dismantling of the President's new "army of spies" by having the use of the Secret Service explicitly restricted to presidential protection and Treasury Department investigations. Roosevelt responded to this rebuke in his last annual message. He declared that the restrictions meant that the government would harbor criminals, and he added a suggestion that congressional resistance to his fight against corruption indicated a fear in that branch that its own members might be implicated.

This was the last straw, for it seemed to confirm rumors that the Secret Service was being used to accumulate embarrassing information on the activities of the President's enemies in Congress. As Cannon organized a committee to formally censure the President, Roosevelt threatened to expose specific congressmen in one great "political slaughter." Aldrich then drew up a resolution to condemn the President in the Senate. The chief executive responded with Secret Service data on Democratic Senator Benjamin Tillman, suggesting his involvement in land fraud and abuse of the franking privilege. On January 8, 1909, the House formally rejected all the President's actions and accusations on the matter. The vote was 212 to 35. The Senate followed with a reprimand that counter-charged the President with involvement in an illegal corporate merger.[23]

Theodore Roosevelt had carried the challenge of an executive-professional reconstitution of civil administration to the brink of party revolt and constitutional crisis. His seven-year reform initiative fundamentally altered the position of civil administration and civil administrators within the federal government. Driving a wedge between national administration and local politics, he jolted long-established governing arrangements and permanently altered national institutional politics. But the limits of his stewardship strategy for a reconstitution of institutional power relationships were reached before the organizational, procedural, and intellectual determinants of a new governmental order could be consolidated. Rank-and-file federal employees now looked to Congress for relief from executive controls. A professional cadre of top administrators looked to the President to secure their new positions in the high affairs of state. A bipartisan bloc in Congress demanded respect for the interests and prerogatives of the legislative branch. Old Guard Republican leaders served notice that they would fight their own chief executive for the control of civil administration regardless of the popularity of his reform position or the strength of his electoral mandate. It was not at all clear what direction remained open for American state building when the new Republican President assumed office.

The confrontation

William Howard Taft rejected the abrasive theory of presidential stewardship but not the need to develop executive prerogatives within their proper sphere. Having learned the lessons of 1907–09, the new President took office with protestations of respect for Congress and soon made his strategic decision to work further reforms through Cannon and Aldrich. By recognizing the prerogatives and interests of the congressional leadership, Taft tried to use his party's strength in government to reassert executive control over civil administration and to place it on a foundation more secure than that provided by his predecessor.

The Taft strategy got off to an auspicious start. In 1909, Congress requested the President's advice on how to make estimates of governmental appropriations coincide more accurately with estimated revenues. Aldrich went further early in 1910 by proposing a joint administrative investigation of the problem including representatives, senators, and executive appointees. Understanding the bitter opposition evoked by Roosevelt's in-house investigation but desiring full control over his own administrative commission, Taft asked for congressional authorization for an executive commission employing outside experts in conjunction with federal administrators. The President's Inquiry into Re-Economy and Efficiency (later reorganized as the President's Commission on Economy and Efficiency) was born in a spirit of partisan cooperation and trust between the President and Congress.[24]

Having bowed to congressional authority to sanction his administrative study, Taft selected personnel who were likely to tell him what he wanted to hear. Taft's pet administrative project was the creation of an executive budget. He saw the budget as his personal legacy to a revitalized presidency and to administrative modernization. A budget would provide the chief executive with administrative responsibilities commensurate with his constitutional status as a governmental authority coequal with Congress and the judiciary. As chairman of his commission, Taft chose Frederick Cleveland, father of the budget idea in America. Cleveland was a political scientist of high professional standing, a financial specialist, and technical director of the New York Bureau of Municipal Research. The second outside member was Frank Goodnow, a leader in the field of administrative law at Columbia University and author of the pathbreaking work *Politics and Administration* (1900). The third outside member was Harvey Chase, a New England accountant noted for his financial management reforms in city and state government. The public officials included W. F. Willoughby, past president of the Executive Council of Puerto Rico, Assistant Director of the Census, and future cofounder and director of the Institute for Government Research; Merritt O. Chase, auditor for the Post Office Department and top aid to Elihu Root during his executive reform offensive as Roosevelt's Secretary of War; and Judge Walter Warwick, Associate Justice of the Supreme Court of the Canal Zone.[25]

The budget idea was the central and guiding concept of the commission's work. Its underlying assumption was that the President had to assume responsibility for the coordination and control of the administrative departments, the independent agencies, and federal civil service personnel. With this assumption, the commission branched out into specific studies of governmental organization, personnel procedures, and financial practices. From the commission's reports, which included the first comprehensive chart of the existing organization of the federal government, emerged a plan for the establishment of three permanent presidential agencies to be part of a new executive office. These were: a Bureau of Central Administrative Control, a Central Division of Budgeting within that bureau, and a restructured Civil Service Commission.[26]

It was never more clear how the ideology of economy and efficiency was affected by the institutional interests to which it happened to be attached. The Bureau of Central Administrative Control picked up and extended the idea behind Roosevelt's Interdepartmental Statistics Committee. It was to be the consolidated information and statistical arm of the entire national government. Through the new bureau, the President would direct all offices concerned with accounting, auditing, statistics, bookkeeping, reporting, inspection, and budget making. With the centralization and consolidation of these tasks, the commission believed that "each process would become part of a well-considered *plan* for providing complete, accurate and prompt information on each subject concerning which data are needed, whether for protection and advice of the administration or for laying before Congress a statement of affairs in any summary or detail thought to be desirable."[27]

At the heart of this bureau was the Budget Division. The division was to develop and present "the annual *program of business* for the Federal Government" to be financed by Congress. Here was the commission's answer to Congress's request for advice on balancing revenues with expenditures. Here was also the professionals' promise of a new presidency, a new form of bureaucratic accountability, and a new kind of responsible democracy.

> [I]t may be said that a national budget is the only effective means whereby *the Executive* may be made responsible for getting before the country a definite, well-considered, comprehensive program with respect to which *the legislature* must also assume responsibility for action or inaction. Without such an instrument efficiently used by the Executive, the people and the press of the country, as well as the legislature, must be hopelessly in the dark; without a definite method of getting his concrete proposals before the country, the Executive, as the one officer of the government who represents the people as a whole, lacks the means for keeping in touch with public opinion with respect to administrative proposals – both the Congress and the Executive are handicapped in thinking about the country's needs.[28]

In order for the new budget to lay a well-considered executive program for governmental activity before Congress, the government's classification of expenditures, appropriations, and estimates would have to be revised. This meant changing congressional forms and procedures in response to an executive format. It was at this point that the budget proposal dovetailed with a proposal for a new Civil Service Commission. Because the executive budget would format expenditures for civil service personnel, it provided a vehicle through which the Civil Service Commission could pursue a comprehensive reclassification of positions and salaries. The President's personnel agency, working in conjunction with the President's budget agency, was to fashion and regulate a new civil service career structure. The old alternatives of lump-sum salary appropriations to bureau chiefs or rigid statutory specifications of salaries were to give way to a flexible but centrally controlled system of position definitions and salary ranges. Implicitly, congressional and bureau chief prerogatives in personnel matters would be correspondingly limited.[29]

The new Civil Service Commission outlined by the Commission on Economy and Efficiency was to be charged with a full range of personnel management responsibilities. Beyond administering examinations for appointment and planning the career structure, it was to take charge of promotional examinations, become the arbiter of labor–management disputes, regulate working conditions, and set efficiency standards. In all these tasks, the experts recommended that the Civil Service Commission provide a forum for the expression of "the interests of the individuals in the service as distinct from questions of economy in management and the interests of the manager."[30] By vastly expanding the scope of the commission's duties, the experts seemed to believe that it could become the great reconciler of the labor tensions now growing within the new administrative sphere.

Acting under explicit congressional authorization, the Commission on Economy and Efficiency developed a program that would institutionalize executive control over civil administration in ways that far surpassed the scope and implications of the Roosevelt initiatives. Ironically, however, no sooner had the commission been set in operation than Taft's political strategy for gaining support for reform began to backfire. As the commission charted the path toward an administrative reconstruction, the Taft administration was being pulled into a series of constitutional confrontations over administrative control.

Problems in Taft's strategy first appeared as administrators who had been catapulted into positions of power and prestige by Roosevelt began to feel their interests compromised by the new President's conciliatory approach toward the Old Guard of the party. The conservation program, in particular, appeared to be placed in jeopardy. Roosevelt believed that he had reached an agreement with Taft to retain Garfield as Secretary of the Interior and thus keep the Roosevelt–Pinchot program secure. Garfield, however, had been intimately involved in Roosevelt's controversial decision to withhold public lands from sale by the General Land Office in spite of explicit congressional restrictions on such action. When Taft took office, he appointed Richard Ballinger, former head of the General Land Office, to the post of Interior Secretary. Claiming that neither he nor Garfield had any independent authority to withhold land from sale, Ballinger moved to return control over certain disputed territories to the General Land Office.[31]

As relations between Pinchot and Ballinger began to strain, Taft strengthened the Roosevelt gag order to include bureau, office, and division chiefs. The new gag order was ostensibly issued to prepare the bureaucracy for the President's executive budget initiative. In effect, it prevented top-ranking civil servants like Pinchot from either petitioning Congress in their interests or responding directly to congressional requests for information.[32] With Pinchot gagged and Ballinger presiding over Interior, Taft could claim that his administration had balanced the interests of all Republicans.

The claim soon proved hollow. Louis Glavis, a Land Office agent from Seattle, petitioned Pinchot with an accusation of corruption in Ballinger's administration of Alaskan coal reserves. Pinchot arranged an interview between Glavis and Taft to discuss the charge, but the President dismissed the matter and authorized Ballinger to fire the Seattle agent. Recognizing that he was on shaky political ground, Taft pleaded with Pinchot to drop the Glavis case. The Chief Forester, however, decided to make the President pay for failing to support the conservation program in the Roosevelt mode. He directly petitioned Senator Jonathan Dolliver, one of a group of insurgent midwestern Republicans, for an investigation of the Interior Department.[33] Pinchot dared Taft to fire him and risk a devastating constitutional and partisan confrontation.

In one of the pivotal administrative controversies of modern American state development, Taft faced a bureaucrat openly defying executive authority and implicitly plotting the demise of his governing coalition. Should the President fire Pinchot on the basis of a Rooseveltian administrative rule and, in the process, sever a major political bond between himself and the Roosevelt wing of the party, or should he retain Pinchot for the sake of Roosevelt, expose the gag order as a sham, and open civil administration to trilateral bargaining relationships among Congress, the President, and top bureaucrats? Retaining Pinchot had the added disadvantage of extending a damaging party controversy over conservation policy in Congress. Cannon had already taken his stand, declaring "not one cent for scenery." A choice was imperative. The President decided to cut his losses. Posing as a strong executive, he moved against one of the masterminds of the executive–professional reform coalition. Roosevelt had to admit an understanding of the grounds for Taft's dismissal of Pinchot, but he also expressed his continuing commitment to the policies that Pinchot advocated and Taft had compromised.[34]

Taft's stand on behalf of executive control undermined his early pretensions to holding the various Republican factions together and raised the specter of party disintegration.[35] Ballinger was ultimately exonerated by Congress but not before Louis Brandeis, arguing the case for Pinchot and Glavis, had excoriated Taft and the Republican Old Guard and turned what was essentially a bureaucratic power play into a public call for the forces of democracy to reject the entrenched interests. More troubling still, when the House moved to set up its investigating committee, insurgent Republicans were able to deny Cannon his appointment prerogative. The man whom Taft depended upon to control the House and support his administration had suffered his first major defeat, and a party revolt in Congress threatened to leave the President isolated within the government. The debacle culminated with Ballinger's resignation in 1911. The secretary found Taft's renewed efforts to restore moderation and political balance in conservation policy intolerable.[36]

Taft's second watershed confrontation over the control of civil administration joined the insurgent Republicans with the resurgent Democrats (who took control of the House in 1911) in open rejection of executive controls over civil service personnel. By 1910, Taft was engaged in a thorough patronage purge aimed at bringing wayward Republicans to heel, or at least forcing them to pay a price for their defiance of the Old Guard leadership in Congress. Robert LaFollette was one of the President's chief targets. Decrying these tactics, the insurgent senator from Wisconsin began an investigation of the Railway Mail Service. The hearings dragged on into 1912, exposing administrative corruption, restrictions on union membership, and the dismal plight of federal employees gagged by executive restrictions. LaFollette became the champion of federal employee rights and turned Congress toward positive action to free the public employees from executive controls.[37]

Taft opposed legislation defining the rights of public employees on the grounds that it would destroy discipline and impede efficiency.[38] The shifting sands of electoral politics and political coalition building had, however, placed the President in a weak position. Sensing what was coming, Taft made some last-minute conciliatory moves. To preempt more radical action in Congress, he modified the most controversial of the strong-executive civil service rules. The President directed executive officers to provide written charges for all dismissals and demotions and to allow employees the right of written reply. He also clarified the gag order to guarantee that employee demands submitted to department heads would receive prompt and precise transfer to Congress.[39]

These efforts proved to be too little, too late. LaFollette, working with Democratic Congressman James Lloyd in the House, followed the more sweeping demands of Samuel Gompers and the American Federation of Labor. Gompers had been demanding explicit legislative acknowledgment of the right of federal workers to organize, legislative restrictions on the power of executive officers over public employees, and legislative recognition of the right of federal employees to petition Congress directly in their own interests. The Lloyd–LaFollette Act of August 1911 met each of these demands. It recognized the right of public employees to organize, specified the procedures to be used by appointing officers and the Civil Service Commission in cases of demotion or dismissal, and affirmed that "the right of persons employed in the civil service of the United States, either individually or collectively, to petition Congress, or any member thereof, or to furnish information to either House of Congress, or any committee or member thereof, shall not be denied or interfered with." It should be noted that the bill also explicitly denied the right of federal workers to strike, though this was not seen as an interference with their right to associate with and support the AFL.[40]

The Lloyd–LaFollette Act effectively nullified the Roosevelt–Taft initiatives on behalf of exclusive executive control over civil service personnel. Moreover, Congress explicitly asserted its role as an equal and alternative ear for all administrative interests, whether career, institutional, or policy interests. It was a major defeat for Taft's state-building designs and left his vision of a neat Madisonian reconstitution of civil administration in shambles. A bipartisan bloc had again formed in Congress to assert legislative prerogatives. Pinchot's strategy of appealing to Congress to protect his interests from the executive was vindicated after all, and trade unions emerged victorious in their struggle against castelike executive restrictions. Administrative insulation from institutional politics was a dead letter.

Taft's Commission on Economy and Efficiency completed its *Report to the President* at about the same time as work on the Lloyd–LaFollette Act was being completed in Congress. The summer of 1912 was not a very propitious time for a presidential initiative on behalf of an executive budget and a new Civil Service Commission. Implementation of the budget format required, at a minimum, close cooperation between the President and the chairmen of Congress's seven appropriations committees, and this was, after all, the first Democratic House in almost two decades. Moreover, Congress was eager to serve notice to the President that it had its own views on the civil service and that it would make those views known. Though born in a spirit of cooperation, the Taft Commission on Economy and Efficiency provided the grist for a third, if somewhat anticlimactic, constitutional confrontation over the control of civil administration.

In June 1912, Taft sent a message to the House stating his intent to present a sample budget for the next fiscal year. Both houses replied with a rider to an appropriation bill stating that until Congress specifically requested new procedures for the presentation of appropriations and expenses, the old procedures – following the Treasury Department's presentation of a Book of Estimates – would be adhered to. Congress "knew best the character and extent of the information it desired" and stated explicitly that it would not "abdicate, even by implication, its prerogatives in this matter." Taft directed his department heads to prepare budget estimates anyway. Responding directly to the rider, he argued: "If the President is to assume any responsibility for either the manner in which the business of the Government is transacted or the results obtained, it is evident that he cannot be limited by Congress to such information as that branch may think sufficient for his purpose." The sample budget was submitted to Congress on February 26, 1913, along with the reports of the Commission on Economy and Efficiency. The President denied congressional authority to refuse to receive the executive budget message, but he could not force Congress to act upon it. Presidential insistence was met with congressional indifference.[41]

Meanwhile, in August 1912, just as the Lloyd–LaFollette bill was being signed into law, Congress had moved to reconstruct the Civil Service Commission. It established a new Division of Efficiency within the commission to develop personnel policies. At first, the division seemed a direct response to the Taft Commission's call for a new Civil Service Commission that would take a broad personnel management view of its role. Indeed, the head of the division, Harold Brown, had worked closely with the Economy and Efficiency Commission.[42] In practice, however, Brown turned his division into a watchdog for congressional interests working within the executive personnel agency. Tensions began to grow at the Civil Service Commission over the proper way to proceed with the development of a personnel management program. In general, the commission stressed a more professional career orientation and looked toward presidential controls, whereas the new division stressed labor- and money-saving techniques and looked toward congressional controls.[43] The federal workers, flush with their recent victory over the executive, did not seem to notice that their erstwhile allies in Congress had just created a management division antithetical to their basic material interests.

Taft left office with control of civil administration up for grabs and the size of the permanent civil service pushing 300,000 employees. Between

the Republican party split at the 1912 convention and Wilson's inauguration, the President had blanketed into the merit service 52,236 patronage
appointees, including the remainder of the fourth-class postmasters.[44]
Like the Cleveland classifications of 1896, Taft's sweeping extensions
reflected the rather desperate action of a President lashing out in the face
of the disintegration of his own party as well as the specter of an opposition victory. Yet, with the classification of the postal patronage in the
South and the West, Taft left Wilson with a patronage problem far more
serious than that dealt with by William McKinley sixteen years earlier.

The congressional counteroffensive

Soon after Wilson's inauguration, Joseph Tumulty, the new President's
private secretary and chief party strategist, charged that Frederick Cleveland was in collusion with the Civil Service Commission against the new
regime and ordered all the records of the Economy and Efficiency Commission seized. An interview was arranged in which Wilson explained to
Cleveland that he supported the work of the Economy and Efficiency
Commission in principle but that it was impossible for him to secure its
position at this time.[45] All good causes had to be subordinated to the
passage of the New Freedom legislation on tariff, trade, and banking.
Cleveland tendered his resignation and, with W. F. Willoughby and
Frank Goodnow, made plans to establish an institute for research on the
national government modeled on the New York Bureau of Municipal
Research. The Institute for Government Research, father of today's
Brookings Institution, was founded in 1916 with Willoughby as its first
director. Pushed out of the government proper, the champions of the
professionalization of civil administration took up permanent residence
in the capital and offered their services to government officials on an ad
hoc basis.[46]

    Tumulty's attack on the Economy and Efficiency Commission was
accompanied by charges of political manipulation in the venerable Civil
Service Commission itself.[47] Taken together, these accusations signaled
the beginning of an executive retreat from claims of independent control
over civil administration, a retreat that would lead to a humiliating loss
of legitimacy in the Civil Service Commission in the wake of the World
War I crisis. The fate of the executive bid for independent controls was
sealed in Wilson's early strategy sessions with Tumulty and Postmaster
General Burleson over how best to pursue the New Freedom legislation
in Congress. Here the pivotal decision was made to work through the
regular Democratic party.[48] The southern Bourbons who dominated the
regular party machinery had little intrinsic interest in Wilsonian pro-

gressivism but a tremendous thirst for offices. Moreover, this was a fresh Congress without a clearly defined leadership structure. If Wilson gave up executive pretensions to independent administrative control, he could trade the perquisites of office for party support of his legislative program. On this basis, the President became a legislative leader, and party and Congress advanced with a mixture of old administrative methods and new administrative machinery.

This was a hard pill for the new President to swallow. Wilson was, after all, a former vice president of the National Civil Service Reform League, the father of the study of public administration in America, the professor who had lectured his colleagues on the need to create an administrative elite that would stand outside of politics and embody America's highest cultural ideals. Clearly, more lessons are to be learned about American administration from Wilson's presidency than from the dictum of his academic years that administration is a field of business separate from politics. Wilson the President did resist party pressures for even more drastic reversals of civil service reform, and he never gave up rhetorical support for the professional ideal. But the significant thing about his first term is the abandonment of the idea that administrative control required independent and imposing executive machinery and his turn toward a cooperative system that would join President and Congress through reliance on party and department heads.[49] The limitations of this system and its consequences deserve careful attention.

Wilson's first major pronouncement on civil administration was a declaration that no fourth-class postmaster would be placed under merit appointment unless he had first taken an open competitive examination. This halted Taft's blanketing in of 36,000 Republicans in the South and West and helped Wilson save face as a civil service reformer. Its effect was to give Postmaster General Burleson a fairly free hand over a vast pool of offices in the postal service. The Postmaster General allowed congressmen to choose appointees from among those who had passed the examination, and, in doing so, he implicated the Civil Service Commission itself in a Democratic party spoils raid. Meanwhile, Wilson had to suffer the public statements of his Secretary of State, William Jennings Bryan, which boasted of irreverence for the merit system. Not only did the old Democratic standard bearer have many friends to repay, but he had for years been the nation's most prominent opponent of civil service reform.[50]

As the New Freedom legislation emerged from Congress, Wilson made good his bargain with the party. The major bills carried explicit provisos against the merit classification of administrative personnel. Internal revenue officers, the Federal Trade Commission, the Agricultural Credits Administration, the Tariff Commission – all the great institution-building accomplishments of Wilson's first term bore the stamp of the spoilsmen.[51] Excluding the war emergency, Wilson exercised his own prerogative to extend civil service classifications to cover only 4,904 positions. On the other hand, individual exceptions were made in offices already classified within the merit system in 4,297 cases.[52]

In the excitement of the New Freedom years, the only group that seemed to care very much about what was really going on at the Civil Service Commission was that agency's natural constituency, the National Civil Service Reform League (NCSRL). In 1916, the league asked for access to commission information regarding the methods used in recent postal appointments. The commission denied the request. The league appealed to the President and received an evasive response.[53] The political pressure on the commission began to build as the league, still predominantly Republican, launched an indignant attack on the agency it had fostered and the President it had recently counted among its leaders. The commission's ascent to authority and prestige under Roosevelt and Taft made a proper response to Wilson, Burleson, and the league difficult to discern. Attached to a President who had given the spoilsmen a fairly free hand with the merit service, the commission found that it was more difficult to sustain the withdrawal of support once given than it was to sustain the position of noble isolation it had held within the government in the late nineteenth century.[54]

Wilson's treatment of the civil service issue raises an underlying problem in his political vision. Simply put, the President could not ground his new form of party government in a new kind of party.[55] Rhetorical support for a professional civil service and vague appeals to British ideals only masked the fact that Wilson's national party program was merely traded off against provincial party interests in national offices. Moreover, as Wilson's interaction with the NCSRL indicated, the President was not willing to launch a counteroffensive in the Bryan mode justifying the emasculation of the merit system. The spoils remained an embarrassment to the former professor; yet he could do little to secure the integrity of the Civil Service Commission or the professional ideal, and he had no clear alternative to offer. Wilson failed to place relations between party and bureaucracy on a new plane. His programmatic achievements remained personal and circumstantial and left this basic structural tension between party power and administrative modernization unresolved.

Congress did not just want spoils for deserving Democrats. Once again, the more significant innovations took place in the struggle to control the internal development of the new administrative realm. Obtaining the chief executive's cooperation on spoils matters was followed by a bipartisan congressional initiative in the area of administrative reorganization and investigation. In 1916, Congress removed its pet project of 1912, the Division of Efficiency, from the Civil Service Commission and established an "independent" Bureau of Efficiency. Though nominally still part of the executive branch, the bureau was to function as a special administrative task force for the legislature.[56] It was to pursue special investigations from time to time as Congress saw fit. Bureau Chief Harold Brown explained the role of his agency as follows:

> At the time the Bureau of Efficiency was created in 1916, the leaders of Congress realized the need for some independent establishment that would be available to assist Congressmen by ascertaining essential facts and presenting suggestions for consideration in connection with pending or proposed legislation. These leaders felt that to be of real value this establishment would have no regular administrative duties. It was created as an independent establishment to provide special administrative services to Congress and its committees.[57]

With the creation of the Bureau of Efficiency, the quest for control over the new realm of civil administration effectively passed from the President to Congress. The bureau harkened back to the late nineteenth century, when administrative oversight was a congressional responsibility. At the same time, it reflected Wilson's first-term concern with legislative leadership in substantive policy areas and his efforts to avoid clashes with Congress and party over questions of governmental control. The pretensions of this permanent bureau for administrative oversight to independent status is suggestive of the characteristically ambiguous institutional form taken by the New Freedom program, that is, the independent commission.

The bureau was given projects very similar to those that had occupied the Keep and Taft commissions. It investigated the problem of civil service salaries and position reclassification. It reported on the cost of a civil service pension system, the improvement of methods of finance and accounting, and the need for an executive budget. Like the Keep and Taft commissions, the bureau defined economy and efficiency in terms of the institutional interests of those who lent it support. For example, its proposal for position reclassification looked toward the maintenance of the lump-sum congressional appropriations that gave congressmen and department officials sweeping discretionary authority over promotions and salary adjustments. The permanent reclassification was to be controlled by the bureau and implemented on an incremental basis. This would delay the jolting shift upward in federal salary expenditures threatened by a comprehensive salary equalization plan, and it would substitute for the holistic and centralized reclassification designs of the Civil Service Commission.[58] The bureau's reclassification scheme spoke to the interests of Congress, department heads, and the bureau itself in opposition to those of the Civil Service Commission and the public employees.

On other matters, the bureau reported against a government pension for civil employees as an unnecessary burden on the taxpayer. It acknowledged the administrative advantages of an executive budget but rejected the centralized, programmatic approach of the Taft Commission's Bureau of Central Administrative Control. The Bureau of Efficiency argued for separating budgeting and accounting controls and recommended that no action be taken on budget legislation until Congress, working through the bureau, had restructured its own accounting and auditing procedures with an eye toward legislative supervision.[59]

As if to hammer home the new lines of cleavage emerging in the politics of reconstitution, Congress in 1917 authorized the Bureau of Efficiency to make a special investigation of the administrative methods of the Civil Service Commission.[60] Pressured by Burleson's spoils manipulations, Reform League criticism, and now an investigation by an agency anxious to assume its personnel management role, the commission found its position and its integrity threatened on all sides. By 1916, Wilson's cooperative partnership of President and Congress in administrative affairs had turned into an aggressive congressional counteroffensive for control over civil administration. With a war on the horizon, some dramatic changes in presidential strategy appeared imperative.

The crisis of governmental authority

World War I did more to magnify than to resolve the problems of reconstituting the state in modern America. The institutional direction charted for American government during the New Freedom years was not readily reversed. Only when the course of events threatened the complete breakdown of governmental machinery did Wilson appeal for exclusive control over administration, and by that point, establishing order was an exercise in improvisation. The dream of constitutional cooperation gave way to a temporary presidential stewardship extemporaneously composed. The powers and positions of those contesting the shape of the new governmental order were reshuffled once again, but the results were a makeshift.

The government remained nominally Democratic after the election of 1916, but Republicans and Democrats counted virtually equal numbers in the House. Moreover, there was a growing disaffection within the

Democratic ranks in the Senate, and there was stiff resistance to executive efforts to plan for war from local interests and regional, bipartisan voting blocs in both houses. Wilson spent much of 1917 struggling to coordinate a war mobilization effort in the face of multifaceted and growing unrest in Congress. Congressional impediments to Wilson's control over the administrative apparatus swelled during the severe winter of 1917–18, when the weaknesses of the federal bureaucracy were most dramatically exposed. The President scrambled to defeat Republican-inspired proposals for a Civil War-like Committee on the Conduct of the War, only to face an alternative proposal from Democratic Senator and Military Affairs Committee Chairman George Chamberlain for an industrial War Cabinet. It then became apparent that if the President was not going to capitulate and share control, he would have to take decisive and preemptive action.[61]

In February 1918, Wilson asked administration loyalists in the Senate to sponsor legislation giving the President general discretion to reorganize the executive branch at will. The bill, sponsored by Lee Overman, was transferred to the Senate Judiciary Committee with uncertain prospects. Success was not secured until May, when three Republicans on the committee broke with their own party's opposition and pushed the measure through.[62] The passage of the Overman Act marked the reversal of New Freedom institutional strategy. It authorized the President to abolish, create, or combine agencies within the federal government without specific reference to Congress, and it effectively outflanked unwanted interference from the Democratic leadership. Viewed from the other side, however, the Overman Act was only a temporary delegation of emergency power that transferred to the President full responsibility for what appeared a rather desperate situation in the early months of 1918. Congress merely awaited the end of hostilities before moving to reassert its prerogatives in the new governmental order.

The bureaucracy that Wilson struggled to control in 1917–18 was not the bureaucracy Roosevelt had struggled to build. Although Wilson was given a free hand to establish independent executive machinery, he did not command a strong administrative arm disciplined by professional bureaucratic managers. Rather, Wilson found himself the steward of a public sector on the brink of internal collapse. The President had little choice but to use his vast emergency powers to work out interim governing arrangements with private-sector interests. Bringing the personnel of business and labor into the center of power in the wartime government, the President acknowledged the very different paths that had been traveled in the modernization of the public and private spheres over the past forty years and how far the resources of the latter had outstripped the governing capacities of the former. A massive infusion of private power into public administration at a time when the government's regular machinery was faltering framed the distinctive contribution of the war period to the emerging structure of the new American state.

The kind of men recruited into the very highest levels of war management indicates Wilson's interest in maintaining some kind of distinction between public authority and private power even as he recognized the failure of the public sphere to control the war effort on its own. The President thrust a diverse group of personal loyalists, philanthropists, and independent professionals into the high administrative command posts. Bernard Baruch, Herbert Hoover, Harry Garfield, and Robert Brookings – to name a few – were figures familiar to the business community, but each had left the business world prior to the war to pursue some higher public calling.[63] Wilson relied on the detachment of such retired businessmen, their sense of public reputation, and their personal attachment to the President himself to hold the government together at the top while private power fused with public administration at the middle and lower levels.[64]

For their part, the war managers facilitated the flow of academics into the federal government on an unprecedented scale. By the war's end, some semblance of an executive–professional governing coalition had reappeared. In these circumstances, however, the professional's role was not that of supervising and directing the private sector from positions in a powerful state but mediating and coordinating the actions of a powerful private sector in a weak state.[65]

Though the most dramatic institutional innovations of wartime are more appropriately dealt with in later chapters, changes notable in areas of specific concern to this chapter aptly convey the character of this new phase in the politics of reconstitution. War administration enhanced the position of the organized federal employees, destroyed the credibility of the Civil Service Commission, and revived the idea of central planning at the top. These three disjointed shifts in the shape of civil administration did not fuse a new order. They merely repositioned the contending interests.

The call to arms found the federal employees aroused and restless. In 1916, Congressman William Borland had launched a campaign to increase working hours for federal employees from seven to eight without increasing pay. Borland, a Missouri populist, espoused a view of economy and efficiency with a long and noble history in Congress, and he spiced it with a radical Democratic attack on the rising aristocracy of permanent bureaucrats. The federal employees received the Borland idea as a symbol of the insufferable gap that had developed between their interests and the attitudes of those wielding power in Congress. The AFL came to the aid of the civil servants once again and secured the defeat of Borland's rider to a general appropriations bill. The congressman, however, was not intimidated and vowed to try again.[66]

The federal employees and the AFL were two groups that Wilson could not afford to antagonize in undertaking war preparations. It comes as no surprise, then, that Wilson became a vigorous opponent of the Borland idea and that by 1917 he had turned into a vociferous champion of the civil servants' material and career interests. The President spearheaded a drive to provide an employee salary bonus in 1917, and he promised to press for yearly pay increases until Congress acted upon a comprehensive scheme for the reclassification of salaries and positions. He also gave his assurance that retirement legislation would be introduced with the cessation of hostilities.[67] In June 1918, both houses of Congress passed an appropriations bill containing the Borland rider. Samuel Gompers personally intervened to remind Wilson that the Council of National Defense had advised against increased working hours for federal employees. The President sent a veto message on July 1, 1918.[68]

It will be recalled that Gompers and the AFL had campaigned long and hard during the Roosevelt and Taft years to free public servants from executive controls and restrictions. The Lloyd–LaFollette Act of 1912 climaxed labor's drive to harness congressional fears of executive aggrandizement in the field of public employee management to the interests of federal employees. The reverse strategy was employed in 1918, and another dimension of the new institutional politics came to the fore. This time it was the President who was called upon to protect the interests of civil servants from a hostile Congress and a hostile party.

Using the threat of the Borland rider and the crisis atmosphere of wartime, the AFL pressed its interests in civil administration further. As it took up the fight in Congress against increased hours, it also took up the work of organizing employees in areas other than the postal service. In mid-1916, it joined two employee associations, one in the Bureau of Printing and Engraving and the other in the War Department, into the Federal Employee Union. By 1917, the National Federation of Federal Employees (NFFE) was established as a full-fledged affiliate of the AFL. The union joined some forty federal employee associations located in the field offices to the association in Washington. It drew its membership most heavily from stenographers and lower ranked clerks.[69]

The NFFE capitalized on the organizational momentum created by the Wilson veto by financing an AFL political campaign to defeat Borland in the 1918 primaries. Its success established the federal employees' union as a permanent fixture in American institutional politics. The civil servants outside the post office were prepared to speak on their own behalf in the difficult legislative battles of the postwar years.

Although the World War I crisis enhanced the power and position of new interest groups in civil administration, it did little to bolster the authority of established civil institutions. The President's support for the public employees was not matched by support for executive control over civil service personnel. The Civil Service Commission was left to flounder and ultimately became a victim of the crisis. By 1917, the commission had antagonized the NCSRL, was under investigation by the Bureau of Efficiency, and was rent with internal dissension over how to respond to Burleson's manipulations. Dissension intensified with the pressures of war. When the civil service rules were relaxed during the crisis to facilitate recruitment into the administrative war machine, the commission appeared paralyzed. Its inability to act early in the war led the NCSRL to fill the vacuum and set national policy for the emergency. When the war ended, the commission's position became completely untenable. It appeared to have been harboring a spoils raid for six years, the Republicans were preparing to take control of Congress, and the commissioners had shown themselves unable to agree about how to respond to the conflicting pressures that swirled around them.

The wake of the war pushed the Civil Service Commission to an ignominious fall from its lofty status as the premier symbol of integrity in the new American state. As early as April 1918, Wilson indicated his dissatisfaction with the commission's handling of its duties and informed the NCSRL that changes would be forthcoming. Early in 1919, he tried to sever his connections with the agency and its wartime operations by requesting the resignation of all the commissioners. This action sparked a controversy that extended into the fall. One embittered commissioner refused to resign merely to spare Wilson political embarrassment; instead he appealed to the Republican Congress for support. He then publicly accused Burleson of manipulation of the civil service rules and implicated the commission in the shady dealings.[70] Whatever was left of the myth that the commission would place administration beyond politics was now laid to rest. It remained just another pawn in the still unresolved scramble over the redefinition of institutional power relationships. The forty-year struggle to define a higher standard in personnel administration had lost its credibility under the pressures of its first great test.

Ironically, as the government's permanent machinery for the development of a new order faltered, the cause of professionalism was being elevated elsewhere by institutional outsiders carried into the government by Wilson's extraordinary team of war managers. From the early months of planning for war by the Council of National Defense, personnel from the recently established Institute for Government Research were employed in the management of the war machine. Soon the entire staff of the institute was on special assignment to the government. When Wilson used his authority under the Overman Act to elevate Bernard Baruch to a commanding position in a reorganized War Industries Board (see Chapter 7), this relationship was strengthened further. Robert Brookings, a trustee of the institute, was placed in charge of the Price Fixing Committee of the board. From this important post within the government, Brookings supported the personnel and advocated the ideas of the institute. The war linked Wilson to the men and ideas he had pushed out of the government in 1913 and made the institute another permanent fixture in the Washington establishment.[71]

No single agency epitomized the hastily improvised executive–professional coalition formed in wartime better than the Central Bureau of Planning and Statistics. The bureau was created by Wilson in June 1918 on the recommendation of Baruch. Edwin Gay, dean of the Harvard Business School, was chosen to run it. By the force of his example as head of the planning unit of the wartime Shipping Board, Gay had proven the indispensability of academics in coordinating public and private activities. In his new position as head of the Central Bureau of Planning and Statistics, Gay was placed in charge of compiling information on the operations of all the new war agencies and the regular bureaus of the federal government. This information was presented to the President in weekly reports. By the war's end, Gay had become the key figure controlling the flow of information within the war machine.[72]

The bureau was not in operation long enough to make any significant changes in the internal operations of the established bureaus of the federal government. Like the other war agencies, it represented an ad hoc response to the emergency and was gradually phased out of existence as the emergency subsided. Its enduring significance lay in reviving the idea of the Keep and Taft commissions for some kind of central bureau of administration and in providing a haven in which the skills of the academic community were concentrated and its talents demonstrated. The operations of the bureau provided Robert Brookings and W. F. Willoughby with an important example in their efforts to press for an executive budget in postwar reconstruction politics.

Overall, World War I jolted civil administration but not in any definitive direction. In the final analysis, the impact of the crisis is best understood in terms of the disjointed quality of developments in the unionization movement, in personnel management, and in central planning. Each development was propelled by the extraordinary demands of the war crisis on government, but each was effected differently. Rather than transcending the previous decade and a half of inconclusive political struggle, the state-building imperatives of wartime extended that struggle and further confused the puzzle of reconstitution.

The consolidation

When the various fragments of Progressive reform in civil administration were consolidated in the postwar years, the problems of reconstituting internal governmental order were simply institutionalized. Authoritative controls over the new national bureaucratic apparatus were cast in a constitutional stalemate. The shifting scramble for power and position could not be satisfactorily ended, so it was built into the very structure of the new American state.

The return of the Republican party to control of Congress in 1919 brought with it a scathing attack on Wilson's wartime administration and a renewed determination to set a course for strict economy and efficiency. This change in congressional party leadership certainly did not bode well for institutional cooperation in resolving the outstanding issues of reconstruction in civil administration; yet, what ensued was not entirely a partisan struggle. Democrats joined Republicans in resuming the congressional counteroffensive they had launched between 1912 and 1916. The President was left to his own devices to defend executive prerogatives against bipartisan support for congressional controls.

The first issue to come to a head in the postwar years concerned the status of the Bureau of Efficiency. Late in 1918, the NCSRL took note that the bureau was a "curious anomaly" within the executive branch and recommended that it be rejoined to the Civil Service Commission.[73] Democratic Senator William King and Republican Senator Reed Smoot had other plans. Attempting to formalize the relationship between Congress and the bureau, they sponsored legislation that would take the bureau out of the executive branch altogether and give it sweeping powers over civil administration in the name of strict congressional control.

The King bill of January 1920 proposed to make the chief of the Bureau of Efficiency an appointee of the Speaker of the House and directly accountable to the chairman of the House and Senate appropriations committees. The bureau was to supervise promotions, transfers, and even discharges from the federal service.[74] The Smoot proposal followed King's appointment scheme but was less specific on the scope of the bureau's powers. It simply authorized the Bureau of Efficiency to "investigate any matters relating to the organization, activities or methods of business of the several administrative services of the government."[75]

The Federal Employee, the official publication of the NFFE, vigorously denounced these proposals as designs to take from executive officers "all control over matters of personnel, organization and business methods in their departments, and to vest such control in the Bureau of Efficiency." They would effectively make the bureau chief, Harold Brown, the "Civil Service Czar."[76] Labor had made a complete turnaround from its campaign of 1901–12 against executive control and now appeared to be defending the prerogatives of executive officers and the Civil Service Commission against this threat from Congress and the Bureau of Efficiency.

The Smoot proposal was passed by the Senate as a rider to an appropriations bill in April 1920. Republican William Wood and Democrat Thomas Sisson pushed the proposal in the House, but they ran into heavy opposition from the NFFE and the chairman of the House Select Committee on the Budget, James Good. Good's committee was drafting its own legislation, and the congressman argued that the Senate's Bureau of Efficiency proposal would confuse, if not derail, his own efforts to secure independent administrative control over auditing. Good suggested that the status of the Bureau of Efficiency be considered after action on budget legislation. The Smoot rider was deleted in a House–Senate conference on the appropriations bill, but Senators Smoot and King were now joined by none other than Senator Overman in a determination to attach the Bureau of Efficiency proposal directly to the forthcoming budget bill.[77]

On May 13, 1920, Wilson sent a veto message to Congress objecting to a different rider to this same appropriations bill, which would have established a Public Buildings Commission composed of senators, representatives, and bureaucrats and charged with the allocation of office space. The President took care in this message to outline his position on the Bureau of Efficiency proposal as well. Though that rider had been eliminated in conference, Wilson noted that it had reappeared as a Senate amendment to the pending legislation on the national budget, and he saw in it the same strategy he was rejecting in the veto of the Public Buildings Commission. He objected to plans to give the Bureau of Efficiency "more sweeping powers of investigation than are usually conferred upon the committees of Congress," and he expressed doubt that the creation of a "bureau of Congress" was permissible at all.[78] Congress was duly advised of the President's newfound determination to protect executive prerogatives in civil administration. The formal transfer of the Bureau of Efficiency to the control of Congress was eventually dropped. The bureau remained a curious anomaly within the executive branch with strong informal ties to Congress, a strong antipathy for the material and career concerns of the public servants, and a strong conflict of interest with the Civil Service Commission.

The struggle for administrative control thus centered on the pending budget and accounting bill. A large federal debt, the example of the Central Bureau of Planning and Statistics, and the vigorous support of the National Association of Manufacturers had pushed the House into action on budget legislation early in 1919. Through the efforts of Robert Brookings, James Good obtained the services of W. F. Willoughby to draft a budget bill and, in effect, turned the Institute for Government Research into a legislative staff on the issue.[79] The Good bill secured Willoughby's chief object since his service on the Taft Commission. It created a budget bureau directly under the President acting as a personal administrative staff for the chief executive, as the primary instrument for coordination and control of the executive branch, and as a central statistical arm for the entire federal government. But the bill broke new ground in calling for the removal of the auditing of accounts from the Treasury Department and establishing an independent audit. The independent audit was Congress's quid pro quo for the President's budget bureau. It was to act as a "real critic" and to be in a position to appeal to Congress concerning executive actions "no matter what the political complexion of Congress or the executive might be." It would keep watch over the budget bureau and be free of executive influence in reporting on the legality of any given expenditure before the money left the Treasury. With these assurances, the Good bill was passed by the House on October 21, 1919. The vote was 285 to 3.[80]

The Senate remained wary. In addition to its determination to secure the position of the Bureau of Efficiency as an arm of Congress, it moved to strengthen the position of the independent audit and to weaken the position of the executive budget bureau. The Senate version of the budget bill placed the budget bureau in the Treasury Department and subjected the budget director to the supervision of the Secretary of the Treasury, the cabinet officer traditionally enjoying the closest relations with Congress. It then made the office of the independent audit into a General Accounting Office that could prescribe accounting methods and supervise the financial activities of all government agencies. The Senate passed this version of the budget bill on May 1, 1920.[81]

In this setting, Congress received the President's veto warning against the Bureau of Efficiency proposal and more generally urging caution on any invasion of executive prerogatives in administration. The House–Senate conferees agreed to the Senate's proposal for a strong General

Accounting Office. The Bureau of Efficiency was not mentioned, and a compromise was reached on the status of the Bureau of the Budget. The Budget Chief was to be directly responsible to the President, but the bureau was to be located in the Treasury Department. Thus, the President was to have the responsibility for submitting a budget to Congress, but there was to be no new executive office of the President. The message seemed to be that the budget was an instrument for facilitating congressional business, not for the aggrandizement of presidential power. The Budget and Accounting Act hammered this point home in another particular as well. It acknowledged that all financial requests to Congress from administrative officers would have to be channeled through the budget bureau, but it assured that Congress could, at its discretion, request such information directly from any administrative officer.[82] In all aspects of the bill, Congress was careful to maintain its own lines of communication with the bureaucracy.

Congressional action on budget legislation had been dominated by institutional interests. President Wilson's veto on June 4, 1920, turned on the same grounds. Wilson had warmly endorsed the budget idea, but to the extent that he had been specific about his wishes at all, he had indicated a preference for an audit within the Treasury Department, at least nominally a part of the executive branch.[83] The President saw in the Budget and Accounting Act an attempt to tie the leading officers of the weighty new General Accounting Office directly to Congress, and as he had warned in his message on the Bureau of Efficiency, he considered this kind of arrangement unconstitutional. The act stipulated that the Comptroller General and the Assistant Comptroller General would be appointed by the President with the consent of the Senate to fifteen-year terms and that their removal before that time could be made only by a concurrent resolution of the House and Senate. In effect, this made the leading officers of the new Accounting Office congressional officers subject only to the President's recommendation for appointment. Wilson deemed the Comptroller to be an *executive* officer and saw the removal clause as an infringement on long-established constitutional prerogatives of the chief executive.[84]

This deadlock was broken only when President Warren Harding agreed to an arrangement that actually made the removal of the Comptroller General even more difficult. A joint resolution of both houses and the chief executive was now required. The Budget and Accounting Act, a watershed in the creation of a new American state and the establishment of a new bureaucratic politics, became law in June 1921.

The machinery of administrative oversight for the new American state moved into place with one characteristic overriding all others – the obfuscation of authoritative controls. It is significant that the specific positions of the Civil Service Commission, the Bureau of Efficiency, the Bureau of the Budget, and the General Accounting Office within the federal establishment were all somewhat obscure, but the general implication of parallel sets of controls pitted against each other was unmistakable. The Civil Service Commission and the Bureau of the Budget appeared as presidential instruments for personnel and financial management, whereas the Bureau of Efficiency and the General Accounting Office appeared as corresponding instruments of congressional control juxtaposed to those of the President. Overall, it was a design that promised to keep control over the new realm of civil administration at the center of political contention in the operations of the new American state.

If the new controls established for civil administration appeared problematic, much more so was the government's effort to establish an administrative career structure for federal employees. The first indication of a problem came in the Bureau of Efficiency's report to the Senate arguing against a government contribution to a civil service pension fund. This report foreclosed passage of a fifty-fifty employee–employer retirement plan supported by the NFFE.[85] In the Retirement Act of 1920, the government hedged and dealt a serious setback to the organized federal workers, not to mention the cause of a stable and professional civil service. The act raised all retirement funds from voluntary employee contributions until such time as the amount raised at the given rate could not cover expenditures. In its first year of operation, this long-sought employee program was taken advantage of by only 7,000 civil servants.[86]

The Retirement Act was only a prelude to the battle over the reclassification of positions and salaries. In March 1919, Congress had established a Joint Commission on the Reclassification of Salaries. The commission employed Frederick Cleveland and Lewis Merriam of the Institute for Government Research as expert advisors. Not surprisingly, the plan of this commission closely followed that advocated by the Taft Commission on Economy and Efficiency, the Civil Service Commission, and federal labor. It called for the Civil Service Commission to develop and implement a comprehensive plan for reclassification and salary standardization. The commission's plan would represent the complete salary and career structure for the entire federal service, and it would be implemented all at once. The Civil Service Commission would then become the central agency of personnel management. A personnel advisory board was to be attached to the commission to provide a voice for the interests of the federal employees.[87]

This proposal was defeated by the efforts of Senator Smoot on the grounds of economic extravagance and Civil Service Commission control. The senator argued that economy could be ensured only by congressional controls and that the reclassification scheme should be planned and directed by Congress's personnel agency, the Bureau of Efficiency. The Bureau of Efficiency, it will be recalled, argued for an incremental reclassification worked out through a series of bureau–Congress negotiations and gradual departmental adjustments. Organized federal labor pressed the House for Civil Service Commission control, and the issue was locked in a congressional stalemate.[88]

The passage of the Budget and Accounting Act in 1921 provided an opening wedge into the interminable legislative debates on the subject, and yet the solution arrived at only transferred the political and institutional conflicts at issue to the administrative control agencies themselves. The Classification Act of 1923 created a new and independent Personnel Classification Board composed of one member of the Civil Service Commission, one member of the Bureau of Efficiency, and one member of the Bureau of the Budget. The board was to decide upon the basic approach to be used in reclassification, to develop a plan accordingly, and to supervise its implementation.

Clearly, this was no solution at all, only an abdication of political authority to administrators in the face of political deadlock. The administrators on the Personnel Classification Board proved no better than the elected politicians in reaching agreement. The battle of interests and institutions continued for three years within the board itself until new legislation was passed in 1926. Apropos of its own position in the government, the Bureau of the Budget played the role of mediator in the bitter conflict between the Civil Service Commission and the Bureau of Efficiency.[89] The Personnel Classification Board epitomized America's turn-of-the-century leap from the party state, with its much maligned spoils system, to an institutional stalemate, with administrators themselves being asked to make policy decisions in a political system defiant of authoritative controls.

The Progressive state-building achievement I

Between the party-controlled administration of the nineteenth century and the bureaucratic management of the twentieth century lay the problem of reconstituting the American state. A state organized from the bottom up had to be reorganized from the top down. A state tied together by the procedures of spoils appointment had to be reoriented around the procedures of merit appointment. A state operated in the interests of party workers and party managers had to give way to the interests of a permanent civil service and a new intellectual cadre of independent professionals. The challenge of constructing a new governmental order informed every stage of the process of administrative modernization.

The organizational, procedural, and intellectual determinants of the new American state crystallized around 1920. New overhead machinery for the supervision of an expanding arm of national administration had been put in place. Over 70 percent of the executive civil service was in the merit system. The new intellectuals had made themselves indispensable in and around the high councils of government. Viewed in these terms, Progressive state building appears a paradigm of successful modernization achieved through the gradual evolution of appropriate governmental forms and procedures.

Closer inspection, however, reveals a paradox in this achievement. The outstanding characteristic of Progressive state building was neither efficiency nor rationality. Although the capacities of the new order to meet the growing demands on the national government clearly surpassed those of the old, the American state was also newly constricted in action by the repoliticization of its national bureaucracy around a constitutional stalemate. This recasting of national institutional politics went hand in hand with the building of the new administrative system and was part and parcel of the result. A struggle for political power and institutional position within the state apparatus mediated the modernization process and defied both the ideology of efficiency and the developmental imperatives for rationality.

Reconstructing the administrative system of the American party state was as precarious in its political foundations as it was wrenching in its institutional effects. The period of Republican hegemony (1896–1910) provided the best political opportunities for a decisive break with the governing arrangements of the past, but the bold administrative departures extorted in these years did not yield a consensus on the shape of a new order; instead, they redefined the lines of cleavage in the struggle for institutional power and gave added impetus to the disintegration of the Republican party. Before the issues of reconstitution raised in this period of relative electoral stability could be resolved, American politics entered another period of electoral uncertainty. The scramble for power and position, shifting with the changing shape of electoral politics, ultimately led political authorities into a morass of institutional conflicts, all contesting control of an expanding arm of national administrative power. This is the Progressive achievement to which we can trace the origins of the modern American state.

Inseparable from what was being created in these years was what was being undermined in the process. The reconstruction of civil administration left the institutional resources of the President bolstered and the position of Congress refortified, but at the same time it weakened the internal bonds of party government. None of the various combinations of party power and state-building strategy encountered in these years resolved the developmental contradiction between American party structure and the forging of a bureaucratic mode of operations for the national government. Roosevelt had tried to circumvent his party, Taft had tried to use his party, Wilson had tried to lead his party; but none of them could change the provincial coalition form of party in America, and each of them ultimately found the demand for control over national administration incompatible with party government. The constituent party hovered around the Progressive state-building achievement, alive but decidedly out of step with modern bureaucratic politics. The administrative reform agenda was now attuned to the interests of organized labor and of the Institute for Government Research, and this agenda confounded operations of the American party state.

By 1920, American national government had broken from the grip of local politics and assumed a more independent role in American society. But modernization seemed to confirm Walter Weyl's fears for the future of American democracy. Support for the new national administrative apparatus was consolidated at the expense of political coherence. The new institutional politics established controls over bureaucratic power without defining political responsibility. Machinery for the attainment of efficiency proliferated, but the "system as a whole [was] ill-geared."

7

Reconstituting the army: professionalism, nationalism, and the illusion of corporatism

This is a time of organization. Great results are produced only by that. Individual effort, individual brillance, individual heroism accomplishes but little, except as it has an effect upon masses of men. Effective and harmonious organization is the moving power of the world today. We have lagged behind in the army until now; and now, I believe and trust, we take our place in the front rank of the organizations which are to control the effective action of the future . . . Days of trial for our country are to come, and I confidently believe that, when those days are upon us, the American people will look back to the inauguration of the General Staff, and will look back to the inauguration of a good spirit of brotherhood in arms pervading all branches of the American Army, as the beginning of a new day and the origin of an efficiency never known before in the defenders of our government and of our nation.

Elihu Root, First Annual General Staff Dinner, 1904

Over the first two decades of the twentieth century, the American army was transformed from a standing contradiction operating within the state of courts and parties into a constituent part of a new bureaucratic state. Professionalism, nationalism, and corporatism – ideals as inextricably linked with the modernizing thrust of Progressive state building as economy and efficiency – heralded this reconstitution.[1] Yet, the historical–structural impasse that had developed in American army reform in the late nineteenth century called into question institutional power relationships throughout the governmental system and gave a significant twist to reform ideals. The actual structure and operations of the new American army were determined by a struggle for power and position within the state apparatus, the dimensions of the struggle shifting with the changing shape of electoral politics and institutional opportunities. The terms in which governmental elites dealt with the imperatives for army development parallel the pattern observed in the reconstitution of civil administration and indicate the impact of a distinctive political logic mediating the construction of a new governmental order.

Before 1900, those who had championed a new professionalism and a new nationalism for the American army were able to do little more than eke out a shadow presence within the War Department. The various parts of the army establishment were more closely integrated with Congress, the parties, and the state governors than they were with each other, and multifaceted political opposition stymied all reform efforts aimed at insulating and internally integrating the army hierarchy. After 1901, the politics of army reform changed dramatically. Combining vigorous presidential support and a strong party position, Secretary of War Elihu Root fundamentally altered the positions of the contending actors. The new army professionals gained an institutional power base allied with the executive against the forces of localism, amateurism, and the pork barrel. The questions that Root left unresolved when he retired from the War Department in 1904 – in particular, how far would the executive–professional reform coalition go in displacing the old mode of governmental operations and how would new institutional power relationships be consolidated among the contending actors – dominated War Department politics for the remainder of the Progressive era.

Even the threat of a world war did not spark a consensus on these matters. If anything, the international crisis of 1914 magnified the divisiveness of the politics of reconstituting the army. The War Department was floundering in internal disarray – pulled apart in the vicissitudes of the political struggle to recast the foundations of institutional power – when it turned to the challenge of war mobilization and faced the arrival of a new era in military–industrial relations. At this critical juncture, businessmen and intellectuals held out a vision of corporatism, a cooperative partnership of government and industry, but the War Department was reeling out of control and proved a poor partner. The politics of American state building simply could not sustain the corporate ideal.

The challenge

Elihu Root was an organization man. In the late nineteenth century, he was to be found defending the Tweed Ring when Dorman Eaton was being beaten up by its member for his role in their prosecution (and, in reaction, began to lead the bar association and civil service reform movements). Root was nominated for his first electoral campaign by Chester Arthur and Alonzo Cornell at the very time that the battle for civil service reform raged at the New York Customhouse. Yet, after the election of 1900, Root took charge of a comprehensive administrative reform offensive aimed at reconstructing the American army along the lines of Uptonian professionalism. Later in his career, he became a moving force behind the professionalization of the American bar. Looking back over his early activities and associations, Root explained that the actions of men in power must be judged by the standards of their time.[2] The late nineteenth century was a time for electoral politics and party organization; the early twentieth century was a time for experts and bureaucratic organization. Root not only adapted to the times, he bridged the gap between new and old organizational models.

The distinguishing feature of Root's state-building initiative in the War Department is his personal mediation of the structural tensions between congressional and party interests on the one hand and the professional reform program on the other. His regular party background sensitized him to the threat posed by the coalition of an executive officer with reform-minded professionals in army administration. At the same time, he shared the Republican impulse toward imperial expansion and knew that it required a new kind of governmental machinery, the kind the young professionals championed.[3] Root's dedication to making America fit for its imperial mission coupled with his close associations with the men and machinery of the regular Republican party made for an administrative reform offensive lacking in the abrasiveness of Gifford Pinchot's offensive in the Department of Agriculture. Indeed, Root acted so as to restrain the young military professionals in their zeal for structural clarity. Conciliation was the key to his success in pulling the contending factions in War Department politics through pivotal changes in the early years of Roosevelt's first term. It was also the key to the ability of the interests threatened by those changes to regain their ground in the later years of Roosevelt's second term.

Root waited until after the elections of 1900 had reaffirmed the position of the Republican party, vindicated its imperial policies, and silenced the Democrats in Congress before attempting any significant alteration of army organization. The secretary had plans for a thorough nationalization of the militia on hand, but he let a militia bill pass in June 1900 that raised the federal subsidy from $400,000 to $1 million without reforming militia organization or control.[4] Even after the election, Root moved cautiously. He sidestepped the entreaties of his closest professional advisors (Adjutant General Henry Corbin and his assistant, Colonel William Carter) to move immediately against the autonomy of the War Department's administrative bureaus with General Staff reform. The secretary feared bureau interference as well as National Guard interference with his immediate concern for establishing order in the new territories. He settled for a minimal reorganization program at first. Returning to the

Hull bill of 1899, he asked Congress for an increase in the peacetime size of the regular army to 60,000 men and an organizational structure designed for rapid expansion to 100,000. Preempting opposition from the bureaus and the militia, Root used the Republican victory to accomplish in February 1901 what had been filibustered away in February 1899.[5]

While sidestepping the challenge of General Staff reform in favor of a less threatening increase in the size of the regular force, Root explored the possibility of using reforms in military education as a substitute for the General Staff idea. Early in 1900, he composed a board of rising officers to report on the establishment of an Army War College in Washington and asked them to consider its value as an authoritative agency in War Department planning and coordination. The Ludlow Board reported back that a War College was an essential part of the General Staff concept but distinct from it. The college might draw up plans, but coordination of these plans required a central staff in a position of authority within the administrative hierarchy of the War Department. It was untenable to have central planning without an institutional capacity for administrative supervision.[6] Root accepted the point, but in the meantime he had delayed the contest.

The Army War College was created by executive order in 1901. The Secretary of War then set out to refashion the entire educational hierarchy of the army leading up to the college. The intermediary postgraduate schools founded in the late nineteenth century at Fort Monroe, Fort Leavenworth, and Fort Riley were reorganized to link West Point education to War College service. The lyceum system for continuous officer education was also reinvigorated. The new educational hierarchy was bound together through advancement by merit up to the War College. The militia was invited to raise its standards by opening the educational hierarchy to state-commissioned officers. Root also secured an appropriation from Congress to begin construction on a building to house the War College.[7]

By the end of 1901, Root had accomplished just about all that could be done for professionalism and nationalism in the War Department without directly challenging the entrenched interests of the old army establishment. The young Uptonians were eager for more, and so was the new President. Roosevelt's first annual message to Congress, delivered in December 1901, directed attention to the need for a thorough reform of the military departments.[8] The message coincided with the launching of two legislative proposals that were to ensure Root his pivotal place in American military history. Simultaneously, he moved to impose federal supervision on the state militia and to centralize control over the War Department. By February 1903, these two proposals had been embodied in law, realizing more for the cause of professionalism and nationalism in fourteen months than had been gained in the previous twenty-five years of frustrating efforts on their behalf. Root aimed his reforms at the two junctures of institutional and political power that had stifled the modernization of the War Department in the late nineteenth century: the ties between local political elites and the state militia and the ties between congressmen and the administrative bureaus. Taken together with his initiative on the educational front, these challenges provided concrete institutional grounding for the organizational, procedural, and intellectual reconstitution first articulated by Emory Upton. Just before leaving the War Department, Root gave testimony to his inspiration (or more exactly, the inspiration of his professional military advisors who drafted the original reform proposals) by ordering the publication of Upton's obscure manuscript on the *Military Policy of the United States.*[9]

Yet, in Root's hands, elegant professional designs became pragmatic, indeed, problematic hybrids. As one student of the War Department reforms has noted: "Root was too politic to be an Uptonian."[10] His instinct for compromise on structural reform introduced a range of institutional ambiguities that gave a foothold to reform ideals without displacing the forces of opposition. The cosmopolitan models of the professional reformers were Americanized in a way that redefined institutional conflict in the War Department rather than resolving it.

In pursuing militia reform, Root sought to accommodate National Guard interests with the imperatives of professionalism and nationalism in the army. He hoped to defuse with generosity the political opposition of governors and states' righters to regular army supervision and, at the same time, to limit the role of locally controlled forces in any future military offensive. Specifically, Root was willing to accept the guard as a locally controlled domestic defense force if it limited its national service explicitly to repelling invasion and suppressing insurrection within the Union. In this regard, he appealed directly to the post–Spanish-American War sentiments of northeastern militia officers who were uncomfortable with the prospect of leaving their normal jobs for a two-year tour of foreign duty. His plan restricted the domestic national service of state guard units to nine months. Then with a carrot and a stick, Root offered the guard increased subsidies in return for routine regular army inspections. Rather than attacking the state militia head on, Root offered it more federal support, gave it a limited role in the national military establishment, and asked it to upgrade its standards.[11]

Turning to the Guard's claim to first-line offensive reserve status, Root offered even greater benefits to those who would accept a clean break with the traditional concept of local control. He sought to use the guard's large manpower pool as the foundation for a National Volunteer Reserve fully prepared for international action. Militia officers would be able to obtain federal commissions, and militiamen would be able to obtain higher pay and other compensation if they would submit to federal control and more stringent military standards.[12] On the one hand, they could choose local control upgraded by federal supervision, short-term domestic service, and higher subsidies; on the other hand, they could choose a more thorough professionalization and nationalization, with even higher subsidies and full first-line reserve status for offensive campaigns. Those units that wished to be part of the National Volunteer Reserve were to have all their officers appointed by the President after passing before a board of review composed of regular army officers. Their training standards were to be identical to those of the regulars. But there was no compulsion for a guard unit to submit to the more rigorous national regimen. There would still be a local guard fulfilling its constitutional duty, narrowly construed, even with the National Volunteer Reserve organization.[13]

This vision of the National Guard as a common manpower pool for an upgraded, state-controlled defense force and a militarily superior, nationally controlled offensive reserve force was not without operational ambiguities. How would individual guardsmen and guard units make their choice? When would they make their choice? Could the federal government depend on the independent decisions of local officers to provide the backbone of a national reserve? The questions themselves illustrate Root's determination to ride the horns of a structural dilemma in American state building. He recognized the guard's political power, its diverse interests, and its extant resources; and he set out to reconcile all of these things with the new military needs of an international power.

Congress welcomed Root's conciliatory approach but had little patience with the fine distinctions that he and the professionals were at pains to maintain. The carrot-and-stick approach to more effective state units was thoroughly accepted. Boards of review for militia officers, stricter training standards, and routine inspections by the regulars became the prerequisite for increasing federal subsidies to the states. In this, Root set a new pattern for all future guard reforms: The price of increased federal support and recognition was to be stricter federal regulation and less direct involvement in local politics. But as the idea of improving the quality of locally controlled guard units through greater federal supervision gained acceptance, the proposal for a formally distinct but practically synonymous National Volunteer Reserve with officers appointed by the President appeared confusing, if not superfluous. Root stressed the constitutional point that state-officered units could not serve outside the United States and the sentiment that the amateur soldiers did not necessarily want to be forced into the long period of service required for an offensive army. Yet, governors, congressmen, and the National Guard Association (NGA) saw the issue of control in political terms. In the end, this challenge to guard autonomy and local appointment prerogatives proved to be more than Root could sustain. He sacrificed the national reserve idea in order to gain a state militia ostensibly limited in its functions and subject to more rigorous federal supervision. The governors' appointment powers remained intact, but the guard's role was limited to short-term domestic defense. It might well be said that Root received as much as he did because he presented the case for so much more. [14]

The national reserve question was simply left hanging as the Dick Militia Act now eased through Congress. The reform immediately produced new lines of War Department conflict. Root's congressional compromise led professionals in the War Department to push for an independent reserve officer corps totally under regular army control and subject to presidential appointment and a first-line offensive reserve force completely independent of National Guard personnel. The professionals could accept the new National Guard outlined in the Dick Act only if a clear distinction was now made between it and the need for a national offensive reserve of the regular army. On the other hand, the improvement of the guard units and their submission to professional standards were used by the NGA as the rationale to designate the state guard units as the official and existing organization of the first-line offensive reserve without suffering a confusing distinction between its domestic and international modes. [15] Root's nationalization of the militia gave the professionals a strong foothold in guard affairs, but in doing so it strengthened the guard's position against one of the professionals' most cherished goals. In 1908, after Root had left the War Department, a new militia bill was passed that gave explicit assurance that the guard would be called as the first-line offensive reserve before any other volunteer reserve that might be organized. [16] The challenge of reconstruction had been offered and met.

The nationalization of the militia was pursued by Root in conjunction with a General Staff initiative. To the extent that the General Staff reform institutionalized an executive–professional reform coalition at the top of the War Department hierarchy, it was used by the professionals to push the executive for a limited, defensive role for the National Guard. To the extent that the General Staff reform became, like the militia reform, a political compromise of a structural reform, it provided the basis for congressional appeals by both the War Department's administrative bureaus and the National Guard in opposition to the executive–professional program. As with his guard initiative, Root seemed to begin with the dual purpose of providing the forces of professionalism and nationalism a firm institutional foundation and placing explicit restrictions and controls on the forces of opposition. Again, his political sense led him to accept ambiguity in controlling the old in order to gain a foothold for the new.[17]

The first obstacle to be overcome at the top of the War Department hierarchy was the conflict between the Secretary of War and the Commanding General over control of the War Department. The goal was to unify the chain of command over the administrative bureaus and the line. Not surprisingly, Root's resolution of this conflict drew less directly on Upton's broadside attack on civilian control in the name of professionalism than on Schofield's more moderate view of a unified military hierarchy clearly subordinated to the civilian secretary. Root proposed to abolish the office of Commanding General altogether and to replace it with a Chief of Staff. The secretary, acting under the President, was to direct the operations of both the bureaus and the line. The Chief of Staff was to be the subordinate of the secretary in all department affairs. He was to act as the secretary's professional military advisor with the authority to supervise the bureaus and the line. The Chief of Staff was also to sit atop a new General Staff Corps composed of officers detailed for four-year periods of service according to rules devised by the President. The divisive tradition of dual controls in the War Department was to end in an executive–professional alliance.

The second obstacle to be overcome was to give substance to the term *supervise* as it was used to specify the authority of the Chief of Staff and the General Staff over the administrative bureaus. Was the General Staff to be an advisory body helping to coordinate War College proposals with routine bureau business and the line, or was it to be a management body that could directly intervene in the routine operations of the bureaus? The distinction was a fine one, for it would be hard to gain effective coordination without accepting some kind of intervention in routine operations; yet, it was a distinction that, if blurred, could permit the new hierarchical ordering of departmental controls to coexist with rather than replace the long established lateral ties between Congress and the bureaus. Another question concerned the scope of the Chief of Staff's authority. Was the Chief of Staff to be the exclusive military advisor of the Secretary of War and the sole officer through whom the secretary directed the bureaus and the line, or did the Chief of Staff supervise the bureaus through the work of the General Staff and leave the bureau chiefs their direct line of access to the secretary long established by tradition? On the answer to these questions rested the balance of power between the new executive–professional reform coalition and the old pork barrel politics.

Root gave conflicting signals on these issues. His presentation to Congress placed the emphasis on the need to resolve the tension between the Secretary of War and the Commanding General in the name of unity of command under civilian control. He said that the new military offices at the top were created for purposes of "planning," "coordination," and "preparation" rather than management or control. The General Staff was to act as an "executive" rather than an "administrative" body and would be prevented from assuming "duties of an administrative character." On the other hand, the emphasis on planning, coordination, and preparation did not alter the fact that if the General Staff was to be at all effective, the established position of the bureaus would have to be altered. In this regard, Root called for rotation between bureau and line positions, a procedure that would serve to weaken the bureau's lateral ties, strengthen hierarchical controls, and insulate army administration. More generally, Root proclaimed support for the "Roosevelt rule," which informed Congress that appointments, promotions, and details would be based on merit criteria collected by the department and that congressional advice on such matters would no longer be considered. More significant still was Root's move against the single most powerful administrative figure of the old army establishment, the Adjutant General. He called for abolishing the office altogether, deeming it as incompatible with the General Staff concept as that of the Commanding General. Administrative management responsibilities were to be lodged in the less prestigious position of a Military Secretary, who would be subject to the supervision of the Chief of Staff. Finally, in his boldest attack on bureau autonomy and pork barrel connections, Root called for a consolidation of all the supply services of the bureaus in the General Staff.[18] Because the General Staff, in conjunction with the War College, was to be responsible for the preparation, planning, and coordination of a war effort, it was deemed appropriate that the staff control the procurement and distribution of military supplies. The problems produced by having each bureau provide for itself had been amply illustrated in the Spanish-American War. The proposal to place supply responsibility on the General Staff would have extended the reach of the executive–professional coalition outward into industrial relations and downward throughout War Department operations. On the relationship between the General

Staff and the services of supply would hinge the shape of military–industrial cooperation in the emergent American state.

Congress accepted Root's guarded language concerning the scope of the General Staff's authority in "planning and coordination," rejected his proposed consolidation of the supply services, accepted rotation between the bureaus and the line for future appointments, and accepted the abolition of the Adjutant General's office. Again proving himself a better politician than an Uptonian, Root accepted the supply defeat as "a matter of small importance" in order to receive a new Chief of Staff, a new General Staff, rotation, and the end of the Adjutant General's office as a focus for the old methods of army administration. The executive–professional coalition gained an institutional power base with a somewhat ambiguous scope of authority. In Root's hands, the program that army professionals had struggled to implement for twenty years eased past a once decisive congressional opposition. Knowing where not to press for clarity, the Secretary of War accepted reforms that were at least potentially radical.[19]

The man who rose to meet the challenge of a radical reconstruction by the General Staff was General Fred Ainsworth, chief of the Bureau of Records and Pensions. Ainsworth was a master administrator of the old school. He had turned his bureau into a smooth-running machine dedicated to providing immediate responses to congressional requests and quality services to the Grand Army of the Republic.[20] It was Ainsworth, above all others in the staff bureaus, who perceived and exploited the political and institutional interests of congressmen against the executive–professional reform coalition embodied in the new War Department machinery. Whereas this reform coalition dedicated itself to adjusting Congress to a new mode of governmental operations, Ainsworth dedicated himself to exposing the challenge and using the War Department's established congressional ties to stymie the new departure.

Ainsworth succeeded in getting the Bureau of Records and Pensions exempted from the direct supervision of the General Staff in the legislation of 1903. In 1904, when the Office of Military Secretary was formally established to replace the Adjutant General position, its responsibilities were combined with those of Records and Pensions, and Ainsworth became the leading officer in charge of the details of administrative management in the War Department. The Military Secretary was placed "under the direction of the Secretary of War," but he was "subject to the supervision of the Chief of Staff in all matters pertaining to the command, discipline or administration of the existing military establishment."[21] The ambiguity was symptomatic of the questions that had been hedged in the legislation of 1903. At the moment when clarification was most essential, Root left the War Department, and the amiable William

Howard Taft took his place. Ainsworth immediately began to press the new Secretary of War for a judgment on the respective jurisdictions of the Chief of Staff – ostensibly the military head of the bureaus and line under the Secretary of War but ambiguously tied to administrative management – and the Military Secretary – also directly responsible to the Secretary of War, somehow responsible to the Chief of Staff, and clearly charged with administrative management responsibilities.

Taft respected Ainsworth's administrative talents and political connections, and he had little patience with internecine bureaucratic struggles. Moreover, the secretary was being increasingly lured away from the sticky business of departmental reorganization to promote his future in national politics. In April 1906, Taft attempted to resolve the seemingly endless bickering between the Chief of Staff and the Military Secretary. Apparently thinking he could impose cooperation by fiat, he directed the Chief of Staff to consult with the Military Secretary before reporting to the Secretary of War, and he gave the Military Secretary explicit and exclusive supervision over the civil business of the bureaus. Controls over the bureaus and the line, which Root had tried to consolidate, suddenly appeared to be divided again. In May 1906, the Military Secretary, rather than the Chief of Staff, was given control over the War Department in the absence of the Secretary of War and the Assistant Secretary. In March 1907, Ainsworth advised Congress to abolish the title of Military Secretary and to reestablish the position of Adjutant General. In doing so, Congress also raised Ainsworth's rank to major general so that he could assume the Adjutant General position.[22]

Adjutant General Ainsworth was the dominant figure in the War Department after 1907. His notorious contempt for the new "General Stuff" combined with Congress's affirmation of the militia's first-line reserve status in 1908 to cloud the future of the War Department's reconstruction in the last years of Roosevelt's presidency. The Root–Roosevelt state-building initiative had jolted the War Department loose from the intellectual, procedural, and organizational constraints of the nineteenth-century structure, but its new structure remained an open question. Like the Roosevelt experience in civil administration, the most favorable political conditions for a state-building break with the past yielded new lines of institutional conflict.

The confrontation

Republican party divisions, Democratic party resurgence, and the Roosevelt commitment to structural reform produced a series of seminal political confrontations over the issue of administrative control in which William Howard Taft had the misfortune to play the part of decision maker. In civil administration Taft weathered the Pinchot–Ballinger affair, the executive gag order–unionization battle, and the budget rejection. The parallel in the War Department was the confrontation between Chief of Staff Leonard Wood and Adjutant General Fred Ainsworth.

Like his good friend Gifford Pinchot, Leonard Wood rose to prominence in the government through close association with Roosevelt. Wood had served Roosevelt first as Military Governor of Cuba and then as Military Administrator of the Philippines.[23] Upon his appointment to the position of Chief of Staff in 1910, Wood dedicated himself to the institutionalization of central planning and a new professionalism in the War Department as vigorously as Pinchot had in the Agriculture Department. Wood fought against localism and pork barrel ties through attacks on the local political ties of the militia and the autonomy of the War Department service bureaus; Pinchot fought against localism and the pork barrel through attacks on the General Land Office and the Army Corps of Engineers. When Pinchot left Washington, he rejoined Roosevelt and attempted to popularize the bureaucratic virtues of scientific management and planning in the Progressive conservation crusade. When Wood left Washington, he rejoined Roosevelt and attempted to popularize the military virtues of discipline and peacetime preparation in the Progressive preparedness crusade.[24]

Gifford Pinchot bolted from Taft's governing coalition when his professional bureaucratic program was threatened. Wood, however, found new executive support for the professional bureaucratic program. In the War Department scenario, it was Ainsworth who defied bureaucratic discipline and placed the issue of administrative control on the line. Tactical considerations of the actors aside, the Pinchot–Ballinger affair and the Wood–Ainsworth affair held in the balance the same two alternative modes of governmental operations, and they were linked together by the shaky political position of President Taft as he twisted and turned to maintain his governing coalition in a state torn between these two alternatives. In this regard, it is significant that the Ainsworth–Wood conflict intensified as Taft attempted to ease the strains in his relations with Roosevelt, strains epitomized by his dismissal of Pinchot in 1910.

Taft used an opportunity to appoint a new Secretary of War in 1911 to "polish his tarnished image as a progressive." He gave the nod to Henry Stimson, a well-known associate of both Roosevelt and Pinchot.[25] Thus whereas Taft's appointment of Ballinger as Secretary of the Interior in 1909 suggested an effort to appease Congress and the Old Guard of the Republican party in the wake of the Roosevelt–Pinchot–Garfield conservation offensive, the appointment of Stimson suggests an effort to recover from the political damage that the rejection of Garfield and the dismissal of Pinchot had extracted from that strategy. Secretary Stimson and Chief of Staff Wood did indeed reinvigorate the executive–professional reform coalition in the War Department, but the result was anything but the restoration of political harmony.

The President pulled himself out of the frying pan only to be pushed into the fire as Stimson and Wood joined in battle against the master administrator of the old school. With a strong Secretary of War in alliance with a strong Chief of Staff, the power and position of the Adjutant General in departmental affairs were threatened.[26] Yet long service to congressmen and the rise of a Democratic majority in the House gave Ainsworth the leverage to turn a losing bureaucratic power struggle into another constitutional and partisan confrontation. Democrats had no use for the professional military reform program, and the prospects for Republican unity behind what Stimson and Wood proposed for the army were dim.

Ainsworth and Wood clashed over those points of tension and ambiguity left open in Root's military reforms. Wood sought to take the cause of professionalism and nationalism to a new level of clarity and control in War Department operations. He was skeptical of the militia-based reserve system and opposed its further development. He favored the creation of a new national first-line reserve under full regular control. He favored the consolidation of administrative management under the General Staff, and he favored the consolidation of military posts into fewer and larger units. The consolidated military posts were necessary to take the army beyond the era of the Indian wars and into the era of preparation for international conflict. Consolidated around the nation's larger cities, the new posts were to become the recruitment, training, and mobilization centers for the new national reserve. In these proposals, Wood had the support of Secretary of War Stimson. Ainsworth spoke out against the new national reserve, supported the militia and its further development, called for a consolidation of administrative management under the Adjutant General, and opposed the consolidation of military posts. Ainsworth's chief political support came from the new chairman of the House Military Affairs Committee (and longtime foe of the new professional army), Democrat James Hay, and chairman of the Senate Military Affairs Committee, Republican Francis Warren. Warren's opposition to the new professionalism stemmed from his friendship with Ainsworth and from the fact that his home state of Wyoming was a chief target of Wood's post consolidation plan. Warren had worked hard to secure his state's military outposts and was not about to yield them to federal bureaucrats who preferred to live in the cities and train citizens for some future military service.[27]

This dovetailing of the questions of power and control in War Department affairs with issues of substantive military policy remained in the background of the actual confrontation. Appropriately enough, the catalyst of the crisis came in the form of a minor and apparently unrelated report from one of the subcommittees of the President's Commission on Economy and Efficiency concerning the improvement of administrative methods in the War Department. The commission recommended that the "muster roll," the primary personnel record of the War Department, be abolished and consolidated into a more comprehensive and simplified system of personnel management. Wood and Stimson agreed with the recommendation and sent it to Ainsworth, the officer in charge of the muster roll, for his comment. Ainsworth's reply not only rejected the recommendation but contained a personal attack on Wood and Stimson as "incompetent amateurs." Ainsworth called their support of the muster roll reform "a forcible illustration of the unwisdom of entrusting the preparation or amendment of the forms of the Army to those who have no procedural knowledge of the uses to which those forms are put."[28] This outburst directly challenged both the authority of the Chief of Staff even to recommend reforms in administrative management to the Adjutant General and the principle of civilian control by the Secretary of War. It was to prove the last in a long train of insults directed by Ainsworth against the executive–professional reform coalition in the army.

Wood appealed to Stimson for decisive action. Stimson took the issue to Taft. Not to be outdone by Ainsworth's support in Congress, Stimson asked Root, now a prominent representative of Taft's Republican support in the Senate, to support him against Ainsworth. Root and Stimson, standing together behind the Chief of Staff, were an impressive and persuasive team. They convinced Taft that the time had come to affirm solidly the authority of the Chief of Staff and the principle of civilian control and that court martial proceedings against Ainsworth were in order. Ainsworth was immediately relieved of duty, but before a trial could begin, he voluntarily retired.[29]

Ainsworth's retirement from the War Department was a victory for the executive–professional coalition as important as the defeat that coalition had suffered with Pinchot's dismissal. But the confrontation had just begun. Like Pinchot in 1910, Ainsworth used his freedom from the executive to counterattack from Congress. He remained a consultant to the House Military Affairs Committee, and in this role he continued to wield influence over military policy. Moreover, though Wood had been vindicated, his position remained precarious, and it exposed the political

vulnerability of the President himself. Democrats had no patience with
the Chief of Staff; friends of Ainsworth resented him; representatives
with army posts to protect were angered by him; Progressive Republicans
suspected him because of Taft's support; Taft Republicans attacked him
because he was Roosevelt's man.[30]

The political repercussions of the Ainsworth dismissal became evident
in the army appropriations bill for 1912. Democrat Hay in the House
worked with Republican Warren in the Senate to push through a bill that
followed many of Ainsworth's earlier recommendations. Beyond this, it
reduced the General Staff from forty-five to thirty-six officers, specifically
excluded Wood from the position of Chief of Staff after March 6, 1913
(one year before his official term expired), and established a commission
of congressmen to report on the location and distribution of military
posts.[31] Congress was determined to remove the champion of the new
professionalism in the War Department in return for the chief executive's
removal of the champion of congressional interests in the War Department. It then attacked the General Staff directly by reducing its personnel
and placing military planning directly in congressional hands.

The Republicans' support for this bill caused Taft to waver. Important
administration friends in the Senate wanted Taft to use the bill to rebuke
Roosevelt. Rumors spread that Warren would withhold support from
Taft at the party convention unless Wood's removal was secured. Could
the President afford to support a Roosevelt ally in his administration at
the risk of losing party support in Congress? Seeing the President's position, Root again asserted his dual role as representative of the party
regulars and protector of the War Department reforms. At this point,
Root was Taft's political manager for the party convention. He personally assured the President that his position at the convention was secure
and that a veto of the appropriation bill was necessary to uphold executive authority in the War Department despite its domination by a
Rooseveltian Chief of Staff. (It might be noted that in the Pinchot–
Ballinger controversy, Root had strongly advised Taft to fire the Chief
Forester in the name of executive control over administration.) Persuaded
by Root's unique ability to mediate the inherent conflicts between the old
partisanship and new state building, Taft vetoed the appropriations bill.
The reform coalition had secured a second major victory.[32]

Meanwhile, the House had demanded an investigation of the
Ainsworth retirement. Stimson cooperated, but in his report the Secretary
of War brought the constitutional confrontation over administrative control to its symbolic culmination. He stated:

> I am . . . directed by the President to say that these papers relate to a
> matter of military discipline and executive action which, by the Con-

stitution, is confided exclusively to the President as Commander in Chief of the Army and that their transmittal is not to be construed as a recognition of the authority or jurisdiction of the House or of any of its committees to require of the Chief Executive a statement of the reasons for his official action in such matters or a disclosure of the evidence upon which such official action is based.[33]

The Democratic House officially took issue with the Secretary of War's statement and asserted its powers of investigation.[34] It might be noted that it was in the last weeks of his administration that Taft was also lecturing Congress on his constitutional authority to present a budget and on congressional responsibility to accept it. In the War Department confrontation, Taft asserted his executive prerogative to act without accountability to Congress. Taft's stands on the budget proposal, the army appropriations bill, Pinchot's defiance of the gag order, and Ainsworth's insult to the Secretary of War reflect a willingness to assert the full powers of the Madisonian presidency regardless of the political cost. Though Taft made his point repeatedly in confrontations with Congress, he also exposed the fragility of the Madisonian model as a foundation for government operations in the modern American state.

Overall, the executive–professional reform coalition weathered the Taft years a bit better in the War Department than it had in the realm of civil administration. Wood was able to finish his full term as Chief of Staff. The Adjutant General had been firmly subordinated to the Chief of Staff, and the latter's position as military head of both the staff and the line seemed to be confirmed. Credit for this achievement must rest largely with the strategic position held by Elihu Root in the politics of reconstitution. On the other hand, Congress had taken a strong line against the advance of the new professionalism. It had clearly repudiated Wood. Its revised appropriations bill maintained a reduction in the General Staff from forty-five to thirty-six officers. Post consolidation and bureau consolidation had been blocked. The basic questions of army reconstruction were far from settled when the Democrats swept into power in 1913, and their victory effectively preempted Root's ability to smooth over the rough edges of the professional program.

The *War Department Annual Report for 1912* sharpened enough of those rough edges to ensure the Democrats' opposition for years to come. The Secretary of War used his final report to Congress to present the Army War College's first comprehensive plan for a new American army. The "Organization of the Land Forces of the United States" was conceived in reaction to recent troubles in Mexico. On all points it echoed the brash designs of Wood's earlier congressional testimony.[35] Moreover, coming in the wake of Wood's triumph over Ainsworth, the War College report suggested a consolidation of the army's intellectual, procedural, and organizational break with the past. Riding the high tide of recent administrative victories, the professional reformers ran full steam ahead into the Democratic administration. Unlike Root, they were not too politic to act like true Uptonians.

The congressional counteroffensive

Woodrow Wilson's first Secretary of War, Lindley Garrison, was a political unknown. His appointment seemed significant only in drawing attention to William Jennings Bryan's position as Secretary of State. With Bryan and Garrison, the United States seemed to have set a firm course against militarism, professionalism, and imperialism. But just before leaving office, Stimson led Garrison through the War Department and entrusted his orientation to the new job to Leonard Wood. In the final year of his service as Chief of Staff, Wood dedicated himself to enlightening Garrison on the indispensability of an executive–professional reform coalition in the War Department. He cultivated the new secretary as a voice for the professional program, which would endure after the Chief of Staff himself left the department.

Garrison learned his lessons and demonstrated his own political capability by emerging as one of the most able and trusted members of the Wilson cabinet. Wood had done his work well, perhaps too well, for the new Secretary of War distinguished himself early on by openly criticizing congressmen who requested appointments or promotions for their friends in violation of the "Roosevelt Rule" on army personnel.[36] Garrison's zealous dedication to the cause of army reconstruction was to prove his undoing in Wilson's form of party government. But he was not without political allies.

Wood left Washington confident of Garrison's reform spirit and assumed a military post in New York. There he joined Roosevelt. With the outbreak of war in Europe, these two Progressive Republicans began to agitate for military and industrial preparedness. Wood drilled businessmen in a special camp at Plattsburgh, New York, and turned the camp into a vehicle for promoting his pet plan for universal military training. Roosevelt lectured industrialists and financiers on the need for war preparations and on their role in a war effort.[37] Wood and Roosevelt built an impressive constituency willing to support Garrison in any new initiative on behalf of the professional army program.

War in Europe and preparedness in the Northeast presented serious threats to Wilson's political position. The President had set out to work through a party whose center was southern, western, and decidedly anti-army on behalf of a personal reform program designed to gain northeastern votes for the Democrats. The more the Northeast became preoccupied with the preparedness issue, the more difficult it became to make this strategy work. Preparedness was an issue that threatened to divide the Northeast from the isolationist South and West. Democrats could take some comfort in the fact that the business-oriented preparedness campaign was generally opposed by organized labor; but the constant attacks on America's military weakness, the glorification of America's world mission, and the inevitable ethnic antagonisms raised by involvement in European conflicts combined to produce a formidable force enervating to all that the New Freedom programs promised to accomplish for the Democratic party. Moreover, preparedness was instantly associated with Wilson's chief opponent as a Progressive leader, and Roosevelt was building his movement around New York, a state deemed essential to the success of Wilson's Progressive Democracy.

As a former President and a former Chief of Staff sounded the alarm, Wilson insisted that there was no danger. When Lindley Garrison appeared publicly to contradict the President's position, Wilson tried to ignore him. The President went so far as to endorse Democratic leaders in Congress in their proposal to cut military spending. But on May 7, 1915, Wilson found reason to reconsider. The sinking of the *Lusitania* gave preparedness advocates a tremendous boost and cast serious doubt on the wisdom of the Democrats' present course. The Democrats were in real danger of being labeled the party of national weakness throughout the Northeast.

Unlike Bryan, the President did not have an instinctive revulsion at the thought of rebuilding the American army, and he certainly knew that at present it was in poor shape for war. In July, Wilson asked Garrison for a comprehensive assessment of the army's needs and notified the congressional leadership that he was about to alter his position. The President had decided to lead his party toward a "reasonable preparedness" and to see what the executive–professional coalition in the War Department would come up with.[38]

The second major War College assessment of America's military needs was an elaboration of the first and demonstrated again the penchant of the professional reformers for political confrontation. Their bold "Statement of a Proper Military Force for the United States" called for an army of 1,500,000 men. The regular army was to be increased to 281,000, and it was to be organized to expand to 500,000. Two reserve levels of 500,000 men each were planned. The state militias were to be barred from offensive service by the repeal of all laws that might be construed either as allowing the call of the National Guard for offensive duty or as requiring the guard to be called immediately after the regular force expanded to its full size. The guard would be a reserve of last resort and play a domestic defense role in wartime. In the words of the report:

> No force can be considered a portion of our first line whose control and training is so little subject to Federal authority in time of peace. No force should be considered a portion of our first line in war unless it be maintained fully organized and equipped in peace at practically war strength. This would exclude the Organized Militia from consideration from service in the first line because of the impossibility of giving in peace the training required for such functions.[39]

The new national reserve of the regular army was to be filled through universal military training. Local training centers were to be established throughout the country. To preempt charges of extravagance, the War College emphasized the relative frugality of its proposals when placed next to the size and resources of the belligerent forces.[40] Garrison took the plan to Wilson, eager to claim his place in the Root–Stimson tradition.

Garrison found Wilson receptive. He supported the War College plan in principle, urging modifications that tempered the professionals' zeal without abandoning their basic message. The compromise plan worked out between Wilson and Garrison called for a smaller increase in the regular army, to 141,843 men. Then came what is known as the Continental army reserve. A citizen reserve trained and controlled by the regulars would be organized in three increments of 133,000 men each. The total national reserve of 400,000 was to be on hand and ready for combat within three years. The reserves were to enlist for six years, with periodic service in the first three and on-call service in the last three. The National Guard was to receive an increased subsidy but remain restricted to domestic service and last-line reserve status. The General Staff endorsed the Wilson–Garrison compromise. The executive–professional coalition was cemented once again. On December 7, 1915, the President recommended the Continental army to Congress as a plan for "reasonable preparedness."[41]

Wilson had accepted an enormous political challenge, but the cause was not lost from the beginning. The Senate Military Affairs Committee was chaired by a staunch advocate of preparedness, of the national reserve, of universal training, and of the General Staff. If anything, George Chamberlain (Oregon) wanted to go further in the direction of the original War College proposal than Wilson's Continental army plan. Chamberlain's zeal made Wilson's proposal appear moderate. Opposition centered in the House. Southern and western Democrats and the National Guard lobby found powerful voices in Military Affairs Committee Chairman James Hay and Majority Leader Claude Kitchin. With the antipreparedness forces concentrated in his own party, Wilson made some early efforts to work the measure through the minority leadership in the House. Hay tried to persuade the President of the folly of his course early on. He enlisted the aid of the irrepressible Fred Ainsworth to help work out an alternative that would silence Garrison, the General Staff, and the preparedness Republicans while still allowing the President to save face.

Hay was willing to support a new army if it was organized around the National Guard. At this point, however, Wilson was committed to some version of the Continental army scheme. He calculated that if he could get popular backing from the Midwest and Far West, he could still bring Hay to heel. In January 1916, the President took to the stump, determined to push his recalcitrant party in a direction they had not bargained to go in 1912. The results were disappointing.[42]

Upon his return from the heartland, the President was informed by Hay in no uncertain terms that the Continental army was doomed in the House. The committee chairman then proclaimed that "nine Congressmen in ten" were willing to support his own alternative based on a National Guard strengthened by more stringent federal controls. The President yielded his support. Garrison resigned.[43]

The brief Wilson offensive of July to February on behalf of nationalism and professionalism in the army had been decisively turned back. Trying to respond to the political pressures for preparedness, the chief executive was given a forcible demonstration of the limitations of his party leadership in Congress. When the House passed the Hay bill, the only questions that remained involved the extent to which the executive would be forced to retreat and the extent to which Congress would launch a counteroffensive against the professional reformers. The answer awaited Hay's settlement with the Senate's key Democratic champion of professionalism and nationalism, George Chamberlain. Chamberlain did what he could, but he emerged from the conference unsatisfied and began to assume the role of War Department critic as the crisis approached. The result of the congressional compromise was something that Wilson could still call "reasonable preparedness" but that the War Department reformers understood as a crushing defeat. The party spared their President as much embarrassment as possible, but it did not spare the professionals this opportunity to destroy their sixteen-year offensive on behalf of a departmental reconstruction and to secure its own interests in their place. The Democratic party would be able to stand for a strong America in an election year, but in Leonard Wood's evaluation, it would have been "far better to have [had] no Army legislation at all than to have [had] this measure put through."[44]

The National Defense Act of 1916 was the most comprehensive piece of military legislation ever passed by Congress. It provided for a peacetime regular army enlarged to 175,000 men (more than Wilson had requested). The number of units and officers was vastly increased, and a plan was included for a five-year expansion of these skeletal units to a regular army of 298,000 men. A reserve officer training program was instituted whereby regular army officers would be detailed to the nation's colleges and universities as professors to train a leadership cadre for the expanded regular force. The President was authorized to institute a draft in wartime to fill out the ranks of the regular army. The most controversial section of the act ensured the National Guard its position as the first-line offensive reserve to be called directly after the expansion of the regular army. The guard also received drill pay and other material benefits. The cost of this new recognition and support was a significant detachment from local politics. For the first time, the President could prescribe the number and type of units that the states had to organize. The President was authorized to approve or annul any commission issued by a governor. Physical requirements, drill regulations, and uniforms were placed on the standards of the regulars. Guard enlistments were lengthened to three years active and three years reserve duty. A dual oath to the state and federal governments was required of all guardsmen so as to allow them to serve outside the United States. The new guard would substitute for Wilson's Continental reserve army by growing to a size of 450,000 men. Some lip service was given to the idea of a second-line National Volunteer Reserve, but there was no specific provision concerning its substance or training.[45]

If the plan for a new National Guard could be made to work (a condition that the professionals rejected on its face), these provisions of the Defense Act could hardly be considered a portent of disaster. The Root compromise of giving up the national reserve idea, providing the guard with greater benefits, and imposing higher professional standards and stricter national supervision had only been taken to a new level. Yet, this compromise represented the first major defeat for the executive–professional coalition that had been institutionalized in the relationship among the War College, the General Staff, the Chief of Staff, and the Secretary of War. The heart of the "Proper Military Policy" championed by the alliance – the national first-line reserve and the limitation of the guard's wartime role – had been soundly rejected. The rejection was punctuated in another provision of the act that made the Militia Division of the War Department an independent bureau in its own right. The guard had traded increased detachment from local politics for increased autonomy within the national bureaucracy.

This peculiar change in the guard's position was but part of a major congressional counteroffensive against professional reform advances. Ainsworth and Hay had not forgotten 1912. The National Defense Act represented a "magna carta for the bureaus" and a broadside attack on the General Staff.[46] The War College was formally separated from the staff, and the number of General Staff officers serving in Washington at any given time was limited to twenty. Congress limited hierarchical control by the executive by defining the authority of each bureau and its commanding officer in the statute. An effort was made to eliminate any lingering ambiguity concerning the scope of General Staff authority over the bureaus by explicitly prohibiting the General Staff from "assuming or engaging in work of an administrative nature" or work that "being assumed or engaged in by members of the general staff corps, would involve impairment of the responsibility or initiative of such bureaus or offices, or would cause injuries or unnecessary duplication of or delay in the work thereof."[47] Overall, the bureaus were defended against executive control, War College planning was separated from General Staff coordination, and General Staff coordination was separated from departmental administration.

Thus, the rejection of the War College proposal of 1915 and the reaffirmation of the National Guard's position in national defense went hand in hand with a resurgence of bureau autonomy, a formal restriction on General Staff authority, and a limitation on the staff's effective capacities by hiving off its parts and reducing its Washington-based personnel. The organizational, procedural, and intellectual reconstitution that seemed to be coming together in 1912 was shattered in 1916. America prepared for world war by rejecting the professional standard of army organization.

The pattern of executive challenge, constitutional confrontation, and congressional counteroffensive notable in the reconstruction of the War Department between 1900 and 1916 parallels the state-building pattern observed in civil administration. It will be recalled that 1916 was also the year that Congress took its first major step toward becoming an alternative center of control over the new realm of civil administration by establishing the Bureau of Efficiency. On the surface, the Bureau of Efficiency and the new army outlined in the National Defense Act of 1916 both appear as progressive governmental adaptations to changing environmental conditions, but in their form and content these adaptations reveal a government thoroughly caught up in an internal struggle over the reconstitution of political and institutional power relationships. As a different look into this same historical–structural problem, the War Department case provides a particularly clear illustration of the impact of the struggle for power within the state apparatus on the formation of new relations between state and society in the industrial age. In this regard, it is significant that in 1916, Congress gave formal recognition to the role of industrialists in a modern war effort.

As early as 1910, the Army War College had advocated the creation of a formal connection between the War Department and industry for the purpose of coordinating a mobilization effort.[48] The preparedness movement had linked the Republican political leadership, the champions of professional army reform, and the northeastern business community behind a corporatist vision of cooperation between business and government in war mobilization.[49] The reforms that Roosevelt, Root, Wood, Stimson, and the War College had championed within the government looked toward grounding such cooperation in a strong state sector represented by a hierarchically controlled and internally insulated War Department. Ironically, the Democratic Congress of 1916 appealed to the interests of the northeastern business community and embraced the principle of military–industrial cooperation while it lashed out against the executive–professional design for governmental control. The Army Appropriation Act of 1916 gave Wilson the authority to organize business advisory committees under an interdepartmental Council of National Defense. The advisory committees were to assist the cabinet members of the council in preparing and coordinating plans for industrial mobilization. The army legislation of 1916 allowed Wilson to meet the political challenge of preparedness by bringing its business constituency directly into the government, but at the same time, it denied the President the administrative infrastructure that the political leaders of preparedness had advocated.

America embarked upon a new era of military–industrial relations with a congressional offensive against hierarchical control and professional coordination in departmental administration. Business–government cooperation was introduced into the War Department as the cosmopolitan standard for administrative development was being rejected. This peculiar intersection of private power with state-building politics posed a threat to the business community no less than the government. Perhaps this is what Wood had in mind when he quipped that it would have been better had no army legislation been passed at all.[50]

The crisis of governmental authority

Forty years after Emory Upton launched his professional diatribe against the provincial republican virtues in military organization, America entered World War I. Elihu Root's General Staff represented the heart of the Uptonian reconstruction, and it had been placed in operation a full fourteen years before America's entry into the war specifically to prepare for just such "days of trial." Yet, because war preparations in 1916 had taken the form of an attack on the General Staff, the basic difference between the War Department on the eve of World War I and the War Department on the eve of the Spanish-American War seemed to rest in the depth of internal governmental divisions produced by the extended and inconclusive reconstruction initiatives that had intervened. The War Department of 1917 was structured to turn the major international crisis of the era into a display of administrative impotence.

At the center of the crisis stood Newton D. Baker, an outspoken pacifist and antimilitarist from Cleveland. After the defeat of the Continental army plan, Wilson had chosen Baker as his new Secretary of War. Through Baker the President attempted to reassure his party of his peaceful intentions and to mollify a Congress angered by Garrison's militant and abrasive style. The appointment followed a political rather than a military logic, but the new secretary had more than symbolism to offer the President.[51] Once in office, he endeared himself to his chief by displaying unflinching loyalty, an instinctive protection of the regular machinery and prerogatives of the government, and undying efforts to conciliate the departmental conflicts that threatened an administrative collapse.

Even before the war began, Baker showed an interest in piecing his department back together in the wake of the damage done by the National Defense Act. Soon after assuming office, he asked the Judge Advocate General for an interpretation of the impact of the act on the General Staff. This bureau chief took a hard line in his reply. He advised the new secretary that Congress had intended to bar the General Staff from any interference with the activities of the bureaus and that the Chief of Staff had been barred from even advising the secretary on matters relating to the bureaus. According to the Judge Advocate General, administrative operations had been freed from any effective coordination or professional supervision. Baker rejected this interpretation and, with it, the likely sentiments of James Hay. The secretary insisted that the National Defense Act had merely reaffirmed the position and role of the General Staff outlined in Root's original formulation of 1903. The staff was indeed an executive, not an administrative, agency, but coordination and supervision might at times involve it in issues bearing on bureau operations. With this ruling, Baker began to limit the impact of Congress's handiwork and to set himself up as the department mediator.[52]

The attempt to save the General Staff from irrelevance appeared somewhat academic in April 1917. In accordance with other provisions of the Defense Act, there were nineteen officers serving on the General Staff in Washington and eleven serving in the Army War College when the war began. Whatever arguments might be made on behalf of the formal authority of the staff, its effective capacities at the outset of the war were nil.[53] In comparison, the German General Staff had 650 officers in 1914, the French 644, the English 232, and the Japanese 234.[54] America was most clearly distinguished among the belligerent powers by the weakness of its bureaucratic machinery for controlling the war effort and by the intensity of the struggles being waged within the bureaucracy (and ultimately between the bureaucracy and the private sector) over the question of control.[55] With its administrative arm in disarray, America could achieve neither the collegial cooperation of high military officers and industrialists found in Germany nor the clear separation of military supply from the military services found in Britain and France.[56] In this context, corporatist cooperation was little more than an ideological illusion; the reality was an intensified but still inconclusive scramble for power and position.[57]

The dollar-a-year men who came from the business community into the government met Secretary Baker in his role as chairman of the Council of National Defense. Baker organized the business advisory committees of the council and served as Wilson's chief advisor on industrial mobilization. These private-sector volunteers were heralded as America's answer to the bureaucratic statism of Europe, the ultimate vindication of the liberal tradition.[58] But necessity was the better part of virtue. America's weak state made the talents and resources of American business all the more indispensable to the mobilization effort, but it also posed an inescapable problem for all concerned. Whereas political leaders, business leaders, and bureaucrats shared the goal of cooperation, relations between government and business were structured to maximize insecurity. When it came to defining the terms of cooperation, ideology gave way to mutual suspicion and self-protection.[59]

The leading lights among the volunteers had an interest in cooperation far beyond that of winning the war and making a short-term profit. Direct involvement in the war effort provided an opportunity to prove the modern corporation and the great entrepreneur worthy of public confidence. A sterling display of order and self-discipline among businessmen might catalyze a reevaluation of the government's antitrust disposition and policelike attitudes toward business. Government and business might emerge from the war as partners working together in the management of the private economy. By their own example, the businessmen and professionals who espoused this new partnership had to convince the politicians, the public, and indeed the business community itself that cooperation could work to maximize efficiency and minimize corruption.[60]

The inability of the War Department to maintain order within its own sphere threatened to turn the largest cooperative venture and corporate opportunity of all time into an economic debacle that would directly implicate the business community. Business leaders found it difficult enough to make voluntary cooperation work among themselves, and they quickly discovered that a government unable to control itself was also unable to focus and stabilize business efforts. Indeed, the weaknesses of the state threatened the maintenance of order among businessmen as much as it did the cooperation between business and government. The lack of central controls in administration blurred responsibility and lowered the standards of business practice at the middle levels of the bureaucracy. Without government providing authority and direction, business became even more susceptible to charges of profiteering and corruption.[61]

The major obstacle to business success was the independence of the War Department bureaus in dealing with purchase, supply, and transport. The onset of war had pushed the army bureaus beyond all authoritative control. The General Staff was overwhelmed and spent more time trying to reorganize and expand its personnel in order to take control than in the act of coordination itself.[62] Each bureau looked after its own domain, and each had its own purchasing staff, financial accounts, storage facilities, and transportation connections to do so. The failure to consolidate these supply services under the General Staff, which Root had accepted as a matter of small importance, was now crippling business efforts to coordinate industry with War Department demands. There was no central assessment of needs, no ordering of priorities, no accumulation of like purchases, and no locus of authority capable of managing such activities. More troubling still, the organization of the bureaus bore no relationship to the organization of the economy. Business advisory committees proliferated, and each was left to its own devices in trying to meet bureau demands. Finally, as long as army supply and purchase remained disjointed and out of step with industrial organization, efforts to coordinate supply and purchase for other government departments were futile.[63]

A strong administrative arm within the government was the key to the success of a cooperative partnership, but the government's administrative arm was fast being exposed as the weakest link in the mobilization effort. America's answer to European statism was proving to be no answer at all. With the promise of a new corporate order being sacrificed to an incompetent administration, businessmen began to look beyond voluntary cooperation toward taking control themselves. The business advisory committees prepared to demand substantive authority over business, over the economy, and over military procurement for the army and navy.[64]

The advisory committees were consolidated into a War Industries Board in July 1917. This board was the first centralized agency for the supervision of business activity and economic performance, yet it remained a creature of the Council of National Defense under the tutelage of the Secretary of War. It functioned as a clearinghouse for the business committees and still acted in what was essentially an advisory capacity. The position of the board chairman carried tremendous responsibility but little effective power, and it soon became the focus of business frustration. As the severe winter of 1917–18 began to take its toll on the industrial mobilization effort, businessmen openly appealed to an irate Congress for real power over both the economy and the bureaucracy.

The Senate Military Affairs Committee, under the chairmanship of George Chamberlain, provided the businessmen with a forum by opening an investigation of the War Department in December. The businessmen's message was clear. Cooperation with the War Department was impossible; industrial mobilization was in jeopardy; a center of authoritative controls had to be established under business supervision. Government by businessmen had to substitute for the failure of business–government cooperation.[65]

The precariousness of business's political position and the need to appear virtuous as it pursued power and position in the war effort were matched by paranoia in the War Department and its determination to maintain control of its prerogatives. Wilson himself welcomed business cooperation with government, but he too hesitated when it came to business control of government.[66] His fears for the integrity of government were mild compared to those of Secretary Baker, the General Staff, and the War College. After decades of struggle to gain control over the War Department bureaus, the secretary and the professionals now faced an attempt to have them officially stripped out of the military hierarchy and placed under the control of industrialists. Professional reformers outside the military such as Robert Brookings and W. F. Willoughby could point to Britain and France as models of administrative rationality in separating military procurement and supply from the administration of the military departments, but the professionals on the General Staff saw in this a new political assault on the military establishment. The Secretary of War saw this radical departure from established governmental organization as a grave tactical mistake and suspected profiteers eager to gain power at the expense of true public authorities. It might be noted that the army's adamant opposition to the transfer of supply and purchase to a separate civilian department was shared by the navy.[67]

The question was, did Baker have a workable alternative to abdicating governing power to business? He had been constantly reorganizing and expanding the General Staff since 1917, hoping to find a way to coordinate supply, to maintain all department prerogatives intact, and to keep business in an advisory capacity. The consolidation of the advisory boards under the War Industries Board in July 1917 had been planned and executed by Baker to meet the demand for industrial reorganization while keeping business firmly under the arm of the Council of National Defense and out of the War Department's domain. In November, he appointed Cleveland businessman Benedict Crowell Assistant Secretary of War to coordinate supply with industry without suffering external controls. When business turned to Congress to demand independent controls and exposed Baker's leadership to severe criticism, the secretary grasped a more radical War College proposal for buttressing the department and preempting its dismemberment. Two assistant chiefs of staff were created, one a Director of Purchase and the other a Director of Storage. Each was to work at a coordinate level in conjunction with a civilian Surveyor General who would, in turn, act as a link with industry within the department. This reform was carried out in mid-January with Edward Stettinius, a J. P. Morgan partner, appointed to the position of Surveyor General.[68]

The leaders of the War Industries Board portrayed the Stettinius appointment as a futile, last-ditch effort to block a desperately needed munitions department under independent civilian control. They had a point. The War Department bureaus remained intransigent in the face of Baker's effort to impose General Staff supervision, viewing even this as too radical a step. Moreover, when General George Goethals, the builder of the Panama Canal, assumed the position of Director of Storage, ambiguity in his relationship to Stettinius degenerated into conflict at the top.[69]

Baker simply did not have the time or resources to sustain the supremacy of the War Department. The winter crisis in supply and transport combined with the bitterness expressed in the Senate investigations took a heavy toll on the secretary. At this point, George Chamberlain offered his proposal for a civilian War Cabinet. Republicans demanded the appointment of Root, Roosevelt, or Wood to a high leadership position in war administration. Democrats wavered, fearing Republican control, suspecting a rape of government by businessmen, and perhaps most of all, foreseeing public recrimination on the horizon for a Democratic administration's bungling of the war effort. The Secretary of War signaled his readiness to resign.[70]

Wilson moved to rescue the mobilization effort late in January. He admonished Chamberlain for his criticism and rejected proposals for an industrial War Cabinet or a munitions ministry. At the same time, he expressed confidence in Baker. But the President understood the reasons for business dismay and the failure of Baker's efforts to remedy the situation. He decided to catapult business into a dominant position, but to do so under his own authority. Lee Overman set in motion the congressional machinery that would allow the President to handle the emergency on his own terms. The President then ordered Baker, as chairman of the Council of National Defense, to meet with Bernard Baruch, representing the War Industries Board, to reach agreement on an effective coordination of the war effort.

Baker insisted that the army and navy departments retain their control over the determination of the military needs to be served by the board, but beyond this he yielded. He recognized that the War Industries Board would become a "legal, authoritative, responsible, centralized agency" acting under the President; that it would have the power to "commandeer plants, products, equipment, manufacturing facilities, mines, and materials"; that it would procure military supplies, control the industry of the nation, and regulate prices and compensation; and that the chairman of the board would have final authority over the allocation and distribution of the program of needs submitted by the various departments. Baruch was appointed chairman of the new War Industries Board on March 4, 1918.[71]

The demand for central authority in wartime worked to catapult the private-sector volunteers over governmental institutions. But the business victory over Baker remained a limited one. At least as important as the President's decision to place the War Industries Board in a commanding position was his rejection of the War Industries Board's call for a munitions ministry and Chamberlain's War Cabinet scheme. By sustaining Baker in the War Department and bringing the War Industries Board under his own authority as an emergency measure, Wilson accepted the creation of an industrial czar as a necessary but temporary expedient. Moreover, Baker maintained control over the War Department bureaus, and the President's emergency power could be used to secure that control against further business encroachment as readily as it could be used to secure Baruch's position. Significantly enough, on the day that Wilson appointed Baruch chairman of the War Industries Board, Baker appointed a new Chief of Staff. General Peyton March, recently returned from the European front, was not one to step softly. When the Overman

Act finally passed in May and Wilson shifted the War Industries Board from the Council of National Defense to his own emergency authority, Baker used that same authority to unleash March against the War Department bureaus.[72] In a sense, Wilson's action in the spring of 1918 saved the War Department from external dismantling by the industrialists from above and from internal disintegration from the bureaus below.

Under March's leadership, the General Staff grew to about 1,000 officers. Assistant Chief of Staff Goethals had his hand strengthened in a Staff Division of Purchase, Storage, and Traffic. Baker spent much of his time mollifying the bureau chiefs as March and Goethals realized the long awaited consolidation of the supply services. Goethals completed the work on October 24, when the supply activities of the engineer corps, the medical corps, and the signal corps were transferred to his division. The General Staff was finally ready to meet the War Industries Board as a full-fledged partner in a new corporate order, but in less than three weeks the war was over.[73]

In developing the capacities to work with the War Industries Board, the General Staff also sought to delimit the board's domain. The army and industry struggled to a standoff over the terms of their wartime cooperation, and the joint effort that ended the war never fully transcended self-protection, suspicion, or the expectation of future struggle. Baruch and March knew that their working arrangements were temporary and that military–industrial relations would emerge as a major postwar issue.[74] The military–industrial complex of the fall of 1918 rested on the most precarious political and institutional foundations, and each actor recognized that congressional, executive, business, bureau and military staff interests would soon be scrambling for positions of advantage in the postwar consolidation.

Had the consolidation of supply activities been secured in 1903, 1912, or 1916 (let alone sometime between 1877 and 1900), it is possible that business and military interests would have been spared their mutual insecurities. America did not lack the designs, skills, or interests for the development of a strong administrative arm; it did not lack an ideology of business–government cooperation; it did not lack the will of businessmen to cooperate with the state. The corporate ideal went unfulfilled because government officials, acting collectively, could not sustain or secure the requisite reconstitution of institutional power relationships. Neither military reformers nor business ideologues could control the structural changes they championed. Reconstitution followed a political logic, and shifts in the political calculus of power and position determined the awkward terms upon which the army and business met during the war.

The consolidation

The significance of the President's strategy for dealing with government by businessmen in the spring of 1918 became apparent immediately after the armistice. Wilson rejected all entreaties to allow the War Industries Board to continue to operate in the postwar period for purposes of planning and stabilizing the demobilization. Taking a short-term view of the emergency, he summarily disbanded the board effective January 1, 1919, and dissociated himself from any implication of a change in the government's normal posture toward business. Moreover, the War Department's demobilization plan was sustained despite differences with the board's plan. Emergency powers allowed the President to catapult the business community to a commanding position in the executive branch in the spring and to usher it out with all deliberate speed in the winter.[75]

There was, however, no returning to prewar conditions. Power relationships within the War Department and between the War Department and industry had been fundamentally disrupted by the war, and Wilson's decision to terminate the War Industries Board effectively passed to Congress the task of deciding what to do about those new relationships. The tenuous but clear arrangements that had emerged in the autumn of 1918 under the President's emergency powers gave way to congressional interests early in 1919.

A flood of proposals for the War Department's reorganization engulfed Congress in the aftermath of the war. Several distinct points of view can be identified. Baker and March attempted to seize the initiative early and consolidate the professional–executive coalition as it had evolved during the crisis. They pressed for new General Staff legislation that would centralize management controls over the bureaus in the General Staff and permit a permanent staff division of Supply, Traffic, and Storage to concentrate supply and military–industrial planning responsibilities in the army's central planning agency. General Goethals also wanted to end the conflict between the staff and the bureaus and to concentrate military–industrial planning in professional military hands. He believed, however, that this could best be accomplished not by bureau consolidation under the General Staff but by preventing the bureaus from having contact with the General Staff. He called for a consolidated supply service corps kept under military management and organized as a hierarchical line of authority running parallel to the services of the line up to the Secretary of War. The General Staff and Chief of Staff would be concerned with war plans, military intelligence, and military operations, whereas parallel *military* machinery would be concerned with industrial mobilization plans, industrial liaison, and military supply. Assistant Secretary of War Benedict Crowell, the War Department's chief business liaison between Goethals and the War Industries Board, also agreed that supply services should be consolidated but argued against military control. He suggested the creation of a new Assistant Secretary of War responsible to the Secretary of War for military supply and industrial mobilization but recruited directly from the nation's enlightened entrepreneurs. Finally, the Institute for Government Research, whose members had close relations with the War Industries Board, proposed a consolidated supply department for the army and the navy. It would be independent of the military departments themselves, headed by an enlightened industrialist, and directly responsible to the President.[76]

The various points of view represented in these proposals reflect the respective positions held by their proponents during the period of the President's emergency reorganization. Apart from their differences, each called for an end to the bureau autonomy that had proven so enervating to the mobilization efforts of both the War Department and industry in 1917. A strong, clear vertical line of control over military supply was to be realized in each case. Executive authority was to reign supreme and provide a focus for military–industrial interactions. Differences among the proposals related to the specific structure of executive authority and the nature of the relations between the military professionals and industry.

On these matters, Congress had some ideas of its own. The return of the Republicans to control in the House and Senate in 1919 may have contributed marginally to the confusion of controls evident in the Army Act of 1920, but that act appears most notable for turning the Democrats' National Defense Act of 1916 into a nonpartisan statement of congressional interests in the new military establishment. Indeed the 1920 legislation took the form of a long amendment to the National Defense Act written with an eye toward acknowledging a new state of affairs while securing a strong congressional connection to all parts of the new structure. At every turn, Congress checked and balanced the wartime progress of the champions of nationalism, professionalism, and corporatism, and, in doing so, it pushed the new American state into a maze of authoritative confusion.

The new order of cooperation between government and industry emerged as one part of the consolidation of twenty years of political struggle over the reconstitution of power relationships in the War Department. For the first time, Congress took note of the professionals' argument that preparedness should not end with the end of a war. The regular army was to maintain the potential strength of 298,000 men provided in the act of 1916, and its peacetime limit was raised to

280,000 men. Also for the first time, the details of organizing the military units were left to the President and the War Department. Three new bureaus were created: Air Services, Chemical Warfare, and Finance. The reserve officer training program, established in 1916, was continued. Beyond this, however, Congress rejected regular army pleas for compulsory military training and, much to the professionals' dismay, it strengthened the position of the National Guard. The act envisioned 400,000 guard volunteers serving as a first-line reserve to be called into service in conjunction with the regular army. Enlistments could be for either one or three years, and pay was increased substantially as an inducement for volunteers. Moreover, the National Guard Bureau, which had been given independent status within the department in 1916, was taken out of the hands of the regulars in 1920. National Guard Association complaints about the demobilization procedures used by the regulars led Congress to secure even more autonomy for the organized militia within the War Department by entrusting its administration directly to a guard officer.[77]

When it came to the General Staff, Congress looked for some alternative to the cut-and-slash approach it had used in 1916. It decided to increase the permanent size of the staff to eighty-eight, and at the same time, it expressed a new interest in the institution. In one of the most striking innovations of the act, the General Staff was separated from the exclusive control of the Secretary of War. Congress stipulated that all recommendations for legislation from the Secretary of War were to be accompanied by a report from the appropriate division of the General Staff, and that staff reports could be presented directly to Congress without the consent or oversight of the secretary. Here was an assault on the executive–professional reform coalition couched in terms of an invitation to the professional military reformers to petition Congress in their own interests. Instead of attacking the centerpiece of the new American army broadside, as it had in 1916, Congress now decided to join it and, in so doing, permitted the General Staff to play off executive controls against congressional influence. In this, as in other particulars of the act, it was the authority of the Secretary of War that was now being challenged most directly.[78]

In this spirit of recognizing a new order and protecting its political and institutional interests within it, Congress approached the major question of postwar army reconstruction: military supply. Bowing to strong bureau opposition, Congress rejected the Baker–March proposal to permit a permanent consolidation of procurement activities in the General Staff. The wartime experience of centralized professional control gave way to a modified system of bureau autonomy. The quartermaster corps was given responsibility for the procurement of all supplies used by two or more bureaus, leaving the procurement of supplies used by only one bureau to that bureau's own control. Moreover, the strong language of 1916 prohibiting General Staff interference with the operations of the bureaus was reaffirmed. Yet, having stripped the General Staff of its direct control over supply and having reaffirmed the autonomy of the bureaus, Congress allowed the General Staff to "plan" for "supplying, equipping and mobilizing" the army.[79] Then, in another striking innovation, Congress established a direct connection to industry through the office of the Assistant Secretary of War. The assistant secretary was charged with the "supervision of the procurement of all military supplies and other business of the War Department pertaining thereto and the assurance of adequate provision for the mobilization of material and industrial organization essential to wartime needs."[80] Baker objected to this statutory specification of the role of the assistant secretary because it gave a subordinate of the Secretary of War undue independence from the regular chain of command and limited the discretion of the superior officer.[81] Indeed, it appeared that Congress had linked industry, the Assistant Secretary of War, and the semiindependent bureaus in a separate line of authority running directly to Congress.

The assistant secretary's charge followed the general outlines of Benedict Crowell's proposal for centralizing control over military–industrial relations in the hands of a reputable industrialist. But the other sections of the act dealing with supply clouded the picture considerably. There was a hint of the Baker–March proposal in having the General Staff engage in supply planning. There was a hint of the Goethals proposal in the provision for some consolidation of supply outside the General Staff in the quartermaster corps. There was also the reaffirmation of the 1916 language concerning bureau autonomy. In essence, Congress acknowledged the claims of all the contending actors and, after assuring its own involvement with each, merely institutionalized the scramble among them.

The results were predictable. Chief of Staff March created a permanent Supply Division in the General Staff in accordance with the planning responsibilities outlined in the act. When General Pershing became Chief of Staff in 1921, he appealed to Baker's arguments of 1916 and broadly reinterpreted congressional restrictions on staff authority so as to strengthen the staff's position vis-à-vis the bureaus. In the mid-1920s, the Assistant Secretary of War established an Industrial War College in accordance with his responsibilities for supervising supply activities and began to use the Supply Division of the General Staff as his personal staff. Conflicts between the Assistant Secretary of War and the Chief of Staff over the control of supply, the bureaus, and the General Staff focused a new round of struggle within the War Department.[82] Once again, cooperation and coordination fell victim to a confusion of governmental authority.

The Progressive state-building achievement II

In nineteenth-century America, the basic operating structure of the state was clear and simple; yet, it worked to destroy the organizational integrity of the army. Progressive state builders set out to resolve this problem, but in the process, they encountered a new paradox. The reconstruction of the army left the basic operating structure of the state in confusion.

A similar outcome has been observed in the reconstruction of civil administration. There, the party bureaucracy of the nineteenth century gave way to a nonpartisan bureaucracy newly politicized around a constitutional stalemate of administrative controls. In the case of the army, a parallel political struggle over the reconstitution of institutional power relationships was focused within a single bureaucracy. The American army of 1920 emerged as a constituent part of a new bureaucratic state, its interior structure illuminating another piece of this larger state-building achievement.

The American army of the 1870s and the American army of the 1920s were two entirely different institutions. The institution that late-century military professionals scorned as a debased appendage of local interests and an all-consuming democratic politics had, in the intervening years, undergone an organizational, procedural, and intellectual transformation. The newly empowered Secretary of War, the new Assistant Secretary of War, the Chief of Staff, the General Staff, the Army War College, the Industrial War College, the nationalized militia system, and the reserve officer training program – all the new machinery of the War Department – embodied an institutional accommodation to the champions of nationalism, professionalism, and corporatism. The army had become a powerful bureaucratic institution in its own right, able to claim a distinctive place in the national government, the corporate economy, and the universities.

Yet, merely listing the parts of this new bureaucratic machine distorts the meaning of the state-building achievement. The peculiar character of the army of 1920 and the more enduring characteristics of the new American state are to be discerned in the relations structured among the parts of the machine. The militia had indeed been nationalized, but its autonomy within the War Department had also been secured. Interest-group pressure had been built into the interior structure of the new bureaucratic establishment. Although the General Staff had been institutionalized as the centerpiece of the new professionalism, its relationships to the Secretary of War above and the bureaus below were clouded by lateral connections to Congress. Although the position of Assistant Secretary of War had been established to integrate the War Department with the corporate community, his relations to the Chief of Staff, the regular army hierarchy, and Congress were mired in confusion. In all, the champions of nationalism, professionalism, and corporatism made their way into the War Department only to end up locked in alternative and competing systems of control.

Professional insulation and executive control failed to displace lateral political ties and particularistic interests. Under the new mode of governmental operations, the former were accepted by being structured to coexist with the latter. Thus, the cosmopolitan professional was not freed from local politics but fused to it. Nationalism came to mean a proliferation of semiindependent and competing power centers at the national level rather than the establishment of a national center of power. Institutions that promised to provide the corporatist planning of a strong bureaucratic state turned into avenues for promoting particular interests in a weak bureaucratic state.

The expansion of national administrative capacities opened a new range of possibilities for state action, but at the same time, the politics of reconstitution forged a new set of operational constraints. Governing power was concentrated at the national level, but when it came to the control of this power, efficiency yielded to uncertainty, and responsibility yielded to competition. The blessing of power restrained became linked to a curse of confusion. Twentieth-century state builders broke through the structural limitations imposed by the nineteenth-century mode of governmental operations only to find themselves caught in a constitutional standoff. A tangle of authority arrayed around bureaucratic power defined the new institutional politics and distinguished the new state.

8

Reconstituting business regulation: administrative justice, scientific management, and the triumph of the independent commission

Although under the decision of the courts the National Government had power over the railways, I found, when I became President, that this power was either not exercised at all or exercised with utter inefficiency. The law against rebates was a dead letter ... the scrupulous and decent railway men had been forced to violate it themselves under penalty of being beaten by their less scrupulous rivals. It was not the fault of these decent railway men. It was the fault of the Government.

Theodore Roosevelt, *An Autobiography*, 1913

The Interstate Commerce Commission (ICC) emerged in 1920 as the signal triumph of the Progressive reconstitution. Here, the old mode of governmental operations was most completely superseded, and the reintegration of the American state with the new industrial society most clearly consummated. The agency gained powers hitherto dispersed among the states, Congress, the courts, and the executive. With these powers, it acquired the responsibility for supervising all aspects of the national railway system in accordance with the most advanced precepts of scientific management. The revival of the ICC was heralded as a vindication of the independent expert over the narrow interests of political managers and the usurpations of jealous judges. It became a symbol of a new democracy and a new political economy. It was all the promises of the new American state rolled into the expansion of national administrative capacities.

It was also a political response to a developmental dilemma. Beneath the rhetoric of reform lay the problems of reconstituting institutional power relationships and the implications of past failures. The early ICC had been caught between the vitality of the electoral–representative system on one side and the vitality of judicial discipline on the other. A Congress geared to guarantee the particular interests of all contending factions, coupled with a Supreme Court that had no patience for ambiguity in the delegation of legislative power to an administrative tribunal, stifled efforts to implement a Progressive theory of regulation and left the government with nothing new to offer in resolving the conflicts of the marketplace. By 1900, it appeared that relations between the American state and the industrial economy would become increasingly distorted so long as the old governmental order remained strong. Translating reform rhetoric into the logic of American state building, lawmakers and judges were obstacles to be overcome in developing the administrative capacities necessary to bring order and stability to the nation's railway network.

This historical–structural impasse was negotiated through the political shifts of the Progressive era and the now familiar pattern of contentious institutional maneuvering that accompanied these shifts. The rehabilitation of the ICC touched upon several alternative models for the reestablishment of internal governmental controls, but none of these could be sustained over time. Ultimately, the extended politics of reconstitution rejoined state and society by simply turning the governmental dilemma of late-century regulation inside out. The rise of the independent commission in modern American government ultimately shattered political responsibility and judicial discipline in the exercise of regulatory power and left the state itself in internal disarray. To understand this gradual inversion of institutional power relationships between 1900 and 1920 is to understand why the signal triumph of the Progressive reconstitution was destined to become the nemesis of reform in the new American state.[1]

The challenge

The aborted experiment in administrative regulation had left the railroads of the 1890s to their own devices to seek stability in consolidation. The personnel of the ICC and the progressive economists of the American Economic Association (AEA) recognized the inevitability of consolidation but took to the leading journals to argue the case for administrative control over the rate structure and administrative supervision of business practices.[2] Tensions between railroads and shippers still ran high, and the manners of the marketplace let the most unscrupulous set the fashion. Commissioners and economists alike spoke for a clarification of the relationship between judicial authority and administrative authority that would facilitate the exercise of the latter and for an expansion of administrative powers that would allow the government to develop a coordinated and cooperative system of railroading.[3] As rates began to increase after 1900, the commission's plea to reopen the regulatory issue began to gain a receptive audience.[4]

The first concrete manifestation of the new support for regulatory reform came in February 1903, when the Elkins Anti-Rebating Act passed the Senate with no dissenting vote and the House with only six negative votes. Stephen Elkins, a West Virginian with substantial shipper and railroad interests of his own, had taken over the chairmanship of the Senate Committee on Interstate Commerce from Shelby Cullom in 1901. He immediately disposed of a comprehensive reform measure written by the commission and sponsored by Cullom that would have given sweeping rate-making powers to the ICC.[5] He chose instead to reopen the regulatory issue by strengthening one of the few stipulations of the act of 1887 that had sparked little opposition even in the original debates. Indeed, only the very largest shippers gained from rebates and drawbacks. The railroads engaged in the practice to increase their traffic, but their long-term interest lay in the promotion of rate standardization and the prevention of rate cutting. Pennsylvania Railroad officials were instrumental in helping Elkins draft his new antirebating proposal. For their part, the shippers had recently reorganized to fight rate discriminations as well as rate increases. As a group, they too offered the bill support.[6]

The Elkins Act gave teeth to the antirebating clause of the act of 1887 without broaching any of the questions of institutional power and governmental operations that lay at the heart of the problem of American state building. The railroads were permitted to set their own rates, but the mere fact of a deviation from the rate formally filed with the commission was made a criminal violation, with each party involved subject to a fine of $20,000. As soon as the ICC or the Attorney General suspected such a deviation, proceedings were to be initiated directly in a federal circuit court.[7] Elkins sidestepped the most divisive issues in administrative regulation in order to strengthen the government's traditional surveillance posture toward business.

Behind the Elkins consensus, a heated debate was developing over the shape of a more positive form of administrative regulation. Between 1901, when the comprehensive Cullom–ICC bill was tabled, and 1906, when the Hepburn Act was passed, Congress confronted the full scope of the problem of reconstitution. During these years, it became clear that there were three fairly distinct governmental tasks to be performed in railroad regulation. First, there was the task of adjudicating disputes between railroads and shippers. Second, there was the legislative task of setting rates that would be binding in the future. Third, there was the administrative or executive task of managing or supervising the private management of a consolidated railway system.[8]

As the various dimensions of railroad regulation were being distinguished, a number of proposals were circulated to strengthen the ICC in some of its regulatory functions and to separate the others. In most proposals, the commission was to remain an arm of Congress, to which the parent body would explicitly delegate rate-making powers. Beyond this, however, there were numerous possibilities. The government could establish a specialized railroad court of appeals, it could establish an executive bureau or department for railroad management (the idea was to transfer the ICC to the new Department of Commerce and Labor), or it could hive off both the judicial and executive management functions and restrict the ICC to the business of setting rates.[9] It is likely that what the more extreme proposals for separating functions and powers into different institutions gained in terms of clarifying constitutional authority and political control, they would have lost in terms of coordination and institutional conflicts of interest. In fact, judicial control, legislative control, and executive control would each be tested before 1920, only to collapse back into an ever more powerful and independent ICC.

Contending economic interests were, of course, intimately involved in the debates over the reconstitution of institutional power relationships. Yet, perhaps the most important thing about the carriers and the shippers is that when it came to the specifics of administrative reconstruction they each spoke with many conflicting voices. Any general exposition of their interests only indicates the direction in which they tended to lean.[10]

The railroads were generally interested in the potential for federal regulation to bolster private management. So far as they supported the revival of the regulatory effort, they wanted the federal government to legalize pooling, to guarantee their financial solvency, to consider the credit ratings necessary to take advantage of reinvestment opportunities, and to secure industrial stability. Some were willing to accept rate-making powers if they were designed with these overall industrial management functions in mind. They stood in favor of a broad judicial review of administrative decisions and argued that the agency that fixed rates should not be the same agency that adjudicated disputes. They supported the establishment of a specialized railroad court to hear disputes as well as appeals from ICC decisions.

The shippers were even less unified in their interests than the railroads. More than anything else, their positions tended to relate to the transportation needs and services of their particular locality. But they were generally interested in using the government to check railroad rate increases, and they were opposed to governmental involvement in the management of the railroad industry. A concern for management suggested governmental support for further consolidations, for the elimination of competition, for massive new capital investments, and for the arbitration of labor demands for higher wages – all of which spelled higher rates for the shippers. They also tended to support broad administrative discretion in the adjudication of disputes and restrictions on the scope of judicial review of commission decisions. A specialized administrative court appeared to the small shipper as a railroad check on his own appeals to the commission.

The institutional issues in regulation were always more than a mere facade for private group interests.[11] Whereas the reconstitution of institutional power relationships directly engaged the interests of economic factions in securing positions of advantage in new relations with the state, government officials had concerns of their own in approaching these matters. In this regard, it is important to note that key figures on the commission around the turn of the century were at the forefront of the effort to distinguish the various dimensions of federal railroad regulation. They gave their own arguments for establishing new institutions to perform various tasks.

Commissioner Charles Prouty was one of the more skeptical members of the ICC when it came to railroad interests, but he endorsed the idea of creating a specialized court to hear railroad appeals. By placing a special court between a refortified ICC and the Supreme Court, Prouty saw a possibility of easing the tensions in a most difficult institutional relationship. Prouty, like many Progressives, was keenly aware of the judicial obstacles to the effective exercise of administrative power, but he thought that these obstacles might be overcome most amicably by establishing a new kind of court whose judges were especially attuned to the technical and extralegal questions that arose in administrative regulation. Moreover, a specialized court to hear railroad appeals might help speed commission decisions through the judiciary and thus give them more immediate effect. In this sense, the railroad court idea represented a Progressive state-building reform. It looked toward the development of a new body of administrative law and procedure that would facilitate the rise of administrative regulation by eliminating the intellectual, procedural, and organizational obstacles that had left the commission impotent for so many years. It acknowledged an important role for the judiciary in administrative regulation and sought to develop mutual understanding and cooperation among specialists.[12]

Another leading figure at the ICC, Henry Carter Adams, approached

the question of industrial management with the interests of the professional economist in mind. He argued throughout this period that the
central problem in railroad regulation was not high rates. Instead, he
detailed the need for the management of railroad credit, the supervision
of railroad finances, and a public valuation of railroad properties. Adams
had never been enthusiastic about the commission form of regulation,
and he was quite receptive to the idea of having the industrial management tasks of regulation separated from the others and placed under
executive control. He had long advocated the creation of a Bureau of
Railway Statistics where trained economists could gather more complete
and accurate public information and with it pursue the scientific management of a national railway system.[13]

Beyond the interests of the private groups and the ideas of public
administrators lay the all-important problem of building a political coalition among elected officials for concerted action on these institutional
issues. Here, still other kinds of interests were superimposed on the revival of administrative regulation. Three positions of particular significance can be distinguished among elected officials.

Most Democrats and the Republicans of the West and Midwest viewed
the regulatory issue as a battle between the people and the corporations.
Their political base lay in the traditional strongholds of agrarian
radicalism, and they championed the small shippers. They spoke out
against railroad consolidation and against the rise in railroad rates. They
opposed a positive role for the government in the support of the railroad
industry and, more importantly still, they were enraged by any regulatory
proposal that allowed the judiciary to check the will of the people's
representatives. Not only was an administrative court viewed as a
mouthpiece for the railroads, but during the 1890s the judicial branch as
a whole had become the archenemy of the forces of populism. The nullification of state regulatory laws in the 1890s and the nullification of the
federal income tax law in 1895 identified the judiciary as the opponent of
democracy upholding a plutocracy of eastern capital.[14] The representatives of the South and the West were determined to overthrow this judicial imperialism, and one way of doing so was to grant sweeping rate-
making powers to the ICC and radically restrict the scope of judicial
review.

It will be recalled that the agrarian radicals of the 1870s had been
suspicious of regulation by commission, preferring instead restrictive
legislation enforced directly by the courts. The courts' subsequent defiance of legislative will caused a reevaluation of the commission as the
more appropriate instrument for carrying out the legislature's regulatory
mandate. More than any other single factor, the radicals' attack on the

judiciary in the name of popular control gave the rise of the ICC its democratic symbolism. Moreover, in calling for restrictions on the judiciary and a strengthening of the commission, the radicals approached the state-building position of the new professionals and opened the door to a limited political coalition. On the other hand, separating the judiciary from administrative regulation in order to turn the regulatory machinery into a political arm of Congress for restricting the corporations gave the champions of insulated institutions controlled by experts reason for caution.

Spearheading the interests of the experts in regulation was Theodore Roosevelt. Unlike populists and southerners, Roosevelt approached the regulatory issue as a problem of restoring order in the market and cooperation in relations between the railroads and the shippers. He supported the legalization of pooling and was favorably disposed toward the development of an executive management role for the government in the development of a consolidated national railway system. He also supported the shippers in their desire to give the commission control over rates, but he cautioned that this power must not be used to deprive the railroads of a fair return on their property.[15] In these sentiments, Roosevelt also echoed the views of a number of moderate Republicans in the House.

The distinctiveness of Roosevelt's position is most clearly revealed in his approach to Congress and the courts. He had little faith in the capacities of either to meet the challenges of government in an industrial society. The role of the President in regulatory reform was, in his view, to restrict the penetration of each into what was essentially an administrative task.[16] The President was unconvinced by those Progressive reformers who saw some constructive purpose to be served in the creation of courts of special jurisdiction. "All the wise friends of the effort to secure government control of corporations know that this government control must be exercised through administrative and not judicial officers if it is to be effective. Everything possible should be done to minimize the chance of appealing from the decisions of administrative officers to the courts."[17] In this, Roosevelt held open the door to a coalition with the radicals, but it was not until 1912 that he took full advantage of this option. He preferred not to go so far as the "zealots" who wished to "totally abolish the judicial appeal," for he believed that this was unconstitutional and would merely invite the courts to nullify all efforts to create an autonomous realm of administrative action.[18] Nor would he tie administrative power to the dominant opinion in Congress. It was not Congress, the Supreme Court, or even the small shipper who best embodied the public interest in regulation; it was the independent professional and the administrative expert.[19] Roosevelt's goal was a concentration of national administrative power and an insulation of expertise that would facilitate stability, harmony, and further growth in the industrial economy.

On the right stood the Old Guard Republicans. Their center of political strength lay in the industrial North, and their center of institutional strength lay in the Senate. Like Roosevelt, they would shield the railroads from broadside political attacks. But unlike the President, they were suspicious of broad legislative delegations of regulatory powers to administrators, and they supported a broad interpretation of judicial review. They were content to leave the commission in its nineteenth-century status as a ward of the courts. They were also increasingly suspicious of Roosevelt's challenges on behalf of national administrative expansion, recognizing in these a calculated executive strategy to circumvent the prerogatives and prestige of Congress. They were the least politically disposed to any change in established institutional power relationships.[20]

The regulatory interests of private groups and the ideas of public administrators could make themselves felt only through some coalition of these political actors. The array of positions suggested a number of alternative political combinations and regulatory compromises, but the potential for an enduring solution was more questionable. The institutional issues raised by the revival of regulation were charged with political symbolism, and they carried great significance for institutional incumbents in terms of the future shape of power relationships within the government. Twenty years of irresolution and volatility in the politics of reconstitution were in the offing.

Roosevelt launched his initiative on behalf of administrative regulation of the railroads in the campaign of 1904.[21] Soon after the election, the House passed a fairly comprehensive bill that gave the ICC broad rate-making powers and added a special railroad court of appeals. The House had given the bill an overwhelming endorsement, but it stood no chance of passage in the more conservative Senate.

The President was determined to use his landslide victory and strong party position to push a railroad bill through both houses of Congress. Seeing that one comprehensive measure could not possibly be enacted, he looked toward the implementation of a series of less sweeping measures that would gradually expand administrative powers. His rhetoric called for reforms that would secure the interests of the "honest shipper" and the "honest railroad man." Making overtures to the shippers without threatening the railroads translated into a political strategy to gain party unity on the issue by making overtures to moderate Republicans without threatening the Old Guard. It translated into an institutional strategy for strengthening the commission with a limited rate-making power that would invite a graceful retreat by the courts. The Roosevelt challenge focused all the political resources of the most advantageous state-building position of the era in an effort to make a small but decisive break through the structural obstacles to administrative expansion.

Working closely with James Garfield, now head of the Bureau of Corporations, Roosevelt set upon a most cautious proposal. It would allow the commission to fix a maximum rate, but only upon a specific complaint. It would also strengthen the commission's control over railroad finances and accounts. In essence, Roosevelt did not plan to give the commission much more power than it had already claimed under the act of 1887 but was denied because of legislative ambiguity. The Court itself had acknowledged the principle of rate making by the federal commission but had not found that power clearly delegated in the original legislation. Shippers were certain to want more from the government. The railroads could take heart that the President had significantly tempered more sweeping legislative proposals. There was little here to evoke forceful interest opposition. The proposal was designed more as a display of executive leadership than as an experiment with new administrative ideas. When the Old Guard in the Senate balked and took Roosevelt to the mat, it was less because of the substance of the President's attack on the railroads or the substance of his attack on the courts than because Roosevelt was championing another in a series of reform causes in a way that would enhance executive prestige and build administrative power at the expense of those tied to the old governmental order. Overtures to party unity notwithstanding, the challenge of Roosevelt's presidential stewardship could not go unmet.

A regulatory bill sponsored by Congressman William Hepburn contained all the essentials of the President's plan except that it provided for a railroad court of appeals. Roosevelt persuaded Hepburn to remove the court provision and then threw his full support behind the bill. The measure glided through the House. The opposition took its stand in the Senate under the leadership of Old Guard Republican Nelson Aldrich. Aldrich was determined to stall passage of the measure long enough to embarrass the President politically and force the issue of judicial review of administrative decisions to take center stage in the discussion of regulatory reform.

When the Senate Committee on Interstate Commerce reported the Hepburn bill to the floor, Aldrich maneuvered to place South Carolina Democrat and arch Roosevelt foe Benjamin Tillman in charge of the floor debate. Aldrich not only forced Roosevelt to woo one of his most bitter political enemies but threatened to push him far to the left as Democrats and radical Republicans began adding restrictions on judicial review of administrative decisions. Aldrich then made his own stand in favor of either a special railroad court or the broadest possible judicial review if explicit rate-making powers were to be granted to the commission. This was precisely the issue that had broken regulatory legislation in the Senate in the recent past and precisely the issue Roosevelt had tried to sidestep with his original strategy of moderation. Aldrich made it plain that the price of presidential leadership would be a public breach with the party leadership in Congress and that, if the President chose to lead the country, he would have to move toward the honest shipper in a political coalition with the Democrats and appear to be against the honest railroad men, who deserved the full consideration of due process of law in court.

Once again, Roosevelt's electoral mandate and strong party position had not produced institutional harmony. His effort to assert executive leadership on behalf of regulatory reform exacerbated party fragmentation and turned the regulatory debate into a constitutional test of wills over how the prerogatives of the executive, the legislature, and the judiciary were to develop in the new American state. Yet, the President was willing to accept Aldrich's terms for asserting executive leadership and restricting the courts. He worked with Tillman and altered his political strategy toward building a coalition of Democrats and left-leaning Republicans. Aldrich, however, gained his point when the bill as amended to restrict the courts failed to pass the Senate.

Roosevelt could not win in Congress with the conservative wing of his own party leading the opposition. He was forced to switch back and find some accommodation with the Old Guard. The challenge of executive leadership had been met by the Senate leadership. In returning to something very much like his original position, the President now drew cries of betrayal and retreat from Republican radicals as well as Democrats. Under these conditions, a regulatory bill finally passed by an overwhelming majority in the Senate.

The Hepburn Act of June 1906 provided the ICC with the power to set a maximum rate on complaint from a shipper, but it was not much clearer on the scope of judicial review than the act of 1887. It provided that "if upon such hearing as the [circuit] court may determine to be necessary, it appears that the order [of the commission] was regularly made and duly served, and that the carrier is in disobedience of the same, the court shall enforce obedience to such order."[22] All sides in the controversy could claim victory. The Old Guard and the railroads had secured a clause that would allow the court to determine for itself how far-reaching its review of commission decisions should be. Past experience in the federal circuit courts suggested that substantive findings of fact might be reconsidered and new evidence might be presented in the appeal. In this, the Hepburn Act seemed to keep the commission a ward of the courts, allowing it to offer expert opinions for the judges' consideration but not authoritative decisions. On the other hand, radicals, Progressives, and shippers could take heart that the court was being asked by Congress only to ensure that the orders of the commission were "regularly made and duly served." Moreover, the court had been reminded once again, in other sections of the act, that the findings of the commission were to be considered prima facie evidence in any appeal. In this view, because the Court had indicated that it would accept administrative controls over rates if clearly delegated, the Hepburn Act had made an appropriate and sufficient response. The commission, they insisted, had been removed from judicial tutelage and turned into an arm of the legislature.[23]

Roosevelt's compromise with the Old Guard left changes in institutional power relationships an open question. Robert LaFollette, embittered by Roosevelt's settlement, pointed to the commission's new powers over railway accounts and reports as the most concrete advances in the act of 1906.[24] In the end, the courts, the commission, the railroads, and the shippers were left to scramble over exactly what Congress and the President had accomplished.

Roosevelt's moderate regulatory challenge had led him into a costly political and institutional battle. Contrary to his original intentions, parties fragmented and institutional harmony dissolved over the terms of expanding administrative capacities. After the Hepburn Act was signed into law, Roosevelt continued with his plan to pursue regulation one step at a time. With the recession of 1907, he turned his attention to the problems of railroad management and finance. He indicated his sympathy with railroad arguments for a rate increase but advised against pressing this issue until after the elections of 1908. He openly advocated a legalization of pooling, a federal incorporation of the railroads, a public valuation of railroad properties, and federal regulation of railroad securities.[25] No action was taken. Executive resources in this area, as in the other reform areas dealt with in this study, had been fairly well exhausted by the end of 1906. The Hepburn Act represented the limits of Progressive state building under Roosevelt's presidential stewardship.

To recognize the limits is not, however, to dismiss the accomplishment.[26] Roosevelt had turned his electoral mandate into a mandate for federal regulatory reform, and he proved willing and able to see the legislative struggle through to a necessary compromise with the Republican conservatives. A legislative power had been clarified and delegated to an administrative body. The administrative management functions of the federal government had been strengthened. The courts were informally asked to retreat with dignity. The President had moved against that institutional juncture in the early American state where representative pluralism and legislative stalemate fused with judicial supremacy, and in doing so, he jolted an entire mode of governmental operations. As with the other state-building challenges of the Roosevelt years, the results of the effort were uncertain, the shape of the new governmental order still unclear. In each case, Roosevelt broached the basic questions of state structure and governmental operations in America, and though he failed to resolve them, he gave the champions of the administrative reconstitution a new institutional foundation on which to build.

The confrontation

The Supreme Court had several options in reviewing ICC decisions under the Hepburn Act. It could have denied congressional authority to delegate a legislative power such as rate making to an administrative body. This was unlikely, however, because it had already recognized the principle. It could have accepted the rate-making power and interpreted judicial discretion under the act broadly to include a review of the substance of the commission's opinion or to allow new evidence to be offered in judicial appeals. In so doing, it would have allowed the courts to duplicate the work of the commission, rule on the reasonableness of the actual rate set by the commission, and block the rise of an authoritative sphere of administrative action. This was what Aldrich had in mind. Lastly, the Court could have voluntarily restricted its review of the commission's orders to "questions of law," that is, to the legal authority under which the commission acted and the procedures it employed in reaching its decisions. This, of course, was the path toward an administrative reconstitution.

In 1910, the Court indicated its willingness to explore the third alternative and to nurture the administrative instrument it had recently stifled. In the leading case heard under the Hepburn Act, Interstate Commerce Commission *v* Illinois Central Railroad Company, the Court used its broad discretion to restrict voluntarily judicial review of the commission's rulings to questions of law and procedure. With Justice Brewer now alone in dissent, the Court refused to "assail the wisdom of Congress in conferring upon the Commission the power that has been lodged in that body . . . or to attack as crude or inexpedient the action of the

Commission in performance of the administrative functions vested in it, and upon such assumption invoke the exercise of unwarranted judicial power to correct assumed evils."[27] The decision was a landmark in the development of a new American state. By reviewing only "the power to make the order and not the mere expediency or wisdom of having made it," the Court deferred to the commission on the substantive matters of regulation and recognized the integrity of the national administrative domain.[28] Roosevelt and the anticourt forces had gained through judicial self-restraint what they had failed to impose on the judiciary through Congress.

The question immediately arises as to why the Court did not take up the Aldrich invitation to accept the new delegation of rate-making power while continuing with a broad review of commission actions. It is doubtful that the Court was acting on behalf of economic interests, that it had turned proshipper or antirailroad. It is more likely that the Court understood the volatile political nature of the question at hand and the growing precariousness of its own political position. In declaring its determination to refrain from "unwarranted" exercises of judicial power, the Court seemed to be searching for a new and more secure position before the growing democratic attack on the judiciary got out of hand and caused some real damage to its prerogatives and its prestige.

Several pieces of circumstantial evidence lend credence to this view. In the first place, both political parties were pledged to move forward with further reforms in the area of railroad regulation. The debates under the Taft administration had already begun when the *Illinois* decision was rendered, and it was clear that the role of the judiciary in administrative supervision was going to be a major, if not the major, point of contention once again. The Court stood to gain more by redefining its position on its own than having it done by others. Second, Democrats and insurgent Republicans were bringing the movement for the recall of judges and judicial decisions into high gear at this time. Both parties were pledged to judicial reform as well as regulatory reform.[29] Commissioner Charles Prouty, imploring the Court to adopt a narrow review in 1910, revealed how far the political and constitutional questions on railroad regulation had become intertwined. Writing in the *Yale Law Journal,* Prouty warned that if "no substantial progress" was made toward the affirmation of administrative authority and legislative will, there would ensue a renewal of popular agitation against the judicial system "which would not stop until the Constitution itself had been so altered as to enable the people to deal properly with these public servants."[30]

Moreover, the Court's deference to Congress and its recognition of commission authority in the *Illinois* decision did not mark a judicial retreat so much as a determination to work out gradually some modus vivendi with a new kind of governmental agency. Indeed, the Court protected itself by asserting that its prerogative to engage in a more substantive review could not be curtailed and might in a "proper case" become unavoidable. Only a few weeks after the landmark decision, the Court exercised this prerogative, handing down a unanimous opinion nullifying a commission order upon a substantive review of its evidence and findings. The case and the opinion were less sweeping than *Illinois* in their scope and implications, but they served notice to the commission that its new relationship to the judiciary could not be taken for granted. The case, Interstate Commerce Commission *v* Northern Pacific Railroad Company, concerned the commission's new power to determine a through rate upon appeal. The Court refused to allow the commission to "trifle away" an explicit statutory condition of the exercise of this power.[31] Thus, after recognizing a new state of affairs, the Court set out to assert its role in defining a new balance of judicial and administrative authority in interpreting the laws of business regulation. The Court knew that it had a power with explosive political implications and seemed to go out of its way to accommodate the commission in a way that would best preserve its own prerogatives. Its actions suggested that it would now use judicial discretion more cautiously so as to move with, rather than against, the mounting political pressures for change, and that in doing so, it would readjust its position in the new state on its own terms.[32]

As the Court was trying to maneuver quietly into a new institutional position on the regulatory question, the political position and governmental vision of William Howard Taft combined to bring the state-building challenge of business regulation to another explosive constitutional confrontation. Politically, Taft faced a growing Republican insurgency demanding more sweeping regulatory action. At the same time, he was tied to the Old Guard of the party, which had sought protection for the railroads in broad court review. Personally, Taft looked at the railroad regulation issue as a problem of separating powers and compartmentalizing different governmental functions under the appropriate constitutional authorities. Combining political strategy and governmental vision, the President came up with a new formula for joining his party behind business regulation. He gave his support to new legislation that would increase the powers of the ICC so long as provision was made for a specialized railway court.

What the establishment of an executive budget was to Taft's view of the necessary and proper scope of executive authority in a new American state, the establishment of a Commerce Court was for his view of the necessary and proper scope of judicial authority. Both were pet projects perceived by the President as his personal legacy to the reconstitution of government in the face of irresistible demands for an expansion of national administrative services and supports. Both projects were designed to clarify lines of governmental authority and internal control. Roosevelt opposed a specialized court standing over the ICC in the name of building administrative power; Taft championed the court idea as a Progressive reform designed to upgrade the quality and responsibility of judicial decision making in an era of administrative specialization and professional expertise. Specialized administrative courts (Taft envisioned many) would reaffirm constitutional guarantees at a time of expanding administrative discretion. The administrative courts would not only provide close supervision of administrative action, they would aid in the exercise of administrative power by speeding up the appeals process and giving more timely effect to administrative decisions. They promised to institutionalize a cooperative judicial–administrative partnership behind the formation of a new body of administrative law and procedure. Rather than becoming overwhelmed by experts and ultimately accepting its retreat as a fait accompli, the judiciary could use its specialized courts to keep pace with administrators in replacing the formalistic posture of late-century regulation.[33]

Taft was, of course, a vigorous opponent of the political attack on the judiciary, and the railroad court was, of course, a railroad demand. But to treat Taft's position on regulation simply in anti-democratic, prorailroad terms is no more satisfactory than to treat Roosevelt's position in 1906 as populist and antirailroad. Neither President wanted to antagonize powerful railroad or shipper interests in the formulation of regulatory policy. Both envisioned an accommodation of economic interests. Moreover, both sought a political coalition that would bring the divergent strands of the Republican party together, and both knew that the heart of the problem of administrative regulation lay in the reconstitution of institutional power relationships. With regard to this last point, Roosevelt's great insight lay in the institutional obstacles to expanding regulatory powers in the state of courts and parties. It did not, in this instance, extend to the challenge of reestablishing constitutional controls in the face of administrative power. Roosevelt aimed to extort administrative powers from Congress and the courts in order to gain more effective regulatory machinery for dealing with the new problems of the marketplace, but he did not seem to see that success in concentrating administrative powers and insulating them from the Congress and the courts threatened to throw governmental authority itself into internal disarray. Taft accepted the Progressives' zeal for expanding federal regulatory power and matched it with an acute sense of the need to control that power once it was created. He saw that Roosevelt's approach would not solve the problem of American state building; it would merely invert that problem.

Taft's proposal for a Commerce Court was fairly simple on its face. Instead of first adjudicating appeals from the commission's decisions through one of the federal circuit courts of general jurisdiction, one court of special jurisdiction, having the full status of a court of appeals within the federal judicial system, would be created to hear all controversies arising from the commission's decisions. Appeals were to be handled by the Attorney General, thus strengthening the hand of the executive in regulation and separating the tasks of investigation (ICC), prosecution (Attorney General), and adjudication (Commerce Court). Appeals from the Commerce Court were to be referred to the Supreme Court. The new court was to be composed of five judges holding permanent appointments.[34]

The proposal suggested a major revision of the common law view of the judge as a generalist in technical matters with an eye toward a Progressive ideal of making the judge a technical as well as a legal expert. The thrust of the reform was for greater specialization, greater proficiency, and greater clarity in governmental operations. Yet, however genuine, however innovative, however farsighted Taft's vision of Progressive regulatory reform was, it raised political and institutional questions that were as untimely as they were unavoidable. The proposal ran directly against the grain of the radicals' vision of legislative supremacy, and the subtlety of Taft's constitutional theory was lost on those who knew a concession to the railroads and the Old Guard when they saw one. Moreover, cooperation among experts and institutional harmony were long-term prospects. Turning judges into experts on technical matters was bound to rekindle an old and bitter struggle to redefine the administrative domain and the judicial prerogative. Finally, a Commerce Court was bound to throw a wrench into the Supreme Court's own quest for a quiet accommodation to administrative power by pressing an issue it had sought to defuse. The Court would be saddled with a new ward to oversee administrative operations just as it was defining its own limits in the field. It would have to handle the inevitable disruptions in institutional power relationships and, in the high tide of the Progressive insurgency, its decisions were likely to take on a significance beyond its control.

Working through his Attorney General, George Wickersham, Taft championed a comprehensive regulatory proposal that contained the basic demands of all the economic interests and Republican party factions.[35] In addition to a Commerce Court, he proposed the legalization of pooling. On the other side, he supported an extension of ICC rate-making power that would allow the agency to suspend a rate on its own initiative and investigate its reasonableness without waiting for a specific complaint from a shipper. He also supported federal regulation of railroad securities and shipper control over routing. This regulatory package far surpassed the Hepburn Act in its scope and implications, but in addressing the major demands of all groups, it also gave each that much more to oppose.

Insurgent Senator Albert Cummins stymied the President's bill by adding scores of amendments in committee. He then seized the initiative for the radicals. He personally questioned the value of the railroad court proposal, seeing it as redundant at best, as a usurpation of ICC (and legislative) authority at worst. It was challenged by the radicals as a distortion of the traditional and proper role of the judiciary and as a special support for the railroads against the people (and the shippers). Yet, Cummins understood what the court proposal meant to the President, and he held out support for it in return for pushing the remainder of the legislation far to the left.

The insurgents' proposal prohibited pooling and revived the long- and short-haul clause. It extended the time the commission had to suspend a rate for investigation and placed the burden of proving the reasonableness of rates squarely on the railroads. Even the sacred Commerce Court proposal was modified. The insurgents limited the term of office for Commerce Court judges to five years, after which they would rotate back to the regular circuit courts. If the whole idea behind the Commerce Court was specialization and technical expertise, this rotation provision cast doubt upon its value. Moreover, the rotation provision made the court an even more odd and suspect institution within the judicial system as a whole. From the beginning, its claim to full status as a federal court of appeals was undermined.[36]

The Old Guard senators balked at the insurgents' handiwork but found their President willing to ride along with the compromise. The best they could do was to remove the clause concerning federal regulation of railroad securities and replace it with a special federal commission to study the securities problem.[37] The Mann–Elkins Act, named for the two reluctant supporters who happened to head the House and Senate committees on interstate commerce, passed with overwhelming bipartisan support in June 1910. An awkward coalition of insurgents intent on making the ICC a strong arm of the legislature for restricting the railroads and a President intent on revitalizing the role of the judiciary in administrative regulation had seen the bill through. Neither the concept, the coalition, nor the institutional arrangements gave much hope for a stable resolution of the regulatory question.

The first omen of the fate of the new form of judicial supervision was Taft's appointment of Martin Knapp as Chief Justice of the Commerce Court. Knapp had been the leading ICC commissioner for over a decade, and the President may well have believed that this appointment would ensure cooperation between commission and court on technical matters. But Knapp had recently found himself holding a minority position in commission decisions. He perceived the growing political bias in favor of the shippers in the legislature, and he was instinctively more sympathetic with the railroads' position than the emergent new majority of commissioners.[38] Knapp accepted the court position to check legislative agitation against the railroads and to resolve regulatory issues as he would have wanted them resolved as a commissioner.

Under the very best of circumstances, establishing a good working relationship between the new court and the ICC would have been a difficult and extended process, but Knapp's appointment transformed a healthy conflict within the commission into a stark, destructive conflict between two institutions vying for position within the regulatory arena. Soon Knapp's court was giving a thorough review to the commission's evidence and findings and indelicately overturning one commission order after another. Commissioners who had previously supported the special court idea as a Progressive reform now perceived it as a new obstruction and a usurpation of authority duly granted the commission by Congress.[39] The actions of the new court appeared all too reminiscent of the judicial imperialism of the late nineteenth century and threatened to rob the commission of the authority it had struggled for decades to gain. Knapp's exercise of judicial authority dashed visions of cooperation among experts and numbered the days of Taft's experiment with revitalizing the judiciary in the age of administrative expansion.

Appeals from the Commerce Court to the Supreme Court thrust the latter institution into the center of the political debate it had cautiously avoided in 1910. The scope of judicial review of administrative decisions was the critical question once again. Knapp tried to articulate a position that would give some teeth to his new charge while recognizing an appropriate sphere for administrative action. He argued that the Commerce Court was bound to the commission's findings of fact but that it held inalienable prerogatives as a court and equal authority as an expert tribunal to make an independent judgment of those findings.[40] Indeed, why else create a specialized administrative court if not to accept the results of administrative investigations and give an authoritative opinion about administrative decisions? In dealing with this assertion of judicial authority, the Supreme Court overturned four of the first five Commerce Court decisions.[41] By elaborating the line of argument outlined in its *Illinois* decision, the Supreme Court may well have been trying to save its new ward by imposing moderation, but its actions were inevitably taken as a judicial condemnation of the entire experiment. The reversals of the Commerce Court confirmed the radicals' conviction that judicial controls were, in fact, an irrelevance and hardened relationships among the Court, the commission, and Congress that had been quite flexible in 1910. In its annual report for 1911, the commission used the Supreme Court's own arguments to declare itself the authoritative voice of legislative will and to press for some relief from this new judicial intrusion.[42] It found a receptive audience.

The election of 1910 had fanned the fires of anticourt sentiment throughout the nation. The Commerce Court was an all too obvious national target for the Progressive and Democratic campaigns for the recall of judges and court decisions at the local level. The fire raged out of control in 1912. In that year, the Supreme Court denied the Commerce Court the authority to hear the appeals of shippers whose petitions had been denied by the ICC. In effect, the Commerce Court was only open to the grievances of the railroads. Even worse, impeachment proceedings were opened against one of the judges of the Commerce Court for using his office to promote his own private interests in the railroads. By August 1912, both houses of Congress had passed legislation to abolish the new institution.[43]

Beneath the attack on the Commerce Court lay the disintegration of the Republican party. It was at this time that Roosevelt cast his support for the judicial recall. This decision, more than any other, made his break with Taft and Root irreversible and secured his leadership of a new Progressive party. As Roosevelt had made clear to Aldrich in the legislative struggle of 1906, the restriction of the courts was a form of democracy he could live with. Roosevelt, of course, opposed the Commerce Court as an unfortunate setback to his own bold offensive for administrative regulation of the railroads.[44] Taft met the movement to abolish the railroad court squarely on the issue of recall. He stood firmly by his strict constitutional vision against the Progressive insurgency. The President's veto message declared complete and "utter opposition to the abolition of a court because its decisions may not always meet the approval of a majority of the Legislature. It is introducing a recall of the judiciary, which in its way, is quite as objectionable as the ordinary popular method proposed."[45]

The Attorney General pleaded the administration's case for continuing the experiment. Wickersham garnered evidence to prove that the Commerce Court had succeeded in eliminating delay and that despite differences with the commission and reversals by the Supreme Court, it had established a much better overall record of upholding the ICC than the regular circuit courts. He argued that the heart of the problem was that neither Congress nor the Supreme Court had yet given any authoritative definition to the relationship between administrative orders and judicial review. He proposed a statutory specification of the Commerce Court's powers of review that would limit it to questions of law and enable it to hear the appeals of shippers who had been denied relief by the commission.[46]

But the radicals had little patience for working out the bugs. They were no longer bound by the political compromise of 1910; they no longer needed the administration's support. Abolishing the court promised to complete their work and to turn administrative regulation into an uncompromising extension of legislative power to restrict the railroads. Once again Taft's efforts to reconstitute the government in the first half of his term dissolved under the shifting political sands of the second half. The awkward coalition he had entered into to gain the Commerce Court broke down in a constitutional confrontation over its survival. In October 1913, Woodrow Wilson ignored the protestations of his own Attorney General and signed the bill abolishing this cornerstone of Taft's Madisonian revival.[47]

The demise of the Commerce Court ushered out the era of judicial review of administrative findings of fact and ushered in a new era of administrative justice. Commissioners made policy and judges reviewed the procedures employed. Ironically, however, administrative detachment from the courts had tied the ICC more closely than ever before to Congress. There was no mandate here for independent administrative action. Insurgents expected deference to Congress, and through the vicissitudes of the politics of reconstitution, they had succeeded in doing what had hitherto been impossible: They had secured a regulatory mandate that clearly articulated one particular point of view. As President Wilson soon discovered, this new arrangement was far from satisfactory.

Scientific management in the new democracy

The regulatory proposals of Roosevelt and Taft looked toward a balance of governmental support for the interests of both the railroads and the shippers. By 1913, however, the railroads had emerged as the big losers in securing an institutional endorsement of their concerns. Presidential efforts on behalf of legalized pooling had failed. The special court for railway appeals had been abolished. The railroads carried the full burden of proving the reasonableness of any given rate to the ICC. The smaller shippers, on the other hand, found just what they wanted – a commission with sweeping controls over rates, a limited court review, and a new regime that lacked any obvious center of political support for railroad management concerns.

Beyond the continued ban on pooling and the abolition of the special court of appeals, the most striking failure of the railroads in the prewar years was their inability to convince the newly empowered ICC that general rate increases were necessary to maintain and improve rail services. Since the debates of the Roosevelt administration, railroad managers had argued that although rates were rising, they were still too low to guarantee the continued stability, solvency, and reinvestment necessary for the continued development of the railroad industry as a whole. This point of view found impressive support among professional economists. As far back as 1905, Henry Carter Adams had identified the problem of railroad credit and capital deficiency as the concern that should be primary in the government's approach to railroad regulation.[48] In 1911, the special commission created under the Mann–Elkins Act to study the problem of railroad securities reported sympathetically on the railroads' plea for financial relief and recommended that the government adopt a long-term view of the problem of capital investments. This commission, chaired by the prestigious Arthur Hadley, found that "neither the rate of return actually received on the par value of American railroad bonds and stocks today, nor the security which can be offered for additional railroad investments in the future will make it easy to raise the needed amount of capital . . . A 'reasonable' return [to the carrier] is one which, under honest accounting and responsible management, will attract the amount of investor's money needed for the development of our national railroad facilities."[49] Moreover, in 1910 the railroads established a Bureau of Railway Economics to propagate a theory of scientific management that would direct the plans and policies of the state toward corporatist cooperation in the development of the national railway system.[50] Still, the voice of the professional and the power of the corporation notwithstanding, the cooperative vision in regulation did not make its way into ICC policies in its early years of power.

Ironically, after decades of struggle to gain an unprecedented concentration of national administrative controls, the ICC emerged from its legislative victories of 1910–13 a bit bewildered as to how to approach the railroads' financial difficulties. At the heart of the problem lay the fact that Congress had specifically designed the commission's mandate to check the rise of railroad rates. There was nothing in the law directing it to consider the impact of the overall rate level on the health and well-being of the railroad industry. As the commission stated in 1910, "We must not regard too seriously ... the effort of railroad counsel to establish this Commission *in loco parentis* to the railroads ... The Government has not undertaken to become the directing mind in railroad management."[51] Added to this was the fact that those who had led the commission in its twentieth-century struggle for power and who were most inclined toward independent action left the commission between 1910 and 1914. Martin Knapp, Charles Prouty, and Franklin Lane took their cues from the long struggle to expand the scope of the regulatory vision. They were replaced by men who tended to view the commission's powers in terms of the specific mandate of 1910. Moreover, even the independent thinker had to admit that the commission's formal powers had far outstripped its ability to make informed judgments about railroad needs. As Prouty continually pointed out, railroad management's protestations of inadequate returns could not be confirmed by independent experts until a public valuation had been made of the railroads' physical assets and liabilities. The reasonableness of a rate was of necessity a political rather than a scientific judgment at this time, and the political calculus for the commission was fairly clear. Indeed, underlying all the reasons for ICC hesitation in this period was the commission's certain knowledge that action taken to relieve the railroads would raise the wrath of the agency's most ardent supporters in Congress. Those whose powers were so recently won were reluctant to cross those who had catapulted them to the commanding heights.[52]

In these circumstances, the commission latched on to an alternative view of scientific management in setting railroad policy. During hearings on the railroads' request for a rate increase in 1910, shippers' attorney Louis Brandeis had offered a compilation of statistical data and expert opinion as scientific proof that waste and mismanagement on the part of the railroad corporations were largely responsible for their financial difficulties. Taking inspiration from Frederick Winslow Taylor's work on increasing industrial efficiency, Brandeis presented an eminently respectable argument for denying governmental support to the railroads. In this view, to indulge the industry with higher rates was to make the public bear an extra burden for corporate extravagance. This was not only deemed unnecessary, it was considered highly ineffective. Only by denying rate increases could the government hope to force the railroads to adopt sound principles of scientific management in their own operations and thus get to the root cause of their financial difficulties.[53]

The Brandeis view of scientific management allowed a politically insecure and institutionally limited ICC to take refuge in a strong disciplinary posture in administrative regulation. The commission could recognize, even sympathize, with the railroads' financial difficulties, but it stead-fastly avoided direct involvement in their relief by withholding support and proposing to pressure the industry into economy and efficiency. Of course, to hold the alternative corporatist view of scientific management, one did not have to deny the existence of waste and mismanagement in the industry or the need to have these corrected. One merely had to interpret these shortcomings as further signs that the government needed to take positive steps to save the railroads from themselves and argue that a public resource as vital as the national railway network needed to be nurtured and protected by governmental supervisors.[54] Scientific man-agement, like all the other great Progressive standards of institutional reform, underscored very different visions of the new mode of gov-ernmental operations and of the interests to be served by the state. Be-neath the apparent consensus on reform rhetoric lay a new phase in the politics of reconstitution.

After denying the railroads their rate requests in 1910, the commission retained Brandeis as its special counsel. The signs of a new organiza-tional, procedural, and intellectual synthesis were unmistakable. Between 1910 and 1917, the commission weathered a constant barrage of railroad pleas for across-the-board rate relief. Its decisions were divided, but only in 1914 did a majority concede a 5 percent increase across two major classification territories, and then only on special prodding from the President.[55] The commission's general disposition on the rate question closed the only possibility left to the railroads for turning the Progressive regulatory machinery of 1910 toward their interests. Railroad manage-ment received encouraging words of support and sympathetic under-standing, but the commission's policies were decidedly proshipper.

The commission's use of its new powers may be faulted as both shortsighted and one-sided. Yet, it also represented a paradigm of admin-istrative deference to Congress. The agency sought refuge from an explo-sive political issue by interpreting its charge narrowly, and there can be little doubt that it was acting much as its sponsors had originally in-tended. Ironically, after throwing off the shackles of court review, the commission adopted the perspective of the strict constructionist. It acted as a ward of Congress and refused to break new ground in public policy without a new mandate. There was growing suspicion in all quarters that something had to be wrong with a regulatory posture that pushed a vital industry further down the path of financial crisis. The organizational, procedural, and intellectual synthesis of 1910–13 was outdated from its inception. But the machinery of government had just begun to move in concert, and it would prove difficult to alter course.

Woodrow Wilson, leader of the triumphant new Democracy, bore the full weight of the regulatory dilemma. The center of his party lay in the South, a stronghold of support for the sentiments of the small shipper. Moreover, Wilson's electoral campaign on behalf of the average "man on the make" had earned him the respect of the insurgent Republicans from the West. To consolidate a Progressive–Democratic coalition in the area of railroad policy, the President had only to seal the fate of the Commerce Court.

Yet, Wilson soon became uncomfortable with the political economy of his Progressive–Democracy. Demand for rail services was increasing, and the outbreak of war in Europe emphasized the nation's dependence on rail transportation for national defense. Under existing national policy, badly needed terminal facilities were not being built, capital stock was deteriorating, and investors were becoming reluctant to loan money for capital redevelopment.[56] The leader of the new Democracy grew increasingly sympathetic to the plight of the railroad managers and increasingly frustrated by the timid and narrow outlook of the ICC. The question was, could the President turn his regime around?

The new regime's first major statement on the issue of railroad regulation was a request for more information. In 1913, a Valuation Act was signed into law authorizing a massive governmental study of railroad assets and liabilities. The purpose was to give the government some standards by which to judge whether or not the railroads were getting a fair return on the value of their property. Robert LaFollette had long been an enthusiastic supporter of the idea, but at this point there was little opposition. All interested parties were confident that their position would be vindicated by independent experts. The undertaking vastly expanded the responsibilities and staff of the ICC. It also put off concrete action for railroad relief. In passing the measure, Congress indicated that it might at some future time redefine the commission's rules for rate making. In the short term, however, it only agreed to start an investigation that was expected to take about a decade to complete. Charles Prouty left his position as commissioner to direct the valuation project.[57]

The President wanted more immediate changes. As early as January 1914, he announced his support for the railroads' new plea for a general rate increase. The commission responded lamely with piecemeal action. When the war broke out in Europe, the railroads renewed their request.

Wilson now wrote directly to Commissioner Winthrop Daniels, calling attention to the railroads' desperate financial situation. The commission relented with an extension of its earlier action, but then returned to a policy of denial and piecemeal action in 1915.[58] With this sign of renewed administrative intransigence, Wilson decided to go to the heart of the problem. He appealed to Congress.

The appeal was delivered early in December 1915. The President made clear his interest in a basic reconsideration of the present course of regulatory policy: "The transportation problem is an exceedingly serious and pressing one in this country. There has from time to time of late been reason to fear that our railroads would not much longer be able to cope with it successfully, as at present equipped and coordinated." He then endorsed the principle of regulation by federal commission and acknowledged that it had "fully justified the hopes and expectations of those by whom the policy of regulation was originally proposed." He also avoided a frontal assault on the Progressive–Democratic solution of 1913. "The question is not what we should undo. It is whether there is anything else we can do." He refrained from making a specific policy recommendation, asking only for "a new commission of inquiry to ascertain by a thorough canvass of the whole question whether our laws as at present framed and administered are as serviceable as they might be in the solution of the problem."[59]

Wilson's growing sense of the urgency of the railroad situation was combined with a sense of the delicate political and institutional maneuver in which he was engaged. He appeared caught between a determination to change the ICC and a determination to maintain his cooperative partnership with Congress. He had to disengage the legislature from the railroad solution of 1913 without pushing himself into a confrontation with his governing coalition. The master legislative leader of the era found the complex procedure of working through Congress to change the commission to favor the railroads painstakingly slow and ultimately ineffective.

Francis Newlands, chairman of the Senate Committee on Interstate Commerce, rallied to the President's call and became Wilson's chief congressional ally in the effort to change federal regulatory policy. There was, however, little enthusiasm elsewhere in Congress. The President had asked for little, but the House leadership stalled. Wilson informed House leaders that the inquiry was more than a suggestion; it was an integral part of his legislative program. Still, it was not until November 20, 1916, a precious year after the original call, that a joint congressional committee under Newlands's leadership began to hear testimony.[60]

The Newlands committee reopened the debates of 1910 with few surprises. The small shippers of the South and West defended the status quo. Shippers in the larger northern cities were more sympathetic to reforms that would relieve congestion, upgrade carrying capacities, and improve terminal facilities. On the other hand, state railroad commissioners argued vigorously against railroad pleas for a nationalization of all regulation. The railroads stressed the irrationality of the crazy quilt of state regulatory laws and called attention to new Supreme Court rulings in support of establishing a single regulatory system. This issue touched a sensitive nerve in the South and the West. William Jennings Bryan was paraded before the committee to remind the party in power of its roots and to defend the traditions embodied in state regulatory laws.[61] The committee continued to meet through 1917, but the pace of events made their deliberations irrelevant.

Meanwhile, railway labor unions had capitalized on the threat of war and the drive toward preparedness. To avert a nationwide strike in the fall of 1916, Wilson threw his support behind legislation to grant labor an eight-hour day. The President's proposal contained two provisions designed to meet the interests of railroad management. The first would increase the number of commissioners and thus allow the President to change regulatory policy through new appointments. The second would establish a special commission to report on the impact of increased labor costs on the railroads. The small shippers had long feared the demands of organized labor and found this linkage of labor and management concerns insufferable. Newlands informed the President that his proposals would tie up the Senate in extended debates. The House responded by passing the eight-hour-day bill without either of the President's provisions. Wilson decided against putting the matter to a test.[62] The Adamson Eight Hour Day Act brought railway labor into its own as an interest to be reckoned with in regulation and left the railroads squeezed by the government from two sides.

Wilson reaffirmed his determination to change the commission's attitudes in January 1917, when he nominated Commissioner Winthrop Daniels for a second term. Daniels was Wilson's personal confidant on the commission. He was generally credited with securing the rate increases of 1914, and he was the most consistent and outspoken advocate of railroad management's position. The nomination was secured by loyal Democrats, but it threw the small shippers and the old insurgent Republicans into a rage. Albert Cummins, architect of the system of 1913, led the assault on Daniels and all who sought to twist the mandate of Congress into support for the railroads. Progressive Republicans used the Daniels affair to saddle the Democrats with the prorailroad label and to ally powerful shipper groups behind them in opposition to the administration. Afterward, the President's determination to alter the commission seemed to fade. Late in 1917, he had the opportunity to make three other appointments to the agency, but he chose figures who offered the railroads little hope for a new direction.[63] Wilson had not changed his position, but he had changed his strategy. The crisis at hand had grown to a magnitude requiring an entirely different form of control. In the end, the President yielded the commission to Congress.

Considering the pressures of war preparedness, Wilson's resolve to turn federal regulatory policy around is most remarkable for its paltry results. Symbolically, he had gone a long way toward discrediting the system of 1913 and pulling his party away from it, but substantively, he was reduced to skirmishing around the edges of Congress's handiwork while the transportation situation became increasingly chaotic. Like the retreat on civil service reform and the defeat on army reorganization, the failure to spark concerted action in support of the railroads shows a President who was as much the captive as the leader of the new Democracy. In each case, Wilson was caught between the imperatives for institutional development and the nature of his governing coalition. In each case, the President's cosmopolitan reform vision ran counter to the provincial interests of his congressional power base. In each case, the institutional machinery of the new American state was brought to the brink of a war poised for a display of impotence.

The crisis of governmental authority

Soon after the Newlands committee opened its inquiry, the magnitude of the nation's railroad problem was revealed in full. America had not yet entered the war, but it was actively engaged in supplying war materials to Britain and France. Severe car shortages and inadequate terminal facilities backed up shipments from New York to Chicago in the winter of 1916–17. National freight exceeded the carrying capacity of the railroads by upward of 100,000 carloads.[64] The long predicted transportation crisis had arrived.

So had a crisis of governmental authority. The government's first response to the freight glut was to appeal to the railroad managers for help. The Council of National Defense called upon the carriers to merge their "individual and competitive activities" and create a single national system of transportation. A Special Committee on National Defense of the American Railroad Association was formed on April 11, 1917. The Railway War Board, as the committee was called, was heralded as a demonstration of the capacities of the railroad managers to make their industry work through voluntary cooperation. It was America's answer to public ownership. But it had not worked in the 1880s, and it did not work now.[65]

As suggested in the preceding chapter, the enthusiasm of the captains of industry for voluntary cooperation under the Council of National Defense did not readily translate into action. The regional managers of the Railway War Board found it difficult to overcome the competitive instincts of the railroads in their areas so as to make common use of their facilities. Not only was the coercive power of the state missing, but official government policy still rested on the side of competition. Voluntary cooperation was seriously impeded by repeated warnings from the Attorney General that the antitrust and antipooling laws were still in effect and that railroad managers were liable for any violations. Moreover, the government had no machinery to indicate to the carriers what shipments were to receive priority.[66] Voluntary cooperation could not substitute for state direction because state action was a bundle of contradictions. The government was simply too incoherent to support the private remedy.

Contradictions in the government's policy toward the railroads in 1917 were most clearly manifested at the ICC. At first, the ICC lent its full support to the program of voluntary unification. Commissioner Edgar Clark sat as an ex-officio member on the Railway War Board. When, in May, Congress established a Division of Car Service at the commission to deal with the problem of car shortages, the agency chose a prominent railroad official to head it. E. H. DeGroot worked closely with the War Board's Committee on Car Service and lent the voluntary effort the aura of ICC authority.[67] Still, the ICC steadfastly refused to extend its cooperation with railroad management to the issue of rates.

The railroads asked for a 15 percent rate increase in March 1917 and again in October. The first request was denied in June and the second in December. The railroads argued that under the Adamson Act labor costs had jumped dramatically. They pointed out that bank loans were becoming increasingly difficult to obtain and that the government's own efforts to finance the war interfered with railroad efforts to obtain money for capital improvements. National defense alone justified financial support. The rate request tested the government's capacity to sustain a new and consistent course of action, to put all its efforts behind the program of maximizing the efficiency of the transportation network through voluntary cooperation. The ICC responded by denying that it had the authority to grant an across-the-board rate increase to alleviate the railroads' financial problems, by pointing to recent increases in corporate profits, and by turning its early support for the Railway War Board into criticism of the inefficiencies and deficiencies of the railroad managers' efforts.[68]

The commission's response was obviously inadequate and its position increasingly untenable. Absolving itself of responsibility, it sent a special message to Congress in early December proclaiming the failure of the government's entire approach to the railroad problem. The agency outlined two alternative courses of action. The government either had to commit itself formally to railroad unification under private operation by lifting all antitrust and antipooling restrictions and providing the railroads with government loans, or it had to take control of the railroads and unify operations itself.[69] Although the commission's message appeared to substitute for its refusal to reopen the case for a 15 percent rate increase, it did not implicate its rate decisions directly. Indeed, either unification plan promised to lessen the need for further rate increases. There was no suggestion of an abdication of power by the ICC or any acknowledgment that a unification of railway operations would necessarily impair the statutory authority of the agency over rates.

At the moment of truth, the commission protected itself, criticized the railroads, and passed the hard decisions to Congress.[70] Wilson quickly seized the initiative. Preempting debate, he advised Congress on December 26 that he was invoking powers granted in the Army Appropriation Act of 1916 to take direct control of the railroads.[71] The President proposed to resolve the contradictions in government policy himself and to place all the powers of the executive branch behind the effort to reestablish order in the transportation industry. The doors were opened to a third alternative for the coherent articulation of internal governmental controls in the area of business regulation.

The railroad managers would have preferred to keep unification in private hands, but the President had several good reasons for overruling them and invoking the public option. Private controls offered little hope of defusing shipper opposition or appeasing labor. Public operation suggested the possibility for a reconciliation of these divergent interests under the auspices of the state. Moreover, federal control offered the most efficient means of overcoming the railroads' critical financial problems and of circumventing the crazy quilt of local regulatory laws. Finally, public operation allowed Wilson to sustain the supremacy of public men and personal loyalists in the extraordinary machinery of wartime government. The President chose his son-in-law, Secretary of the Treasury William McAdoo, as Director General of the United States Railroad Administration.[72]

The railroads accepted public operation as a temporary measure and looked forward to the return to private control. Ironically, however, McAdoo's inevitable dependence on the railway managers in making public operation work turned shippers into the most vigorous opponents of the new experiment in executive control. McAdoo tried to present the Railroad Administration as a showcase for the cooperative ideal in scientific management, but he was forced to go to extremes. Executive control was first and foremost an improvisation in which crisis conditions and limited governmental resources dictated institutional form, procedure, and policy. The imperatives of moving freight outweighed shipper interests in economy and the high ideals of harmony in the marketplace. McAdoo packed the inner cabinet of the Railroad Administration with the nation's top railroad executives and shut the shippers out.[73] The cooperative ideal in scientific management looked suspiciously like executive capitulation to the railroads.

The strength of executive control lay in administrative management by executive order. The major obstacle to the free exercise of the executive order in the government's operation of the railroads was the voice of the shipper, the ICC. Neither the shippers nor the commissioners linked railroad consolidation under executive control with the curtailment of the commission's powers. McAdoo did. Early in 1918, when the administration proposed legislation specifying the terms and conditions of federal control of the railroads, McAdoo asked for a total suspension of the ICC's rate-making powers. He argued that the ICC could make no special claims to knowledge of what a reasonable rate was and that war operations made flexibility under a single authority imperative.[74]

Albert Cummins took up the shippers' cause in an effort to maintain the commission's powers intact. A compromise was finally reached that permitted rates to be set by executive order, stripped the commission of its power to suspend rates, but appeared to grant the ICC the appellate status it had held between 1906 and 1910. In fact, however, the commission's power to investigate rates upon complaint from a shipper had been limited further in recognition of the new state of affairs. The agency was directed to recognize that competition had given way to consolidation. It was told to consider the impact of rates on the unified railway system and to take account of the findings and recommendations of the President and the Director General. McAdoo accepted this as a clear subordination of the commission to executive control.

Wilson made passage of the Federal Control Act a test of party loyalty to the administration. Despite a few defections from the South and the West, the Democrats carried the measure in March. Embracing McAdoo's system of executive control, they also assumed the political burden of having sponsored government by railroad managers.[75]

The new system of rate making was tested in the spring of 1918. The Railroad Wage Commission, under the direction of Interior Secretary Franklin Lane, recommended a $300 million wage increase for railroad labor. McAdoo accepted the recommendation with a promise to railroad management of a corresponding increase in railroad rates. On May 25, he announced a general 25 percent rate increase to take effect the following month. The Director General then bypassed the ICC grievance mechanism and set up his own system for making adjustments at the local level. The new grievance machinery was composed of thirty local traffic committees representing management and shipper interests. It was characteristic of McAdoo's directorship that railroad managers were ensured a majority on these committees. Shippers remained disaffected and pressed for a revival of the ICC. It was also characteristic of McAdoo's directorship that ICC personnel were involved in decision making in an advisory capacity but that the commission itself was compelled to take a subordinate position at the periphery of power in war administration. When McAdoo openly challenged the commission's determination to exercise its limited powers to review shipper grievances caused by the June rate increase, the agency's disaffection came to the surface. "It is inconceivable," the commission protested, "that the Congress did a vain thing in conferring on this Commission power to determine whether or not the rates initiated by the Director General are just and reasonable."[76]

The Federal Control Act specified that the Railroad Administration would remain in operation for twenty-one months after the end of hostilities. McAdoo resigned his post as Director General in November 1918, and Wilson appointed Walker Hines, chairman of the board of the Santa Fe Railroad, to head the agency in the postwar period. During 1918, Hines had emerged as McAdoo's chief advisor on federal operations. He had a well-known history of contempt for shipper and labor interests, but these sentiments gave way to a determination to fend off attacks on the authority of the Railroad Administration and to place the executive management alternative in the best possible light in postwar politics.[77]

Hines took on a most difficult task. A shift in electoral politics had given the Republicans control of Congress. The Railroad Administration had been a campaign issue, and Senator Albert Cummins and Representative John Esch, the new chairmen of the commerce committees, had announced their intention to revive the ICC before the official end of federal operations. The new Director General scrambled to redress the imbalance of interests in the Railroad Administration and to forestall the Republican attack. He gave shippers equal representation on the local traffic committees. He involved federal and state railway commissioners more closely in Railroad Administration decisions. Most importantly, he pledged to avoid further rate increases. Hines's actions turned the Railroad Administration from an organization of railroad managers appeasing labor into an organization of railroad managers appeasing shippers. But then, the Director General surely knew that labor would oppose the revival of the ICC as adamantly as railroad management.[78]

These concessions did delay congressional action, but in the fall of 1919 a bill was passed to restore the full authority of the federal and state commissioners. Hines appealed to Wilson, claiming that the bill interfered with the fulfillment of executive responsibilities, that it created an undesirable division of federal authority, and that it gave the state commissions a dangerous check on federal operations. Wilson vetoed the measure, but he rested his objections solely on the need to maintain federal control over intrastate traffic.[79] Hines's victory was clearly only a temporary stay. Like Taft's reprieve for the Commerce Court and the ideal of judicial authority, Wilson's veto merely delayed the demise of executive authority. The politics of reconstitution had already entered a new phase.

Like the War Industries Board, the United States Railroad Administration intruded into an ongoing struggle over the reconstitution of institutional power relationships within American government. In both cases, the scramble for political power and institutional position shifted sharply but never ended. After May 1918, a set of new institutional ties began to emerge in the Railroad Administration that reached out to all the interests contending for federal services and supports, but time was short and the patience of the aggrieved parties thin.[80] The railroads never had any intention of suffering federal operation beyond the emergency, and for others, the legitimacy of the experiment had been fatally undermined at the outset by the executive's dependence on the administrative capacities of the railroad managers. The Railroad Administration could not fulfill the dreams of those who championed executive control or the cooperative ideal in scientific management. Suspended in an inchoate state, it sustained the government through a major crisis of authority but failed to resolve the dilemma of reconstituting authority.

The consolidation

After the elections of 1918, McAdoo and Hines pressed Congress and the President for a five-year extension of the experiment with federal operation and executive control. They argued that the potential benefits to be derived from the unification and standardization of the national railway system had not yet been tapped and that these benefits would become apparent only with the return to normalcy. McAdoo, in particular, also feared that a thorough airing of the regulatory issue at the scheduled time of reconversion to private control (August 1920) would make the Railroad Administration a campaign issue once again and further damage the prospects of the Democratic party. This political calculus was, of course, reason enough to preclude a favorable response from Congress. The alternative became an early termination of the experiment that would place the burden of the regulatory issue on the Republicans and allow the Democrats to share in the solution. But too early a return to private control might endanger a badly needed federal appropriation for the railroads. The President decided to revert to private control on January 1, 1920, later extending the date in the midst of a legislative deadlock to March 1.[81]

The President offered no proposals for regulation. He professed that he had no solution and only hoped that Congress would recognize the limitations of the regulatory posture of the prewar years.[82] Wilson's detachment freed his fellow partisans from the administration's identification with the carriers and focused responsibility on the congressional leadership. Presidential indifference set the stage for the final solution to America's historical–structural dilemma in regulation – the mandate for administrative independence. Unable to sustain judicial or executive supervision and no longer able to agree on a clear policy of its own, Congress opted for expanding the range of regulatory possibilities and transferring full responsibility for making the decisive choices to the commission.

The contending interests would have preferred something a little more definite. Organized labor lobbied a bold plan for permanent government ownership. The Association of Railway Executives lobbied for the establishment of a Secretary of Transportation who, like the Director General of wartime, would give an executive opinion concerning rate requests before they were reviewed by the commission. Failing this, they pressed for a Transportation Board that would inform the ICC of the rate of return necessary for the maintenance of efficient rail service. Shippers spoke with regional biases but generally opposed labor and management efforts to circumvent the ICC. Those from the South and West feared the specification of a new rule of rate making or new labor policies that would guarantee rate increases in the future.[83] No group would be able to claim a clear victory from the action the government took, but then again, none was totally ignored.

Working under the pressures of the President's January 1 deadline, the House passed a regulatory bill in late November; the Senate, in late

December. The proposals signaled the demise of the Progressive Republican consensus. John Esch and Albert Cummins had championed two very different pieces of legislation and faced each other in a standoff.

It was Cummins, the architect of the regulatory system of 1913, who had the more dramatic change of heart. Sometime during 1919, he became an ardent convert to the cooperative ideal in scientific management. His bill called for compulsory consolidation of the national railway network by merging the weak with the strong roads. He called for professional supervision of the consolidated railway network by a new Transportation Board. The ICC was to continue to regulate rates, but the Transportation Board was to assume all management functions. Together the ICC and the Transportation Board were to guarantee the railroads a specified minimum income so as to meet the nation's need to maintain rail services. Although touching base with railroad management interests in some particulars, the Cummins plan diverged from them in others. Most importantly, it called for a recapture of excessive earnings from the stronger roads to support the weaker ones. The plan also antagonized organized labor by prohibiting railroad strikes.[84]

The Iowa Progressive emerged in 1920 as the true independent in railroad regulation. He offered a coherent and specific law directing the positive use of administrative power in the interests of securing harmony in the marketplace and maintaining the railroads as a public resource. He found his old friend, Robert LaFollette, an unreconstructed radical and his most formidable opponent on the Senate floor. The right to strike and the guaranteed income for the railroads became the major points of contention. Cummins yielded the guaranteed minimum income to a compromise that directed the ICC to provide a 5.5 percent return on the fair value of railroad property for a five-year postwar transition period. Passage was secured without other major changes, but only with the help of Senate Democrats.[85]

The Esch bill was more specifically in the prewar regulatory tradition and gained its support from shipper interests. It did not specify a new rule of rate making. It did not establish a new agency to supervise railroad management. It did not specify a plan for consolidation. It guaranteed railroad earnings for only six months after the return to private control. The bill was amended in a floor debate to address the labor problem. It created a Railroad Labor Board to settle disputes and did not specifically prohibit strikes. The Esch bill passed the House in a Republican vote. House Democrats were now bending over backward to dissociate themselves from the war experience and attacked the bill as too favorable to the railroads.[86]

With neither house willing to concede to the other, the President offered a two-month extension of his deadline. Surrounded by conflicting interest group pressures, the Republican leaders battled for six weeks in conference. In the end, Cummins yielded on structure and definition, Esch on the potential scope of the regulatory vision.

The Transportation Act of 1920 turned the ICC into the authoritative voice of the federal government on the national transportation system. On the forty-year-old question of competition versus consolidation, Congress hedged and let the commission decide. The ICC was to "plan" for railroad consolidation and to approve proposals for railroad pooling if it deemed them appropriate. At the same time, it was directed to preserve as much competition as possible. The commission was given the power to regulate railroad securities, railroad safety, railroad services, railroad construction, and railroad abandonments. It was to protect the weak roads and accumulate a contingency fund from the excess profits of the strong ones. It was to coordinate the use of facilities and equipment, and it was given sweeping authority over intrastate commerce. Only on the labor issue was the regulatory power of the commission qualified. Congress set up a separate Railroad Labor Board to impose settlements, but it did not explicitly outlaw strikes. The Railroad Labor Board was abolished in 1926.[87]

At the heart of the Transportation Act lay a new approach to rate making. Here the dual impulse to expand regulatory possibilities and avoid decisions was most clearly manifest. The commission was now permitted to set minimum as well as maximum rates. More importantly still, it was directed to set rates so that railroads that were run in an "honest," "efficient," and "economical" way received a "fair return" on the value of their property. The substitution of the "fair return" principle for the "just and reasonable principle" indicated a basic change in the spirit of regulation. Protection for the shipper was no longer the sole concern of the government. The ICC was charged with considering the nation's need for adequate transportation services.[88]

This change conferred on the commission an enormous responsibility and considerably modified the antirailroad posture of prewar legislation. But the shippers had lost less than appears at first glance. Indeed, they had succeeded in preventing Congress from guaranteeing the railroads anything beyond a two-year transition to private operation. Most importantly, they had prevented the creation of a separate institution to articulate management standards. Rate making was to be a bargaining process in which there were no binding standards and from which there was little hope in appeal. In adopting the fair return rule, Congress chose a more expansive concept but declined to make any commitments. The new rule allowed the commission to address more basic questions than the old one, and it gave the railroads an equal opportunity to press their interests upon the agency; but the way in which Congress wanted the basic issues resolved was, if anything, more ambiguous than before. When it came to determining what "adequate" transportation services were or what future transportation needs required, Congress cut the strings of 1910 and ushered in the age of administrative independence.

The Progressive state-building achievement III

The Transportation Act of 1920 framed a new order in the relations between state and society in industrial America. National administrative authority extended outward to farmers, shippers, carriers, laborers, investors, and passengers with a mandate to deal with virtually all conceivable transportation problems that might arise among them. Nationalism superseded localism; system superseded fragmentation; administrative flexibility superseded legal formalism; expert managers superseded political agitators; supervision superseded surveillance; public financiers superseded private profiteers. In short, national administrative authority superseded the limits of courts and parties and in the process transformed the organizational, procedural, and intellectual landscape of American government. The ICC embodied a new mode of governmental operations designed for the relief of a "distended society" and the establishment of "a more orderly system of control."[89]

Yet, to conclude with the reintegration of the state with society is to distort the achievement by telling only half the story. The emergence of a distended state tells the other. Both the state-building process and the structure of the outcome defy neat functional interpretations. The signal triumph of the Progressive reconstitution carried the full weight of the paradox of American state building.

The ICC was, as Charles Francis Adams lamented, "a necessity but nonetheless an excrescence." Its development required the destruction of a clearly articulated governmental order, and its triumph reflected the failure to reestablish governmental order. The achievement, in all its dimensions, was correspondingly limited, its governing potential inevitably a disappointment.

The shifting political opportunities for reconstituting institutional power relationships mediated and delimited a rather tortuous transition to a regulatory mode of governmental operations. In the end, the politics of reconstitution yielded only a flip-flop between two equally problematic extremes. At one extreme, the state stifled the exercise of administrative power through the vitality of irrelevant internal controls; at the other extreme, the state released administrative power by short-circuiting internal controls. Herein lies the essential difference between regulation under the Interstate Commerce Act of 1887 and regulation under the Transportation Act of 1920. The structural obstacles to the reintegration of state and society in industrial America were ultimately overcome by preempting the prerogatives of lawmakers and judges and, in the process, undermining the integrity of the state.

The inversion of institutional power relationships notable between the regulatory legislation of 1887 and that of 1920 was not an isolated curiosity but an integral part of the broader pattern of American state building. The same historical–structural impasse and the same reform sequence that produced the ICC's mandate for independence produced a constitutional stalemate in the national management of civil administration and laced individual bureaucracies like the War Department with alternative and competing systems of control. In each case, the expansion of national administrative capacities broke through the political and institutional constraints imposed by the old order, only to become stuck in authoritative confusion. In each case, institutional politics were reoriented around a new realm of national bureaucratic power, whereas the reconstitution of political and institutional power relationships was severely attenuated. In each case, the limitations of the new order were created in the very process of overcoming the limitations of the old.

Epilogue: Beyond the state of courts and parties – American government in the twentieth century

So thoroughly have the Judges, with very few exceptions, been imbued with the liberal spirit in later years, that the danger at present does not seem to lie in a reluctance of the Court to bow to the Legislative will, but rather in a too facile readiness to confirm whatever the Legislature may temporarily have chosen to decree.

Charles Warren, *The Supreme Court in United States History*, Vol. II, 1947

Anything as close to the vital process of representative government as the party system is bound to affect the nation's political life in more than one way. Whatever impairs the essential operation of the party system also produces serious difficulties in other spheres of national existence.

American Political Science Association, "Towards a More Responsible Two-Party System," 1950

Reform and the limits of regeneration

State building is prompted by environmental changes, but it remains at all times a political contingency, a historical–structural question. Whether a given state changes or fails to change, the form and timing of the change, and the governing potential in the change – all of these turn on a struggle for political power and institutional position, a struggle defined and mediated by the organization of the preestablished state. Herein lies the key to the state-building achievement in twentieth-century American development. Modern American state building successfully negotiated a break with an outmoded organization of state power. The modern American state represents an internal governmental reconstruction worked out through incremental political reform.

A gradual accretion of national administrative forms and procedures may be traced in American government since the late nineteenth century, but American state development is not all of a piece. Modern American state building did not extend the governing arrangements elaborated during the nineteenth century. It was, in fact, stymied by those arrangements and had to challenge them in order to chart a new course. A historical–structural impasse was encountered midstream in American development, and the problem of reconstituting political and institutional power relationships became a central preoccupation affecting the government's response to the social, economic, and international disruptions of the industrial age. The government's response to industrialism was mediated by the politics of recasting an already highly developed but functionally limited state of courts and parties to support an independent arm of national administrative action.

The agenda for building a new American state was defined by an intellectual vanguard of university-trained professionals. They articulated the limitations of the state of courts and parties and championed specific bureaucratic alternatives that promised functional responses to new environmental demands. They were America's single most valuable state-building resource, yet they never controlled the state-building process. To analyze the construction of the new American state solely in terms of their ideals and aspirations is to dismiss the state-building problems they so clearly perceived. In this volatile democracy, the opportunities for challenging the old order were few, fleeting, and inconsistent. The pace and the path of change in government would not mesh neatly with the course of change in other spheres. New governing arrangements emerged out of a political pattern of partial institutional breakthroughs and untimely reversals, a pattern that confounded the logic of functional proficiency and altered the meaning of reform ideals. The drive toward a responsible new democracy organized around executive leadership, the drive toward a new political economy based upon central planning in cooperation with industry, the drive toward administrative rationality grounded in scientific principles of public administration – all were caught in and transformed by the politics of reconstitution.

To follow these politics through is to unravel the paradox of Progressive state building. The incremental struggle simultaneously to break with the governing arrangements articulated over the course of a century and to build a whole new range of governing capacities ultimately produced a state in disarray. As the American state was being fortified with an independent arm of national administrative action, it was also becoming mired in operational confusion. Its newfound strengths were riddled with structural weaknesses. The national administrative apparatus was freed from the clutches of party domination, direct court supervision, and localistic orientations only to be thrust into the center of an amorphous new institutional politics.

In coming to terms with the limits of America's achievement in regenerating the state through political reform, we ultimately confront two overriding considerations: the constancy of the Constitution of 1789 and the destructive consequences of constructive reform initiatives. Forged in the wake of a liberal revolt against the state, the American Constitution has always been awkward and incomplete as an organization of state power. It was the ingenious extraconstitutional framework of courts and parties, developed in the early decades of the nineteenth century, that articulated a coherent mode of governmental operations, balanced the state's support for electoral democracy and the private economy, and facilitated the release of state power within the limited demands of the times. But at the turning point in American state development, when the nature of the demands on government began to change, courts and parties came under direct attack as the pillars of the old order.

Modern American state building was pursued in the name of reharnessing the vital energies of political democracy and the private economy to ever higher levels of achievement, but to do so it had to assault two institutional resources invaluable to governing under the Constitution. National administrative capacities expanded through cracks in an edifice of rules of action and internal governmental controls articulated by courts and parties. The bureaucratic advance pushed against those two special instrumentalities of government and left state power tangled in a constitutional stalemate.

Modern American state building shattered an outmoded judicial discipline. But it failed to reconstruct a vital role for the judiciary in regulating the new political economy. The courts were gradually swamped by Congress's expansion of bureaucratic authority into economic regulation, and ultimately they decided to focus their attention elsewhere. Modernization thus sapped the new American state of a precious source of standards for governmental action. Modern American state building also shattered an outmoded form of party government. But it failed to reconstruct a vital role for party in the new democracy. The foundations of party government were also weakened by Congress's expansion of bureaucratic services. Modernization sapped the new American state of the energies of strong party organizations and the coherence that strong party ties tend to lend to institutional politics. In short, modern American state building progressed by replacing courts and parties with a national bureaucracy, and this dynamic yielded a hapless confusion of institutional purposes, authoritative controls, and governmental boundaries.

Thus, although the Progressive state-building achievement was marked by disjunction rather than continuity with the past, the old and the new remained joined in an intimate if paradoxical relationship. The state-building process led to an exchange of governing strengths and weaknesses. The "weak springs of government" in 1877 were functional. They can be traced to the operational vitality of courts and parties in the industrial age and the limits this placed on national administrative development. The "weak springs of government" in 1920, however, were operational. They can be traced to the state-building thrust against courts and parties and the concomitant expansion of national administrative power. The further we move into the twentieth century, the more pronounced this irony becomes.

Toward maturity

One anomaly begets another. American exceptionalism has not been transcended by twentieth-century state building; it has only taken a new form. The Progressive state-building sequence has been extended and elaborated over the course of this century, but the path of institutional development and the terms of the contest for state control have not been fundamentally altered. Administrative expansion accompanied by a withering of party machinery and judicial restrictions on state action has defined America's peculiar approach to modernity.

The fate of courts and parties in the new American state was sealed during the New Deal. The three great institutional struggles of Franklin Roosevelt's second term are especially telling in light of the Progressive experience. First, in the Court battle of 1937, the President pushed the judiciary into a full retreat in the face of the bureaucratic advance to power. Then, in the party purge of 1938, Roosevelt suggested that a new party might lend coherence to relationships among the President, Congress, and the bureaucracy. He attempted to use New Deal patronage appointees to prod recalcitrant Democrats into line behind his programs, but the Democratic Congress would have none of it. The Hatch Acts formally removed federal civil servants from electoral politics and stunted the further development of this revival of party government. Finally, in 1939, the President made his famous bid for control of the new administrative machinery. Following the latest prescriptions of political science as articulated by his Commission on Administrative Management, Roosevelt sought to transfer the Bureau of the Budget from the Treasury Department to a new Executive Office of the President, to undercut the power and position of the Comptroller General, and to modify the independent status of the regulatory commissions by transferring most of their operations to new executive departments. Here the Democratic Congress yielded enough to keep the new machinery running but steadfastly refused to sanction the commission's sweeping conception of presidential management.

The second round of twentieth-century state building left the courts to search for a new domain in which to exercise judicial creativity. It left party government to degenerate as a remnant of an earlier state of things. It left the President with enormous responsibilities but with sanctions that were, in Harold Laski's words, "not continuous enough in their operation to make his leadership continuously effective except under conditions the avoidance of which is the purpose of every scheme of government."[1]

The major constructive contribution of the New Deal to the operations of the new American state lay in the sheer expansion of bureaucratic services and supports. Pushing courts and party organizations further out of the center of governmental operations, the New Deal turned bureaucracy itself into the extraconstitutional machine so necessary for the continuous operation of the constitutional system. Like party patronage in the old order, bureaucratic goods and services came to provide the fuel and the cement of the new institutional politics. They became something valuable for Presidents to offer and for congressmen to support. They articulated a new set of concrete institutional ties between the state and the citizenry. This bureaucratic solution to the problems of governing under the Constitution promised to work in benign confusion as long as administrative services and supports could expand.

The coming to maturity of the new American state was marked by a growing restlessness among the organic intellectuals. The first premonitions of serious structural problems in the new order entered political analysis around mid-century. Scholars began to describe the informalities in the "governmental process" with forebodings of a "morbific politics."[2] The political and intellectual rehabilitation of the judiciary was received with concern about an uncontrolled expansion of governmental activity.[3] The exhaustion of party government was linked to excessive dependence on the limited offices of the presidency and the portent of constitutional crisis.[4]

The bureaucratic expansion of the 1960s pushed the intellectual revolt into high gear. Like the Mugwumps of old, the new critics dedicated themselves to exposing the limitations of the established governmental order. But unlike the originals, the new mugwumps offered no clear reconstructive vision, had no concrete reform agenda, and mobilized no persuasive reform constituencies. They were left with little more than a lament for the damage done by their predecessors. They lamented the quality of national government in the bureaucratic state and appealed to the virtues of the nineteenth century.[5] They lamented uncontrolled administrative discretion, with its degradation of the rule of law, and appealed to the judicial discipline of old.[6] They lamented the Progressives' bureaucratic offensive against party and harkened back to the politics of machines and bosses.[7]

The disaffection of the new mugwumps was the ultimate despair. It bespoke an exhaustion of alternatives for governing under the Constitution. The very path of modernization seemed to foreclose the possibilities for further change. One possibility, however, was never seriously considered. Following the logic of the late-century assault on party patronage, major changes in government might follow a direct attack on the motor force of the new state. Reverse, halt, or even slow the expansion of bureaucratic goods and services, and the structure of state power might once again be thrown into contention.

Beyond the hapless giant?

Beyond the state of courts and parties lay a hapless administrative giant, a state that could spawn bureaucratic goods and services but that defied authoritative control and direction. State development between the 1870s and the 1970s turned out to be a grand historical flip-flop of problematic extremes. A governmental order in which party destroyed the integrity of bureaucracy gave way to a governmental order in which bureaucracy destroyed the integrity of party. A governmental order in which judicial standards stymied the expansion of administrative capacities gave way to a governmental order in which judicial standards fueled that expansion.

American state development has come full circle. The old solution has become the problem. The limitations of the new mode of governmental operations have been displayed as vividly in recent years as the limitations of the old were displayed in the late nineteenth century. The economic and international changes of the past decade have thrown the administrative expansion of twentieth-century state building into serious question. A new governing impasse has been exposed, and a reform challenge unprecedented since the late nineteenth century has emerged. Once again, the organization of state power itself has been made a major political issue.

The shape of the present challenge is a developmental inversion of the first. The political attack on all-consuming parties has been replaced by a political attack on all-consuming bureaucracies. The plight of Presidents severely constrained in their leadership by the normal routines of the party state has been replaced by the plight of Presidents constrained by the normal routines of the bureaucratic state. Even the imperial judiciary has reappeared, this time overextended and under siege for its zealous expansion of civil rights and guarantees. Once again, we have seen how institutions and procedures created to serve socioeconomic development become self-perpetuating perversions of that purpose. Once again, we have heard that a constructive solution to our governing problems requires a new declaration of independence, a shattering of traditional illusions about government, and an emancipation from the institutional routines and orientations of the past.

Reform efforts during the 1970s offered only patchwork solutions. We saw futile and self-defeating attempts to circumvent the bureaucracy by concentrating the operations of the federal government more directly in the Executive Office of the President and the White House staff. We saw a symbolic dismantling of the Civil Service Commission and a renewed appeal to spoils incentives in order to gain control over top-level bureaucrats. But hitherto, we have not seen a successful assault on the centerpiece of the new American state. Only now have election results created political opportunities for a concerted campaign to roll back domestic bureaucratic programs and regulatory activities. It is far too soon to know whether such a campaign can succeed at all in the long run, let alone predict its scope and depth; but the structure of the present situation should alert us to the lessons of history and the implications of success.

Obviously, the attack on bureaucracy does not herald the dismantling of the American state. But like the Progressive attack on courts and parties, it may signal the end of patchwork politics and the opening of a new reconstruction sequence. Instead of a return to an earlier state of things, we face the possibility of a great departure in the terms of the struggle over institutional development and governmental control. Enthusiasm for stimulating the economy by halting the expansion of administration should not preclude serious concern for how political and institutional power relationships might be recast in the process of this struggle. Bureaucracy is not an isolated evil; for good or ill, the entire constitutional system has been fashioned to work through and around it. To tug at the bureaucratic lynchpin is to challenge the way government officials gain and maintain their positions, the way they relate to each other within and across institutions, and the way they relate back to social and economic groups.

On the optimistic side, one may speculate that a concerted attack on bureaucratic programs might spark a revival of party organization and that a concerted attack on administrative regulation might push the courts back into the business of articulating coherent standards of state action. The result would be a happy if long-delayed redress of the Progressive imbalance. This new cycle of reconstruction politics might end with reenergized parties, a vigilant judiciary, and disciplined bureaucracies all working in harmony under the Constitution. It hardly need be said, however, that this millennium for reform will not be reached through a series of reflex reactions. The political and intellectual vanguard for such a transformation has yet to announce itself, and the very structure of the Constitution may well bar any such outcome, at least insofar as party is concerned.

More likely, an attack on bureaucracy would allow us to begin anew as we began before. Reconstruction would probably follow a twisted and halting course, its path marked by institutional struggles rooted in the structure of the bureaucratic state and mediated by shifts in electoral politics. The results would be incremental reform, partial institutional breakthroughs, and untimely stalemates. This path may still yield adequate, if largely unintended, results. But it hardly need be said that the costs of regeneration in this manner are increasing. Unlike the last time, we no longer have the luxury of decades to work out the problems in a new mode of governmental operations.

This raises another alternative. The magnitude of the governing problems at hand, the press of time, and popular outrage aimed at bureaucratic bungling may ultimately work to complete the Progressives' break with the past. The search for control and direction may yet persuade us to move beyond our unwieldy Constitution. It hardly need be said that this path toward a regeneration of American government requires the utmost caution, lest in disgust with bureaucracy we stumble upon a sense of the state far more threatening than any we have yet known.

Notes

Preface

1 Alan Wolfe, *The Limits of Legitimacy: Political Contradictions of Contemporary Capitalism* (New York: Free Press, 1977).
2 J. Rogers Hollingsworth, "The United States," in Raymond Grew, ed., *Crises of Political Development in Europe and the United States* (Princeton, N.J.: Princeton University Press, 1978), pp. 163–95.
3 Walter Dean Burnham, *Critical Elections and the Mainsprings of American Politics* (New York: Norton, 1970), pp. 1–10.

Chapter 1. The new state and American political development

1 See below for a discussion of Hegel's rejection of America as a state. For a more contemporary view see J. P. Nettl, "The State as a Conceptual Variable," *World Politics* 20, 4 (July 1968), pp. 559–92.
2 This organizational view of the American state is developed more fully in the next chapter. See Alexander Passerin d'Entreves, *The Notion of the State: An Introduction to Political Theory* (London: Oxford University Press, 1967), pp. 114–23; Gianfranco Poggi, *The Development of the Modern State: A Sociological Introduction* (Stanford University Press, 1978), pp. 97–8; Max Weber, "Politics as a Vocation," H. H. Gerth and C. Wright Mills (trans. and eds.), *From Max Weber: Essays in Sociology* (New York: Oxford University Press, 1958), p. 78; Charles Nixon, "Relations Between States and Economies in Marx and Weber," paper delivered at the International Political Science Association, Moscow, August 12–18, 1979.
3 Alexis de Tocqueville, *Democracy in America,* 2 vols. (New York: Vintage Books, 1945), I, pp. 72–5.
4 *Ibid.,* p. 59.
5 Georg Friedrich Hegel, *The Philosophy of History* (New York: Dover, 1956), pp. 84–7; George A. Kelly, "Hegel's America," *Philosophy and Public Affairs* 2 (Fall 1972), pp. 2–36. Compare Nettl, "Conceptual Variable."
6 *Ibid.*
7 Karl Marx and Frederick Engels, *The German Ideology,* C. J. Arthur, ed. (New York: International, 1970), p. 80.
8 Karl Marx, *Critique of Hegel's 'Philosophy of Right,'* Joseph O'Malley, ed.;

Annette Jolin and Joseph O'Malley, trans. (Cambridge University Press, 1970), pp. 29–32.

9   Marx, *Critique of Hegel*, p. 31; Kelley, "Hegel's America," p. 9.

10 Marx, *Critique of Hegel*, p. 31; Marx and Engels, *German Ideology*, pp. 79–81.

11 Daniel Bell, "The End of American Exceptionalism," *The Public Interest* 41 (Fall 1975), pp. 193–225.

12 See Jürgen Habermas, *Legitimation Crisis* (Boston: Beacon Press, 1973); Ralph Miliband, *The State in Capitalist Society: An Analysis of the Western System of Power* (New York: Basic Books, 1969); John H. Schaar, "Legitimacy in the Modern State," Philip Green and Sanford Levinson, eds., *Power and Community: Dissenting Essays in Political Science* (New York: Vintage Books, 1970), pp. 276–327; Alan Wolfe, *The Limits of Legitimacy: The Political Contradictions of Contemporary Capitalism* (New York: Free Press, 1977).

13 Charles Tilly, ed., *The Formation of National States in Western Europe* (Princeton, N.J.: Princeton University Press, 1975); Gabriel Almond, Scott C. Flanagan, and Robert Mundt, eds., *Crisis, Choice and Change* (Boston: Little, Brown, 1973); Leonard Binder et al., *Crises and Sequences in Political Development* (Princeton, N.J.: Princeton University Press, 1971); Raymond Grew, ed., *Crises of Political Development in Europe and the United States* (Princeton, N.J.: Princeton University Press, 1978); see in particular J. Rogers Hollingsworth on "The United States," pp. 163–95; Otto Hintze, *The Historical Essays of Otto Hintze,* Felix Gilbert, ed. (New York: Oxford University Press, 1975), pp. 90–215.

14 Morton Keller, *Affairs of State: Public Life in Late Nineteenth Century America* (Cambridge, Mass.: Belknap Press, 1977), pp. 1–238.

15 Frederick Engels, *The Family, Private Property, and the State,* Eleanor Leacock, ed. (New York: International, 1972); Wolfe, *Limits of Legitimacy.*

16 Thomas C. Cochran and William Miller, *The Age of Enterprise: A Social History of Industrial America* (New York: Harper & Row, 1961); Edward C. Kirkland, *Industry Comes of Age: Business, Labor and Public Policy 1860–1897* (New York: Holt, Rinehart & Winston, 1961); Glenn Porter, *The Rise of Big Business 1860–1910* (Arlington Heights, Ill.: AHM, 1973).

17 Emile Durkheim, *Professional Ethics and Civic Morals* (Glencoe, Ill.: Free Press, 1958).

18 Samuel P. Hays, *The Response to Industrialism, 1885–1914* (University of Chicago Press, 1957), p. 2.

19 Robert Wiebe, *The Search for Order, 1877–1920* (New York: Hill and Wang, 1967), p. xiv.

20 Scholars will argue about the weight to be attached to these factors in an evaluation of the primary cause of state building. In the chapter studies on specific administrative reforms, consideration is given to the environmental imperatives that seem most pressing in each case. The major task of this study is, however, not to show how a particular environmental stimulus evokes a particular kind of response but to explore how a distinctly political

problem intervened and fashioned responses in a similar way regardless of the specific stimulus. We may thus avoid the knotty problem of specifying a primary cause in order to distinguish the full variety of forces pressing for a new departure in American government at this time.

21 Theda Skocpol, *States and Social Revolutions: A Comparative Analysis of France, Russia, and China* (New York: Cambridge University Press, 1979).

22 It is important to note that parties, courts, the President, Congress, and the individual states were changing at this time independently of the challenge posed by bureaucratic expansion. These changes, as they affected administrative developments, are treated in the chapter studies on individual reforms. See Loren Beth, *The Development of the American Constitution 1877–1917* (New York: Harper & Row, 1971). Also see *Origins and Development of Congress* (Washington, D.C.: Congressional Quarterly, Inc., 1976); Nelson Polsby, "The Institutionalization of the House of Representatives," *American Political Science Review* 62, 1 (March 1968), pp. 144–68; David Rothman, *Politics and Power: The United States Senate, 1869–1901* (Cambridge, Mass.: Harvard University Press, 1966).

23 For the contending interpretations of political reform in the Progressive era, see the following: Walter Dean Burnham, "Theory and Voting Research: Some Reflections on Converse's 'Change in the American Electorate,'" *American Political Science Review* 68, 3 (September 1974), pp. 1002–23; Philip E. Converse, "Comment," *American Political Science Review* 68, 3 (September 1974), pp. 1023–7; Jerrold G. Rusk, "Comment," *American Political Science Review* 68, 3 (September 1974), pp. 1028–49; Walter Dean Burnham, "Rejoinder," *American Political Science Review* 68, 3 (September 1974), pp. 1050–7; Jesse F. Marquette, "Social Change and Political Mobilization in the United States: 1870–1960," *American Political Science Review* 68, 3 (September 1974), pp. 1058–74; Richard Hofstadter, *The Age of Reform: From Bryan to FDR* (New York: Vintage Books, 1955); Gabriel Kolko, *The Triumph of Conservatism: A Re-Interpretation of American History, 1900–1916* (Chicago: Quadrangle Books, 1963); Wiebe, *Search for Order*.

24 Many scholars have noted the significance of the political-institutional dimension in relation to specific developments. See, for example, Robert Cuff, *The War Industries Board* (Baltimore: Johns Hopkins University Press, 1973); Samuel P. Hays, *Conservation and the Gospel of Efficiency: The Progressive Conservation Movement, 1890–1920* (New York: Atheneum, 1974); Ari Hoogenboom, *Outlawing the Spoils: A History of the Civil Service Reform Movement, 1865–1883* (Urbana: University of Illinois Press, 1961).

Chapter 2. The early American state

1 Lawrence Henry Gipson, *The Triumphant Empire: Britain Sails into the Storm, 1770–1776* (New York: Knopf, 1965); A. F. Pollard, *Factors in American History* (New York: Macmillan, 1925), p. 32. On conflicts be-

tween imperial claims and domestic power in colonial politics, see Bernard Bailyn, *The Origins of American Politics* (New York: Vintage Books, 1967), pp. 59–105.

2 Charles C. Thach, Jr., *The Creation of the Presidency, 1775–1789: A Study in Constitutional History* (Baltimore: Johns Hopkins University Press, 1923), pp. 1–75.

3 On the search for a new American science of politics, see Gordon Wood, *The Creation of the American Republic 1776–1787* (New York: Norton, 1969).

4 The quoted passage is from John Quincy Adams, cited in Alpheus Thomas Mason, *Free Government in the Making* (New York: Oxford University Press, 1965), p. 329.

5 Wood, *American Republic*, pp. 519–64.

6 The quoted passage is again from John Quincy Adams, cited in Alpheus Thomas Mason, "Political System without a Model," *The Supreme Court: Palladium of Freedom* (Ann Arbor: University of Michigan Press, 1962), p. 2.

7 Samuel P. Huntington, *Political Order in Changing Societies* (New Haven, Conn.: Yale University Press, 1968), p. 109.

8 Huntington, *Political Order*, pp. 93–139; J. P. Nettl, "The State as a Conceptual Variable," *World Politics* 20, 4 (July 1968), pp. 559–92.

9 Lynton K. Caldwell, *The Administrative Theories of Hamilton and Jefferson: Their Contribution to Thought on Public Administration* (New York: Russell and Russell, 1944); Jacob E. Cook, ed., *The Reports of Alexander Hamilton* (New York: Harper & Row, 1964). For Hamilton on the military, see Richard H. Kohn, *Eagle and Sword: The Federalists and the Creation of the Military Establishment in America, 1783–1802* (New York: Free Press, 1975). For Hamilton on taxation, see Dall W. Forsythe, *Taxation and Political Change in the Young Nation, 1781–1833* (New York: Columbia University Press, 1977); Leonard White, *The Federalists: A Study in Administrative History* (New York: Macmillan, 1948).

10 On notions of institutional thickening and union in Whig thought, see Major L. Wilson, *Space, Time and Freedom: The Quest for Nationality and the Irrepressible Conflict, 1815–1861* (Westport, Conn.: Greenwood Press, 1974).

11 On the Federalist institutional program and its transformation into a party platform, see William Chambers, *Political Parties in a New Nation: The American Experience, 1776–1809* (New York: Oxford University Press, 1963). On the Whigs, see Lynn L. Marshall, "The Strange Stillbirth of the Whig Party," *The American Historical Review* 72, 2 (January 1967), pp. 445–69.

12 Samuel Beer, "The Modernization of American Federalism," *Publius* 3, 2 (Fall 1973), pp. 59–63.

13 Daniel Elazar, *The Federal Partnership: Intergovernmental Relations in the Nineteenth Century United States* (University of Chicago Press, 1962), p. 109; Malcomb Rohrbough, *The Land Office Business: The Settlement and*

Administration of American Public Lands 1789–1837 (New York: Oxford University Press, 1968); Leonard D. White, *The Jacksonians: A Study in Administrative History* (New York: Macmillan, 1954); Leonard D. White, *The Jeffersonians: A Study in Administrative History* (New York: Macmillan, 1951).

14   Forest G. Hill, *Roads, Rails and Waterways: The Army Engineers and Early Transportation* (Norman: University of Oklahoma Press, 1957).

15   William Riker, *Soldiers of the States: The Role of the National Guard in American Democracy* (Washington, D.C.: Public Affairs Press, 1957); John K. Mahon, *The American Militia: Decade of Decision 1789–1800, University of Florida Monograph in Social Science*, No. 6, Spring 1960 (Gainsville: University of Florida Press, 1960); Kohn, *Eagle and Sword*.

16   Theodore J. Lowi, *The End of Liberalism: The Second Republic of the United States* (New York: Norton, 1979), p. 272. Theodore J. Lowi, "Parallels of Policy and Politics: The Political Theory in American History" (paper delivered to the Organization of American Historians, New Orleans, April 15, 1971).

17   Beer, "American Federalism"; Theodore J. Lowi, "Parties, Policy and Constitution in America," William Nisbet Chambers and Walter Dean Burnham, eds., *The American Party Systems: Stages of Political Development* (New York: Oxford University Press, 1967), pp. 238–76.

18   Standard historical studies of evolving institutional power relationships in Washington are Wilfred Binkley, *President and Congress* (New York: Vintage Books, 1962); Edward Corwin, *The President: Office and Powers* (New York University Press, 1957); Charles Haines, *The American Doctrine of Judicial Supremacy* (New York: Russell and Russell, 1959); *Origins and Development of Congress* (Washington, D.C.: Congressional Quarterly, Inc., 1976); Ernest Sutherland Bates, *The Story of Congress, 1789–1935* (New York: Harper & Brothers, 1936).

19   John R. Commons, *The Legal Foundations of Capitalism* (Madison: University of Wisconsin Press, 1968, reissued from 1924), p. 123.

20   Huntington, *Political Order*, pp. 9–12.

21   Commons, *Legal Foundations*, pp. 148–50.

22   White, *The Federalists*, pp. 253–94; White, *The Jeffersonians*, pp. 336–69; Carl Russell Fish, *The Civil Service and the Patronage* (New York: Longmans, Green, 1905), pp. 1–63; James Sterling Young, *The Washington Community, 1800–1828* (New York: Harcourt Brace Jovanovich, 1966).

23   Binkley, *President and Congress*, pp. 33–59; Young, *Washington Community*.

24   Young, *Washington Community*, p. 252.

25   James W. Ceaser, *Presidential Selection: Theory and Development* (Princeton, N.J.: Princeton University Press, 1979), pp. 132–69; Richard Hofstadter, *The Idea of a Party System* (Berkeley: University of California Press, 1969), pp. 212–71; Richard P. McCormick, "Political Development and the Second Party System," *American Party Systems*, pp. 90–116; Roy Nichols, *The Invention of the American Political Parties* (New York: Macmillan,

1967), pp. 263–377; Robert V. Remini, *Martin Van Buren and the Making of the Democratic Party* (New York: Columbia University Press, 1959).

26 Theodore J. Lowi, "Party, Policy and Constitution in America," *American Party Systems,* pp. 238–76.

27 Ceaser, *Presidential Selection;* Matthew Crenson, *The Federal Machine: Beginnings of Bureaucracy in Jacksonian America* (Baltimore: Johns Hopkins University Press, 1975); Elazar, *Federal Partnership,* p. 303; Fish, *Civil Service,* pp. 63–114; Howard Roberts Lamar, *Dakota Territory 1861–1889: A Study in Frontier Politics* (New Haven, Conn.: Yale University Press, 1956), pp. 1–86; McCormick, "Political Development"; Martin Shefter, "Party, Bureaucracy and Political Change in the United States," Louis Maisel and Joseph Cooper, eds., *Political Parties, Development and Decay* (Beverly Hills: Sage, 1978), pp. 218–25; James Q. Wilson, "The Rise of the Bureaucratic State," *The Public Interest* 41 (Fall 1975), pp. 77–106.

28 It is worth noting, further, with Arthur Schlesinger, Jr., that "the spoils system, whatever its faults, at least destroyed peaceably the monopoly of officers by a class which could not govern, and brought to power a fresh and alert group which had the energy to meet the needs of the day." *The Age of Jackson* (Boston: Little, Brown, 1945), p. 47.

29 Woodrow Wilson, *Constitutional Government in the United States* (New York: Columbia University Press, 1908), p. 206.

30 Lowi, "Party, Policy and Constitution," pp. 238–41; Wilson, *Constitutional Government.*

31 Walter Dean Burnham, *Critical Elections and the Mainsprings of American Politics* (New York: Norton, 1970), p. 11; Hofstadter, *Party System,* p. 246.

32 Binkley, *President and Congress,* pp. 105–32; Marshall, "Whig Party"; Nichols, *Invention,* pp. 331–41.

33 Ceaser, *Presidential Selection;* Hofstadter, *Party System;* Lowi, "Party, Policy and Constitution," p. 243; Robert Remini, *Martin Van Buren and the Making of the Democratic Party* (New York: Columbia University Press, 1959), esp. pp. 123–46.

34 Note Tocqueville's discussion of the great power of American judges and the inherent passivity of judicial institutions. "Judicial Power in the United States and Its Influence on Political Society," *Democracy in America,* 2 vols. (New York: Vintage Books, 1945), I, pp. 102–09.

35 Alpheus Thomas Mason and William M. Beany, *The Supreme Court in a Free Society* (Englewood Cliffs, N.J.: Prentice-Hall, 1959), pp. 1–27. It should come as no surprise that the Supreme Court was bitterly attacked in the early nineteenth century for betraying the antistatist principles of the Revolution and the Constitution. By asserting the unity of the state and by protecting the vitality of its national prerogatives, the Court seemed to have turned the Constitution into an altered form of the same tyranny experienced in Britain. See John Taylor, *Construction Construed and Constitutions Vindicated* (Richmond, Va.: Shepherd and Pollard, 1820).

36 John R. Schmidhauser, *The Supreme Court as Final Arbiter in Federal–State Relations, 1789–1957* (Chapel Hill: University of North Carolina Press,

1958). On the institutional history of the Court before the Civil War and the practical limits on its supervision imposed by the system of circuit riding, see Felix Frankfurter and John Landis, *The Business of the Supreme Court: A Study in the Federal Judicial System* (New York: Macmillan, 1927), pp. 4–55; Erwin C. Surrency, "A History of the Federal Courts," *Missouri Law Review* 28, 2 (Spring 1963), pp. 214–44.

37   The decline of public works was abrupt after the panic of 1837. Carter Goodrich, *Government Promotion of American Canals and Railroads, 1800–1890* (New York: Columbia University Press, 1960). Administrative problems with state public works projects are detailed by Louis Hartz, *Economic Policy and Democratic Thought: Pennsylvania, 1776–1860* (Cambridge, Mass.: Harvard University Press, 1948), pp. 148–80; James Willard Hurst, *The Legitimacy of the Business Corporation in the Law of the United States: 1780–1970* (Charlottesville: University of Virginia Press, 1970). Hurst writes: "The regulatory goals set by legislatures could be achieved only through steady, strong, capable executive or administrative effort. In the 19th century situation it was almost inevitable that we could not provide the necessary executive or administrative resources. From the American Revolution we inherited a stubborn distrust of committing power to the executive. In an economy hard pressed for fluid capital, taxes were difficult to raise for public ventures let alone for the support of a swelling bureaucracy" (p. 40). Harry N. Scheiber, "Federalism and the American Economic Order 1789–1910," *Law and Society Review* 10, 1 (Fall 1975), pp. 57–118.

38   Hurst, *Legitimacy*, pp. 40–57; Morton Horwitz, *The Transformation of American Law 1780–1860* (Cambridge, Mass.: Harvard University Press, 1977).

39   Elazar, *Federal Partnership*, pp. 183–225.

40   Alexander H. Pekelis, "Legal Techniques and Political Ideologies: A Comparative Study," Reinhard Bendix, ed., *State and Society* (Boston: Little, Brown, 1968), pp. 355–78.

41   Horwitz, *Transformation*, p. 30; James Willard Hurst, *Law and the Conditions of Freedom in the Nineteenth Century United States* (Madison: University of Wisconsin Press, 1956); G. Edward White, "The Path of American Jurisprudence," *University of Pennsylvania Law Review* 124 (May 1976), pp. 1212–59.

42   Maxwell Bloomfield, "William Sampson and the Codifiers: The Roots of American Legal Reform 1820–1830," *American Journal of Legal History* 11 (July 1967), pp. 234–52; Richard Ellis, *The Jeffersonian Crisis: Courts and Politics in the Young Republic* (New York: Norton, 1974); Perry Miller, ed., *The Life of the Mind in America: From the Revolution to the Civil War* (New York: Harcourt, Brace and World, 1965), pp. 239–69.

43   The practical limits on federal court authority are emphasized by Scheiber, "Federalism."

44   R. Kent Newmyer, *The Supreme Court under Marshall and Taney* (Arlington Heights, Ill.: AHM, 1968), pp. 119–46; Roy Nichols, *The Disruption of American Democracy* (New York: Collier Books, 1962).

45 Eric L. McKitrick, "Party Politics and the Union and Confederate War Efforts," *American Party Systems*, pp. 117–51. McKitrick suggests the importance of two-party competition in fusing together Republican power in government during the war. On the courts in this period, see Stanley I. Kutler, *Judicial Power and Reconstruction Politics* (University of Chicago Press, 1968), pp. 7–29.

46 "Oneida County Proceedings of the Republican Party Convention" held at Rome, N.Y., September 26, 1892, published in the *Utica Morning Herald*, Utica, N.Y.

47 David Donald, *Lincoln Reconsidered* (New York: Vintage Books, 1956), pp. 57–82, 103–27; McKitrick, "Party Politics"; Hans L. Trefousse, *The Radical Republicans: Lincoln's Vanguard for Racial Justice* (Baton Rouge: Louisiana State University Press, 1968). The problems of maintaining unity in the Republican ranks are emphasized by T. Harry Williams, *Lincoln and the Radicals* (Madison: University of Wisconsin Press, 1941). The problems of national administrative mobilization at the outset of the war are dealt with by A. Howard Meneely, *The War Department, 1861: A Study in Mobilization and Administration* (New York: Columbia University Press, 1928). The problems of running a war in a radically decentralized political system are dealt with by William B. Hesseltine, *Lincoln and the War Governors* (New York: Knopf, 1955).

48 David Montgomery, *Beyond Equality: Labor and the Radical Republicans, 1862–1872* (New York: Vintage Books, 1972) p. 47.

49 Morton Keller, *Affairs of State: Public Life in Late Nineteenth Century America* (Cambridge, Mass.: Belknap Press, 1977), pp. 37–285; Montgomery, *Beyond Equality*, pp. 72–84.

50 Antonio Gramsci, *Selections from the Prison Notebooks*, Quinton Hoare and Geoffrey Nowell Smith, eds. and trans. (New York: International, 1971). Gramsci writes of the relationship between the intellectuals and the development of the state (pp. 3–23). America's peculiarity as a state was, in Gramsci's view, intimately related to the kind of intellectual it offered. America never developed "traditional" intellectuals in the European sense but only "organic" intellectuals who performed routine tasks and changed with social development. See "State and Civil Society," p. 272, and "Americanism and Fordism," pp. 277–8, 316–20. See also Antonio Gramsci, *Letters from Prison* (New York: Harper & Row, 1973), pp. 243–4; Jerome Kanabel, "Revolutionary Contradictions and the Problem of the Intellectuals," *Politics and Society* 6, 2 (1976), pp. 146–65; Joseph Schumpeter, *Capitalism, Socialism and Democracy* (New York: Harper & Row, 1950), pp. 143–55.

51 John Armstrong, *The European Administrative Elite* (Princeton, N.J.: Princeton University Press, 1973).

52 Sidney Aronson, *Status and Kinship Ties in the Higher Civil Service: Standards of Selection in the Administration of John Adams, Thomas Jefferson and Andrew Jackson* (Cambridge, Mass.: Harvard University Press, 1964).

See also White, "American Jurisprudence"; Crenson, *Federal Machine,* pp. 11–30.

53 S. E. Finer, "Patronage and the Public Service: Jeffersonian Bureaucracy and the British Tradition," *Public Administration* 30 (Winter 1952), pp. 329–30.

54 A Tenure of Office Act was passed in 1820 but applied to a limited number of offices. Moreover, in all offices tenure continued to be de facto during good behavior. The notion of property in office as it grew at this time is treated by David H. Rosenbloom, *The Federal Service and the Constitution* (Ithaca, N.Y.: Cornell University Press, 1971), pp. 41–4.

55 White, *The Jacksonians,* pp. 300–16; Fish, *Civil Service,* pp. 105–30, 158–69.

56 Tocqueville, *Democracy in America,* I, pp. 282–90.

57 R. Kent Newmyer, "Daniel Webster as Tocqueville's Lawyer: The Dartmouth College Case Again," *American Journal of Legal History* 11 (April 1967), pp. 127–47.

58 Newmyer, "Daniel Webster," pp. 143–5.

59 Maxwell Bloomfield, "Lawyers and Public Criticism: Challenge and Response in Nineteenth Century America," *American Journal of Legal History* 15 (October 1971), pp. 274–75.

60 *Ibid.* See also Maxwell Bloomfield, "Law vs. Politics: The Self Image of the American Bar (1830–1860)," *American Journal of Legal History* 12 (October 1968), pp. 306–23.

61 Anton-Hermann Chroust, *The Rise of the Legal Profession in America,* 2 vols. (Norman: University of Oklahoma Press, 1965), II, pp. 129–73; Perry Miller, *The Life of the Mind in America: From the Revolution to the Civil War* (New York: Harcourt, Brace, and World, 1965), pp. 99–116.

62 Crenson, *Federal Machine,* pp. 11–47; Chroust, *Legal Profession,* pp. 129–73; James Willard Hurst, *The Growth of American Law: The Lawmakers* (Boston: Little, Brown, 1959), pp. 249–94; Charles Warren, *A History of the American Bar* (Boston: Little, Brown, 1911), pp. 211–40; Richard Hofstadter, *Anti-Intellectualism in American Life* (New York: Vintage Books, 1963).

63 Bloomfield, "Law vs. Politics"; Gerald W. Gawalt, "Sources of Anti-Lawyer Sentiment in Massachusetts, 1740–1840," *American Journal of Legal History* 14 (June 1970), pp. 283–307; Gary B. Nash, "The Philadelphia Bar and Bench 1800–1860," *Comparative Studies in Society and History* 7, 2 (January, 1965), pp. 203–20.

64 Maxwell Bloomfield, *American Lawyers in a Changing Society* (Cambridge, Mass.: Harvard University Press, 1976); Magali Sarfati Larson, *The Rise of Professionalism: A Sociological Analysis* (Berkeley: University of California Press, 1978), pp. 105–35; David Calhoun, *Professional Lives in America: Structure and Aspiration* (Cambridge, Mass.: Harvard University Press, 1965), pp. 59–87, 178–98; Compare James Bryce with Tocqueville on the American bar. *The American Commonwealth,* 2 vols. (New York: Macmillan, 1920), II, pp. 665–78.

65 Bloomfield, "Lawyers and Public Criticism," p. 271.

66 For alternative means of maintaining legal standards after the decline of the local bars, see Elizabeth Gasper Brown, "The Bar on the Frontier: Wayne County, 1796–1836," *American Journal of Legal History* 14, 2 (April 1970), pp. 136–56; Gerald W. Gawalt, "Massachusetts Legal Education in Transition 1776–1840," *American Journal of Legal History* 17, 1 (January 1973), pp. 27–50.

67 For emphasis on technical competence and service in the American army, see Samuel P. Huntington, *The Soldier and the State: The Theory and Practice of Civil–Military Relations* (New York: Vintage Books, 1957), pp. 195–203.

68 For a striking comparison with the Prussian experience, see Hans Rosenberg, *Bureaucracy, Aristocracy, Autocracy: The Prussian Experience, 1660–1815* (Boston: Beacon Press, 1958).

Part II. Introduction

1 David Montgomery, *Beyond Equality: Labor and the Radical Republicans* (New York: Vintage Books, 1972), p. 359; Morton Keller, *Affairs of State: Public Life in Late Nineteenth Century America* (Cambridge, Mass.: Belknap Press, 1977), pp. 37–285.

2 Matthew Josephson, *The Politicos, 1865–1896* (New York: Harcourt, Brace and World, 1963); John M. Dobson, *Politics in the Gilded Age: A New Perspective on Reform* (New York: Praeger, 1972), pp. 40–52.

3 See Robert Wiebe's notion of late-century American as a "distended society." *The Search for Order, 1877–1920* (New York: Hill and Wang, 1967), pp. 11–44.

4 Frederick Engels, "Introduction" to the 1891 edition of Karl Marx's *The Civil War in France* (Peking: Foreign Language Press, 1966), p. 15. A similar view of American party government is presented by Maurice Ostrogorski, *Democracy and the Organization of Political Parties*, Frederick Clark, trans. 2 vols. (London: Macmillan, 1902), II, pp. 550–7. Engel's analysis also echoes the sentiments of America's own Mugwump reformers. See below.

5 William M. Wiecek, "The Reconstruction of Federal Judicial Power, 1863–1875," *The American Journal of Legal History* 13 (October 1969), pp. 333–59; Keller, *Affairs of State*, p. 370.

6 Felix Frankfurter and James M. Landis, *The Business of the Supreme Court: A Study of the Federal Judicial System* (New York: Macmillan, 1927), pp. 56–103; Erwin C. Surrency, "A History of the Federal Courts," *Missouri Law Review* 28, 2 (Spring 1963), pp. 232–4.

7 Wiecek, "Federal Judicial Power," p. 355.

8 Robert McCloskey, *The American Supreme Court* (University of Chicago Press, 1960), pp. 101–36; Arnold M. Paul, *Conservative Crisis and the Rule of Law: Attitudes of the Bar and Bench, 1887–1895* (Gloucester, Mass.: Peter Smith, 1976); Edwin White, *The American Judicial Tradition: Profiles*

of Leading American Judges (Oxford University Press, 1976), pp. 84–108.

9   Alan Jones, "Thomas M. Cooley and 'Laissez Faire Constitutionalism': A Reconsideration," *Journal of American History* 53, 4 (March 1967), pp. 751–71; Charles McCurdy, "Justice Field and Jurisprudence of Government–Business Relations: Some Parameters of Laissez-Faire Constitutionalism, 1863–1896," *Journal of American History* 61, 2 (March 1975), pp. 970–1003.

10 E. L. Godkin, "The Duty of Educated Men in a Democracy," *Forum* 17 (March 1894), p. 4.

11 Magali Sarfatti Larson, *The Rise of Professionalism: A Sociological Analysis* (Berkeley: University of California Press, 1978), pp. 137–207; Lawrence R. Veysey, *The Emergence of the American University* (University of Chicago Press, 1965).

12 Lawrence M. Friedman, *A History of American Law* (New York: Simon & Schuster, 1973), pp. 560–4.

13 Thomas L. Haskell, *The Emergence of Professional Social Science: The American Social Science Association and the Nineteenth Century Crisis of Authority* (Urbana: University of Illinois Press, 1977); George M. Fredrickson, *The Inner Civil War: Northern Intellectuals and the Crisis of the Union* (New York: Harper & Row, 1965), pp. 199–216.

14 Haskell, *Professional Social Science*; Mary O. Furner, *Advocacy and Objectivity: A Crisis in the Professionalization of American Social Science* (Lexington: University of Kentucky Press, 1975); A. W. Coates, "The First Two Decades of the American Economic Association," *The American Economic Review* 50, 4 (September 1960), pp. 255–74.

15 Samuel P. Huntington, *The Soldier and the State: The Theory and Practice of Civil–Military Relations* (New York: Vintage Books, 1957), pp. 243–7.

16 On the growth of the professional ethic in America generally, see Barton J. Bledstein, *The Culture of Professionalism: The Middle Class and the Development of Higher Education in America* (New York: Norton, 1976). More to the point, see David G. Grossman, "Professors and Public Service, 1885–1925: A Chapter in the Professionalization of the Social Sciences" (Ph.D. diss., Washington University, 1973). For some qualifications on the relationship between professionalization and bureaucratization that will be borne out in the examination of the cases, see Wayne K. Hobson, "Professionals, Progressives and Bureaucratization," *The Historian* 39 (August 1977), pp. 639–58.

17 See, for example, Leonard W. Bacon, *The Defeat of Party Despotism by the Re-Enfranchisement of the Individual Citizen* (Boston: Rockwell and Churchill, 1886); Godkin, "Duty of Educated Men"; George William Curtis, *The Public Duty of Educated Men* (Albany: J. Munsell, 1878); Moorfield Story, *Politics as a Duty and as a Career* (New York: Putnam, 1889). The absence of a similar attack on the Court at this time reflects the positive identification of most of these reformers with the laissez-faire orientation of the Court and, more generally, with the Court's assertion of authority, principle, and in-

tellectual leadership in government. The important exception to this rule is dealt with in the Chapter 5 on the early ICC.

18   On reform as an expression of the political frustration and decline of an older gentleman class, see John G. Sproat, *The Best Men: Liberal Reformers in the Gilded Age* (Oxford University Press, 1968); Stow Persons, *The Decline of American Gentility* (New York: Columbia University Press, 1973). Other analyses of reform shed doubt on the adequacy of this characterization of the reformers. That the reform standard also gained considerable support from a young, newly organized professional class is argued by Gerald W. McFarland, "The New York Mugwumps of 1884: A Profile," *Political Science Quarterly* 71, 1 (March 1963), pp. 40–58; Gordon S. Wood, "The Massachusetts Mugwumps," *The New England Quarterly* 33, 4 (December 1960), pp. 435–51. See also, Haskell, *Professional Social Science;* Fredrickson, *Inner Civil War.* These works suggest that the institutional reform movements of the late nineteenth century represent a linkage between an older patrician style of deference politics and a new professional style based on expertise.

19   Godkin, "Duty of Educated Men."

20   Keller, *Affairs of State,* p. 290; John Tomsich, *A Genteel Endeavor: American Culture and Politics in the Gilded Age,* (Stanford University Press, 1971).

21   Dobson, *Politics in the Gilded Age,* p. 189.

22   Woodrow Wilson, "The Study of Administration," *Political Science Quarterly* 2, 2 (June 1887), p. 220.

23   Ernst Freund, "The Law of Administration in America," *Political Science Quarterly* 9, 3 (Fall 1894), pp. 403–25.

24   Ostrogorski, *Democracy;* Wallace D. Farnham, "The Weakened Springs of Government: A Study in Nineteenth Century History," *Journal of American History* 68, 3 (April 1963), pp. 662–80; Wiebe, *Search for Order,* pp. 11–52. On the courts, see McClosky, *American Supreme Court;* Benjamin Twiss, *Lawyers and the Constitution: How Laissez-Faire Came to the Supreme Court* (New York: Russell and Russell, 1962).

25   On parties, see Walter Dean Burnham, *Critical Elections and the Mainsprings of American Politics* (New York: Norton, 1970), and Walter Dean Burnham, "Theory and Voting Research: Some Reflections on Converse's 'Change in the American Electorate,'" *American Political Science Review* 68, 3 (September 1974), pp. 1002–23; Philip E. Converse, "Comment," *American Political Science Review* 68, 3 (September 1974), pp. 1023–7; Jerrold G. Rusk, "Comment," *American Political Science Review* 68, 3 (September 1974), pp. 1028–49; Walter Dean Burnham, "Rejoinder," *American Political Science Review* 68, 3 (September 1974), pp. 1050–7; Jesse F. Marquette, "Social Change and Political Mobilization in the United States: 1870–1960," *American Political Science Review* 68, 3 (September 1974), pp. 1058–74. On the courts, see Jones, "Thomas M. Cooley"; McCurdy, "Justice Field"; White, *American Judicial Tradition.*

Chapter 3. Patching civil administration

1 Max Weber, "Bureaucracy," *From Max Weber: Essays in Sociology* (New York: Oxford University Press, 1958), pp. 196–244.

2 R. G. S. Brown, *The Administrative Process in Britain* (London: Methuen, 1971), p. 5; Henry Parris, *Constitutional Bureaucracy: The Development of British Central Administration since the Eighteenth Century* (London: Allen & Unwin, 1969). The first major innovations in the British civil service date from the Northcote–Trevelyan Report of 1854, but the establishment of the system envisioned in that report awaited an Order in Council of 1870. American reforms in 1853 and 1855 paralleled the earliest British moves. Leonard White finds them "fully equivalent" in "Centennial Anniversary," *Public Personnel Review* 14 (January 1953), pp. 3–7.

3 Fritz Morstein Marx, *The Administrative State* (University of Chicago Press, 1957), pp. 76–80.

4 Carl Russell Fish, *The Civil Service and the Patronage* (Cambridge, Mass.: Harvard University Press, 1920), p. 209.

5 U.S. Congress, Joint Select Committee on Retrenchment, "The Civil Service of the United States," *Reports,* 39th Cong., 2nd sess., 1867; U.S. Congress, Joint Select Committee on Retrenchment, "The Civil Service of the United States," *Reports,* 40th Cong., 2nd sess., 1868.

6 Dorman B. Eaton, *The Civil Service in Great Britain: A History of Abuses and Reform and Their Bearing on American Politics* (New York: Harper & Brothers, 1880), pp. 361–428; Paul Van Riper, "Adapting a British Invention to American Needs," *Public Administration* 31 (Winter 1953), pp. 317–30.

7 Marx, *Administrative State*, p. 79; Hans Rosenberg, *Bureaucracy, Aristocracy, Autocracy: The Prussian Experience 1660–1815* (Boston: Beacon Press, 1958).

8 Samuel Beer, *British Politics in the Collectivist Age* (New York: Vintage Books, 1969), pp. 32–68; Brown, *Administrative Process,* pp. 3–25; S. E. Finer, "Patronage and the Public Service: Jeffersonian Bureaucracy and the British Tradition," *Public Administration* 30 (Winter 1952), pp. 329–60; J. Donald Kingsley, *Representative Bureaucracy* (Yellow Springs, Ohio: Antioch Press, 1944), pp. 19–140; Parris, *Constitutional Bureaucracy;* E. E. Schattschneider, *Party Government* (New York: Farrar and Rinehart, 1942), p. 40.

9 E. L. Godkin, "Money at Elections," *Nation* (November 17, 1881), p. 384; E. L. Godkin, "Which Raised Most Money for the Canvass," *Nation* (November 10, 1881), p. 369; Matthew Josephson, *The Politicos, 1865–1896* (New York: Harcourt, Brace and World, 1963), pp. 61, 168, 221, 299; Robert Marcus, *Grand Old Party: Political Structure in the Gilded Age, 1880–1896* (New York: Oxford University Press, 1971), pp. 28–9; Thomas C. Reeves, "Chester A. Arthur and Campaign Assessments in the Election of 1880," *The Historian* 31, 4 (August 1969), pp. 573–82;

Schattschneider, *Party Government*, pp. 176–83; Frederick W. Whiteridge, "Assessments," John L. Lalor, ed., *Cyclopedia of Political Science, Political Economy and Political History of the United States by the Best American and European Writers*. 3 vols. (New York: C. E. Merrill, 1890), I, pp. 152–5.

10 Leonard White, *The Republican Era, 1869–1901: A Study in Administrative History* (New York: Macmillan, 1958); Fish, *Civil Service*, p. 229. By 1896 seven-tenths of the federal payroll was going to employees in the merit service. *United States Civil Service Commission Annual Report* 13 (1895–6), p. 16. Hereafter cited as *Annual Reports*.

11 Allen Schick, "Congress and the 'Details of Administration'," *Public Administration Review* 36, 5 (September–October 1976), pp. 516–28; White, *The Republican Era*, p. 2.

12 In response to the first civil service reform proposal presented to Congress by Charles Sumner in 1864, the *New York Times* wrote: "The work of government will henceforth be too vast and varied, the sum of money too great, the details with which it will have to deal too complicated, to render it possible to perform without a staff of trained officials, furnished with the usual motives to behave well and make the public service the whole and sole business of their lives" (May 10, 1864, p. 4).

13 Carl Schurz, "Congress and the Spoils System," address delivered at the annual meeting of the National Civil Service Reform League, December 12, 1895 (New York: National Civil Service Reform League, 1895).

14 Schurz, "Congress and the Spoils System."

15 *Congressional Record*, 52nd Cong., 2nd sess., 1893, pp. 1302–3, 1341–4, 2482, 2483; see also Oscar Kraines, "The Dockery–Cockrell Commission, 1893–1895," *Western Political Quarterly* 7, 3 (September 1959), pp. 417–62.

16 "The Business Side of Reform," *New York Times* (September 9, 1881), p. 4.

17 "The Civil Service – A Question of Efficiency and Retrenchment," *New York Times* (January 30, 1867), p. 4.

18 *Congressional Globe*, 39th Cong., 2nd sess., 1867, pp. 838–9.

19 Ari Hoogenboom, *Outlawing the Spoils: A History of the Civil Service Reform Movement, 1865–1883* (Urbana: University of Illinois Press, 1968), pp. 42–3.

20 Ari Hoogenboom, "An Analysis of Civil Service Reformers," *The Historian* 23, 1 (November 1960), pp. 54–78; Edward C. Kirkland, *Dream and Thought in the Business Community, 1860–1900* (Ithaca, N.Y.: Cornell University Press, 1956), pp. 139–40.

21 Dorman B. Eaton, "Civil Service Reform in the New York City Post Office and Custom House," *House Executive Documents*, 46th Cong., 3rd sess., 1881; *Congressional Record*, 47th Cong., 1st sess., 1881, pp. 79–85.

22 *New York Times*, "The Business Side of Reform."

23 This is not to suggest that merchant support was insignificant. It is doubtful that reform would have achieved the success it did without this politically

salient constituency behind it. Merchants were also helpful in financing the reform campaign. New York businessman Orlando Potter, for instance, financed much of the propaganda circulated in the critical months after Garfield's assassination. Finally, as we shall see, the Pendleton Act was most effective in appeasing the specific interests of urban merchants.

24 Hoogenboom, *Outlawing*, pp. 42–3, 63.

25 E. L. Godkin, "The Monopolists and the Civil Service," *The Nation* 32, 835 (June 1881), p. 453.

26 James Parton, "The Power of Public Plunder," *North American Review* 133 (July 1881), pp. 42–64. Also, and more generally, see Ruth M. Berens, "Blueprint for Reform: Curtis, Eaton and Schurz" (master's thesis, University of Chicago, 1943).

27 William Dudley Foulke, *Fighting the Spoilsmen, Reminiscences of the Civil Service Reform Movement* (New York: Putnam, 1919), p. 9.

28 George Curtis, "The Evil and the Remedy," *Harper's Weekly* (October 7, 1871), p. 930; Herbert Storing, "Political Parties and the Bureaucracy" in Robert Goldwin, ed., *Political Parties, U.S.A.* (Chicago: Rand McNally, 1964), pp. 139–42.

29 Albion W. Tourgee, "Reform versus Reformation," *North American Review* 132, 293 (April 1881), pp. 305–17. Tourgee supported reform but rejected the leading reformers' grander designs for the government. Dorman Eaton's reply and critique were presented two issues later. "A New Phase of the Reform Movement," *North American Review* 132, 295 (June 1881), pp. 546–58.

30 Grover Cleveland quoted in Allan Nevins, *Grover Cleveland: A Study in Courage* (New York: Dodd, Mead, 1962), p. 200; see also William Graham Sumner, "Elections and Civil Service Reform," *Collected Essays in Political and Social Science* (New York: Henry Holt, 1885), pp. 140–51; Storing, "Political Parties and Bureaucracy."

31 Hoogenboom, "Analysis," p. 59.

32 George Fredrickson, *The Inner Civil War: Northern Intellectuals and the Crisis of the Union* (New York: Harper & Row, 1965), pp. 199–216; Henry Bellows, head of the U.S. Sanitary Commission, became chairman of the first New York Civil Service Reform Association, formed in 1877.

33 Thomas Haskell, *The Emergence of Professional Social Science: The American Social Science Association and the Nineteenth Century Crisis of Authority* (Urbana: University of Illinois Press, 1977), pp. 115–23.

34 Lawrence M. Friedman, *A History of American Law* (New York: Simon & Schuster, 1973), p. 561; Gerald McFarland, "The New York Mugwumps of 1884: A Profile," *Political Science Quarterly* 78, 1 (March 1963), pp. 47–69; Gerald McFarland, *Mugwumps, Morals and Politics* (Amherst: University of Massachusetts Press, 1975), pp. 173–7; Berens, "Blueprint for Reform," pp. 30–65.

35 *Annual Report* 8 (1890–1), p. 13.

36 George Curtis, quoted in Frank Stewart, *The National Civil Service Reform League* (Austin: University of Texas Press, 1929), p. 8.

37   Charles Bonaparte, quoted in Paul Van Riper, *History of the United States Civil Service* (Evanston, Ill.: Row, Peterson, 1958), p. 83.

38   Parton, "Public Plunder," p. 62.

39   Theodore Roosevelt, *An Autobiography* (New York: Macmillan, 1913), p. 162.

40   Parton, "Public Plunder."

41   Henry Adams, "Civil Service Reform," *North American Review* 190, 225 (October 1869), p. 456.

42   Charles Bonaparte, quoted in Robert Wiebe, *The Search for Order, 1877–1920* (New York: Hill and Wang, 1967), p. 60.

43   George Curtis, "The Last Assault Upon Reform," *Harpers Weekly* 31 (May 21, 1887), p. 358.

44   Schurz, "Congress and the Spoils System," pp. 5–6.

45   Carl Schurz, "Civil Service Reform and Democracy," address delivered at the annual meeting of the National Civil Service Reform League (New York: National Civil Service Reform League, April 25, 1893), pp. 1–26.

46   Contemporary scholars who have analyzed presidential reform interests in these terms include Hoogenboom, *Outlawing*, p. 179; Schattschneider, *Party Government*, pp. 139–40; White, *Republican Era*, p. 26.

47   Schurz, "Congress and the Spoils System," p. 73.

48   Rutherford B. Hayes, *Diary and Letters*, Charles R. Williams, ed. 5 vols. (Columbus: Ohio State Archaeological and Historical Society, 1922–1926), III, July 14, 1880, pp. 612–13.

49   Edward A. Huth, "Rutherford B. Hayes: Civil Service Reformer" (Ph.D. diss., Case Western Reserve University, Cleveland, 1943), pp. 239–312; John M. Dobson, *Politics in the Gilded Age: A New Perspective on Reform* (New York: Praeger, 1972), p. 62; Josephson, *The Politicos*, p. 274.

50   Presidential distaste for the consuming duty of patronage distribution is documented by Huth, "Rutherford B. Hayes"; Margaret Leech, *In the Days of McKinley* (New York: Harper & Brothers, 1958), pp. 134–6; Nevins, *Grover Cleveland*, pp. 515–16.

51   Morton Keller, *Affairs of State: Public Life in Late Nineteenth Century America* (Cambridge, Mass.: Belknap Press, 1977), pp. 297–9; H. Wayne Morgan, *From Hayes to McKinley: National Party Politics, 1877–1896* (Syracuse University Press, 1969); Josephson, *The Politicos*, pp. 61–466.

52   16 Stat. 475 at 514, March 3, 1871; Revised Stat. sec. 1753.

53   In the 41st Congress (1869–71) there were 149 Republicans and 63 Democrats in the House and 56 Republicans and 11 Democrats in the Senate. In the 42nd Congress (1871–3) there were 134 Republicans and 104 Democrats in the House and 52 Republicans and 17 Democrats in the Senate.

54   Adams, "Civil Service Reform."

55   Josephson, *The Politicos*, p. 155.

56   Lionel V. Murphy, "The First Civil Service Commission 1871–75," parts I, II, III, *Public Personnel Review* 3, nos. 1, 3, 4 (1942); Hoogenboom, *Outlawing*, pp. 88–117.

57   Quoted in Murphy, "First Civil Service Commission," part III, p. 319.

58 Even Grover Cleveland, who led reformers to bolt the Republican party for a promise of a principled reform and who successfully challenged the Tenure of Office Act, found it difficult to maintain good relations with reformers once he assumed power. Like Hayes, Cleveland was personally contemptuous of many of the local bosses who controlled his party, but unlike Hayes, he remained sensitive to party interests through his first term. In handling the merit service, at least through 1894, Cleveland differed from Grant, Garfield, Arthur, Harrison, and McKinley only in degree. Even his sympathetic biographer draws attention to the practical political constraints that limited the President's effective support for the reform in this era. See Nevins, *Grover Cleveland*, pp. 234–52. For Godkin's assessment of Cleveland, see "Civil Service Reform," *The Nation* (September 27, 1900), p. 246. Theodore Roosevelt's assessment of Cleveland is presented in William Dudley Foulke, *Roosevelt and the Spoilsmen* (New York: National Civil Service Reform League, 1925), pp. 30–3. For Cleveland's view of the reformers, see Morgan, *From Hayes to McKinley*, pp. 250–1.

59 On the Stalwarts, see David M. Jordan, *Roscoe Conkling of New York: Voice in the Senate* (Ithaca, N.Y.: Cornell University Press, 1971); Josephson, *The Politicos*, pp. 90–293; Marcus, *Grand Old Party*, pp. 24–81; Dobson, *Politics in the Gilded Age*, pp. 41–102; Morgan, *From Hayes to McKinley*, pp. 43–187.

60 *Ibid.*; Richard E. Welch, Jr., *George Frisbie Hoar and the Half-Breed Republicans* (Cambridge, Mass.: Harvard University Press, 1971), esp. pp. 2–4, 90–1.

61 Josephson, *The Politicos*, pp. 301–4.

62 C. Vann Woodward, *Reunion and Reaction: The Compromise of 1877 and the End of Reconstruction* (Boston: Little, Brown, 1951), pp. 20, 105–6.

63 Jordon, *Roscoe Conkling*, pp. 248–80. Jordon points out that Conkling actually supported the Hayes electoral compromise, much to the dismay of other Stalwarts.

64 William J. Hartman, "Politics and Patronage: The New York City Custom House, 1852–1902" (Ph.D. diss., Columbia University, 1952), pp. 12, 206; White, *Republican Era*, p. 34.

65 Huth, "Rutherford B. Hayes," pp. 106–19; Jordon, *Roscoe Conkling*, pp. 270–2; "Commission to Examine Certain Custom Houses of the United States," *House Executive Documents*, 45th Cong., 1st sess., 1877.

66 Huth, "Rutherford B. Hayes," p. 109. Jordon, *Roscoe Conkling*, pp. 281–7.

67 Hoogenboom, *Outlawing*, p. 161; William Hartman, "Pioneer in Civil Service Reform: Silas W. Burt and the New York Custom House," *New York Historical Society Quarterly* 39, 4 (October 1955), pp. 369–79.

68 Hoogenboom, *Outlawing*, pp. 155–78; Hartman, "Politics and Patronage," pp. 201–31.

69 Some amusing replies to this order are reprinted in Huth, "Rutherford B. Hayes," pp. 245–56.

70 Jordon, *Roscoe Conkling*, pp. 309–20; Josephson, *The Politicos*, p. 274.

71 Hartman, "Politics and Patronage," pp. 231–56; Jordon, *Roscoe Conkling*, pp. 360–409; *Nation* (March 31, 1881), pp. 213–17; *Nation* (April 21, 1881), pp. 272–3.

72 *Ibid.;* Hoogenboom, *Outlawing*, pp. 254–5; Hartman, "Pioneer," p. 375.

73 Dorman Eaton, "A New Phase."

74 Stewart, *Civil Service Reform League*, pp. 20–45.

75 Stewart, *Civil Service Reform League*, pp. 24–5; A. Bower Sageser, *The First Two Decades of the Pendleton Act: A Study of Civil Service Reform*, University of Nebraska Studies 34–5 (1934–5), (Omaha: University of Nebraska Press, 1935), pp. 37–40.

76 The legislative history of the Pendleton Act is collected in Irving J. Sloan, ed., *American Landmark Legislation*, 10 vols. (New York: Oceana Press, 1977), I, pp. 465–735.

77 Sageser, *Pendleton Act*, pp. 37–40; Hoogenboom, *Outlawing*, pp. 215–35; Reeves, "Chester A. Arthur."

78 Sageser, *Pendleton Act,* p. 42. Republican Henry Dawes of Massachusetts proposed a compromise bill which was basically a restatement of the Grant reform of 1871. It did not deal with assessments at all, and it placed responsibility for examinations with individual department heads rather than with a separate administrative agency. It was, in short, the status quo in new dress. *Congressional Record,* 47th Cong., 1st sess., 1882, p. 1085.

79 Fish, *Civil Service,* p. 217; Hoogenboom, *Outlawing,* pp. 213, 229–38.

80 *Ibid.*

81 Chester Gordon Hall, Jr., "The United States Civil Service Commission: Arm of President or Congress?" (Ph.D. diss., American University, 1965), pp. 1–45.

82 The Senate vote was divided as follows: 38 affirmative (23 Republicans, 14 Democrats, and 1 Independent), 5 negative (all northern Democrats and 1 Independent). In the house the vote was 155 to 47.

83 These are United States Census figures collected in Darrell H. Smith, *The United States Civil Service Commission* (Baltimore: Johns Hopkins University Press, 1928), p. 37.

84 Sageser, *Pendleton Act*, pp. 224–40; Ismar Baruch, "History of Position Classification and Salary Standardization in the Federal Service 1789–1941 (Report, U.S. Civil Service Commission Personnel Classification Division, Washington, D.C., September 30, 1941), pp. 15–23.

85 Ari Hoogenboom, "The Pendleton Act and the Civil Service," *American Historical Review* 64, 2 (January 1959), pp. 301–18.

86 *Annual Report* 13, (1895–6), p. 12; Dorman Eaton, "Civil Service Reform."

87 Wayne E. Fuller, *The American Mail: Enlarger of the Common Life* (University of Chicago Press, 1972), pp. 302–15.

88 Foulke, *Fighting the Spoilsmen*, pp. 5, 58–66; Dorothy Fowler, *The Cabinet Politician* (New York: Columbia University Press, 1943), pp. 216–17.

89 *Ibid.*

90   Sageser, *Pendleton Act*, pp. 74–173.
91   *Nation* (May 14, 1896), p. 370; *Harper's Weekly* (May 23, 1896), pp. 677–8.
92   Sageser, *Pendleton Act*, pp. 201–23. As noted above, Congress exempted from merit examination all those hired under the Spanish-American War emergency appropriation (about 3,500 positions). Later, the Census Act of 1900 reversed Cleveland's classification of that bureau by returning its field service to the spoils.
93   *Annual Report* 2 (1884–5), p. 27, and *Annual Report* 3 (1886–7), p. 143, show confidence in this decline. In the early 1890s hesitation was notable due to the Wanamaker investigations described below. See *Annual Report* 7 (1889–90), pp. 23–5; see also White, *Republican Era*, pp. 335–40. Confidence that the problem of assessments had been largely solved is expressed after the McKinley election. See *Annual Report* 15 (1897–8), p. 34.
94   Marcus, *Grand Old Party*, pp. 129–38.
95   Fowler, *Cabinet Politician*, p. 209.
96   Marcus, *Grand Old Party*, p. 179.
97   *Harper's Weekly* (February 2, 1889), pp. 675–6.
98   Herbert Adams Gibbons, *John Wanamaker*, 2 vols (New York: Harper & Row, 1926), I, 3–260. After leaving the Harrison administration, Wanamaker ran unsuccessfully for governor and U.S. Senator in Pennsylvania in an effort to upset the Republican machine controlled by Matthew Quay.
99   Fuller, *American Mail*, p. 215; Gibbons, *John Wanamaker*, pp. 281–321.
100 Gibbons, *John Wanamaker*, p. 302; Sageser, *Pendleton Act*, p. 156.
101 Mary S. Schinagl, *History of Efficiency Ratings in the Federal Government* (New York: Bookman, 1966), pp. 18–26. Sageser, *Pendleton Act*, p. 156; *Annual Report* 8 (1890–1), p. 3; *Annual Report* 9 (1891–2), pp. 8, 97–8; *Annual Report* 19 (1901–2), pp. 22–3.
102 Fowler, *Cabinet Politician*, pp. 116–9; Edmund Morris, *The Rise of Theodore Roosevelt* (New York: Coward, McCann and Geoghegan, 1979), pp. 394–457; Sageser, *Pendleton Act*, pp. 147–9; Foulke, *Fighting the Spoilsmen*, pp. 289–90; *Annual Report* 11 (1893–4), pp. 230–9; "Violations of the Civil Service Law in Baltimore," *House Reports*, 52nd Cong., 1st sess., 1892.
103 For the independent investigations of the NCSRL during the Harrison administration, see Stewart, *National Civil Service Reform League*, pp. 54–7; Foulke, *Fighting the Spoilsmen*, pp. 46–72; *The Civil Service Record* (publication of the NCSRL) 9–11 (1890–1). On the problem of inadequate staff and congressional appropriations, see *Annual Report* 6 (1888–9), p. 6; *Annual Report* 9 (1891–2), pp. 8–10; *Annual Report* 10 (1892–3), p. 8.
104 Sageser, *Pendleton Act*, p. 64; *Annual Report* 6 (1888–9), pp. 1–2; *Annual Report* 8 (1890–1), pp. 8–10. One indication of the way the commission's institutional priorities were perceived in Congress is provided by the fact that in 1899, the Civil Service Commission was still requesting

permanent office space for its Washington staff within a federal building. *Annual Report* 16 (1898–9), pp. 27–9.

105 Leonard White, "Centennial Anniversary," *Public Administration Review* 14, 1 (January 1953), pp. 3–7.

106 Baruch, "Position Classification," pp. 15–23.

107 Sageser lists this among many ways to circumvent the merit system. *Pendleton Act*, pp. 224–40.

108 Cleveland approved a modification of the 1853 classification system in order to extend the merit service, but the basic problems of relating work and salary were not addressed. *Annual Report* 4 (1886–8), p. 42; Baruch, "Position Classification," pp. 15–23. Leonard White overstates the accomplishment in the area of career planning in these years. A look at the struggle over reform in the years 1900–20 helps to put this back in perspective. White, *The Republican Era*, pp. 346–64.

109 Fish, *Civil Service*, pp. 222–3.

110 Hoogenboom, "The Pendleton Act and the Civil Service," p. 312.

111 David Grossman, "Professors and Public Service, 1885–1925: A Chapter in the Professionalization of the Social Sciences" (Ph.D. diss., Washington University, 1973), pp. 36–7.

112 Cited in Hoogenboom, "The Pendleton Act and the Civil Service," p. 311.

113 Fish, *Civil Service*, p. 233.

114 *Annual Report* 14 (1896–7), p. 24; Sageser, *Pendleton Act*, p. 212.

115 E. L. Godkin, "Civil Service Reform," *The Nation* (September 27, 1900), pp. 246–7.

116 It is important to note again that progressive elements within the parties themselves were frustrated in their own efforts to "bureaucratize" from within. Robert Marcus's analysis of the Republican party in this era shows that despite important changes the Half-Breeds could not reach their goal of a centrally controlled, nationally oriented party structure. See Marcus, *Grand Old Party*.

Chapter 4. Patching the army

1 Stephen Ambrose, *Upton and the Army* (Baton Rouge: Louisiana State University Press, 1964), p. 95; Captain Francis V. Green, "The Important Improvements in the Art of War During the Past Twenty Years and Their Probable Effects on Future Military Operations," *Journal of the Military Service Institution* (JMSI) 4, 1 (January 1883) pp. 1–35; J. D. Hittle, *The Military Staff: Its History and Development* (Harrisburgh, Pa.: Stackpole, 1944), p. 154; Samuel P. Huntington, *The Soldier and the State: The Theory and Politics of Civil–Military Relations* (New York: Vintage Books, 1957), p. 53; Lieutenant-Colonel William Ludlow, "The Military Systems of Europe and America," *North American Review* 160, 1 (January 1895), pp. 72–84.

2 Compare William Ganoe, *The History of the United States Army* (New

York: Appleton, 1924), pp. 355–462, with Russell Weigley, *History of the United States Army* (New York: Macmillan, 1967), pp. 256–82. See also Jack D. Foner, *The United States Soldier between the Wars: Army Life and Reforms, 1865–1898* (New York: Humanities Press, 1970).

3 J. G. A. Pocock, *The Machiavellian Movement: Florentine Political Thought and the Atlantic Republican Tradition* (Princeton, N.J.: Princeton University Press, 1975), pp. 410–15.

4 It is this close integration of the nineteenth-century army with the local political structure and operations of nineteenth-century American government that makes the army more interesting than the navy in the study of state-building politics. Navy reforms came easier in this period and were more extensive, but they did not raise so serious a challenge to established political power relationships and overall institutional structures. Indeed, this may be one important reason why the navy was more successful in its early reform efforts.

5 C. Joseph Bernardo and Eugene H. Bacon, *American Military Policy: Its Development Since 1775* (Harrisburgh, Pa.: Stackpole, 1957) pp. 36–9; Ganoe, *United States Army,* pp. 298–355; James A. Garfield, "The Army of the United States, Part I," *North American Review* 61 (March–April 1878), p. 196; Otis A. Singletary, "The Negro Militia during Radical Reconstruction," *Military Affairs* 19, 4 (Winter 1955), pp. 177–86; Weigley, *United States Army,* pp. 262–3. On the army that fought the Civil War, see Fred Shannon, *The Organization and Administration of the Union Army 1860–1865* (Gloucester, Mass.: Peter Smith, 1928).

6 Philip Taft, "Violence in American Labor Disputes," *Annals of the American Academy of Political and Social Science* 364 (March 1966), p. 128. With regard to expansion, William Appleman Williams notes that political debate centered on the issue of territorial acquisition, not the search for markets. Even antiimperialists supported commercial expansion. *Contours of American History* (New York: New Viewpoints, 1973), p. 368. See also Walter Karp, *The Politics of War* (New York: Harper & Row, 1979), pp. 3–118; Charles S. Campbell, *The Transformation of American Foreign Relations 1865–1900* (New York: Harper & Row, 1976).

7 General George McClellan, "The Militia and the Army," *Harper's New Monthly Magazine* (January 1886), pp. 294–303. McClellan also gave attention to the revival of the Indian Wars, but since this issue did not place qualitatively new kinds of demands on the army, it will not be addressed in this analysis.

8 For Admiral Mahan's view of the army, the navy, seacoast defense, and commercial expansion, see Graham Cosmas, *An Army for Empire: The United States Army in the Spanish-American War* (Columbia: University of Missouri Press, 1971), pp. 40–1.

9 Bernardo and Bacon, *American Military Policy,* p. 239; for another view, see Major William P. King, "The Military Necessities of the United States, and the Best Provisions for Meeting Them," *JMSI* 5, 19 (September 1884), pp. 355–395.

10 "The War on the Army," *Army and Navy Journal* 16 (December 7, 1878), p. 293; Huntington, *Soldier and the State*, pp. 222–69.

11 In the military literature, Upton is often regarded as "the army's Mahan," but again, the extent to which the professional reform program of the army challenged the existing state structure makes the comparison with civil service reform more interesting from the point of view of state-building politics. The following works were consulted in this review of Upton's program: Emory Upton, *The Armies of Asia and Europe* (New York: Appleton, 1878); Emory Upton, *The Military Policy of the United States* (Washington, D.C.: Government Printing Office, 1904); Ambrose, *Upton and the Army*, pp. 71–135; Peter S. Michie, *The Life and Letters of Emory Upton* (New York: Appleton, 1885); Russell F. Weigley, *Towards an American Army: Military Thought from Washington to Marshall* (New York: Columbia University Press, 1962), pp. 100–26.

12 The work of General John Palmer was devoted to a refutation of Upton's program, especially his position on the potential of the militia. See, for example, *America in Arms: The Experience of the United States with Military Organization* (Washington, D.C.: Infantry Journal, 1943) and *Washington, Lincoln, Wilson: Three War Statesmen* (Garden City, N.Y.: Doubleday, Doran, 1930). For a recent historical account of the problems the Federalists had in dealing with the regular army and the militia, see Richard H. Kohn, *Eagle and Sword: The Federalists and the Creation of the Military Establishment, 1783–1802,* (New York: Free Press, 1975).

13 Weigley, *Towards an American Army,* takes issue with Upton on the feasibility of an expansible army with a regular core this small. Upton's reorganization of regulars called for larger and fewer regiments with more small battalions. Three or four battalions to a regiment were best for the expansible plan.

14 In the mid-1880s, Sherman expressed the views of most regulars in calling for an expansible army at the national level and a revitalized militia system supervised by the regulars and limited to state duty. It is significant that this more moderate position was articulated after the revival of the militia had already become an inescapable fact of army politics, after the regulars had already been excluded from a dominant role in strike breaking, and after several legislative defeats for the professional's interest. See General William T. Sherman, "The Militia," *JMSI* 6, 21 (March 1885), pp. 1–26. See also William T. Sherman, "Our Army and Militia," *North American Review* 151, 405 (August 1890), pp. 129–45. For other professionalist variations on Uptonian themes, see "Organization and Training of a National Reserve for Military Service" (n.n.), *JMSI* 8, 1 (March 1889), pp. 29–45; William B. King, "The Military Necessities of the United States and the Best Provisions for Meeting Them," *JMSI* 5, 19 (September 1884), pp. 56–78; Arthur L. Wagner, "The Military Necessities of the United States and the Best Provisions for Meeting Them," *JMSI* 5, 20 (December 1884), pp. 183–204.

15 Major General James B. Fry, "Origins and Progress of the Military Service Institution of the United States," *JMSI* 1, 1 (May 1879), p. 29.

16 *Army and Navy Journal* 16 (October 5, 1878), p. 140; (November 16, 1878), p. 236–40; (November 23, 1878), p. 254–58; (November 30, 1878), p. 276; (December 7, 1878), p. 294; Louis Cantor, "The Creation of the Modern National Guard: The Dick Militia Act of 1903" (Ph.D. diss., Duke University, 1963), pp. 51–9.

17 Some constitutional and historical background on the early militia system will facilitate a better understanding of the guard's late-nineteenth-century position. The militia clauses of the Constitution have long been distinguished as archetypical examples of the founding fathers' ambiguity and hesitation when spelling out the relations between the federal and state governments. The powers of the national government extend to calling forth the militia "to execute the laws of the Union, suppress Insurrections, and repel Invasions." Apparently the militia was not to be used as an offensive force for campaigns on foreign soil, but it could be nationalized and its units used across state lines. Congress could further provide for organizing, arming, and disciplining the militia and would "govern such Part of them as may be employed in the Service of the United States." When employed in the service of the individual states, the militia was not subject to command by the federal government. The states reserved the authority to appoint militia officers and to train troops in "accordance with the discipline prescribed by Congress." Thus, Congress might provide some uniform standards for organization, but actual administration was to be left to the states.

The early militia acts of Congress established the universal liability for the militia duty of all white males between eighteen and forty-five and provided a permanent and annual appropriation of $200,000 for the purchase of muskets to be distributed to the states on the basis of the proportion of their militia enrollments. The rest was left to the states themselves. One of the many points that was left unclear was what specific procedures would govern a call for state troops by the national government. The relationship between regulars and militia and, more particularly, the responsibilities and status of the state-appointed officers when the militia units were nationalized are examples of some obvious points that were not elaborated.

By the 1840s the militia system envisioned in the early days of the republic was a dead letter. Universal military training fell victim to a general lack of interest and administrative incompetence at both the federal and state levels. What developed in its place was a more informal system of volunteer companies. These varied greatly in their military interests and skills. In the South they reflected the martial spirit of the ruling class; in the Northeast, they often became identified with ethnic groups and were predominantly composed of the skilled working class and small merchants. In both cases, they became a center of social activity and blended into their sociopolitical environment. The election of local officers within each unit combined with the governors' powers of appointment to staff positions to integrate the leaders of these social and ethnic groups into party and patronage politics. Leadership in the militia became both a social distinction and a means of political advancement. Officer appointments became a matter of electoral coalition building and party reward.

The citizen soldiery survived in this condition, and many of the state volunteer groups distinguished themselves in the Mexican War and on both sides of the Civil War. It was the veteran militia officers who instigated and led the NGA's campaign for revival in the late nineteenth century. See Amy Bridges, "The Working Classes in Ante-Bellum Urban Politics: New York City 1828–1863" (manuscript, University of Chicago, June 1977); Marcus Cunliffe, *Soldiers and Civilians: The Martial Spirit in America, 1775–1865* (New York: Free Press, 1973); Jim Dan Hill, *The Minute Man in Peace and War: A History of the National Guard* (Harrisburgh, Pa.: Stackpole, 1964); William H. Riker, *Soldiers of the States: The Role of the National Guard in American Democracy* (Washington, D.C.: Public Affairs Press, 1957); Paul Tincher Smith, "Militia of the United States from 1846–1860," *Indiana Magazine of History* 15, 1 (March 1919), pp. 20–47; Frederick Todd, "Our National Guard: An Introduction to Its History," *Military Affairs* 5, 2 (Summer 1941), pp. 77–86; 5, 3 (Fall 1974), pp. 147–62.

18   Martha Derthick, *The National Guard in Politics* (Cambridge, Mass.: Harvard University Press, 1965), pp. 15–29. Derthick details the guard's good fortune in having its interest group demands coincide with both the needs and the interests of political elites.

19   Two factions contested the NGA program. One, composed predominantly of southern officers, took a strict states' rights position and was hostile to the regular army; the other, composed predominantly of northeastern units and led by General George Wingate of New York, sought major reforms at the national level and closer relations with the regulars. Wingate became the foremost advocate for the NGA at this time, although it is questionable whether or not he truly represented the views of the entire organization. See material cited in note 16.

20   Cantor, "Modern National Guard," pp. 69–78; E. B. Hamilton, "National Guard of Illinois," *United Service* 12 (June 1885), pp. 702–5; John Logan, *The Volunteer Soldier of America* (Chicago: Peale, 1887); William H. Powell, "The National Guard and the Necessity for Its Adoption by the General Government," *United Service* 12 (January 1885), pp. 19–31; Weigley, *Towards an American Army*, pp. 127–37.

21   Cantor, "Modern National Guard"; *Army and Navy Journal* 16 (November 30, 1878), pp. 276–7, and 16 (January 18, 1879), pp. 420–1; Powell, "National Guard."

22   Captain H. R. Brinkerhoff, "The Regular Army and the National Guard," *United Service* (n.s.) 13 (June 1895), p. 502; Alexander Webb, "The Mili-

tary Service Institution: What It Is Doing; What It May Do; Its Relations to the National Guard," *JMSI* 5, 17 (March 1884), pp. 3–28.

23 "The National Military Element," *Army and Navy Journal* 16 (January 18, 1879), p. 414. The traditional unpopularity of the regulars is treated by Cunliffe, *Soldiers and Civilians,* pp. 99–144; Webb, "Military Service Institution."

24 For a guardsman's critique of Upton centering on issues of centralization versus decentralization, states' rights versus national consolidation, and the American tradition in general, see the southern presentation of the militia reform issue in *Army and Navy Journal* 16 (December 7, 1878), p. 294. The regulars' reply is contained in the articles cited in note 14 above.

25 General Theodore F. Rodenbough, "The Militia of the United States," *United Service* (n.s.) 1 (April 1879), pp. 283–5; *Army and Navy Journal* 16 (November 23, 1878), p. 258 and 16 (November 30, 1878), p. 276.

26 Huntington, *Soldier and the State,* pp. 163–92; Leonard White, *The Republican Era: A Study in Administrative History* (New York: Macmillan, 1958), pp. 137–42; Bernardo and Bacon, *American Military Policy,* pp. 251–6. The efforts of Commanding General Schofield to reconcile professional leadership and civilian control are treated below.

27 White, *Republican Era,* p. 55.

28 The Adjutant General's Office and the Inspector General's Department had dual responsibilities to the Secretary of War for supervision of the other staff bureaus and to the Commanding General for line command. They were to become the building blocks of the new General Staff Bureau. The other bureaus were the Quartermaster Department, Subsistence Department, Ordinance Department, Corps of Engineers, Medical Department, Signal Corps, Pay Department, and the Judge Advocate General Department.

29 Huntington, *Soldier and the State,* pp. 193–270.

30 Raphael D. Thian, *Legislative History of the General Staff of the United States from 1775–1901* (Washington, D.C.: Government Printing Office, 1901). The heads of the nineteenth-century staff bureaus were often referred to as the General Staff. See also General William T. Sherman, *Memoirs of General Sherman,* 2 vols. (New York: Appleton, 1875), II p. 405; James Garfield, "The Army of the United States," *North American Review* 126, part 1 (March–April 1878), pp. 442–65.

31 Upton clearly saw his reform program in terms of this conflict between staff and line. In a letter of 1879 he writes: "Truth and honesty are on the side of the line, and the country will yet see the general of the army, under the President, in full exercise of the authority belonging to his position." Quoted in Michie, *Life and Letters of Emory Upton,* p. 455.

32 C. Vann Woodward, *Reunion and Reaction: The Compromise of 1877 and the End of Reconstruction* (Boston: Little, Brown, 1966).

33 *Congressional Record,* 44th Cong., 2nd sess., 1877, pp. 2111–20, 2246–8, 2151–2, 2156–62, 2178, 2214–38, 2252.

34 Robert Bruce, *1877: Year of Violence* (Chicago: Quadrangle Books, 1959); Jerry Marvin Cooper, "The Army and Civil Disorder: Federal Intervention in American Labor Disputes, 1877–1900" (Ph.D. diss., University of Wisconsin, 1971), pp. 69–115; Gerald Eggert, *Railroad Labor Disputes: The Beginnings of Federal Strike Policy* (Ann Arbor: University of Michigan Press, 1967), pp. 24–53; Philip Foner, *The Great Labor Uprising of 1877* (New York: Monad Press, 1977); Philip E. MacKry, "Law and Order, 1877: Philadelphia's Response to the Railroad Riots," *Pennsylvania Magazine of History and Biography* 96 (1972), pp. 183–202; Goldwin Smith, "The Labor War in the United States," *The Contemporary Review* 30 (September 1877), pp. 529–41.

35 Cooper, "The Army and Civil Disorder," pp. 69–115.

36 *Ibid;* Elwell S. Otis, "The Army in Connection with the Labor Riot of 1877," *JMSI* 5, 19 (September 1884), pp. 292–323; Bennett Milton Rich, *The Presidents and Civil Disorder* (Washington, D.C.: Brookings Institution, 1941), pp. 70–87; Frederick Wilson, *Mass Violence in America: Federal Aid in Domestic Disturbances 1787–1903* (New York: Arno Press, 1969), pp. 189–203.

37 Derthick, *National Guard in Politics*, p. 17; Riker, *Soldiers of the States*, pp. 50–1; Cooper, "Army and Civil Disorder," p. 73.

38 Cooper, "Army and Civil Disorder," p. 131; Foner, *Great Labor Uprising*.

39 *Chicago Tribune*, July 24, 1877, p. 4; July 26, 1877, p. 4; July 28, 1877, p. 4.

40 *New York Times*, July 25, 1877, p. 4; also July 24, 1877, p. 4.

41 Foner, *Great Labor Uprising*, p. 212; Matthew Josephson, *The Politicos, 1865–1896* (New York: Harcourt Brace and World, 1963), p. 255. Schurz had been a "political general" during the Civil War.

42 Thomas Scott, "The Recent Strikes," *North American Review* 125 (October 1877), pp. 258–62.

43 *Chicago Tribune*, July 28, 1877, p. 4.

44 *War Department Annual Report*, 1877 1, pp. 5–6; Barton C. Hacker, "The United States Army as a National Police Force: The Federal Policing of Labor Disputes, 1877–1898," *Military Affairs* 33, 1 (April 1969), pp. 24–36.

45 Bruce, *1877*, p. 291; *Congressional Record*, 45th Cong., 1st sess., 1877, p. 287.

46 Upton, *Armies*, p. 269. In later endorsing Upton's manuscript, Congressman James Garfield wrote to the author: "I think the country will just now bear a good deal of plain talk on the whole subject, in view of the dangers of communism. Your plan for a national army, modeled somewhat on the German plan of a regular active force, Landwehr and Landstrum, is excellent, and I hope you will work it out so fully in its details that we can embody it in a bill to be introduced into Congress. I am satisfied we shall never be able to organize an effective national militia on the old plan." Garfield to Upton, July 22, 1878, quoted in Michie, *Life and Letters of*

Emory Upton, p. 451. For Garfield's public endorsement of the professional view, see Garfield, "The Army of the United States."

47 Bruce, *1877,* pp. 309–88. Foner, *Great Labor Uprising,* pp. 189–202.

48 *Congressional Record,* 45th Cong., 1st sess., 1877, pp. 285–302, 306–26, 328–39, 345–52, 398, 415–23, 510–14, 525, 549–60. Arthur Ekirch, Jr., *The Civilian and the Military* (New York: Oxford University Press, 1956), p. 112. Allan Nevins, *Abram S. Hewitt* (New York: Harper & Bros., 1935), p. 403.

49 M. A. De Wolfe Howe, ed., *Home Letters of General Sherman* (New York: Scribners, 1909), p. 387.

50 See note 48.

51 The passage of the *posse* rider did not end the battle to restrict the use of federal troops in the South or to protect their role in riot control in the North. The House passed at least seven riders to various bills amending an act of February 25, 1865, which had empowered federal authorities to employ troops "to keep peace at the polls." All were vetoed by Hayes until some compromise language was agreed upon late in 1878 in which the army was excluded from civil but not military action. On December 1, 1879, Congress again restricted the army. This time there seemed to be a clear effort to separate electoral supervision from suppression of domestic violence. The former was forbidden, the latter sanctioned. Ernest Sutherland Bates writes of this as the "capitalist form" of the act that the President could accept. *The Story of Congress 1789–1935* (New York: Harper & Brothers, 1936), p. 284. This sanction for the use of the army in labor riots did not significantly affect its actual employment. See also White, *Republican Era,* pp. 35–8; James Ford Rhodes, *History of the United States from the Compromise of 1850 to the McKinley–Bryan Campaign of 1896.* 8 vols. (New York: Macmillan, 1920), 8, pp. 281–3; Wilson, *Mass Violence in America,* pp. 187–8; Nevins, *Abram S. Hewitt;* Colonel Elwell S. Otis, "The Army in Connection with the Labor Riots of 1877," *JMSI* 6, 32 (June 1885), pp. 117–18. For the debates of May 1878, see *Congressional Record,* 45th Cong., 2nd sess., pp. 3535–53, 3579–88, 3616–42, 3670–84, 3717–34, 3760–3898, 4180–4358, 4647–81.

52 The important exception to this rule was the Chicago strike of 1894, in which Cleveland sent in troops against the governor's explicit wishes on the basis of interference with mail and interstate commerce. Rich, *Presidents and Civil Disorder,* pp. 87–109; Cooper, "Army and Civil Disorder," pp. 227–80; Matthew Josephson, *The Politicos, 1865–1896* (New York: Harcourt, Brace and World, 1963), pp. 559–81.

53 Robert W. Coakley, "Federal Use of Militia and the National Guard in Civil Disturbances," Robin Higham, ed., *Bayonets in the Streets: The Use of Troops in Civil Disturbances* (Lawrence: University Press of Kansas, 1969), p. 27.

54 Hacker, "United States Army."

55 Lieutenant William Wallace, "The Army and the Civil Power," *JMSI* 17 (March 1895), p. 254.

56 *Congressional Record,* 45th Cong., 2nd sess., 1878, pp. 3538–9.

57 Ronald Gephart, "Politicians, Soldiers and Strikers: The Reorganization of the Nebraska Militia and the Omaha Strike of 1882," *Nebraska History* 46, 2 (June 1965), pp. 89–120; Cyril B. Upham, "Historical Survey of the Militia of Iowa, 1865–1898," *Iowa Journal of History and Politics* 18, 1 (January 1920), pp. 3–93. Other state histories consulted include Frederic Gilbert Bauer, "The Massachusetts Militia," Albert Bushnell Hart, ed., *Commonwealth History of Massachusetts.* 5 vols. (New York: State's History, 1930), 5, pp. 570–97; William P. Clarke, *Official History of the Militia and the National Guard of the State of Pennsylvania* (Williamsport, Pa.: Gazette and Bulletin Printing House, 1887). For a history of the most famous and best-organized Guard unit in the nation, see Emmons Clark, *History of the Seventh Regiment of New York* (New York: Seventh Regiment, 1890).

58 Riker, *Soldiers of the States,* pp. 41–66; Cantor, "Modern National Guard," pp. 50–1.

59 Cantor, "Modern National Guard," p. 78.

60 Major Winthrop Alexander, "Ten Years of Riot Duty," *JMSI* 19, 82 (July 1896), pp. 2–26. Alexander's figures include the years 1886–95. Before 1886, see "Efficiency of the Militia," *House Reports* 3, 754, 52nd Cong., 1st sess. After 1895, see Report of the Army War College 9744-C, "Duty Performed by the Organized Militia in Connection with Domestic Disturbances, 1894–1906" (General Staff War College Division RG165 National Archives, General Catalogue, Washington, D.C.).

61 Francis V. Green, "The New National Guard," *The Century Magazine* 43, 4 (February 1892), pp. 488–9. The northeastern states mentioned received a total of $89,300 from Washington and spent $1,136,000. The militia states spending over $100,000 on troops in 1896 include New York ($448,000), Pennsylvania ($350,000), Ohio ($317,235), Massachusetts ($264,000), New Jersey ($171,654), Connecticut ($140,000), Wisconsin ($118,000), and California ($111,800). Adjutant General Office, War Department, Military Information Division, "The Organized Militia of the United States in 1896," p. 4.

62 See note 58.

63 Green, "New National Guard," pp. 488–9, estimated the annual cost of each regular in the U.S. army at $1,000, whereas the annual cost to the state of each militiaman was $24, of which the federal government contributed one-sixth.

64 Cantor, "Modern National Guard," pp. 51–2.

65 Proceedings of the 12th Annual American Federation of Labor Convention, 1892, quoted in Cooper, "Army and Civil Disorders," p. 23. There was also a military sentiment often expressed in the *Army and Navy Journal* to ban working men from the militia. Though such choices were presented to labor time and again, it does not seem that the guard ever became a strictly propertied class force. See also Riker, *Soldiers of the States,* pp. 50–1.

66 Green, "New National Guard," pp. 491–7; Cantor, "Modern National Guard," pp. 70–8.

67 Cantor, "Modern National Guard," pp. 63–6.

68 Cantor, "Modern National Guard," pp. 66–71.

69 *Army and Navy Journal* 17 (January 17, 1880), p. 474.

70 National Guard Association *Proceedings,* quoted in Cantor, "Modern National Guard," p. 59.

71 Cantor, "Modern National Guard," pp. 59–63, 78–83; W. Boerum Wetmore, "The National Guard Bill in Congress," *United Service* 6 (March 1882), pp. 336–42; Thomas M. Anderson, "Our Militia, State or National?" *United Service* 5 (July 1881), pp. 22–30. By distributing federal equipment rather than money, Congress ensured that the states would not use the subsidy for other purposes. This cleared the way for a federal accounting of goods rendered.

72 Bernardo and Bacon, *American Military Policy,* pp. 247–51.

73 *U.S. Statutes at Large* 24, February 12, 1887.

74 "House and Senate Joint Committee Report on the Reorganization of the Army," *Senate Reports,* 2, 555, 45th Cong., 3rd sess., 1878. The only major military figure to openly oppose the Uptonian professional views was General Hancock, who was on his way toward the Democratic nomination for President in 1880. Weigley, *History,* p. 283.

75 Bernard Boylan, "The Forty-fifth Congress and Army Reform," *Mid-America* 41, 3 (July 1959), pp. 185–6. Army opposition to the troop reductions can be read in the *Army and Navy Journal* 16 (January 25, 1879), pp. 436–7. This bill's administrative reorganization scheme is reviewed in the *Army and Navy Journal* 16 (December 21, 1878), pp. 325–41.

76 Ambrose, *Upton and the Army,* p. 116.

77 *Army and Navy Journal* 16 (December 21, 1878), p. 342.

78 *Army and Navy Journal* 16 (January 25, 1879), p. 488.

79 *Congressional Record,* 45th Cong., 3rd sess., 1879, 8, part 2, p. 1757; Boylan, "Forty-fifth Congress."

80 Quoted in Ira Reeves, *Military Education in the United States* (Burlington, Vt.: Free Press, 1914), p. 205.

81 Reeves, *Military Education,* pp. 204–8; Huntington, *Soldier and the State,* p. 231; Bernardo and Bacon, *American Military Policy,* p. 311; Foner, *United States Soldier between the Wars,* pp. 77–113; Elvid Hunt and Walter Lorence, *History of Fort Leavenworth, 1827–1937* (Fort Leavenworth, Kan.: Command and General Staff School Press, 1937), pp. 221–36; Lieutenant E. M. Weaver, "The Military Schools of the United States," *United Service* (n.s.) 3 (May 1890), pp. 457–69; Lieutenant Arthur Wagner, "An American War College," *JMSI* 10, 39 (July 1889), pp. 287–304.

82 Foner, *United States Soldier between the Wars;* Bernardo and Bacon, *American Military Policy,* pp. 243–4. In 1877 there were over 200 army garrisons in the nation. By 1896, they had been consolidated to 77.

83 *Ibid.;* Ganoe, *United States Army,* pp. 365–6.

84 *Ibid.;* Elizabeth Bethel, "The Military Information Division: Origin of the Intelligence Division," *Military Affairs* 11, 1 (Spring 1947), pp. 17–24.

85 John M. Schofield, *Forty-Six Years in the Army* (New York: Century, 1897), esp. pp. 420–2 and 535–40; see also Weigley, *Towards an American Army,* pp. 162–76.

86 Bethel, "Military Information Division."

87 Weigley, *History,* pp. 283–4.

88 W. B. Franklin, "National Defense," *North American Review* 137 (December 1883), pp. 1179–98; H. A. Smally, "A Defenseless Seacoast," *North American Review* 137 (March 1884), pp. 387–409; Eugene Griffen, "Our Seacoast Defense," *North American Review* 97 (July 1888), pp. 564–89.

89 Edward Ranson, "The Endicott Board of 1885–86 and the Coast Defenses," *Military Affairs* 21, 2 (Summer 1967), pp. 74–84; Weigley, *Towards an American Army,* pp. 141–4.

90 "Report of the Board on Fortification of Seacoast Defenses," 49th Cong., 1st sess., *House Executive Document* 1, 49, 1885.

91 The board had asked for $126 million to complete the project by 1900. Congress appropriated $2 million a year until 1898. Ranson, "Endicott Board."

92 Bernardo and Bacon, *American Military Policy,* p. 249; Ranson, "Endicott Board," p. 79. The seacoast plan also instigated proposals to reorganize the army's own artillary units. See *Army and Navy Journal* 35 (April 16, 1898), p. 621.

93 Cosmas, *An Army for Empire,* esp. pp. 139–40, 144–5, 284–94. On Republican party designs, see Walter Karp, *The Politics of War* (New York: Harper & Row, 1979), pp. 3–118.

94 Cosmas, *An Army for Empire,* pp. 83–6.

95 Cosmas, *An Army for Empire; Army and Navy Journal* 35 (March 19, 1898), pp. 532, 534, 541; 35 (March 26, 1898), p. 555.

96 *Army and Navy Journal* 35 (April 2, 1898), pp. 578, 582, 585; 35 (April 16, 1898), pp. 619, 627; 35 (April 23, 1898), p. 656; Graham Cosmas, "From Order to Chaos: The War Department, the National Guard and Military Policy, 1898," *Military Affairs* 29, 3 (Fall 1965), pp. 105–21.

97 John Hull, "The Army Appropriation Bill," *The Forum* 25 (May 1898), p. 399.

98 *Congressional Record,* 55th Cong., 2nd sess., 31, part 4, 1898, pp. 3624–93. The professional army reply to these sentiments may be summed up by an editorial note entitled "Congressional Ignorance," *Army and Navy Journal* 35 (April 16, 1898), p. 627. "What has the war-talk about liberally educated young men, 'gamest blood,' etc., to do with the question of how we can make the best use of such military knowledge and military training as we have? Given equal intelligence, is it not reasonable to assume that men who have devoted themselves for many years to the study of a particular profession should be better fitted to the exercise of its functions in a time of emergency ... than those whose minds are absorbed with other

pursuits and whose interests in military matters is that of an amateur? . . . Even patriotism should be expended wisely and it is not right to take advantage of the zeal of young men who volunteer for service without any just appreciation of what this involves, and who are offering to their country much more than they can afford to give and much more than she needs to ask." See also *Army and Navy Journal* 35 (April 9, 1898), p. 605.

99   Cantor, "Modern National Guard," pp. 113–14. Regarding the opposition of the governors in the debates, see *Congressional Record,* 55th Cong., 2nd sess., 1890, pp. 4114–15.

100 Cantor, "Modern National Guard," pp. 114–18. Statutes at Large, 30, Act of April 22, 1898, p. 361. Hull quoted in *Congressional Record,* 55th Cong., 2nd sess., 1898, p. 4114.

101 Cosmas, *An Army for Empire,* pp. 108–9.

102 *Army and Navy Journal* 35 (April 30, 1898), pp. 678, 681.

103 Cantor, "Modern National Guard," pp. 121, 122; Cosmas, *An Army for Empire,* pp. 113–14.

104 Edward Ranson, "Nelson A. Miles as Commanding General: 1895–1903," *Military Affairs* 29, 4 (Winter 1965–6), pp. 183–9.

105 Margaret Leech, *In the Days of McKinley* (New York: Harper & Brothers, 1959), pp. 233–40.

106 Cosmas, *An Army for Empire,* pp. 145–8.

107 For a general discussion of the mobilization problems, see Cosmas, *An Army for Empire,* pp. 139–77. See also "Commission to Investigate the Conduct of the War Department in the War with Spain, Report I," *Senate Documents,* 221, 56th Cong., 1st sess., 1900, p. 113. Hereafter cited as *Dodge Commission Report.*

108 *Dodge Commission Report,* pp. 133–4.

109 *Dodge Commission Report,* pp. 134–5.

110 *Dodge Commission Report,* p. 115; Edward Ranson, "The Investigation of the War Department, 1898–99," *The Historian* 34, 1 (November 1971), pp. 78–99.

111 Ranson, "Nelson A. Miles," pp. 187–9; *Dodge Commission Report,* pp. 156–7; Cosmas, *An Army for Empire,* pp. 304–7.

112 Leech, *McKinley,* pp. 366–78; Cosmas, *An Army for Empire,* pp. 304–7.

113 *Army and Navy Journal* 36 (December 10, 1898), pp. 345–6; 36 (December 17, 1898), p. 161; 36 (March 4, 1899), p. 625; Alexander Bacon, "Is Our Army Degenerate?" *The Forum* 27 (March–August 1899), pp. 10–23.

114 *Army and Navy Journal* 36 (December 31, 1898), pp. 415–16; 36 (January 28, 1899), pp. 513; 36 (February 4, 1899), p. 537; 36 (February 11, 1899), p. 551; 36 (February 25, 1899), p. 613; Graham Cosmas, "Military Reform after the Spanish-American War: The Army Reorganization Fight of 1898–1899," *Military Affairs* 35, 1 (February 1971), pp. 12–17.

115 John Hull, "The Organization of the Army," *North American Review* 168, 509 (April 1899), pp. 385–98.

116   *Army and Navy Journal* 36 (March 23, 1899), p. 633.
117   Leech, *McKinley,* pp. 379–83; Philip C. Jessup, *Elihu Root,* 2 vols. (New York: Dodd Mead, 1938), I, p. 215.
118   *Ibid.* See Chapter 7 for Root's reform strategy before the 1900 election.
119   Lieutenant-Colonel James Pettit, "How Far Does Democracy Affect the Organization and Discipline of Our Armies?" *JMSI* 38, 139 (January–February 1906), pp. 1–38. This essay was awarded the Seaman Prize by the institution in 1905.

Chapter 5. Patching business regulation

1   Charles Francis Adams, Jr., *The Railroads: Their Origin and Problems* (New York: Putnam, 1887), pp. 117–18, 214.
2   Lee Benson, *Merchants, Farmers and Railroads: Railroad Regulation and New York Politics, 1850–1887* (Cambridge, Mass.: Harvard University Press, 1955), p. 6; James Willard Hurst, *The Legitimacy of the Business Corporation in the United States, 1780–1970* (Charlottesville: University of Virginia Press, 1970).
3   Ironically, the work that comes closest to taking a public interest view of the ICC still stands above all others as the classic and standard treatment: I. L. Sharfman, *The Interstate Commerce Commission: A Study in Administrative Law and Procedure,* 4 vols. (New York: Commonwealth Fund, 1931). For the pressure group literature, see below.
4   This discussion of the environmental imperatives for railroad regulation draws from a number of works, including: Adams, *The Railroads;* Benson, *Merchants, Farmers and Railroads;* Ari and Olive Hoogenboom, *A History of the ICC: From Panacea to Palliative* (New York: Norton, 1976), pp. 1–6; Gabriel Kolko, *Railroads and Regulation, 1877–1916* (New York: Norton, 1965), pp. 7–29; Edward Chase Kirkland, *Industry Comes of Age: Business, Labor, and Public Policy* (Chicago: Quadrangle Books, 1961), pp. 43–96; Sharfman, *Interstate Commerce Commission,* I.
5   This was Charles Adams's basic definition of the railroad problem. Adams, *The Railroads,* p. 6.
6   This discussion owes much to the insights of Theodore Lowi on the relationship between politics and policy. Theodore Lowi, "American Business and Public Policy: Case Studies and Political Theory," *World Politics* 16, 4 (July 1964), pp. 677–715. Lowi distinguishes constitutional (or institution-building) policies and their politics from regulatory policies and their politics. We are concerned, however, with the constitutional or institution-building problems in this first great national regulatory effort. Civil service reform, army organization, and national railroad regulation shared a similar institution-building problem despite the fact that the specifics of the politics in each area differed.
7   Solon Buck, *The Granger Movement: A Study of Agricultural Organization and Its Political, Economic and Social Manifestations 1870–1880* (Cambridge, Mass.: Harvard University Press, 1913).

8   *Ibid.*, pp. 216, 225; Robert Cushman, *The Independent Regulatory Commissions* (London: Oxford University Press, 1941), p. 26.

9   "Report of the Select Committee on Transportation-Routes to the Seaboard," *Senate Reports* 1, 43rd Cong., 1st sess., 1874.

10 Buck, *Granger Movement;* p. 227–9.

11 George Miller, *Railroads and the Granger Laws* (Madison: University of Wisconsin Press, 1971).

12 *Ibid.*, p. 170.

13 *Ibid.*, p. 94.

14 Gerald D. Nash, "Origins of the Interstate Commerce Act of 1887," *Pennsylvania History* 24 (July 1957), p. 182.

15 Benson, *Merchants, Farmers and Railroads,* pp. 212, 223.

16 *Ibid.*, p. 52.

17 *Ibid.*, p. 118.

18 *Ibid.*, p. 230.

19 Kolko, *Railroads and Regulation,* p. 3.

20 Quoted from G. R. Blanchard in Kolko, *Railroads and Regulation,* p. 38.

21 *Ibid.*, p. 5.

22 Robert W. Harbeson, "Railroads and Regulation, 1877–1916: Conspiracy or Public Interest?" *Journal of Economic History* 27 (June 1967), p. 233. A more sympathetic reviewer observes that Kolko missed the central theoretical issue raised by his discussion of the big business theory of governmental action, that is, why must regulation aimed at reestablishing order and stability in the private economy necessarily be an abandonment of the public interest? Robert B. Carson, "Railroads and Regulation Revisited: A Note on Problems of Historiography and Ideology," *The Historian* 34, 3 (May 1972), pp. 437–46.

23 Kolko, *Railroads and Regulation,* pp. 64–83.

24 Harbeson, "Railroads and Regulation"; Albro Martin, "The Troubled Subject of Railroad Regulation in the Gilded Age – A Reappraisal," *Journal of American History* 61 (September 1974), pp. 339–71. Paul W. MacAvoy argues that despite the antipooling clause in the Commerce Act, de facto pooling agreements in the form of traffic associations were maintained in the 1890s with the implicit sanction of the commission. Yet, whereas the ICC's enlightened neglect of the antipooling clause may have served the railroads' interest, this kind of policy making by default, followed by the Supreme Court's rulings against traffic associations and the commission's position regarding them, only serves to highlight the fact that American national government was incapable of taking concerted and consistent action on its own behalf in regulation. Paul W. MacAvoy, *The Economic Effects of Regulation: The Trunk Line Cartels and the Interstate Commerce Commission Before 1900* (Cambridge, Mass.: MIT Press, 1965). See note 103.

25 Edward Purcell, Jr., "Ideas and Interests: Business and the Interstate Commerce Act," *Journal of American History* 54 (December 1967), pp. 561–78.

26　Ibid., p. 578.

27　Mary O. Furner, *Advocacy and Objectivity: A Crisis in the Professionalization of American Social Science, 1865–1905* (Lexington: University of Kentucky Press, 1975), pp. 72–9.

28　On Henry Carter Adams, see the following: Lawrence Bigelow et. al., "Henry Carter Adams 1851–1921," *Journal of Political Economy* 30, 2 (April 1922), pp. 201–11; A. W. Coats, "Henry Carter Adams: A Case Study in the Emergence of the Social Sciences in the United States 1850–1900" *Journal of American Studies* 2, 2 (October 1968), pp. 177–97; Joseph Dorfman, ed., *Two Essays by Henry Carter Adams* (New York: Columbia University Press, 1954), pp. 3–54; David Grossman, "Professors and Public Service, 1885–1925: A Chapter in the Professionalization of the Social Sciences" (Ph.D. diss., Washington University, 1973); Marvin B. Rosenberry, "Henry Carter Adams," Earl D. Babst and Lewis G. Vander Velde, eds., *Michigan and the Cleveland Era: Sketches of the University of Michigan Staff Members and Alumni Who Served the Cleveland Administrations 1885–89, 1893–97* (Ann Arbor: University of Michigan Press, 1948), pp. 23–41; Tazar Volin, "Henry Carter Adams, Critic of Laissez Faire," *Journal of Social Philosophy* 3, 3 (April 1938), pp. 235–50.

29　Henry Carter Adams, "The Relation of the State to Industrial Action," reprinted in Dorfman, *Two Essays*. See also the opinion of another AEA cofounder, Edwin R. A. Seligman, "Railway Tariffs and the Interstate Commerce Law," *Political Science Quarterly* 2 (June 1887), pp. 223–64, and 3 (September 1887), pp. 369–413.

30　Adams, "Relation of the State," pp. 66–7.

31　*Ibid.*; Dorfman notes (p. 31) that Adams was no champion of the commission idea. He would have preferred an executive bureau. His later writings on a Bureau of Railway statistics confirm this view (see below). Seeing the inevitability of the commission form in 1886, Adams advocated a "strong commission." See also Henry Carter Adams, "Interstate Commerce Act: Discussion," *Michigan Political Science Association Publications* 1, 2 (November 1894), pp. 137–43.

32　Henry Carter Adams, "Relation of the State," pp. 65–6.

33　Others not reviewed in this paragraph include Thomas McIntyre Cooley (discussed later) and Joseph Nimmo, head of the Treasury Department's Bureau of Statistics. Nimmo first became interested in the railroad problem as an investigator for the Windom Committee. He became estranged from the ICC in the 1890s over the issue of rate-making power but came to support it as a leader of the Progressive-oriented Industrial Commission around the turn of the century. His views and others' can be read in C. C. McCain, ed., *A Compendium of Transportation Theories* (Washington, D.C.: Kensington, 1893). The views of all these men can be found in Cullom Committee Report, *Report of The Senate Select Committee on Interstate Commerce*, vol. 2, *Testimony*, 49th Cong., 1st sess., 1886.

34　The evolution of Charles Adams's career and his opinions on railroad regulation can be read in the following: Edward Chase Kirkland, *Charles*

Francis Adams, Jr., 1835–1915: The Patrician at Bay (Cambridge, Mass.:
Harvard University Press, 1965); Edward Chase Kirkland, *Business in the
Gilded Age: The Conservative's Balance Sheet* (Madison: University of
Wisconsin Press, 1952), pp. 3–20. Adams's own writing on the subject
include: "The Railroad System," *North American Review* 104 (April
1867), pp. 345–68; "Legislative Control over the Railway Centers,"
American Law Review 1 (April 1867), pp. 25–46; "Railroad Inflation,"
North American Review 108 (January 1869), pp. 30–106; "A Chapter of
Erie," *North American Review* 109 (July 1869), pp. 30–106; "The
Granger Movement," *North American Review* 120 (April 1875), pp.
394–424; *The Railroads: Their Origin and Problems* (1887); "The Interstate Commerce Law," (December 1888), C. C. McCain, ed., *Compendium of Transportation Theories* (Washington, D.C.: Kensington, 1893),
pp. 178–84.

35 Sterne served with E. L. Godkin and William Evarts on the Tilden Commission. The commission recommended sweeping electoral reforms to crush
machine power, including a restriction of suffrage to propertyholders. The
evolution of Sterne's career can be read in John Foord, *The Life and Public
Service of Simon Sterne* (New York: Macmillan, 1903). Sterne's progress
from the singleminded pursuit of the merchants' immediate demands to a
more moderate and Progressive view is evident in Benson's treatment of the
Hepburn investigation in *Merchants, Farmers and Railroads*. From Sterne
himself, see the following: "The Railway in Its Relation to Public and
Private Interests," address of Simon Sterne before the Chamber of Commerce and New York Board of Trade and Transportation, April 19, 1878
(Press of the New York Chamber of Commerce, 1878); "Information Furnished by Simon Sterne Esq. of New York in regard to the Application of
the Law of Corporations to Policy Arrangements and to Discriminations in
Rail Rates," June 27, 1879 (Library of Congress catalogue); "An Address
on Interstate Railway Traffic" at the Tenth Annual Meeting of the National Board of Trade, December 11, 1879 (Boston: Tolman and White,
1880); *Constitutional History and Political Development in the United
States* (New York: Cassell, Pelten, Golpin, 1882); "Relations of the Governments of the Nations of Europe to the Railways," *Senate Misc. Documents*, no. 66, 49th Cong., 2nd sess., 1887; "The Railway Question:
Statement of Simon Sterne Made to the United States Select Committee on
Interstate Commerce at the Fifth Avenue Hotel of New York"
(Washington, D.C.: Government Printing Office, 1885); "Railway Reorganization," *Forum* 10 (September 1890), pp. 636–8; "Railways," John J.
Falor, ed., *Cyclopedia of Political Science*, 3 vols. (New York: Merrill,
1890), 3, pp. 520–32; *Railways in the United States* (New York: Putnam,
1912).

36 On Hadley's life and career, see Morris Hadley, *Arthur Twining Hadley*
(New Haven, Conn.: Yale University Press, 1948); Grossman, "Professors
and Public Service." It is interesting to note that Hadley refused to join the
AEA at first because of its ideological divisiveness. He later became presi-

dent of the association. For Hadley on railroads, see *Railroad Transportation: Its History and Laws* (New York: Putnam, 1885); "Railroad Business Under the Interstate Commerce Act," *The Quarterly Journal of Economics* 3 (January 1889), pp. 170–87.

37 The quotation is from Henry Poor at the Cullom Committee hearings. *Report of the Senate Select Committee on Interstate Commerce*, p. 232.
38 Simon Sterne, "Relations of the Governments," p. 4.
39 *Ibid.*, p. 5.
40 Benson, *Merchants, Farmers and Railroads*, p. 6; Sterne, "Railways," *Cyclopedia*, pp. 512–13.
41 Charles F. Adams, *Railroads*, pp. 94–9, 116. See also an English view of this American problem: W. M. Acworth, "English and American Railroads: A Comparison and Contrast," *Compendium of Transportation Theories*, pp. 138–40.
42 Hadley, *Railroad Transportation*, pp. 145, 252–8.
43 Henry C. Adams, "Service of a Bureau of Railway Statistics and Accounts in the Railway Question," *Compendium of Transportation Theories*, pp. 129–38.
44 Sterne, "Railways," *Cyclopedia*, p. 529; Charles Francis Adams, *Railroads*, pp. 113–18; Hadley, *Railroad Transportation*, p. 256.
45 Sterne, "Railways," *Cyclopedia*, p. 531.
46 Clyde E. Jacobs, *Law Writers and the Courts: The Influence of Thomas M. Cooley, Christopher Tiedman and John F. Dillon upon American Constitutional Law* (Berkeley: University of California Press, 1954); Thomas A. Mason and William M. Braney, *The Supreme Court in a Free Society* (Englewood Cliffs, N.J.: Prentice-Hall, 1954), pp. 218–31; Arnold M. Paul, *Conservative Crisis and the Rule of Law: Attitudes of the Bar and Bench, 1887–1895* (Gloucester, Mass.: Peter Smith, 1976); Paul L. Rosen, *The Supreme Court and Social Science* (Champaign: University of Illinois Press, 1972), pp. 23–45; Benjamin Twiss, *Lawyers and the Constitution: How Laissez-Faire Came to the Supreme Court* (New York: Russell and Russell, 1942).
47 Henry Carter Adams, "Publicity and Corporate Abuses," *Michigan Political Science Association Publications* 1, 2 (November 1894), pp. 116–18; Henry Carter Adams, "Economics and Jurisprudence" (February 1897), reprinted in Dorfman, *Two Essays*, pp. 137–62.
48 Henry Carter Adams, "The Interstate Commerce Act: A Discussion," *Michigan Political Science Association Publications* 1, 1 (May 1894), p. 141.
49 This is not to say that all those who wrote about the issue took the Progressive line. For the radical agrarian, procompetition view, see James F. Hudson, *The Railways and the Republic* (New York: Harper & Brothers, 1886). Hudson's work was referred to frequently in the legislative debates as a counter to the Progressive viewpoint.
50 *Congressional Record*, 49th Cong., 2nd sess., 1887, p. 844.
51 Munn *v* Illinois, 94 U.S. 113 (1877).

52 Miller, *Railroads and the Granger Laws.*

53 Paul, *Conservative Crisis.*

54 Charles McCurdy, "Justice Field and the Jurisprudence of Government–Business Relations: Some Parameters of Laissez-Faire Constitutionalism, 1863–1896," *Journal of American History* 61, 2 (March 1975), pp. 970–1003; Carl Brent Swisher, *Stephen J. Field, Craftsman of the Law* (University of Chicago Press, 1969), pp. 372–92.

55 Ben H. Proctor, *Not without Honor: The Life of John H. Reagan* (Austin: University of Texas Press, 1962).

56 Republicans who opposed the Reagan bill often offered amendments extending coverage to passenger traffic. To defend southern Jim Crow practices, Reagan would refuse to concur and the bill would be stalled.

57 For a view of an expert of the times see Seligman, "Railway Tariffs." For more recent views, see George W. Hilton, "The Consistency of the Interstate Commerce Act," *Journal of Law and Economics* 9 (October 1966), pp. 87–113; Albro Martin, "The Troubled Subject of Railroad Regulation in the Gilded Age – A Reappraisal," *Journal of American History* 61 (September 1974), pp. 339–71.

58 *Congressional Record,* 48th Cong., 2nd sess., 1884, p. 366.

59 *Congressional Record,* 45th Cong., 3rd sess., 1878, pp. 100–2.

60 *Congressional Record,* 45th Cong., 2nd sess., 1878, pp. 3392–5.

61 *Congressional Record,* 45th Cong., 2nd sess., 1878, pp. 3096–7, 3275–80, 3392–3413.

62 *Congressional Record,* 45th Cong., 3rd sess., 1878, pp. 93–102.

63 Proctor, *Not without Honor,* pp. 233–7; *Congressional Record,* 46th Cong., 2nd sess., 1880, pp. 1081, 4018–32.

64 *Ibid.*; Peter Stephen McGuire, "The Genesis of the Interstate Commerce Commission" (Ph.D. thesis, Cornell University, 1922), pp. 145–50.

65 *Congressional Record,* 48th Cong., 2nd sess., 1884, pp. 42–55.

66 *Congressional Record,* 48th Cong., 2nd sess., 1884, p. 329.

67 James W. Neilson, "Shelby M. Cullom: Prairie State Republican," *University of Illinois Studies in the Social Sciences* 51 (1962), pp. 93–9.

68 *Ibid.*

69 *Senate Committee Report,* 1886, p. 177.

70 For a discussion of the strong and weak commission models, see Robert Cushman, *The Independent Regulatory Commissions* (London: Oxford University Press, 1941), pp. 20–30. See also, Shelby M. Cullom, *Fifty Years of Public Service* (Chicago: McClurg, 1911), pp. 305–32.

71 *Senate Committee Report,* 1886, p. 177.

72 *Ibid.*

73 *Congressional Record,* 48th Cong., 2nd sess., 1885, pp. 1246–54.

74 *Senate Committee Report,* 1886.

75 Kolko, *Railroads and Regulation,* pp. 32–3.

76 Neilson, "Shelby M. Cullom," p. 113.

77 *Congressional Record,* 49th Cong., 1st sess., 1886, pp. 4423, 7755–7818.

78 Wabash, St. Louis, and Pacific R.R. Co. *v* Illinois, 118 U.S. 557 (1886).

79   The railroad's disappointment and anger are nicely summarized by Charles Francis Adams in "The Interstate Commerce Law," (December 1888), *Compendium of Transportation Theories*, pp. 178–84.

80   For the final debates, see also Irving J. Sloan, ed., *American Landmark Legislation*, 10 vols. (New York: Oceana Press, 1977), 2.

81   *Ibid.; Congressional Record*, 49th Cong., 2nd sess., 1887, pp. 632–66, 881, 1435; Hoogenboom and Hoogenboom, *History of the ICC*, pp. 13–17. 24 Statutes at Large 379, passed February 4, 1887; amended 25 Statutes at Large 832, passed March 2, 1889; amended 26 Statutes at Large 743, passed February 10, 1891; additional control over safety was conferred on the commission March 2, 1893, 27 Statutes at Large 531.

82   *Second Annual Report of the Interstate Commerce Commission* (1888), p. 27. Hereafter cited as *Annual Report*.

83   For the thesis that late-century regulation emerged stillborn from the legislative arena, see Martin, "Railroad Regulation."

84   Honorable David J. Brewer, "The Nation's Safeguard," *Report of the New York State Bar Association Proceedings* (1893), pp. 37–47, and "The Protection of Private Property from Public Attack," *The New Englander and Yale Review* 256 (August 1891), pp. 97–110.

85   See case references below; see also William Z. Ripley, *Railroads: Rates and Regulation* (New York: Longmans, Green, 1913) pp. 464–5.

86   Adams, "Interstate Commerce Act," p. 140.

87   Henry Carter Adams, "A Decade of Federal Railway Regulation," *Atlantic Monthly* (April 1898), p. 436.

88   On Cooley's life and career, see: Harry B. Hutchins, "Thomas M. Cooley," William Draper Lewis, ed., *Great American Lawyers*, 8 vols. (Philadelphia: Winston, 1909), 7, pp. 431, 491; Clyde E. Jacobs, *Law Writers and the Courts;* Alan Jones, "Thomas M. Cooley and the Michigan Supreme Court: 1865–1885," *Journal of American Legal History* 10 (April 1966), pp. 97–121; Benjamin R. Twiss, *Lawyers and the Constitution;* Louis G. Vander Velde, "Thomas McIntyre Cooley," *Michigan and the Cleveland Era;* O. Douglas Weeks, "Some Political Ideas of Thomas McIntyre Cooley," *Southwestern Political Science Quarterly* 6, 1 (June 1925), pp. 30–9.

89   Compare Cooley's early attitudes in "Limits to State Control of Private Business," *The Princeton Review* (n.s.) 1 (March 1878), pp. 233–71, and "Labor and Capital Before the Law," *North American Review* 139 (December 1884), pp. 503–16, with later attitudes expressed in "State Regulation of Corporate Profits," *North American Review* 137 (September 1883), pp. 207–17, and "Arbitration in Labor Disputes," *Forum* 1 (June 1886), pp. 307–13. See also Alan Jones, "Thomas M. Cooley and 'Laissez-Faire Constitutionalism': A Reconsideration," *Journal of American History* 53, 4 (March 1967), pp. 751–77.

90   Alan Jones, "Thomas M. Cooley and the Interstate Commerce Commis-

sion: Continuity and Change in the Doctrine of Equal Rights," *Political Science Quarterly* 81, 4 (December 1966), p. 611.

91 *Ibid.; Annual Report* 4 (1890), pp. 11–21.

92 Henry Carter Adams, "A Decade of Federal Railway Regulation."

93 Two series of cases stand somewhat outside the pattern noted below. The first concerned an 1889 amendment to the Commerce Act (supported by the commission) to extend criminal penalties to the shipper who took a lower rate in an illegal bargain as well as to the railroad official who offered it. This allowed both parties to rebates and drawbacks to plead the Fifth Amendment at commission hearings. In 1890, a shipper refused to testify before the commission on these grounds, and he was sustained by the Supreme Court (Counselman *v* Hitchcock 142 U.S. 547 [1892]). The decision crippled the commission by making it dependent on voluntary testimony. In 1893, Congress came to the commission's aid by enacting an expediting act stipulating that no person could be excused from testifying on grounds of self-incrimination but that no prosecution could ensue from such testimony. The commission's authority to compel testimony remained uncertain and was flagrantly ignored until 1896, when the Court upheld the 1893 amendment (Brown *v* Walker 161 U.S. 591 [1896]). See also *Annual Report* 6 (1892), pp. 28–30, 39, 70. For the amendments, see note 81. The second series of cases also concerned the validity of the commission's authority to compel witnesses and papers. A circuit court declared Section 12 of the act conferring this authority invalid. Hitherto only courts and the legislatures had such power, and the court questioned whether the act would not make the Court a "mere adjunct and instrument" of an administrative authority. The circuit court deemed it "beneath the dignity of the court" to render such support to a nonjudicial body, but the Supreme Court reversed that ruling in a 1894 decision written by Justice Harlan (ICC *v* Brimson 154 U.S. 447 [1894]).

94 Cincinnati Ry. Co. et al. *v* ICC, 162 U.S. 184 (1896); ICC *v* Alabama 164 U.S. 144 (1897).

95 Ripley, *Railroads*, pp. 461–3; A. M. Tollefson, "Judicial Review of the Decisions of the Interstate Commerce Commission," *Minnesota Law Review* 2, 5 (April 1927), pp. 385–421.

96 *Annual Report* 10 (1896), pp. 6–16.

97 Sharfman, *Interstate Commerce Commission*, p. 25.

98 *Annual Report* 1 (1887), p. 84.

99 ICC *v* Alabama Midland Ry. Co. et al., 168 U.S. 144 (1897).

100 *Maximum freight rate* case, 167 U.S. 479 (1897).

101 *Annual Report* 2 (1888), p. 27.

102 Gerald D. Nash, "The Reformer Reformed: John H. Reagan and Railroad Regulation," *Business History Review* 29, 2 (June 1955), pp. 189–97.

103 *Annual Report* 10 (1896), pp. 87–91.

104 *Annual Report* 12 (1898), pp. 18–95.

105 *Annual Report* 15 (1901), p. 16.

106 Ripley, *Railroads*, pp. 460–3, 486, 523.
107 Arthur T. Hadley, "The Relation between Economics and Politics," *Economic Studies* 4, 1 (February 1899), pp. 7–28.
108 See note 24.

Part III. Introduction

1 It is possible to specify specific new pressures on the old order in each of the areas of state concern under study here. In the area of civil administration, the executive civil service grew by about 162,000 positions in the first decade of the twentieth century compared to a growth of about 50,000 in the last decade of the nineteenth century. Moreover, a relative decline in customs revenue and expenditures on projects like the Panama Canal strained old financial arrangements. In the area of army organization, colonial possessions kept the professional reform program alive, and the outbreak of war in Europe in 1914 further intensified the reform imperative. In the area of national railroad regulation, a gradual rise in rates at the turn of the century and the progress of railroad consolidations and combinations revived the clamor for federal action.

2 Walter Dean Burnham, "The Changing Shape of the American Political Universe," *American Political Science Review* 59 (March 1965), pp. 7–28; E. E. Schattschneider, *The Semi-Sovereign People* (New York: Holt, Rinehart & Winston, 1960), pp. 78–96; Walter Dean Burnham, "Theory and Voting Research: Some Reflections on Converse's 'Change in the American Electorate.'" *American Political Science Review* 68, 3 (September 1974), pp. 1002–23; Philip E. Converse, "Comment," *American Political Science Review* 68, 3 (September 1974), pp. 1023–7; Jerrold G. Rusk, "Comment," *American Political Science Review* 68, 3 (September 1974), pp. 1028–49; Walter Dean Burnham, "Rejoinder," *American Political Science Review* 68, 3 (September 1974), pp. 1050–7; Jesse F. Marquette, "Social Change and Political Mobilization in the United States: 1870–1960," *American Political Science Review* 68, 3 (September 1974), pp. 1058–74.

3 As we saw in the case of civil administration, Cleveland's actions became more aggressive in the desperate years after 1894, when his party support began to disintegrate. The reader may find interesting comparisons between Cleveland's actions in the 1894–6 period and Taft's actions in the 1910–12 period. The latter are described in Chapter 6.

4 Christopher Lasch, "The Moral and Intellectual Rehabilitation of the Ruling Class," Christopher Lasch, *The World of Nations* (New York: Knopf, 1973), pp. 80–99. Lasch correctly draws a distinction between the Roosevelt style of reform and the nineteenth-century Mugwump style. Roosevelt challenged Wanamaker, Clarkson, and Harrison in the name of civil service reform, but he never cut himself off from the centers of political power. Unlike the Mugwumps, he did not join the bolt from Blaine to Cleveland in 1884.

5 Lasch, "Ruling Class." For an example of the nineteenth-century administrative reformers' opposition to imperialism, see William Graham Sumner, "Elections and Civil Service Reform," William Graham Sumner, ed., *Collected Essays in Political and Social Science* (New York: Henry Holt, 1885) and William Graham Sumner, "The Conquest of the United States by Spain," *Yale Law Journal* 8 (January 1899), pp. 187–219. Significantly, Woodrow Wilson, like Roosevelt, was able to combine support for institutional reform with support for territorial expansion. See his article "Democracy and Efficiency," *Atlantic Monthly* 87 (March 1901), pp. 187–205.

6 In one of his most controversial patronage appointments, Roosevelt gave James Clarkson, Assistant Postmaster General under Wanamaker, the position of Surveyor of the Port of New York. This helped to preempt a Hanna-led anti-Roosevelt coalition at the 1904 convention, but it also put Roosevelt's former foe in the fight for civil service reform in charge of the merit service in the single most important field office in the land. Roosevelt later wrote in his own defense that "in politics we have to do a great many things we ought not to do." Roosevelt maintained the priorities in his governing coalition, however, by subjecting Clarkson's administration of the civil service rules in the Port of New York to the direct supervision of his trusted ally in institutional reform, James R. Garfield. See Henry Pringle, *Theodore Roosevelt* (New York: Harcourt, Brace and World, 1956); see also *Theodore Roosevelt, an Autobiography* (New York: Scribners, 1913); John Morton Blum, *The Republican Roosevelt* (New York: Atheneum, 1975); John Morton Blum, *The Progressive Presidents* (New York: Norton, 1980), pp. 23–60.

7 *New York Times*, June 30, 1906, pp. 1, 3.

8 William Howard Taft, *The President and His Power* (New York: Columbia University Press, 1916); Donald F. Anderson, *William Howard Taft: A Conservative's Conception of the Presidency* (Ithaca, N.Y.: Cornell University Press, 1968); John L. Withers, "The Administrative Theories and Practices of William Howard Taft" (Ph.D. diss., University of Chicago, 1957).

9 Arthur Link, *Wilson: The New Freedom* (Princeton, N.J.: Princeton University Press, 1965), pp. 144–75; James W. Ceaser, *Presidential Selection: Theory and Development* (Princeton, N.J.: Princeton University Press, 1979), pp. 170–212; Woodrow Wilson, *Leaders of Men* (Princeton, N.J.: Princeton University Press, 1952).

10 Arthur M. MacMahon, "Woodrow Wilson as a Legislative Leader and Administrator," *American Political Science Review* 50, 3 (September 1956), pp. 641–75. Without doubt, Wilson's greatest administrative achievement in his first term was the legislation for the Federal Trade Commission. With this bill, Wilson secured administrative discretion in determining the difference between a monopoly that restrained trade and a big business that deserved public commendation. He had been at pains to draw this distinction in his campaign, and with it he softened the antiindustrial tone of his party. On the FTC Act, see Douglas Jaenicke, "Herbert Croly, Progressive Ideology and the FTC Act," *Political Science Quarterly* 3, 93 (Fall 1978),

pp. 471–94. See also the perceptive, if partisan, analysis of Wilson's political position in 1916 given in *The New Republic* (February 5, 1916), pp. 17–19. Herbert Croly writes: "Manifestly the sacrifice of administrative standards was the price which Mr. Wilson and his country had to pay for the attempt to resurrect and consolidate the Democracy."

Chapter 6. Reconstituting civil administration

1 Samuel Haber, *Efficiency and Uplift: Scientific Management in the Progressive Era, 1890–1920* (University of Chicago Press, 1964), pp. 99–116; Robert Wiebe, *The Search for Order, 1877–1920* (New York: Hill and Wang, 1967).

2 William Dudley Foulke, *Fighting the Spoilsmen: Reminiscences of the Civil Service Reform Movement* (New York: Putnam, 1919), p. 212.

3 In his seven years in office, Roosevelt classified 34,766 positions by executive order. There were 234,940 federal positions in the merit service by March 3, 1909. The postal classification of 1908 accounted for 15,488 positions. United States Civil Service Commission, "The Classified Civil Service of the United States Government," Form 2909, 1933.

4 *Civil Service Commission Annual Report* (hereafter cited as *Annual Report*) 19 (1902–3), pp. 120, 134–47; *Annual Report* 21 (1903–4), pp. 69–70; *Annual Report* 23 (1905–6), p. 75; William Dudley Foulke, "Restriction of the Political Activities of Office Holders," *Good Government* 24 (December 1907), pp. 105–17; William Dudley Foulke, *Roosevelt and the Spoilsmen* (New York: National Civil Service Reform League, 1925), p. 52. On the general implications of these rules, see David Rosenbloom, *Federal Service and the Constitution: The Development of the Public Employment Relationship* (Ithaca, N.Y.: Cornell University Press, 1971), pp. 94–119.

5 *Annual Report* 21 (1903–4), p. 22.

6 Frank M. Kiggins, "The Establishment of Civil Service Districts: An Administrative Reform," *Good Government* 21 (December 1904), pp. 96–106.

7 Sterling Spero, *The Labor Movement in a Government Industry* (New York: Doran, 1924), pp. 96–117; Geniana R. Edwards, "Organized Federal Workers: A Study of Three Representative Unions" (M.A. thesis, George Washington University, 1939), pp. 1–15; Harvey Walker, "Employee Organizations in the National Government Service: The Period Prior to the World War," *Public Personnel Studies* 10, 3 (August 1941), pp. 67–73.

8 Spero, *Labor Movement.*

9 *Annual Report* 19 (1901–2), pp. 22–5; *Annual Report* 24 (1906–7), p. 16; Paul Van Riper, *History of the United States Civil Service* (Evanston, Ill.: Row, Peterson, 1958), pp. 192–4.

10 Van Riper, *Civil Service,* 188–9; *Annual Report* 20 (1902–3), pp. 147–50.

11 Spero, *Labor Movement;* Edwards, "Organized Federal Workers."

12 Walker, "Employee Organizations."

13 Oscar Kraines, "The President versus Congress: The Keep Commission, 1905–1909: First Comprehensive Presidential Inquiry into Administration,"

Western Political Quarterly 23, 1 (March 1970), pp. 5–54; Harold Pinkett, "Keep Commission, 1905–1909: A Rooseveltian Effort for Administrative Reform," *Journal of American History* 52, 2 (September 1965), pp. 297–312.

14 Kraines, "President versus Congress."

15 *Ibid.;* Gifford Pinchot Files, boxes 598, 599, 1934, Manuscript Division, Library of Congress. The commission's reports were found in these files, along with Pinchot's notes on commission activities. See also Gustavus A. Weber, *Organized Efforts for the Improvement of Methods of Administration in the United States* (New York: Appleton, 1919), pp. 74–80; David Michael Grossman, "Professors and Public Service, 1885–1925: A Chapter in the Professionalization of the Social Sciences" (Ph.D. diss., George Washington University, 1973), p. 159.

16 Kraines, "President versus Congress."

17 Samuel P. Hays, *Conservation and the Gospel of Efficiency: The Progressive Conservation Movement, 1890–1920.* (New York: Atheneum, 1969), pp. 122–37.

18 Committee on Department Methods, "Methods of Administration in the Department of the Interior," October 22, 1906, Gifford Pinchot Files; Kraines, "President versus Congress."

19 Kraines, "President versus Congress."

20 Carl E. Hatch, *The Big Stick and the Congressional Gavel: A Study of Theodore Roosevelt's Relations with His Last Congress, 1907–1909* (New York: Pageant Press, 1967), pp. 27–57.

21 Kraines, "President versus Congress."

22 Hatch, *Big Stick.*

23 *Ibid.; A Compilation of the Messages and Papers of the Presidents,* 20 vols., prepared under the direction of the Joint Committee on Printing (New York: Bureau of National Literature, 1912), 15, pp. 7238–53.

24 Walter Otto Jacobsen, "A Study of President Taft's Commission on Economy and Efficiency and a Comparative Evaluation of Three Other Commissions," (M.A. thesis, Columbia University, 1941), pp. 1–138; John Lovelle Withers, "The Administrative Theories and Practices of William Howard Taft" (Ph.D. diss., University of Chicago, 1956), pp. 46–124; Weber, *Methods of Administration,* pp. 84–103; A. N. Holcombe, "Administrative Reorganization in the Federal Government," *Annals of the American Academy of Political and Social Science,* 41 (May 1921), pp. 47–58; Bess Gordon, "History of the Commission on Economy and Efficiency," prepared for the National Archives Seminar, June 8, 1956, Washington, D.C. (Washington, D.C.: National Archives Catalogue).

25 *Ibid.,* Jane S. Dahlberg, *The New York Bureau of Municipal Research* (New York University Press, 1966).

26 *Ibid.*

27 President's Commission on Economy and Efficiency, "The Need for the Organization of a Bureau of Central Administrative Control," *Message of the President of the United States: The Need for a National Budget, House*

Documents, 62nd Cong., 2nd sess., 1912, app. 2, pp. 189–205.

28 *Ibid.,* p. 138.

29 U.S. Senate, "Message of the President of the United States, Submitting for the Consideration of Congress a Budget, with Supporting Memoranda and Reports," *Senate Documents,* 63rd Cong., 3rd sess., 1913; W. F. Willoughby, "Reclassification and the Budget," *The Congressional Digest* 2 (April 1923), p. 212; Ismar Baruch, "History of Position Classification and Salary Standardization in the Federal Service 1789–1941" (Washington, D.C.: U.S. Civil Service Commission Personnel Classification Division, September 30, 1941), pp. 30–5. Catalogued in the Civil Service Commission Library.

30 U.S. Senate, "Message of the President," p. 117.

31 Blair Bolles, *Tyrant from Illinois: Uncle Joe Cannon's Experiment with Personal Power* (New York: Norton, 1951), pp. 210–13; Alpheus Thomas Mason, *Bureaucracy Convicts Itself: The Ballinger–Pinchot Controversy of 1910* (New York: Viking Press, 1941), pp. 28–9; Hayes, *Conservation,* pp. 140–60.

32 *Annual Report* 27 (1909–10), p. 47; Spero, *Labor Movement,* pp. 138–9.

33 Mason, *Bureaucracy Convicts Itself,* pp. 37–98; Martin L. Fausold, *Gifford Pinchot: Bull Moose Progressive* (Syracuse, N.Y.: Syracuse University Press, 1961), pp. 21–32; Kenneth W. Hechler, *Insurgency: Personalities and Politics of the Taft Era* (New York: Columbia University Press, 1940), pp. 154–62.

34 *Ibid.* Bolles, *Tyrant from Illinois,* p. 120.

35 Donald F. Anderson, *William Howard Taft: A Conservative's Conception of the Presidency* (Ithaca, N.Y.: Cornell University Press, 1973), pp. 72–7, 154–201.

36 Mason, *Bureaucracy Convicts Itself,* pp. 99–107; Fausold, *Gifford Pinchot;* Hayes, *Conservation,* p. 171; Hechler, *Insurgency.*

37 Spero, *Labor Movement;* pp. 138–81; Edwards, "Organized Federal Workers," pp. 4–17.

38 Walker, "Employee Organizations," p. 72; Anderson, *William Howard Taft.*

39 Van Riper, *United States Civil Service,* pp. 216–17.

40 Walker, "Employee Organizations"; Spero, *Labor Movement;* Chester Gordon Hall, Jr., "The United States Civil Service Commission: Arm of President or Congress?" (Ph.D. diss., American University, 1965), pp. 38–52. U.S. Statutes 555, August 24, 1912.

41 Jacobsen, "Taft's Commission," pp. 54–60; Withers, "Theories and Practices," pp. 105–10; Gordon, "History," pp. 35–7; *New York Times,* February 27, 1913, pp. 5, 12.

42 Weber, *Methods of Administration,* pp. 104–14; Me Hsin Chiang, "The Bureau of Efficiency" (Ph.D. diss., Harvard University, 1940), pp. 1–114; Mary S. Schinagl, *History of Efficiency Ratings in the Federal Government* (Ann Arbor: University of Michigan Press, 1963), pp. 33–45; Van Riper, *United States Civil Service,* p. 240.

43 Van Riper, *United States Civil Service*, pp. 222–3, 242.
44 Civil Service Commission, "Classified Executive Civil Service."
45 Gordon, "History."
46 Brookings Institution, *Institute for Government Research: An Account of Research Achievements* (Washington, D.C.: Brookings Institution, 1956), pp. 1–16; Dahlberg, *Bureau of Municipal Research*, pp. 81–91.
47 *New York Times*, May 23, 1913, p. 8.
48 Arthur S. Link, *Wilson: The New Freedom* (Princeton, N.J.: Princeton University Press, 1956), pp. 145–75.
49 Van Riper, *United States Civil Service*, pp. 230–5; Arthur W. MacMahon, "Woodrow Wilson as a Legislative Leader and Administrator," *American Political Science Review* 50, 3 (September 1956), pp. 641–75.
50 Van Riper, *United States Civil Service*, p. 236; Foulke, *Fighting the Spoilsmen*, pp. 233–54.
51 *Ibid.; Good Government*, January 1914, p. 6, and November 1914, p. 102.
52 Civil Service Commission, "Classified Executive Civil Service."
53 *Good Government*, September 1916, pp. 81–3; *New York Times*, September 7, 1916, p. 4.
54 Tensions within the commission are evident in a dispute among the commissioners about Burleson's tactics. *Annual Report* 33 (1915–16), pp. 11–20 and 25–45.
55 Herbert Croly, "Unregenerate Democracy," *The New Republic* (February 5, 1916), pp. 17–19. Croly's is obviously a politically biased view, but it is nonetheless perceptive on the tradeoffs that Wilson was forced to make in the New Freedom years.
56 See note 42.
57 Letter of Harold Brown of the Bureau of Efficiency reporting on H.R. 8388 to abolish the Bureau of Efficiency (Washington, D.C.: National Archives, Bureau of Efficiency Papers, 1936).
58 See sources cited in note 42; see also *Annual Reports of the United States Bureau of Efficiency* for 1916 through 1920 (Washington, D.C.: Civil Service Commission Library).
59 *Annual Report of the United States Bureau of Efficiency, 1919*, pp. 26–35; *Annual Report of the United States Bureau of Efficiency, 1920*, pp. 15–19.
60 *Annual Report of the United States Bureau of Efficiency, 1917*, pp. 22–3; *Annual Report of the United States Bureau of Efficiency, 1919*, p. 26; *Annual Report of the United States Bureau of Efficiency, 1920*, pp. 12–13.
61 Seward W. Livermore, *Woodrow Wilson and the War Congress, 1916–1918* (Seattle: University of Washington Press, 1966), pp. 1–90.
62 *Ibid.*, pp. 97–9.
63 Bernard Baruch made his fortune as a New York financier. He retired early in life and had become a New Freedom devotee in the early years of Wilson's first term. He was chosen to head the War Industries Board after its reorganization in 1918. Herbert Hoover was an engineer who left the business world in 1915 to run the Belgium relief effort. Harry Garfield had left the business world to join Wilson at Princeton. He later became president of

Williams College. During the war he served as the head of the Fuel Administration. Robert Brookings had been a commercial lawyer and businessman but left his practice in the early years of the century to pursue a life of philanthropy. He was one of the founders of the Institute for Government Research. During the war he served as head of the Price Fixing Committee.

64 Robert Cuff, "We Band of Brothers: Woodrow Wilson's War Managers," *Canadian Review of American Studies* 5, 2 (Fall 1974), pp. 135–48; W. F. Willoughby, *Government Organization in War Time and After: A Survey of the Federal Civil Agencies Created for the Prosecution of the War* (New York: Appleton, 1919).

65 Grossman, "Professors and Public Service," pp. 135–88.

66 Sterling Spero, *Government as Employer* (New York: Remsen Press, 1948), pp. 144–52, 175–7; Edwards, "Organized Federal Workers," pp. 15–26.

67 Paul Van Riper, "Reconverting the Civil Service: What Happened after the First World War," *Public Personnel Review* 9, 1 (January 1948), pp. 3–10.

68 Harvey Walker, "Employee Organizations in the National Government Service: The Formation of the National Federation of Federal Employees," *Public Personnel Studies* 10, 4 (October 1941), pp. 133–4.

69 *Ibid.;* Spero, *Government as Employer*. The NFFE counted 10,000 members in 1917. In the wake of Borland's defeat, membership rose to 50,000.

70 Van Riper, "Reconverting"; Van Riper, *United States Civil Service*, pp. 271–3; *Good Government*, February 1918, p. 27, and December 1918, pp. 184–90; *New York Times*, March 13, 1919, p. 19, September 7, 1919, p. 1, September 12, 1919, p. 17, September 16, 1919, p. 14, September 20, 1919, p. 14.

71 Brookings Institution, *Institute for Government Research*, pp. 18–21.

72 Grossman, "Professors and Public Service," pp. 154–63; Herbert Heaton, *A Scholar in Action: Edwin F. Gay* (Cambridge, Mass.: Harvard University Press, 1952).

73 *Good Government*, October 1918, p. 145.

74 *Congressional Record*, 66th Cong., 2nd sess., 1920, p. 1018.

75 *Congressional Record*, 66th Cong., 2nd sess., 1920, p. 5091.

76 R. J. Quinn, "Shall the Civil Service Have a Czar?" *The Federal Employee* 5, 8 (February 21, 1920), pp. 2–12.

77 *The Federal Employee* 5, 16 (April 17, 1920), pp. 1–15; 5, 17 (April 24, 1920), pp. 1–14; and 5, 18 (May 1, 1920), pp. 3–12.

78 *The Federal Employee* 5, 21 (May 22, 1920), pp. 1–14; *Congressional Record*, 66th Cong., 2nd sess., 1920, pp. 7026–7.

79 Brookings Institution, *Institute for Government Research*, pp. 18–20; Frederick Cleveland and Eugene Buck, *The Budget and Responsible Government* (New York: Macmillan, 1920). For an alternative view critical of executive power, see Edward Fitzpatrick, *Budget Making in a Democracy* (New York: Macmillan, 1918).

80 Charles Wallace Collins, "Historical Sketch of the Budget Bill in Congress," *The Congressional Digest* 2, 2 (November 1922), p. 38; Fritz Morstein Marx, "The Budget Bureau: Its Evolution and Present Role, I," *American*

Political Science Review 39, 4 (August 1945), pp. 653–84; Fritz Morstein Marx, "The Background of the Budget and Accounting Act," Catheryn Seckler Hudson, ed., "Budgeting: An Instrument of Planning and Management," (collection, American University School of Social Sciences and Public Affairs, 1944. Catalogued in the Library of the Office of Management and Budget); Frederick C. Mosher, *The GAO: The Quest for Accountability in American Government* (Boulder, Colo.: Westview Press, 1979), pp. 47–54; House Select Committee on the Budget, *National Budget System, House Documents,* 2, 362, 66th Cong., 1st sess., 1919, pp. 1–10.

81   *Ibid.;* Darrel Henover Smith, *The General Accounting Office* (Baltimore: Johns Hopkins University Press, 1927), pp. 58–66; Harvey C. Mansfield, *The Comptroller General* (New Haven, Conn.: Yale University Press, 1939), pp. 65–70; *Congressional Record,* 66th Cong., 2nd sess., 1920, pp. 6389–95; "National Budget System: Report of the Special Committee on the National Budget," *Senate Documents,* 66th Cong., 2nd sess., 1920.

82   *Ibid.;* Donald Hansen, "Legislative Clearance by the Bureau of the Budget" (manuscript, Office of Management and Budget Library, Washington, D.C., 1947). Despite the opposition of the Director of the Bureau of the Budget, the Secretary of the Treasury did, in fact, demand that budget estimates be sent through his office before being transferred to the President. The conflict on this issue continued through the Harding, Coolidge, and Hoover administrations. See correspondence in Bureau of Efficiency Record Group 51, Box 2, Bureau of Budget File, National Archives.

83   MacMahan, "Woodrow Wilson," p. 675.

84   *Congressional Record,* 66th Cong., 2nd sess., June 4, 1920, p. 8509, June 5, 1920, p. 8625.

85   John S. Beach, "Provision for Retired Employees," *The Congressional Digest* 11, 7 (April, 1923), pp. 96–110; Van Riper, "Reconverting"; Van Riper, *History,* pp. 276–7; *The Federal Employee* 4, 4 (April 1919), p. 198; 5, 10 (March 1920), pp. 1–5.

86   Beach, "Retired Employees," p. 102; Harvey Walker, "Employee Organization in the National Government: Retirement Legislation," *Public Personnel Studies* 10, 9 (February 1941), pp. 246–52.

87   "Congress Provides New Classification for Civil Service Employees," *The Congressional Digest* 2, 4 (April 1923), pp. 206–12; Van Riper, *History,* pp. 296–304; Baruch, "Position-Classification," pp. 45–57; Paul V. Betters, *The Personnel Classification Board* (Washington, D.C.: Brookings Institution, 1931), pp. 1–70; Edward Keating, "The Reclassification Problem," *The Federal Employee* 4, 4 (April 1919), pp. 199–200; "Editorial," *The Federal Employee* 4, 5 (May 1919), p. 253; Charles B. Henderson, "The Work of Reclassification," *The Federal Employee* 4, 5 (May 1919), pp. 261–2; John Doyle, "Reclassification of the Service," *The Federal Employee* 4, 5 (May 1919), pp. 264–5; Courtney Hamlin, "More about Reclassification," *The Federal Employee* 4, 6 (June 1919), p. 339; "The Problem of Lump-Sum versus Statutory Salaries," *The Federal Employee* 4, 27 (December 1919), pp. 718–20; *The Federal Employee* 5, 1 (January 1920), pp.

2–3; *The Federal Employee* 5, 2 (January 1920), pp. 10–11; *The Federal Employee* 5, 12 (March 1920), p. 1.

88 Edward Keating, "Reclassification," *The Federal Employee* 5, 30 (July 1920), pp. 1–13; Fred Telford, "The Classification and Salary Standardization Movement in the Public Service," *The Annals of the American Academy of Political and Social Science* 113 (May 1924), pp. 206–15.

89 *Ibid.;* Baruch, "Position Classification"; Betters, *Personnel Classification Board;* Van Riper, *History,* pp. 296–304.

Chapter 7. Reconstituting the army

1   Russell F. Weigley, "The Elihu Root Reforms and the Progressive Era," *Military History Symposium* 20 (December 1968) pp. 11–34; James Weinstein, *The Corporate Ideal in the Liberal State, 1900–1918* (Boston: Beacon Press, 1968).

2   Philip C. Jessup, *Elihu Root,* 2 vols. (New York: Dodd Mead, 1938), esp. vol. I, pp. 114–33.

3   *Ibid.,* I, pp. 215–407, esp. p. 255; Richard Leopold, *Elihu Root and the Conservative Tradition* (Boston: Little, Brown, 1954), pp. 24–47.

4   Louis Cantor, "The Creation of the Modern National Guard: The Dick Militia Act of 1903" (Ph.D. diss., Duke University, 1963), pp. 111–41; Martha Derthick, *The National Guard in Politics* (Cambridge, Mass.: Harvard University Press, 1965), p. 18; *Five Years of the War Department following the War With Spain, 1899–1903, as Shown in the Annual Reports of the Secretary of War* (Washington, D.C.: Government Printing Office, 1904), "Report for 1899," pp. 57–70.

5   James William Pohl, "The General Staff and American Military Policy: The Formative Period 1898–1917" (Ph.D. diss., University of Texas, 1967), pp. 24–62; *Annual Report for 1899,* "The Report of the Secretary of War," pp. 44–55.

6   *Ibid.;* William Harding Carter, "The Creation of the American General Staff," *Senate Documents* 2, 68th Cong., 1st sess., 119, 1903, pp. 12, 67.

7   *Ibid.;* "The New Education of the Army," *The Nation* 73, 1893 (October 10, 1901), p. 276; C. Joseph Bernardo and Eugene H. Bacon, *American Military Policy: Its Development since 1775* (Harrisburg, Pa.: Stackpole, 1957), pp. 308–12; Ira Reeves, *Military Education in the United States* (Burlington, Vt.: Free Press, 1914), pp. 199–211; Jessup, *Elihu Root,* I, pp. 263–4.

8   The relevant parts of this message are excerpted in Walter Millis, ed., *American Military Thought* (Indianapolis: Bobbs-Merrill, 1966), pp. 262–8. On Roosevelt's support for Root's initiative, see Jessup, *Elihu Root,* I, p. 254.

9   Jessup, *Elihu Root,* I, pp. 242–3; Weigley, "Root Reforms"; William Harding Carter, "Elihu Root: His Services as Secretary of War," *North American Review* 178, 566 (January 1904), pp. 110–21.

10 Louis Cantor, "Elihu Root and the National Guard: Friend or Foe?" *Military Affairs* 33, 3 (December 1969), p. 25.

11 Derthick, *National Guard*, pp. 23–7; Cantor, "Elihu Root"; Cantor, "The Creation," pp. 141–215; Eldridge Colby, "Elihu Root and the National Guard," *Military Affairs* 32, 1 (Spring 1959), pp. 28–34. Root's approach to the National Guard, offering increased material benefits for increased control, was similiar to Roosevelt's approach to the public employees.

12 Cantor, "The Creation," pp. 141–215; *Five Years of the War Department,* "Report for 1900," pp. 131–40; "Report for 1901," pp. 160–68; "Report for 1902," pp. 282–92.

13 *Ibid.;* House of Representatives, "Efficiency of the Militia," *House Reports,* 1094, 57th Cong., 1st sess., 1902, pp. 1–38.

14 *Ibid.;* William Harding Carter, "The Evolution of Army Reforms," *United Service* 3, series 3 (May 1903), pp. 1150–98.

15 *Ibid.*

16 Derthick, *National Guard*, p. 28.

17 The following discussion is based on the detailed accounts given by Pohl, "General Staff," pp. 60–88; Barton C. Hacker, "The War Department and the General Staff, 1898–1917," (M.A. thesis, University of Chicago, 1962), pp. 1–52; Philip Semsch, "Elihu Root and the General Staff," *Military Affairs* 27, 1 (Spring 1963), pp. 16–27; Carter, "The Creation"; James Hewes, "The United States Army General Staff, 1900–1917," *Military Affairs* 38, 2 (April 1974), pp. 87–96; Paul J. Hammond, *Organizing for Defense* (Princeton, N.J.: Princeton University Press, 1961), pp. 10–24; John Dickinson, *The Building of an Army* (New York: Century, 1922), pp. 255–61.

18 *Ibid.;* Senate Committee on Military Affairs, "Efficiency of the Army, Statement of Elihu Root" (Washington, D.C.: Government Printing Office, 1902); *Five Years of the War Department,* "Report for 1901," p. 166.

19 Pohl, "General Staff." It might be noted that when the Adjutant General's position was abolished, it was held by Henry Corbin, a strong proponent of the General Staff idea. Corbin agreed to the move to abolish his office.

20 Mabel E. Deutrich, *The Struggle for Supremacy: The Career of General Fred C. Ainsworth* (Washington, D.C.: Public Affairs Press, 1962), pp. 22–88.

21 *Ibid.,* p. 96.

22 *Ibid.,* pp. 96–104; Pohl, "General Staff," pp. 88–120; Hacker, "War Department," pp. 47–51.

23 Hermann Hagedorn, *Leonard Wood: A Biography,* 2 vols. (New York: Harper & Brothers, 1931), II, pp. 1–95.

24 On the progressive conservation crusade, see Samuel P. Hays, *Conservation and the Gospel of Efficiency: The Progressive Conservation Movement, 1890–1920* (New York: Atheneum, 1974), pp. 122–46; On the Progressive preparedness crusade, see John Patrick Finnegan, "Military Preparedness in the Progressive Era, 1911–1917," (Ph.D. diss., University of Wisconsin, 1969).

25 Donald F. Anderson, *William Howard Taft: A Conservative's Conception of the Presidency* (Ithaca, N.Y.: Cornell University Press, 1968), pp. 83–4; Richard N. Current, *Secretary Stimson: A Study in Statecraft* (New Brunswick, N.J.: Rutgers University Press, 1954), pp. 21–3; Henry L. Stim-

son and McGeorge Bundy, *On Active Service in Peace and War* (New York: Harper & Brothers, 1948), pp. 28–31.

26 Deutrich, *Struggle for Supremacy*, pp. 95–107; James E. Hewes, Jr., *From Root to McNamara: Army Organization and Administration 1900–1963* (Washington, D.C.: Government Printing Office, 1975), pp. 12–21.

27 *Ibid.*; Pohl, "General Staff," pp. 120–207; Hacker, "War Department," pp. 54–60; Otto Nelson, *National Security and the General Staff* (Washington, D.C.: Infantry Journal Press, 1946), pp. 102–31; Hagedorn, *Leonard Wood*, II, pp. 95–120; *Annual Report for 1911*, "Report of the Secretary of War," pp. 142–4.

28 *Ibid.*; House Committee on Military Affairs, "Relief of the Adjutant General from the Duties of His Office," *House Reports*, 508, 62nd Cong., 2nd sess., 1912; Nelson, *National Security*, pp. 145–65.

29 Pohl, "General Staff"; Hagedorn, *Leonard Wood*, II, pp. 121–5.

30 *Ibid.*; Hewes, *From Root to McNamara*, p. 19.

31 *Ibid.*; Hacker, "War Department," pp. 56–65; Deutrich, *Struggle for Supremacy*, pp. 107–30.

32 *Ibid.*; Leopold, *Elihu Root*, p. 80. It should be noted that Stimson had by this time declared his allegiance to Taft in the forthcoming electoral contest with Roosevelt.

33 House Committee on Military Affairs, "Relief of the Adjutant General," p. 1.

34 *Ibid.*, pp. 2, 50; *War Department Annual Report for 1912*, pp. 242–3.

35 Army War College, "Organization of the Land Forces of the United States," in "Report of the Secretary of War," *Annual Report for 1912*, pp. 65–153.

36 Arthur S. Link, *Woodrow Wilson: The New Freedom* (Princeton, N.J.: Princeton University Press, 1956), pp. 19–20, 119–21; Pohl, "General Staff," pp. 216–20.

37 Finnegan, "Military Preparedness," pp. 95–120; Hagedorn, *Leonard Wood*, II, pp. 146–62.

38 Finnegan, "Military Preparedness," pp. 122–77; Arthur S. Link, *Woodrow Wilson and the Progressive Era, 1910–1917* (New York: Harper & Row, 1945), pp. 174–96.

39 Army War College, "Statement of a Proper Military Policy for the United States," in "Report of the Secretary of War," *Annual Report for 1915*, pp. 128–9.

40 *Annual Report for 1915*, pp. 20–35, 109–35.

41 *Ibid.*; Pohl, "General Staff," pp. 287–92; Hacker, "War Department," pp. 65–70; Dickinson, *Building of an Army*, pp. 29–44.

42 George C. Herring, Jr., "James Hay and the Preparedness Controversy, 1915–1916," *The Journal of Southern History*, 30, 4 (November 1964), pp. 383–404.

43 *Ibid.*; Link, *Woodrow Wilson and the Progressive Era*, pp. 185–7; Finnegan, "Military Preparedness," pp. 149–78; Pohl, "General Staff," pp. 292–361; House Committee on Military Affairs, "To Increase the Efficiency of the Military Establishment of the United States," *House Reports*, 1, 297, 64th Cong., 1st session, 1915.

44 *Ibid.;* Dickinson, *Building of an Army,* pp. 44–56. The quotation is found in Arthur Link, *Wilson: Confusions and Crisis, 1915–1916* (Princeton, N.J.: Princeton University Press, 1964), p. 332.

45 Act of June 3, 1916, 39 Statutes at Large, p. 166; *Annual Report for 1916,* "Report of the Secretary of War," pp. 18–56.

46 *Ibid.;* Hewes, *From Root to McNamara,* pp. 20–1.

47 *Ibid.*

48 Daniel R. Beaver, *Newton D. Baker and the American War Effort 1917–1919* (Lincoln: University of Nebraska Press, 1966), p. 52; Grosvenor B. Clarkson, *Industrial America in the World War, the Strategy Behind the Line* (Boston: Houghton Mifflin, 1923), pp. 10–25; R. B. Price, "Industrial Mobilization," *Proceedings of the National Security Congress of the National Security League,* Washington, D.C., January 20–2, 1916.

49 *Ibid.;* Hagedorn, *Leonard Wood,* II, p. 174; Finnegan, "Military Preparedness," pp. 194–204.

50 Wood's disgust with the state of the War Department in 1917 is treated by Edward M. Coffman, *The War to End All Wars: The American Military Experience in World War I* (New York: Oxford University Press, 1968), p. 49; Hagedorn, *Leonard Wood,* II, pp. 181–249, esp. page 236.

51 Beaver, *Newton D. Baker,* pp. 1–21.

52 *Annual Report for 1916,* "Report of the Secretary of War," pp. 70–90; Dickinson, *Building of an Army,* pp. 261–71; Beaver, *Newton D. Baker,* pp. 13–16.

53 Hewes, *From Root to McNamara,* p. 40.

54 Dickinson, *Building of an Army,* p. 272.

55 Robert Cuff, "Business, the State and World War I: The American Experience," in R. D. Cuff and J. L. Granatstein, eds., *War and Society in North America* (Toronto: Thomas Nelson, 1970), pp. 1–19.

56 For a comparative evaluation of staff and supply systems, see J. D. Hittle, *The Military Staff: Its History and Development* (Harrisburgh, Pa.: Stackpole, 1961).

57 A contrary argument that analyzes the war as the fulfillment of the corporate ideal is presented by James Weinstein, *The Corporate Ideal in the Liberal State, 1900–1918* (Boston: Beacon Press, 1968), pp. 214–54.

58 Robert Cuff, "Bernard Baruch: Symbol and Myth in Industrial Mobilization," *Business History Review,* 43 (Summer 1969), pp. 115–33; Robert Cuff, "The Cooperative Impulse and War: The Origins of the Council of National Defense and Advisory Commission," in Jerry Israel, ed., *Building the Organizational Society* (New York: Free Press, 1972), pp. 233–46; Robert Cuff, "Herbert Hoover, the Ideology of Voluntarism and War Organization during the Great War," *Journal of American History* 64, 2 (September 1977), pp. 358–72; Robert Cuff, "The Dollar-a-Year Men of the Great War," *Princeton University Library Chronicle* 30 (Autumn 1968), pp. 10–24.

59 Robert Cuff, *The War Industries Board: Business–Government Relations during World War I* (Baltimore: Johns Hopkins University Press, 1973).

60 Weinstein, *Corporate Ideal;* Robert Cuff, "Harry Garfield, the Fuel Administration, and the Search for a Cooperative Order during World War I," *American Quarterly* 30 (Spring 1978), pp. 39–53.

61 Cuff, *War Industries Board;* Cuff, "Business, the State and World War I."

62 Edward M. Coffman, "The Battle against Red Tape: Business Methods of the War Department General Staff 1917–1918," *Military Affairs* 26, 1 (Spring 1962), pp. 1–10; Hewes, *From Root to McNamara,* pp. 21–31; Cuff, *War Industries Board,* p. 110.

63 "Report of the Chief of Staff," *War Department Annual Report for 1919,* pp. 245, 341–4; Paul A. C. Koistinen, "The Industrial–Military Complex in Historical Perspective: World War I," *Business History Review* 41, 4 (Winter 1967), pp. 378–93; Dickinson, *Building of an Army,* pp. 279–87.

64 Cuff, *War Industries Board,* pp. 86–112.

65 *Ibid.,* pp. 112–40; Daniel R. Beaver, "Newton D. Baker and the Genesis of the War Industries Board, 1917–1918," *Journal of American History* 52, 1 (June 1965), pp. 43–74.

66 Robert Cuff, "Woodrow Wilson and Business–Government Relations during World War I," *Review of Politics* 31, 3 (July 1969), pp. 385–407.

67 Cuff, *War Industries Board,* pp. 140–4; Beaver, "Newton D. Baker and the Genesis of the War Industries Board"; Hewes, *From Root to McNamara,* pp. 21–51; Hammond, *Organizing for Defense,* pp. 10–24, 87–9.

68 Beaver, "Newton D. Baker and the Genesis of the War Industries Board"; Dickinson, *Building of an Army,* pp. 283–5.

69 *Ibid.;* Beaver, *Newton D. Baker,* pp. 166–8.

70 *Ibid.;* Cuff, *War Industries Board,* pp. 112–47; U.S. Congress, Senate Committee on Military Affairs Hearings, Investigation of the War Department, December 12, 1917–February 6, 1918, 65th Cong., 2nd sess., 1918.

71 *Ibid.*

72 *Ibid.;* Edward M. Coffman, *The Hilt of the Sword: The Career of Peyton C. March* (Madison: University of Wisconsin Press, 1966), pp. 64–84.

73 *Ibid.;* John D. Millet, "The Direction of Supply Activities in the War Department: An Administrative Survey I," *American Political Science Review* 38, 2 (April 1944), pp. 254–61; Marvin Kreidberg and Merton Henry, *History of Military Mobilization in the United States Army, 1775–1945* (Washington, D.C.: Department of the Army Pamphlet no. 20-212, June 1955), pp. 241–3; Dickinson, *Building of an Army;* pp. 288–307; Koistinen, "Industrial–Military Complex," pp. 393–403.

74 *Ibid.;* Coffman, *Hilt of the Sword,* pp. 64, 88, 139, 151, 247; Cuff, *War Industries Board,* p. 258.

75 Robert F. Himmelberg, "The War Industries Board and the Antitrust Question in November 1918," *Journal of American History* 52, 1 (June 1965), pp. 59–74.

76 These perspectives can be read in the House and Senate hearings of 1919. U.S. Congress, Senate Committee on Military Affairs, "Reorganization of the Army, Hearings before the Subcommittee on S. 2691," 66th Cong., 1st sess., 1919; U.S. Congress, House Military Affairs Committee, "Army

Reorganization Hearings on H.R. 8287, to Reorganize and Increase the Efficiency of the Army," 66th Cong., 1st sess., 1919; Dickinson, *Building of an Army*, pp. 307–77; Hammond, *Organizing for Defense*, pp. 87–9.

77 *Ibid.;* 41 Statutes at Large 242, June 4, 1920.

78 *Ibid.;* see esp. Dickinson, *Building of an Army*, pp. 318–21.

79 *Ibid.;* John D. Millet, "The Direction of Supply Activities in the War Department: An Administrative Survey, II," *American Political Science Review* 38, 3 (June 1944), pp. 475–84.

80 Act of June 4, 1920, sect. 5a; Millet, "The Direction . . . II," p. 481.

81 Dickinson, *Building of an Army*, p. 318.

82 Millet, "The Direction . . . II," pp. 485–98.

Chapter 8. Reconstituting business regulation

1 For a sampling of twentieth-century opinion on the problems of regulation by an independent commission, see the following: Robert Cushman, "The Problem of the Independent Regulatory Commissions," The President's Commission on Administrative Management: Report with Studies of Administrative Management (Washington, D.C.: Government Printing Office, 1937) pp. 207–48; Marver Bernstein, *Regulating Business by Independent Commission* (Princeton, N.J.: Princeton University Press, 1955); Ari and Olive Hoogenboom, *A History of the ICC: From Panacea to Palliative* (New York: Norton, 1976); Samuel P. Huntington, "The Marasmus of the ICC: the Commission, the Railroads and the Public Interest," *Yale Law Journal* 61 (April 1952), pp. 467–509; Robert C. Fellmeth, *The Interstate Commerce Commission: The Public Interest and the ICC* (New York: Grossman, 1970); Robert B. Carson, *Main Line to Oblivion: The Disintegration of the New York Railroads in the Twentieth Century* (Port Washington, N.Y.: Kennikat Press, 1971).

2 Charles A. Prouty, "The Powers of the Interstate Commerce Commission," *North American Review* 167, 5 (November 1898), pp. 543–57; Charles A. Prouty, "The Powers of the Interstate Commerce Commission," *Forum* 27 (April 1899), pp. 223–36. Commissioner Prouty was engaged in debate by railroad president Milton Smith. Milton Smith, "The Powers of the Interstate Commerce Commission," *North American Review* 168, 1 (January 1899), pp. 2–76; Milton Smith, "The Inordinate Demands of the Interstate Commerce Commission," *Forum* 27 (July 1899), pp. 551–63.

3 Harrison Standish Smalley, "Railroad Rate Control," *Publications of the American Economic Association*, third series, 7, 2 (May 1906), pp. 1–145.

4 Gabriel Kolko, *Railroads and Regulation 1877–1916* (New York: Norton, 1965), pp. 84–101; I. L. Sharfman, *The Interstate Commerce Commission: A Study in Administrative Law and Procedure*, 4 vols. (New York: Commonwealth Fund, 1931), I, pp. 35–40; Hoogenboom and Hoogenboom, *History of the ICC*, pp. 39–46.

5 *Ibid.;* James W. Neilson, *Shelby M. Cullom: Prairie State Republican, University of Illinois Studies in the Social Sciences* 51, (1962), p. 211.

6 See note 4.
7 *Ibid.*
8 Senate Committee on Interstate Commerce, "The Regulation of Railway Rates," *Senate Documents* no. 244, 59th Cong., 1st sess., 1905; House Committee on Interstate Commerce, "Hearing," *House Documents* no. 422, 58th Cong., 3rd sess., 1904; Robert Cushman, *The Independent Regulatory Commissions* (London: Oxford University Press, 1941), pp. 37–146; William Ripley, *Railroads: Rates and Regulation* (New York: Longmans, Green, 1913), pp. 487–521; Kolko, *Railroads and Regulation,* pp. 84–126.
9 *Ibid.*; L. M. Short, *The Development of National Administrative Organization in the United States* (Baltimore: Johns Hopkins University Press, 1923), p. 422. It might be noted here that the original legislation of 1887 placed the ICC in the Department of the Interior. It was removed to a position independent of the regular executive departments by amendment in 1889 out of fear that the Harrison administration would exert a prorailroad influence over its operations.
10 *Ibid.*
11 Gabriel Kolko tends to dismiss institutional issues as merely conflicts of economic interest. See Kolko, *Railroads and Regulation,* p. 133.
12 Charles A. Prouty, "National Regulation of the Railways," *Publications of the American Economic Association,* 3rd series, 4 (February 1903), pp. 6–10. Franklin Lane, who joined the commission in 1906 and shared Prouty's early skepticism toward railroad interests, also shared his position on the value of a Commerce Court. See Keith W. Olson, *Biography of a Progressive: Franklin K. Lane, 1864–1920* (Westport, Conn.: Greenwood Press, 1979), pp. 44.
13 Henry Carter Adams, "A Bureau of Railway Statistics and Accounts," *The Independent* 44 (October 1892), pp. 1384–5; Henry Carter Adams, "Administrative Supervision of Railways under the Twentieth Section of the Act to Regulate Commerce," *Quarterly Journal of Economics* 22 (May 1908), pp. 364–83.
14 Alan Furman Weston, "The Supreme Court, the Populist Movement and the Campaign of 1896," *Journal of Politics* 15, 1 (1953), pp. 3–41; Harding Coolidge Noblitt, "The Supreme Court and the Progressive Era, 1902–1921" (Ph.D. diss., University of Chicago, 1955), pp. 1–35. On the coalition of radical Republicans and Democrats in railroad regulation, see David Sarasohn, "The Democratic Surge, 1905–1912: Forging a Progressive Majority" (Ph.D. diss., University of California, Los Angeles, 1976), pp. 16–28.
15 Kolko, *Railroads and Regulation,* pp. 127–76.
16 John Morton Blum, *The Progressive Presidents* (New York: Norton, 1980), p. 49.
17 Theodore Roosevelt, *Theodore Roosevelt: An Autobiography* (New York: Scribners, 1913), p. 473.
18 *Ibid.*
19 Blum, *Progressive Presidents,* pp. 48–51.

20 John Morton Blum, *The Republican Roosevelt* (Cambridge, Mass.: Harvard University Press, 1954), pp. 73–105.

21 This account of the politics of passing the Hepburn Act draws directly from John Morton Blum, *The Republican Roosevelt.* Other sources used include: Kolko, *Railroads and Regulation,* pp. 155–76; Hoogenboom and Hoogenboom, *History of the ICC,* pp. 46–52; Henry Pringle, *Theodore Roosevelt: A Biography* (New York: Harcourt, Brace and World, 1931), pp. 292–300; George Mowry, *The Era of Theodore Roosevelt* (New York: Harper & Row, 1958), pp. 198–206; Sarasohn, "Democratic Surge," pp. 16–28.

22 Hepburn Act, June 29, 1906, 34 Statutes at Large 584, 590, sect. 16; Frank H. Dixon, *Railroads and Government: Their Relations in the United States 1910–1920* (New York: Scribners, 1922), p. 45; A. M. Tollefson, "Judicial Review of the Decisions of the Interstate Commerce Commission," *Minnesota Law Review* 2, 6 (May 1927), pp. 504–7.

23 Charles A. Prouty, "Court Review of the Orders of the Interstate Commerce Commission," *Yale Law Journal* 18, 5 (March 1909), pp. 297–310.

24 Kolko, *Railroads and Regulation,* p. 145; Henry Carter Adams, "Administrative Supervision."

25 Kolko, *Railroads and Regulation,* pp. 155–76; Roosevelt's first request for further action on railroad regulation was contained in his State of the Union Address for 1906. See *Congressional Record,* 59th Cong., 2nd sess., 1907, pp. 26–7.

26 *New York Times,* June 30, 1906, pp. 1, 3.

27 Interstate Commerce Commission *v* Illinois Central Railroad Co., 215 U.S. 452, 1910.

28 Dixon, *Railroads and Government;* Tollefson, "Judicial Review."

29 Noblitt, "Supreme Court," p. 17. For a sampling of political and intellectual attacks on the court during the Progressive era, see the following: Walter Clark, "Government by Judges," *Senate Document* 610, 63rd Cong., 2nd sess., 1914; L. B. Boudin, "Government by Judiciary," *Political Science Quarterly* 26, 2 (June 1911), pp. 238–70; Robert Z. Owen, "Withdrawing Power from Federal Courts to Declare Acts of Congress Void," *Senate Document* 737, 65th Cong., 2nd sess., 1917; Horace A. Davis, "The Annulment of Legislation by the Supreme Court," *American Political Science Review* 7, 4 (November 1913), pp. 541–87; William Trickett, "Judicial Dispensation from Congressional Statutes," *American Law Review* 41 (January–February 1907), pp. 65–91; Allan L. Benson, "The Usurped Power of the Courts," *Pearson's Magazine* 16 (November 1911), pp. 17–29; Theodore Roosevelt's growing radicalism on the issue of judicial reform can be traced through *The Outlook* between 1910 and 1913.

30 Prouty, "Court Review," p. 310.

31 Interstate Commerce Commission *v* Northern Pacific Railroad Co., 216 U.S. 538, 1910.

32 James Wallace Bryan, "The Railroad Bill and the Commerce Court," *American Political Science Review* 4, 4 (November 1910), pp. 546–54; Noblitt, "Supreme Court," pp. 130–6; Ripley, *Railroads,* pp. 522–54; Carl

McFarland, *Judicial Control of the Federal Trade Commission and the Interstate Commerce Commission, 1920–1930* (Cambridge, Mass.: Harvard University Press, 1933), pp. 100–24.

33 John Lovelle Withers, "The Administrative Theories and Practices of William Howard Taft" (Ph.D. diss., University of Chicago, 1956), pp. 147–94.

34 *Ibid.;* Bryan, "Railroad Bill," pp. 537–47; J. Newton Baker, "The Commerce Court: Its Origins, Its Powers, and Its Judges," *Yale Law Journal,* 20, 7 (May 1911), pp. 555–62; Dixon, *Railroads and Government,* pp. 43–51; "Notes," *New York University Law Quarterly Review* 20, 2 (November 1944), pp. 220–31; Felix Frankfurter, "The Business of the Supreme Court: A Study in the Federal Judicial System," *Harvard Law Review* 39, 5 (March 1926), pp. 587–627; William Z. Ripley, "Present Problems in Railway Legislation," *Political Science Quarterly* 27, 3 (September, 1912), pp. 428–53; George E. Dix, "The Death of the Commerce Court: A Study in Institutional Weakness," *Journal of American Legal History* 8, 2 (July 1964), pp. 238–60; Cushman, "Independent Regulatory Commissions," pp. 85–105; Sharfman, *Interstate Commerce Commission,* I, pp. 52–71; Ripley, *Railroads: Rates and Regulation,* pp. 581–600.

35 For the legislative struggle over the Mann-Elkins bill, see works cited in note 34 and the following: Albro Martin, *Enterprise Denied: Origins of the Decline of American Railroads, 1897–1917* (New York: Columbia University Press, 1971), pp. 183–93; Kolko, *Railroads and Regulation,* pp. 188–95; Sarasohn, "Democratic Surge," pp. 147–55; Kenneth W. Hechler, *Insurgency: Personalities and Politics of the Taft Era* (New York: Columbia University Press, 1940), pp. 163–78.

36 Frank H. Dixon, "The Mann–Elkins Act: Amending the Act to Regulate Commerce," *The Quarterly Journal of Economics* 24, 4 (August 1910), pp. 593–633.

37 Martin, *Enterprise Denied,* p. 234; Sarasohn, "Democratic Surge," pp. 147–55.

38 Hoogenboom and Hoogenboom, *History of the ICC,* pp. 67–71; Kolko, *Railroads and Regulation,* pp. 198–202.

39 Olson, *Progressive,* p. 45; Martin, *Enterprise Denied,* pp. 259–60.

40 Dixon, *Railroads and Government,* pp. 45–51.

41 Hoogenboom and Hoogenboom, *History of the ICC,* p. 67.

42 Dixon, *Railroads and Government,* p. 48; *Annual Report of the Interstate Commerce Commission 1911,* pp. 57–60.

43 See note 34; Kolko, *Railroads and Regulation,* pp. 201–2.

44 Roosevelt, *Theodore Roosevelt,* p. 477.

45 Quoted in Withers, "Administrative . . . Practices," p. 165.

46 Department of Justice, *Annual Report of the Attorney General for 1912,* pp. 55–7, 456.

47 Kolko, *Railroads and Regulation,* p. 201; Dix, "Commerce Court."

48 Martin, *Enterprise Denied,* pp. 38–9, 244.

49 *Ibid.*, pp. 234–37; "Report of the Railroad Securities Commission to the President," *House Document* 256, 62nd Cong., 2nd sess., 1911, pp. 32–3.

50 Martin, *Enterprise Denied*, pp. 167–8, 256–9; Kolko, *Railroads and Regulation*, p. 205; K. Austin Kerr, *American Railroad Politics, 1914–1920: Rates, Wages and Efficiency* (Pittsburgh: University of Pittsburgh Press, 1968), p. 17.

51 Quoted in Dixon, *Railroads and Government*, pp. 15–16.

52 Taft's appointment of Balthasar Meyer to the commission provides the most clear-cut example of the political constraints on independent action. Meyer was the first trained economist to sit on the commission, and his academic reputation was that of a moderate with a clear understanding of railroad problems. But Meyer heralded from the University of Wisconsin and hesitated to cross Robert LaFollette when it came to commission policies. It might also be noted that Meyer's ascendance signaled the decline of Henry Carter Adams's influence as University of Wisconsin economists began to replace Adams's loyal band of University of Michigan economists. See Martin, *Enterprise Denied*, pp. 357–8; See also David Grossman, "Professors and Public Service, 1885–1925: A Chapter in the Professionalization of the Social Sciences" (Ph.D. diss., Washington University, 1973), pp. 200–1.

53 Oscar Kraines, "Brandeis' Philosophy of Scientific Management," *Western Political Quarterly* 13, 1 (March 1960), pp. 191–201; Samuel Haber, *Efficiency and Uplift: Scientific Management in the Progressive Era, 1890–1920* (University of Chicago Press, 1964), pp. 41–54; William J. Cunningham, "Scientific Management in the Operation of the Railroads," *Quarterly Journal of Economics* 25, 3 (May 1911), pp. 539–62.

54 This is not to say that no commissioner articulated this point of view. As we shall soon see, Winthrop Daniels was its most consistent advocate. The important point, however, is that his was the minority view in the prewar years. See Dixon, *Railroads and Government*, pp. 18–21.

55 For a thorough review of the plight of the railroads and the ICC's rate decisions in this period, see Martin, *Enterprise Denied*, pp. 194–351. For a review of ICC rate theory before the Mann–Elkins Act, see M. B. Hammond, "Railway Rate Theories of the Interstate Commerce Commission" *Quarterly Journal of Economics* 25, 1 (November 1910), pp. 1–66; 25, 2 (February 1911), pp. 279–336; 25, 3 (May 1911), pp. 471–538.

56 *Ibid.*

57 Sharfman, *Interstate Commerce Commission, I, pp.* 119–32; Hoogenboom and Hoogenboom, *History of the ICC*, p. 68.

58 Martin, *Enterprise Denied*, pp. 267–304; Hoogenboom and Hoogenboom, *History of the ICC*, pp. 72–4.

59 The President's message is contained in *House Documents* 1, 64th Cong., 1st sess., 1915.

60 Hoogenboom and Hoogenboom, *History of the ICC*, pp. 77–8; Martin, *Enterprise Denied*, pp. 314–15.

61 Joint Committee on Interstate and Foreign Commerce, "Interstate and For-

eign Transportation Hearings," 64th Cong., 1st sess. (November 1916–November 1917), 1917; Max Thelen, "The Newlands Railroad Investigation," *The Utilities Magazine* 3, 2 (February 1917), pp. 1–8; Martin, *Enterprise Denied*, p. 343; Kerr, *American Railroad Politics*, pp. 26–30. The relevant Supreme Court cases are: the *Minnesota* rate cases 230 U.S. 352, 1913; the *Shreveport* cases, 234 U.S. 342, 1914.

62   Martin, *Enterprise Denied*, pp. 329–33; Kerr, *American Railroad Politics*, pp. 33–4.

63   Albert Cummins, "An Address: Winthrop M. Daniels," *Senate Documents* 673, 64th Cong., 2nd sess., 1917; Kerr, *American Railroad Politics*, pp. 25–6; Martin, *Enterprise Denied*, pp. 316–18. Two of the three new appointments were the result of congressional action to expand the commission in the midst of the war crisis.

64   Kerr, *American Railroad Politics*, p. 40.

65   William J. Cunningham, *American Railroads: Government Control and Reconstruction Policies* (Chicago: A. W. Shaw, 1922), p. 25; I. L. Sharfman, *The American Railroad Problem: A Study in War and Reconstruction* (New York: Century, 1921), p. 73.

66   Cunningham, *American Railroads*, pp. 22–37; Kerr, *American Railroad Politics*, pp. 44–55; Sharfman, *American Railroad Problem*, pp. 93–4.

67   Kerr, *American Railroad Politics*, pp. 44–71; Hoogenboom and Hoogenboom, *History of the ICC*, pp. 79–83.

68   *Ibid.*

69   *Ibid.; Annual Report of the Interstate Commerce Commission* (1918), pp. 5–9; Martin, *Enterprise Denied*, p. 349.

70   *Ibid.;* Walker D. Hines, *War History of American Railroads* (New Haven, Conn.: Yale University Press, 1928), p. 17. Commissioner McCord dissented from the commission's presentation of the alternatives, arguing that unification under private operation could not work under any circumstances.

71   Hines, *War History of the Railroads*, pp. 22–3, 256–64.

72   Kerr, *American Railroad Politics*, pp. 59–71.

73   *Ibid.*, pp. 72–83; Dixon, *Railroads and Government*, p. 156. Sharfman, *Interstate Commerce Commission* I, pp. 144–70; Hines, *War History of the Railroads*, pp. 230–3. The academic community was represented at the Railroad Administration by William Cunningham of the Harvard University Business School. Cunningham's role paralleled that of Edwin Gay at the War Industries Board.

74   Kerr, *American Railroad Politics*, pp. 83–91.

75   *Ibid.;* Dixon, *Railroads and Government*, pp. 167–77.

76   Kerr, *American Railroad Politics*, pp. 94–5, 111–24; Dixon, *Railroads and Government*, pp. 172–3. Commission frustration is quoted in Dixon.

77   Kerr, *American Railroad Politics*, pp. 88–100.

78   *Ibid.;* Hines, *War History of the Railroads*, pp. 85–93.

79   Kerr, *American Railroad Politics*, p. 127; Hines, *War History of the Railroads*, pp. 199–201.

80 In addition to the local traffic committees representing management and shippers, McAdoo established a Board of Railroad Wages and Working Conditions and a Division of Labor and Operations after the Lane Commission report.

81 Kerr, *American Railroad Politics*, pp. 142–3, 211–13; Hines, *War History of the Railroads*, pp. 42–5.

82 Dixon, *Railroads and Government*, p. 215.

83 A thorough presentation of these positions is provided by Kerr, *American Railroad Politics*, pp. 128–203; see also Dixon, *Railroads and Government*, pp. 213–25.

84 Kerr, *American Railroad Politics*, pp. 143–56.

85 *Ibid.*, pp. 205–21; Cushman, "Independent Regulatory Commissions," pp. 115–30; Hoogenboom and Hoogenboom, *History of the ICC*, pp. 94–7.

86 *Ibid.*

87 *Ibid.;* Sharfman, *Interstate Commerce Commission*, I, pp. 181–242.

88 *Ibid.;* Cunningham, *American Railroads*, pp. 219–35.

89 On the notion of the distended society, see Robert Wiebe, *The Search for Order, 1877–1920* (New York: Hill and Wang, 1967); On railroad regulation as a search for "a more orderly system of control," see Blum, *The Republican Roosevelt*, pp. 155–76.

Epilogue: Beyond the state of courts and parties

1 Harold Laski, *The American Presidency* (New York: Grosset and Dunlap, 1940), p. 143; see also James MacGregor Burns, *Roosevelt: The Lion and the Fox* (New York: Harcourt, Brace, and World, 1956), pp. 291–380.

2 David Truman, *The Governmental Process: Political Interests and Public Opinion* (New York: Knopf, 1951), pp. 516–25.

3 See the epigraph from Charles Warren at the beginning of the epilogue. *The Supreme Court in United States History* (Boston: Little, Brown, 1947), p. 751.

4 The 1950 *Report of the Committee on Political Parties of the American Political Science Association* warned of four specific dangers related to the decline of party government.

> The first danger is that the inadequacy of the party system in sustaining well-considered programs and providing broad public support for them may lead to grave consequences in an explosive era. The second danger is that the American people may go too far for the safety of constitutional government in compensating for this inadequacy by shifting excessive responsibility to the President. The third danger is that with growing public cynicism and continuing proof of the ineffectiveness of the party system the nation may eventually witness the disintegration of the two major parties. The fourth danger is that the incapacity of the two parties for consistent action based on meaningful programs may rally support for extremist parties poles apart, each fanatically bent on imposing on the country its particular panacea.

5   Robert Pranger, "The Decline of American National Government," *Publius*
    3, 2 (Fall 1973), pp. 97–127; Robert Pranger, *The Eclipse of Citizenship:
    Power and Participation in Contemporary Politics* (New York: Holt,
    Rinehart & Winston, 1968).
6   Theodore J. Lowi, *The End of Liberalism: Ideology, Policy and the Crisis of
    Public Authority* (New York: Norton, 1969), esp. pp. 297–303 on juridical
    democracy.
7   Walter Dean Burnham, *Critical Elections and the Mainsprings of American
    Politics* (New York: Norton, 1970), esp. pp. 175–93.

Selected bibliography

This bibliography offers a general survey of secondary material and commentary on the main topics of concern in this book. It is not meant to provide an exhaustive list but to bring together literatures that have hitherto been kept fairly separate. It should also be noted that government documents, archival material, newspaper articles, editorials, published work by principal actors and associations, memoirs, and general biographies of principal actors do not appear. The Notes must be consulted for a full account of the research.

Two broad areas of primary research that were particularly important in producing this study can be easily summarized. The first lay in government documents. The following were systematically reviewed for the years 1877–1920: *Congressional Record, United States Congress: Serial Set, Annual Reports of the United States Civil Service Commission, Annual Reports of the United States Bureau of Efficiency, Annual Reports of the United States Interstate Commerce Commission, Annual Reports of the War Department.* The second lay in contemporaneous periodicals. The following were consulted extensively for the years 1877–1920: *Atlantic Monthly, The Army and Navy Journal, The Civil Service Record, Commercial and Financial Chronicle, The Congressional Digest, The Federal Employee, Forum, Good Government, Harpers, The Independent, Journal of the Military Service Institution, Nation, The New Republic, The New York Times, North American Review, Political Science Quarterly, Quarterly Journal of Economics, United Service.*

I. Theoretical and comparative considerations

Almond, Gabriel. "Political Systems and Political Change," *The American Behavioral Scientist* 6 (June 1963), 1–14.

Almond, Gabriel, Flanagan, Scott C., and Mundt, Robert, eds., *Crisis, Choice and Change: Historical Studies of Political Development.* Boston: Little, Brown, 1973.

Anderson, Perry. *The Lineages of the Absolutist State.* London: New Left Books, 1974.

Barker, Ernest. *The Development of Public Services in Western Europe 1660–1930.* New York: Oxford University Press, 1944.

Bell, Daniel. *The Cultural Contradictions of Capitalism.* New York: Basic Books, 1976.

Bendix, Reinhard. *Nation-Building and Citizenship: Studies of Our Changing Social Order.* Garden City, N.Y.: Anchor Books, 1969.

Bendix, Reinhard, ed. *State and Society.* Boston: Little, Brown, 1968.

Binder, Leonard, et al. *Crises and Sequences in Political Development.* Princeton, N.J.: Princeton University Press, 1971.

Block, Fred. "The Ruling Class Does Not Rule: Notes on the Marxist Theory of the State," *Socialist Revolution* 33 (May–June 1977), 6–28.

Commons, John R. *The Legal Foundations of Capitalism.* Madison: University of Wisconsin Press, 1924.

d'Entreves, Alexander Passerin. *The Notion of the State: An Introduction to Political Theory.* London: Oxford University Press, 1967.

Durkheim, Emile. *Professional Ethics and Civic Morals.* Glencoe, Ill.: Free Press, 1958.

Eisenstadt, S. N. "Institutionalization and Change," *American Sociological Review* 29 (April 1964), pp. 235–47.

Engels, Friedrich. *The Family, Private Property and the State,* Eleanor Leacock, ed. New York: International, 1972.

Gramsci, Antonio. *Selections from the Prison Notebooks.* Ed. and trans. by Quinton Hoare and Geoffrey Nowell Smith. New York: International, 1971.

Grew, Raymond, ed. *Crises of Political Development in Europe and the United States.* Princeton, N.J.: Princeton University Press, 1978.

Habermas, Jurgen. *Legitimation Crisis.* Boston: Beacon Press, 1973.

Hegel, Georg Friedrich. *The Philosophy of History.* Trans. by J. Sibree. Introduction by C. S. Friedrich. New York: Dover, 1956.

Hegel's Philosophy of Right. Trans. with Notes by T. M. Knox. London: Oxford University Press, 1967.

Hintze, Otto. *The Historical Essays of Otto Hintze.* Ed. by Felix Gilbert. New York: Oxford University Press, 1975.

Huntington, Samuel P. *Political Order in Changing Societies.* New Haven, Conn.: Yale University Press, 1968.

Kingsley, J. Donald. *Representative Bureaucracy.* Yellow Springs, Ohio: Antioch Press, 1944.

LaPalombara, Joseph, ed. *Bureaucracy and Political Development.* Princeton, N.J.: Princeton University Press, 1963.

Larson, Magali Sarfatti. *The Rise of Professionalism: A Sociological Analysis.* Berkeley: University of California Press, 1978.

Laski, Harold. *The State: In Theory and Practice.* New York: Viking Press, 1935.

Lubasz, Heinz, ed. *The Development of the Modern State.* New York: Macmillan, 1966.

MacIver, Robert. *The Modern State.* London: Oxford University Press, 1962.

Marx, Fritz Morstein. *The Administrative State.* University of Chicago Press, 1957.

Marx, Karl. *The Civil War in France, with an Introduction by Frederick Engels.* Peking: Foreign Language Press, 1966.

Critique of Hegel's 'Philosophy of Right', Joseph O'Malley and Annette Jolin, eds. and trans. Cambridge: Cambridge University Press, 1970.

The Eighteenth Brumaire of Louis Bonaparte. New York: International, 1972.

Marx, Karl, and Engels, Frederick. *The German Ideology. Part I With Selections from Parts Two and Three*. Ed. with an Introduction by C. J. Arthur. New York: International, 1970.

Miliband, Ralph. *The State in Capitalist Society: An Analysis of the Western System of Power*. New York: Basic Books, 1969.

Nettl, J. P. "The State as a Conceptual Variable," *World Politics* 20, 4 (July 1968), 559–92.

Neumann, Franz. *Democratic and Authoritarian States: Essays in Political and Legal Theory*, Herbert Marcuse, ed. London: Free Press of Glencoe, 1957.

Ostrogorski, Maurice. *Democracy and the Organization of Political Parties*. Trans. by Frederick Clark. London: Macmillan, 1902.

Parris, Henry. *Constitutional Bureaucracy: The Development of British Central Administration since the Eighteenth Century*. London: Allen & Unwin, 1969.

Parsons, Talcott. *The Social System*. New York: Free Press, 1964.

Poggi, Gianfranco. *The Development of the Modern State: A Sociological Introduction*. Stanford University Press, 1978.

Poulantzas, Nicos. *Political Power and Social Class*. London: New Left Books, 1975.

Redford, Emmette S. *Democracy in the Administrative State*. New York: Oxford University Press, 1969.

Rosenberg, Hans. *Bureaucracy, Aristocracy, Autocracy: The Prussian Experience, 1660–1815*. Boston: Beacon Press, 1958.

Schonfeld, Andrew. *Modern Capitalism: The Changing Balance of Public and Private Power*. London: Oxford University Press, 1965.

Schumpeter, Joseph A. *Capitalism, Socialism and Democracy*. New York: Harper & Row, 1950.

Skocpol, Theda. "Critical Review of Barrington Moore's Social Origins of Dictatorship and Democracy," *Politics and Society*, 4 (Fall 1973), 1–34.

States and Social Revolutions: A Comparative Analysis of France, Russia and China. New York: Cambridge University Press, 1979.

Tilly, Charles, ed. *The Formation of National States in Western Europe*. Princeton, N.J.: Princeton University Press, 1975.

Vile, M. J. C. *Constitutionalism and the Separation of Powers*. Oxford: Clarendon Press, 1967.

Watkins, Frederick. *The State as a Concept of Political Science*. New York: Harper & Brothers, 1934.

Weber, Max. *From Max Weber: Essays in Sociology*. Ed. by Hans Gerth and C. Wright Mills. New York: Oxford University Press, 1958.

Wolfe, Alan. *The Limits of Legitimacy: The Political Contradictions of Contemporary Capitalism*. New York: Free Press, 1977.

Wright, E. O. "To Control or Smash the Bureaucracy: Weber and Lenin on Politics, the State and Bureaucracy," *Berkeley Journal of Sociology* 19 (1974–5), 69–108.

II. American institutional development: general background

Agar, Herbert. *The Price of Union.* Boston: Houghton Mifflin, 1950.

Anderson, Donald. *William Howard Taft: A Conservative's Conception of the Presidency.* Ithaca, N.Y.: Cornell University Press, 1973.

Bailyn, Bernard. *The Origins of American Politics.* New York: Vintage Books, 1967.

Bates, Ernest Southerland. *The Story of Congress, 1789–1935.* New York: Harper & Brothers, 1936.

Beer, Samuel. "The Modernization of American Federalism," *Publius* 3, 2 (Fall 1973), 50–95.

Bell, Daniel. "The End of American Exceptionalism," *The Public Interest* 41 (Fall 1975), 193–225.

Beth, Loren. *The Development of the American Constitution, 1877–1917.* New York: Harper & Row, 1971.

Binkley, Wilfred. *American Political Parties: Their Natural History.* New York: Knopf, 1943.

President and Congress. New York: Vintage Books, 1962.

Bledstein, Barton J. *The Culture of Professionalism: The Middle Class and the Development of Higher Education in America.* New York: Norton, 1976.

Bloomfield, Maxwell. *American Lawyers in a Changing Society.* Cambridge, Mass.: Harvard University Press, 1976.

Blum, John Morton. *The Progressive Presidents.* New York: Norton, 1980.

Boudin, Louis B. "Government by Judiciary," *Political Science Quarterly* 26, 2 (June 1911), 238–70.

Bryce, James. *The American Commonwealth.* 2 vols. Abridged and ed. by Louis Hacker. New York: Putnam, 1959.

Burnham, Walter Dean. "The Changing Shape of the American Political Universe," *American Political Science Review* 59 (March 1965), 7–28.

Critical Elections and the Mainsprings of American Politics. New York: Norton, 1970.

"Theory and Voting Research: Some Reflections on Converse's 'Change in the American Electorate,'" *American Political Science Review* 68, 3 (September 1974), 1002–23.

Calhoun, David. *Professional Lives in America: Structure and Aspiration.* Cambridge, Mass.: Harvard University Press, 1965.

Campbell, Charles S. *The Transformation of American Foreign Relations, 1865–1900.* New York: Harper & Row, 1976.

Ceaser, James W. *Presidential Selection: Theory and Development.* Princeton, N.J.: Princeton University Press, 1979.

Chambers, William Nisbet. *Political Parties in a New Nation: The American Experience, 1776–1809.* New York: Oxford University Press, 1963.

Chambers, William Nisbet, and Burnham, Water Dean, eds. *The American Party Systems: Stages of Development.* New York: Oxford University Press, 1967.

Chandler, Alfred D. *The Visible Hand: The Managerial Revolution in American Business.* Cambridge, Mass.: Belknap Press, 1977.

Chroust, Anton-Herman. *The Rise of the Legal Profession in America.* 2 vols. Norman: University of Oklahoma Press, 1965.

Dobson, John M. *Politics in the Gilded Age: A New Perspective on Reform.* New York: Praeger, 1972.

Dorfman, Joseph. *The Economic Mind in American Civilization.* New York: Viking Press, 1959.

Ekirch, Arthur A., Jr. *Progressivism in America: A Study of the Era from Theodore Roosevelt to Woodrow Wilson.* New York: New Viewpoints, 1974.

Elazer, Daniel. *The Federal Partnership: Intergovernmental Relations in the Nineteenth Century United States.* University of Chicago Press, 1962.

Ellis, Richard. *The Jeffersonian Crisis: Courts and Politics in the Young Republic.* New York: Norton, 1974.

Eulau, Heinz. "Polarity in Representational Federalism: A Neglected Theme of Political Theory," *Publius* 3, 2 (Fall 1973), pp. 153–71.

Farnham, Wallace D. "The Weakened Springs of Government: A Study in Nineteenth Century History," *Journal of American History* 68, 3 (April 1963), 662–80.

Faulkner, Harold U. *The Decline of Laissez Faire, 1897–1917.* New York: Rinehart, 1951.

Fine, Sidney. *Laissez Faire and the General Welfare State: A Study of Conflict in American Thought, 1865–1901.* Ann Arbor: University of Michigan Press, 1965.

Follet, Mary Parker. *The New State.* New York: Longmans, Green, 1920.

Forsythe, Dall W. *Taxation and Political Change in the Young Nation, 1781–1833.* New York: Columbia University Press, 1977.

Frankfurter, Felix, and Landis, John. *The Business of the Supreme Court: A Study in the Federal Judicial System.* New York: Macmillan, 1927.

Fredrickson, George M. *The Inner Civil War: Northern Intellectuals and the Crisis of the Union.* New York: Harper & Row, 1965.

Freund, Ernst. "The Law of Administration in America," *Political Science Quarterly* 9, 3 (Fall 1894), 403–25.

Friedman, Lawrence M. *A History of American Law.* New York: Simon & Schuster, 1973.

Fries, Sylvia. "Staatstheorie and the New American Science of Politics," *Journal of the History of Ideas* 34, 3 (July–September 1973), 391–404.

Fuller, Wayne E. *The American Mail: Enlarger of the Common Life.* University of Chicago Press, 1972.

Furner, Mary O. *Advocacy and Objectivity: A Crisis in the Professionalization of American Social Science: 1865–1905.* Lexington: University of Kentucky Press, 1975.

Gawalt, Gerald W. "Sources of Anti-Lawyer Sentiment in Massachusetts,

1740–1840," *American Journal of Legal History* 14 (June 1970), 287–307.

"Massachusetts Legal Education in Transition 1776–1840," *American Journal of Legal History* 17, 1 (January 1973), 27–50.

Gilbert, James. *Designing the Industrial State: The Intellectual Pursuit of Collectivism*. Chicago: Quadrangle Books, 1972.

Goodrich, Carter. *Government Promotion of American Canals and Railroads, 1800–1890*. New York: Columbia University Press, 1960.

Grossman, David. "Professors and Public Service, 1885–1925: A Chapter in the Professionalization of the Social Sciences." Ph.D. diss., Washington University, 1973.

Haber, Samuel. *Efficiency and Uplift: Scientific Management in the Progressive Era, 1890–1920*. University of Chicago Press, 1964.

Haines, Charles. *The American Doctrine of Judicial Supremacy*. New York: Russell and Russell, 1959.

Hammond, Bray. *Banks and Politics in America: From the Revolution to the Civil War*. Princeton, N.J.: Princeton University Press, 1957.

Hartz, Louis. *Economic Policy and Democratic Thought: Pennsylvania, 1776–1860*. Cambridge, Mass.: Harvard University Press, 1948.

The Liberal Tradition in America. New York: Harcourt, Brace and World, 1955.

Haskell, Thomas L. *The Emergence of Professional Social Science: The American Social Science Association and the Nineteenth Century Crisis of Authority*. Urbana: University of Illinois Press, 1977.

Hays, Samuel P. *The Response to Industrialism, 1885–1914*. University of Chicago Press, 1957.

"The Social Analysis of American Political History, 1880–1920," *Political Science Quarterly* 80, 3 (September 1965), pp. 373–94.

Conservation and the Gospel of Efficiency: The Progressive Conservation Movement, 1890–1920. New York: Atheneum, 1969.

Heale, M. J. *The Making of American Politics, 1750–1850*. New York: Longmans, Green, 1977.

Hechler, K. W. *Insurgency: Personalities and Politics of the Taft Era*. New York: Columbia University Press, 1940.

Hill, Forest G. *Roads, Rails and Waterways: The Army Engineers and Early Transportation*. Norman: University of Oklahoma Press, 1957.

Hobson, Wayne K. "Professionals, Progressives and Bureaucratization: A Reassessment," *The Historian* 39 (August 1977), 639–58.

Hofstadter, Richard. *The Age of Reform: From Bryan to FDR*. New York: Vintage Books, 1955.

Anti-Intellectualism in American Life. New York: Vintage Books, 1963.

The Idea of a Party System. Berkeley: University of California Press, 1969.

Hollingsworth, J. Rogers. *The Whirligig of Politics: The Democracy of Cleveland and Bryan*. University of Chicago Press, 1963.

"The United States." In Raymond Grew, ed., *Crises of Political Development in Europe and the United States.* Princeton, N.J.: Princeton University Press, 1978, pp. 163–95.

Horwitz, Morton. *The Transformation of American Law, 1780–1860.* Cambridge, Mass.: Harvard University Press, 1977.

Huntington, Samuel P. "Political Modernization: America vs. Europe," in *Political Order in Changing Societies.* New Haven, Conn.: Yale University Press, 1968, pp. 93–139.

Hurst, James Willard. *Law and the Conditions of Freedom in the Nineteenth Century United States.* Madison: University of Wisconsin Press, 1956.

The Growth of American Law: The Lawmakers. Boston: Little, Brown, 1959.

The Legitimacy of the Business Corporation in the Law of the United States: 1780–1970. Charlottesville: University of Virginia Press, 1970.

Hyneman, Charles Shang. *Bureaucracy in a Democracy.* New York: Harper & Brothers, 1950.

Israel, Jerry, ed. *Building the Organization Society: Essays in Associational Activities in Modern America.* New York: Free Press, 1972.

Jaenicke, Douglas. "Herbert Croly, Progressive Ideology and the FTC Act," *Political Science Quarterly* 3, 93 (Fall 1978), 471–94.

Josephson, Matthew. *The President Makers: The Culture of Politics and Leadership in the Age of Enlightenment, 1896–1919.* New York: Harcourt, Brace and World, 1940.

The Politicos, 1865–1896. New York: Harcourt, Brace and World, 1963.

Keller, Morton. *Affairs of State: Public Life in Late Nineteenth Century America.* Cambridge, Mass.: Belknap Press, 1977.

Kelly, George A. "Hegel's America," *Philosophy and Public Affairs* 2, 1 (Fall 1972), 2–36.

Kirkland, Edward C. *Industry Comes of Age: Business, Labor and Public Policy.* New York: Holt, Rinehart & Winston, 1961.

Kolko, Gabriel. *The Triumph of Conservatism: A Re-Interpretation of American History, 1900–1916.* Chicago: Quadrangle Books, 1963.

Kutler, Stanley I. *The Judicial Power and Reconstruction Politics.* University of Chicago Press, 1968.

Lasch, Christopher. "The Moral and Intellectual Rehabilitation of the Ruling Class," *The World of Nations.* New York: Knopf, 1973, pp. 80–99.

Link, Arthur S. *Wilson,* 5 vols. Princeton, N.J.: Princeton University Press, 1964.

Woodrow Wilson and the Progressive Era. Princeton, N.J.: Princeton University Press, 1965.

Lively, Robert A. "The American System: A Review Article," *Business History Review* 29 (March 1955), 81–96.

Lowi, Theodore. "American Business and Public Policy: Case Studies and Political Theory," *World Politics* 16, 4 (July 1964), 677–715.

"Party, Policy, and Constitution in America," in William Nisbet Chambers and Walter Dean Burnham, eds., *The American Party Systems: Stages of Development.* New York: Oxford University Press, 1967.

"Parallels of Policy and Politics: The Political Theory in American History." Paper delivered to the Organization of American Historians, New Orleans, April 15, 1971.

The End of Liberalism: The Second Republic of the United States. New York: Norton, 1979.

McClosky, Robert. *The American Supreme Court.* University of Chicago Press, 1960.

McCormick, Richard. *The Second American Party System.* Chapel Hill: University of North Carolina Press, 1966.

McKitrick, Eric L. "Party Politics and the Union and Confederate War Efforts," in William Nisbet Chambers and Walter Dean Burnham, eds., *The American Party Systems: Stages of Development.* New York: Oxford University Press, 1967.

McLaughlin, Andrew C. *The Courts, the Constitution and the Parties.* University of Chicago Press, 1912.

Marcus, Robert. *Grand Old Party: Political Structure in the Gilded Age, 1880–1896.* New York: Oxford University Press, 1971.

Marshall, L. Lynn. "The Strange Stillbirth of the Whig Party," *The American Historical Review* 72, 2 (January 1967), 445–69.

Miller, Perry, ed. *The Legal Mind in America: From Independence to the Civil War.* Ithaca, N.Y.: Cornell University Press, 1962.

The Life of the Mind in America: From the Revolution to the Civil War. New York: Harcourt, Brace and World, 1965.

Morgan, H. Wayne. *From Hayes to McKinley: National Party Politics, 1877–1896.* Syracuse University Press, 1969.

Mosher, Frederick C. *Democracy and the Public Service.* New York: Oxford University Press, 1968.

Mowry, George E. *The Era of Theodore Roosevelt.* New York: Harper & Row, 1958.

Newmyer, R. Kent. "Daniel Webster as Tocqueville's Lawyer: The Dartmouth College Case Again," *American Journal of Legal History* 11 (April 1967), 128–47.

The Supreme Court Under Marshall and Taney. Arlington Heights, Ill.: AHM, 1968.

Nichols, Roy. *The Disruption of American Democracy.* New York: Collier Books, 1962.

The Invention of the American Political Parties. New York: Macmillan, 1967.

Noblitt, Harding Coolidge. "The Supreme Court and the Progressive Era, 1902–1921." Ph.D. diss., University of Chicago, 1955.

O'Neill, William. *The Progressive Years: America Comes of Age.* New York: Dodd, Mead, 1975.

Paul, Arnold M. *Conservative Crisis and the Rule of Law: Attitudes of the Bar and Bench, 1887–1895.* Gloucester, Mass.: Peter Smith, 1976.

Persons, Stow. *The Decline of American Gentility.* New York: Columbia University Press, 1973.

Pollard, A. R. *Factors in American History*. New York: Macmillan, 1925.

Polsby, Nelson. "The Institutionalization of the House of Representatives," *American Political Science Review* 62, 1 (March 1968), 144–68.

Pranger, Robert. "The Decline of American National Government," *Publius* 3, 2 (Fall 1973), 97–127.

Remini, Robert V. *Martin Van Buren and the Making of the Democratic Party*. New York: Columbia University Press, 1959.

Rhodes, James Ford. *History of the United States from the Compromise of 1850 to the McKinley–Bryan Campaign of 1896*, vol. 8, *1877–1896*. New York: Macmillan, 1920.

Robinson, Edgar E. *The Evolution of American Political Parties*. New York: Harcourt, Brace, 1924.

Rohrbough, Malcolm. *The Land Office Business: The Settlement and Administration of American Public Lands 1789–1837*. New York: Oxford University Press, 1968.

Rothman, David. *Politics and Power: The United States Senate, 1869–1901*. Cambridge, Mass.: Harvard University Press, 1966.

Rothman, Stanley. "Intellectuals and the American Political System," in Seymour Martin Lipset, ed., *Emerging Coalitions in American Politics*. San Francisco: Institute for Contemporary Studies, 1978.

Sarasohn, David. "The Democratic Surge, 1905–1912: Forging a Progressive Majority." Ph.D. diss., UCLA, 1977.

Schattschneider, E. E. *Party Government*. New York: Farrah and Rinehart, 1942.

Scheiber, Harry N. "Federalism and the American Economic Order, 1789–1910," *Law and Society Review* 10, 1 (Fall 1975), 57–118.

Schmidhauser, John R. *The Supreme Court as Final Arbiter in Federal–State Relations, 1789–1957*. Chapel Hill: University of North Carolina Press, 1958.

Shefter, Martin. "Party, Bureaucracy and Political Change in the United States," in Louis Maisel and Joseph Cooper, eds., *Political Parties: Development and Decay*. Beverly Hills: Sage, 1978.

Short, L. M. *The Development of National Administrative Organization in the United States*. Baltimore: Johns Hopkins University Press, 1923.

Sprout, John G. *The Best Men: Liberal Reformers in the Gilded Age*. New York: Oxford University Press, 1968.

Storing, Herbert. "Political Parties and the Bureaucracy," Robert Goldwin, ed., *Political Parties, U.S.A.* Chicago: Rand McNally, 1964.

Sumner, William Graham. "The Conquest of the United States by Spain," *Yale Law Journal* 8 (January 1899), 187–219.

Sundquist, James L. *Dynamics of the Party System: Alignment and Realignment of Political Parties in the United States*. Washington, D.C.: Brookings Institution, 1973.

Surrency, Erwin C. "A History of the Federal Courts," *Missouri Law Review* 28, 2 (Spring 1963), 214–44.

Swisher, Carl Brent. *American Constitutional Development.* Cambridge, Mass.: Houghton Mifflin, 1954.

Thach, Charles C., Jr. *The Creation of the Presidency, 1775–1789: A Study in Constitutional History.* Baltimore: Johns Hopkins University Press, 1923.

Tocqueville, Alexis de. *Democracy in America,* 2 vols. Henry Reeve, Francis Brown, and Phillip Bradley, eds. and trans. New York: Vintage Books, 1945.

Tomsich, John. *A Genteel Endeavor: American Culture and Politics in the Gilded Age.* Stanford University Press, 1971.

Veysey, Lawrence R. *The Emergence of the American University.* University of Chicago Press, 1965.

Waldo, Dwight. *The Administrative State: A Study of the Political Theory of American Public Administration.* New York: Ronald Press, 1948.

Warren, Charles. *A History of the American Bar.* Boston: Little, Brown, 1911. *Supreme Court in United States History.* Boston: Little, Brown, 1947.

Weinstein, James. *The Corporate Ideal in the Liberal State, 1900–1918.* Boston: Beacon Press, 1968.

Welch, Richard E., Jr. *George Frisbie Hoar and the Half-Breed Republicans.* Cambridge, Mass.: Harvard University Press, 1971.

White, G. Edward. "The Path of American Jurisprudence," *University of Pennsylvania Law Review* 124, 5 (May 1976), 1212–59.

The American Judicial Tradition: Profiles of Leading American Judges. Oxford: Oxford University Press, 1976.

White, Leonard D. *The Federalists: A Study in Administrative History.* New York: Macmillan, 1948.

The Jeffersonians: A Study in Administrative History. New York: Macmillan, 1951.

The Jacksonians: A Study in Administrative History. New York: Macmillan, 1954.

The Republican Era: A Study in Administrative History. New York: Macmillan, 1958.

White, Morton. *Social Thought in America: The Revolt Against Formalism.* Boston: Beacon Press, 1970.

Wiebe, Robert. *Businessmen and Reform: A Study of the Progressive Movement.* Chicago: Quadrangle Books, 1962.

The Search for Order, 1877–1920. New York: Hill and Wang, 1967.

The Segmented Society: An Introduction to the Meaning of America. New York: Oxford University Press, 1975.

Wiecek, William. "The Reconstruction of Federal Judicial Power, 1863–1875," *The American Journal of Legal History* 13 (October 1969), 333–59.

Wilensky, Norman M. *Conservatives in the Progressive Era: The Taft Republicans of 1912.* University of Florida Monographs in Social Science, no. 25 (Winter 1965). Gainesville: University of Florida Press, 1965.

Williams, William A. *The Contours of American History.* New York: New Viewpoints, 1973.

Wilson, James Q. "The Rise of the Bureaucratic State," *The Public Interest* 41 (Fall 1975), 77–106.

Wilson, Major. *Space, Time and Freedom: The Quest for Nationality and the Irrepressible Conflict, 1815–1861.* Westport, Conn.: Greenwood Press, 1974.

Wilson, Woodrow. *Congressional Government: A Study in American Politics.* New York: Houghton Mifflin, 1885.

Wood, Gordon. *The Creation of the American Republic, 1776–1789.* New York: Norton, 1969.

Woodward, C. Vann. *Reunion and Reaction: The Compromise of 1877 and the End of Reconstruction.* Boston: Little, Brown, 1951.

Young, James Sterling. *The Washington Community: 1800–1828.* New York: Harcourt Brace, Jovanovich, 1966.

III. The reform of civil administration

Aronson, Sidney. *Status and Kinship Ties in the Higher Civil Service: Standards of Selection in the Administrations of John Adams, Thomas Jefferson and Andrew Jackson.* Cambridge, Mass.: Harvard University Press, 1964.

Baruch, Ismar. "History of Position Classification and Salary Standardization in the Federal Service, 1789–1941." Report, Washington, D.C.: U.S. Civil Service Commission Personnel Classification Division, September 30, 1941. Catalogued in the Civil Service Commission Library.

Berens, Ruth M. "Blueprint for Reform: Curtis, Eaton and Schurz. M.A. thesis, University of Chicago, 1943.

Berman, Larry. *The Office of Management and Budget and the Presidency, 1921–1979.* Princeton, N.J.: Princeton University Press, 1979.

Betters, Paul V. *The Personnel Classification Board.* Washington, D.C.: Brookings Institution, 1931.

Brookings Institution. "The Institute for Government Research: An Account of Its Achievements." Washington, D.C.: Brookings Institution, 1956.

Caldwell, Lynton K. *The Administrative Theories of Hamilton and Jefferson: Their Contributions to Public Administration.* New York: Russell and Russell, 1944.

Chiang, Me Hsin. "The Bureau of Efficiency." Ph.D. diss., Harvard University, 1940.

Cleveland, Frederick, and Buck, Eugene. *The Budget and Responsible Government.* New York: Macmillan, 1920.

Crenson, Matthew. *The Federal Machine: Beginnings of Bureaucracy in Jacksonian America.* Baltimore: Johns Hopkins University Press, 1975.

Dahlberg, Jane S. *The New York Bureau of Municipal Research.* New York University Press, 1966.

Eaton, Dorman. *The Civil Service in Great Britain: A History of Abuses and Reform and Their Bearing on American Politics.* New York: Harper & Brothers, 1880.

Edwards, Geniana R. "Organized Federal Workers: A Study of Three Representative Unions." M.A. thesis, George Washington University, 1939.

Finer, S. E. "Patronage and the Public Service: Jeffersonian Bureaucracy and the British Tradition," *Public Administration* 30 (Winter 1952), 329–60.

Fish, Carl Russell. *The Civil Service and the Patronage.* Cambridge, Mass.: Harvard University Press, 1920.

Fisher, Louis. *Presidential Spending Power.* Princeton, N.J.: Princeton University Press, 1975.

Fitzpatrick, Edward. *Budget Making in a Democracy.* New York: Macmillan, 1918.

Foulke, William Dudley. *Fighting the Spoilsmen: Reminiscences of the Civil Service Reform Movement.* New York: Putnam, 1919.

    Roosevelt and the Spoilsmen. New York: National Civil Service Reform League, 1925.

Fowler, Dorothy. *The Cabinet Politician.* New York: Columbia University Press, 1943.

Gordon, Bess. "History of the Commission on Economy and Efficiency." Paper prepared for the National Archives Seminar, June 8, 1956. Washington, D.C.: National Archives Catalogue.

Hall, Chester Gordon, Jr. "The United States Civil Service Commission: Arm of President or Congress?" Ph.D. diss., American University, 1965.

Hartman, William J. "Politics and Patronage: The New York City Custom House, 1852–1902." Ph.D. diss., Columbia University, 1952.

    "Pioneer in Civil Service Reform: Silas W. Burt and the New York Custom House," *New York Historical Society Quarterly* 39, 4 (October 1955), 369–79.

Hatch, Carl E. *The Big Stick and the Congressional Gavel: A Study of Theodore Roosevelt's Relations with His Last Congress, 1907–1909.* New York: Pageant Press, 1967.

Heaton, Herbert. *A Scholar in Action: Edwin F. Gay.* Cambridge, Mass.: Harvard University Press, 1952.

Hoogenboom, Ari. "The Pendleton Act and the Civil Service," *American Historical Review* 64, 2 (January 1959), 301–18.

    "An Analysis of Civil Service Reformers," *The Historian* 23, 1 (November 1960), 54–78.

    Outlawing the Spoils: A History of the Civil Service Reform Movement, 1865–1883. Urbana: University of Illinois Press, 1968.

Huth, Edward A. "Rutherford B. Hayes: Civil Service Reformer." Ph.D. diss., Case Western Reserve University, 1943.

Jacobsen, Walter Otto. "A Study of President Taft's Commission on Economy and Efficiency and a Comparative Evaluation of Three Other Commissions." M.A. thesis, Columbia University, 1941.

Karl, Barry. *Executive Reorganization and Reform in the New Deal.* University of Chicago Press, 1963.

Kaufman, Herbert. "Emerging Conflicts in the Doctrines of Public Administration," *American Political Science Review* 50, 4 (December 1956), 1057–73.

Kraines, Oscar. "The Dockery–Cockrell Commission, 1893–1895," *Western Political Quarterly* 7, 3 (September 1959), 417–62.

"President and Congress: The Keep Commission, 1905–1907, First Comprehensive Presidential Inquiry into Administration," *Western Political Quarterly* 23, 1 (March 1970), 4–54.

McFarland, Gerald. *Mugwumps, Morals and Politics.* Amherst: University of Massachusetts Press, 1975.

MacMahon, Arthur W. "Woodrow Wilson as a Legislative Leader and Administrator," *American Political Science Review* 50, 3 (September 1956), 641–75.

Mansfield, Harvey C. *The Comptroller General.* New Haven, Conn.: Yale University Press, 1939.

Marx, Fritz Morstein. "The Background of the Budget and Accounting Act," Catheryn Seckler Hudson, ed., "Budgeting: An Instrument of Planning and Management." Collection, American University School of Social Sciences and Public Affairs, 1944. Washington, D.C.: Library of the Office of Management and Budget Catalogue.

"The Budget Bureau: Its Evolution and Present Role, I." *The American Political Science Review* 39, 4 (August 1945), 653–84.

Mason, Alpheus Thomas. *Bureaucracy Convicts Itself: The Ballinger–Pinchot Controversy of 1910.* New York: Viking Press, 1941.

Morris, Edmund. *The Rise of Theodore Roosevelt.* New York: Coward, McCann and Geoghegan, 1979.

Mosher, Frederick C. *The GAO: The Quest for Accountability in American Government.* Boulder, Colo.: Westview Press, 1979.

Murphy, Lionel V. "The First Civil Service Commission: 1871–1875," *Public Personnel Review* 3, 1 (January 1942), 29–39; 3, 3 (July 1942), 218–32; 3, 4 (October 1942), 229–322.

Nevins, Allan. *Grover Cleveland: A Study in Courage.* New York: Dodd, Mead, 1962.

Ostrom, Vincent. *The Intellectual Crisis in Public Administration,* rev. ed. University of Alabama Press, 1974.

Polenberg, Richard. *Reorganizing Roosevelt's Government, 1936–1939: The Controversy over Executive Reorganization.* Cambridge, Mass.: Harvard University Press, 1966.

Prinkett, Harold. "Keep Commission 1905–1909: A Rooseveltian Effort at Administrative Reform," *Journal of American History* 52, 2 (September 1965), 297–312.

Reeves, Thomas C. "Chester A. Arthur and Campaign Assessments in the Election of 1880," *The Historian* 31, 4 (August 1969), 573–82.

Rosenbloom, David. *Federal Service and the Constitution: The Development of the Public Employment Relationship.* Ithaca, N.Y.: Cornell University Press, 1971.

Sageser, A. Bower. *The First Two Decades of the Pendleton Act: A Study of Civil Service Reform. University of Nebraska Studies, 34–5*. Omaha: University of Nebraska Press, 1934–5.

Sayre, Wallace S. *The Federal Government Services*. Englewood Cliffs, N.J.: Prentice-Hall, 1965.

Schick, Allen. "Congress and the 'Details of Administration,'" *Public Administration Review* 36, 5 (September–October 1976), 516–28.

Schinagl, Mary S. *History of Efficiency Ratings in the Federal Government*. Ann Arbor: University of Michigan Press, 1963.

Schott, Richard L. *The Bureaucratic State: The Evolution and Scope of the American Federal Bureaucracy*. Morristown, N.J.: General Learning Press, 1974.

Smith, Darrel Henover. *The General Accounting Office*. Baltimore: Johns Hopkins University Press, 1927.

The United States Civil Service Commission. Baltimore: Johns Hopkins University Press, 1928.

Spero, Sterling. *The Labor Movement in a Government Industry*. New York: Doren, 1924.

Government as Employer. New York: Remsen Press, 1948.

Stewart, Frank. *The National Civil Service Reform League*. Austin: University of Texas Press, 1929.

Thatcher, Howard. "Public Discussion of Civil Service Reform." Ph.D. diss., Cornell University, 1943.

Van Riper, Paul. "Reconverting the Civil Service: What Happened after the First World War," *Public Personnel Review* 9, 1 (January 1948), 3–10.

"Adapting a British Invention to American Needs," *Public Administration* 31 (Winter 1953), 317–30.

History of the United States Civil Service. Evanston: Row, Peterson, 1958.

Walker, Harvey. "Employee Organization in the National Government: Retirement Legislation," *Public Personnel Studies* 10, 9 (February 1941), 246–52.

"Employee Organizations in the National Government Service: The Period Prior to the World War," *Public Personnel Studies* 10, 3 (August 1941), 67–73.

"Employee Organizations in the National Government Service: The Formation of the National Federation of Federal Employees," *Public Personnel Studies* 10, 4 (October 1941), 133–4.

Weber, Gustavas A. *Organized Efforts for the Improvement of Methods of Administration in the United States*. New York: Appleton, 1919.

White, Leonard. "Centennial Anniversary," *Public Administration Review* 14, 1 (January 1953), 3–7.

The Republican Era, 1869–1901: A Study in Administrative History. New York: Macmillan, 1958.

Willoughby, W. F. *Government Organization in War Time and After: A Survey of the Federal Civil Agencies Created for the Prosecution of the War*. New York: Appleton, 1919.

Wilson, Woodrow. "The Study of Administration," *Political Science Quarterly* 2, 2 (June 1887), 197–222.

Withers, John L. "The Administrative Theories and Practices of William Howard Taft." Ph.D. diss., University of Chicago, 1957.

Wood, Gordon. "The Massachusetts Mugwumps," *The New England Quarterly* 33, 4 (December 1960), 435–51.

IV. The reorganization of the army

Ambrose, Stephen. *Upton and the Army*. Baton Rouge: Louisiana State University Press, 1964.

Bauer, Frederick Gilbert. "The Massachusetts Militia," in Albert Bushnell Hart, ed., *Commonwealth History of Massachusetts*. 5 vols. New York: State's History, 1930, 5, pp. 570–97.

Beaver, Daniel R. "Newton D. Baker and the Genesis of the War Industries Board," *Journal of American History* 102, 1 (June 1965), 43–74.

Newton D. Baker and the American War Effort 1917–1919. Lincoln: University of Nebraska Press, 1966.

Bernardo, Joseph C., and Eugene H. Bacon. *American Military Policy: Its Development Since 1775*. Harrisburgh, Pa.: Stackpole, 1957.

Bethel, Elizabeth. "The Military Information Division: Origin of the Intelligence Division," *Military Affairs* 11, 1 (Spring 1947), 17–29.

Boylan, Bernard. "The Forty-fifth Congress and Army Reform," *Mid-America* 41, 3 (July 1959), 173–89.

Bruce, Robert. *1877: Year of Violence*. Chicago: Quadrangle Books, 1959.

Cantor, Louis. "The Creation of the Modern National Guard: The Dick Militia Act of 1903." Ph.D. diss., Duke University, 1963.

"Elihu Root and the National Guard: Friend or Foe?" *Military Affairs* 33, 3 (December 1969), 20–9.

Carter, William Harding. "The Creation of the American General Staff," *Senate Documents*, 68th Cong., 1st sess., 119, 1903.

"The Evolution of Army Reforms," *United Service*, 3, Series 3 (May 1903), 1177–95.

"Elihu Root: His Services as Secretary of War," *North American Review* 178, 566 (January 1908), 110–21.

The American Army. Indianapolis: Bobbs-Merrill, 1915.

Clarkson, Grosvenor B. *Industrial America in the World War, the Strategy Behind the Line*. Boston: Houghton Mifflin, 1923.

Coakley, Robert W. "Federal Use of Militia and the National Guard in Civil Disturbances," in Robin Higham, ed., *Bayonets in the Streets: The Use of Troops in Civil Disturbances*, Lawrence: University Press of Kansas, 1969, pp. 3–34.

Coffman, Edward M. "The Battle against Red Tape: Business Methods of the War Department General Staff, 1917–1918," *Military Affairs* 26, 1 (Spring 1962), 1–10.

The Hilt of the Sword: The Career of Peyton C. March. Madison: University of Wisconsin Press, 1966.

The War to End All Wars: The American Military Experience in World War I. New York: Oxford University Press, 1968.

Colby, Eldridge. "Elihu Root and the National Guard," *Military Affairs* 32, 1 (Spring 1959), 28–34.

Cooper, Jerry Marvin. "The Army and Civil Disorder: Federal Military Intervention in American Labor Disputes, 1877–1900." Ph.D. diss., University of Wisconsin, 1971.

Cosmas, Graham. "From Order to Chaos: The War Department, the National Guard, and Military Policy, 1898," *Military Affairs* 29, 3 (Fall 1965), 105–21.

An Army for Empire: The United States Army in the Spanish-American War. Columbia: University of Missouri Press, 1971.

"Military Reform after the Spanish-American War: The Army Reorganization Fight of 1898–1899," *Military Affairs* 35, 1 (February 1971), 12–17.

Cramer, C. H. *Newton D. Baker.* Cleveland: World, 1961.

Cuff, Robert. "The Dollar-a-Year Men of the Great War," *Princeton University Library Chronicle* 30 (Autumn 1968), 10–24.

"Bernard Baruch: Symbol and Myth in Industrial Mobilization," *Business History Review* 43 (Summer 1969), 115–33.

"Woodrow Wilson and Business–Government Relations during World War I," *Review of Politics* 31, 7 (July 1969), 385–407.

"Business, the State and World War I: The American Experience," in R. D. Cuff and J. L. Granatstein, eds., *War and Society in North America.* Toronto: Thomas Nelson, 1970.

"The Cooperative Impulse and War: The Origins of the Council of National Defense and Advisory Commission," in Jerry Israel, ed., *Building the Organizational Society,* New York: Free Press, 1972, pp. 233–46.

The War Industries Board: Business–Government Relations during World War I. Baltimore: Johns Hopkins University Press, 1973.

"We Band of Brothers: Woodrow Wilson's War Managers," *Canadian Review of American Studies* 5, 2 (Fall 1974), 135–48.

"Herbert Hoover, the Ideology of Voluntarism and War Organization during the Great War," *Journal of American History* 64, 2 (September 1977), 358–72.

"Harry Garfield, the Fuel Administration and the Search for a Cooperative Order during World War I," *American Quarterly* 30 (Spring 1978), 39–53.

Cunliffe, Marcus. *Soldiers and Civilians: The Martial Spirit in America, 1775–1865.* New York: Free Press, 1973.

Current, Richard N. *Secretary Stimson: A Study in Statecraft.* New Brunswick, N.J.: Rutgers University Press, 1954.

Derthick, Martha. *The National Guard in Politics.* Cambridge, Mass.: Harvard University Press, 1965.

Deutrich, Mabel E. *The Struggle for Supremacy: The Career of General Fred C. Ainsworth.* Washington, D.C., Public Affairs Press, 1962.

Dickinson, John. *The Building of an Army.* New York: Century, 1922.

Eggert, Gerald. *Railroad Labor Disputes: The Beginnings of Federal Strike Policy.* Ann Arbor: University of Michigan Press, 1967.

Ekirch, Arthur, Jr. *The Civilian and the Military.* New York: Oxford University Press, 1956.

Finnegan, John Patrick. "Military Preparedness in the Progressive Era, 1911–1917." Ph.D. diss., University of Wisconsin, 1969.

Foner, Jack D. *The United States Soldier Between the Wars: Army Life and Reforms, 1865–1898.* New York: Humanities Press, 1970.

Foner, Philip. *The Great Labor Uprising of 1877.* New York: Monad Press, 1977.

Ganoe, William. *The History of the United States Army.* New York: Appleton, 1924.

Gephart, Ronald. "Politicians, Soldiers and Strikers: The Reorganization of the Nebraska Militia and the Omaha Strike of 1882," *Nebraska History* 46, 2 (June 1965), 89–120.

Hacker, Barton C. "The War Department and the General Staff, 1898–1917." M.A. thesis, University of Chicago, 1962.

"The United States Army as a National Police Force: The Federal Policing of Labor Disputes, 1877–1898," *Military History* 33, 1 (April 1969), 24–36.

Hagadorn, Hermann. *Leonard Wood: A Biography.* 2 vols. New York: Harper & Brothers, 1931.

Hammond, Paul J. *Organizing for Defense.* Princeton, N.J.: Princeton University Press, 1961.

Herring, George C., Jr. "James Hay and the Preparedness Controversy, 1915–1916," *The Journal of Southern History* 30, 4 (November 1964), 383–404.

Hewes, James E., Jr. "The United States Army General Staff, 1900–1917," *Military Affairs* 28, 2 (April 1974), 87–96.

From Root to McNamara: Army Organization and Administration, 1900–1963. Washington, D.C.: Government Printing Office, 1975.

Hill, Jim Dan. *The Minute Man in Peace and War: A History of the National Guard.* Harrisburgh, Pa.: Stackpole, 1964.

Himmelberg, Robert F. "The War Industries Board and the Anti Trust Question in November 1918," *Journal of American History* 52, 1 (June 1965), 59–74.

Hittle, J. D. *The Military Staff: Its History and Development.* Harrisburgh, Pa.: Stackpole, 1961.

Hunt, Elvid, and Lorence, Walter. *History of Fort Leavenworth, 1827–1937.* Fort Leavenworth, Kan.: Command and General Staff School Press, 1927.

Huntington, Samuel P. *The Soldier and the State: The Theory and Politics of Civil–Military Relations.* New York: Vintage Books, 1957.

"Equilibrium and Disequilibrium in American Military Policy," *Political Science Quarterly* 76, 4 (December 1961), 481–503.

Jessup, Philip C. *Elihu Root.* 2 vols. New York: Dodd, Mead, 1938.

Karp, Walter. *The Politics of War.* New York: Harper & Row, 1979.

Karsten, Peter. "Armed Progressives: The Military Reorganizes for the American Century," in Jerry Israel, ed., *Building the Organizational Society,* New York: Free Press, 1972, pp. 197–232.

Kohn, Richard H. *Eagle and Sword: The Federalists and the Creation of the Military Establishment in America, 1783–1802.* New York: Free Press, 1975.

Koistinen, Paul. "The Industrial–Military Complex in Historical Perspective: World War I," *Business History Review* 41, 4 (Winter 1967), 378–93.

Kreidberg, Marvin, and Merton, Henry. *History of Military Mobilization in the United States Army, 1775–1945.* Washington, D.C.: Department of the Army Pamphlet No. 20-212, June 1955.

Leopold, Richard. *Elihu Root and the Conservative Tradition.* Boston: Little, Brown, 1954.

Livermore, Seward W. *Woodrow Wilson and the War Congress, 1916–1918.* Seattle: University of Washington Press, 1966.

Logan, John. *The Volunteer Soldier of America.* Chicago: R. S. Beale, 1887.

MacKry, Philip E. "Law and Order, 1877: Philadelphia's Response to the Railroad Riots," *Pennsylvania Magazine of History and Biography* 96 (April 1972), 183–202.

Mahon, John K. *The American Militia: Decade of Decision, 1789–1800.* University of Florida Monograph in Social Sciences, no. 6 (Spring 1960). Gainesville: University of Florida Press, 1960.

Meneely, Alexander H. *The War Department, 1861: A Study in Mobilization and Administration.* New York: Columbia University Press, 1928.

Michie, Peter S. *The Life and Letters of Emory Upton.* New York: Appleton, 1885.

Millet, John D. "The Direction of Supply Activities in the War Department: An Administrative Survey, I," *American Political Science Review* 38, 2 (April 1944), 254–61.

Millis, Walter. *The Martial Spirit: A Study of Our War With Spain.* Boston: Houghton Mifflin, 1931.

   Arms and Men: A Study in American Military History. New York: Putnam, 1959.

Millis, Walter, ed. *American Military Thought.* Indianapolis: Bobbs-Merrill, 1966.

Nelson, Otto. *National Security and the General Staff.* Washington, D.C.: Infantry Journal Press, 1946.

Otis, Elwell S. "The Army in Connection with the Labor Riots of 1877," *Journal of the Military Service Institution* 6, 32 (June 1885), 110–36.

Palmer, John. *Washington, Lincoln, Wilson: Three War Statesmen.* Garden City, N.Y.: Doubleday Doran, 1930.

   America in Arms: The Experience of the United States with Military Organization. Washington, D.C.: Infantry Journal, 1943.

Prucha, Francis Paul. *The Sword of the Republic: The United States Army on the Frontier, 1783–1846.* Bloomington: University of Indiana Press, 1969.

Ranson, Edward. "Nelson A. Miles as Commanding General: 1895–1903," *Military Affairs* 29, 4 (Winter 1965–6), 183–9.

"The Endicott Board of 1885–1886 and the Coast Defenses," *Military Affairs* 21, 2 (Summer 1967), 74–84.

"The Investigation of the War Department, 1898–99," *Historian* 38, 1 (November 1971), 78–99.

Reeves, Ira. *Military Education in the United States.* Burlington, Vt.: Free Press, 1914.

Rich, Bennett Milton. *The Presidents and Civil Disorder.* Washington, D.C.: Brookings Institution, 1941.

Riker, William H. *Soldiers of the States: The Role of the National Guard in American Democracy.* Washington, D.C.: Public Affairs Press, 1957.

Semsch, Philip. "Elihu Root and the General Staff," *Military Affairs* 27, 1 (Spring 1963), 16–27.

Shannon, Fred A. *The Organization and Administration of the Union Army, 1860–1865.* Gloucester, Mass.: Peter Smith, 1928.

Smith, Paul Tincher. "Militia of the United States from 1846–1860," *Indiana Magazine of History* 15, 1 (March 1919), 20–47.

Stimson, Henry L., and Bundy, McGeorge. *On Active Service in Peace and War.* New York: Harper and Brothers, 1948.

Taft, Philip. "Violence in American Labor Disputes," *Annals of the American Academy of Political and Social Science* 364 (March 1966), 114–28.

Thian, Raphael D. *Legislative History of the General Staff of the United States from 1775–1901.* Washington, D.C.: Government Printing Office, 1901.

Todd, Frederick. "Our National Guard: An Introduction to Its History," *Military Affairs* 5, 2 (Summer 1941), 77–86, and 5, 3 (Fall 1974), 147–62.

Upham, Cyril B. "Historical Survey of the Militia of Iowa, 1865–1898," *Iowa Journal of History and Politics* 18, 1 (January 1920), 3–93.

Upton, Emory. *The Armies of Asia and Europe.* New York: Appleton, 1878.

The Military Policy of the United States. Washington, D.C.: Government Printing Office, 1904.

Weigley, Russell F. *Towards an American Army: Military Thought from Washington to Marshall.* New York: Columbia University Press, 1962.

History of the United States Army. New York: Macmillan, 1967.

"The Elihu Root Reforms and the Progressive Era," *Military History Symposium* 20 (December 1968), 11–34.

Wilson, Frederick. *Mass Violence in America: Federal Aid in Domestic Disturbances 1787–1903.* New York: Arno Press, 1969.

V. The emergence of national railroad regulation

Adams, Charles Francis, Jr. *The Railroads: Their Origin and Problems.* New York: Putnam, Sons, 1887.

Baker, Newton J. "The Commerce Court: Its Origins, Its Powers and Its Judges," *Yale Law Journal* 20, 7 (May 1911), 555–62.

Benson, Lee. *Merchants, Farmers and Railroads: Railroad Regulation and New York Politics, 1850–1887.* Cambridge, Mass.: Harvard University Press, 1955.

Bernstein, Marver. *Regulating Business by Independent Commission.* Princeton, N.J.: Princeton University Press, 1955.

Bigelow, S. Lawrence, et al. "Henry Carter Adams, 1851–1921," *Journal of Political Economy* 30, 2 (April 1922), 201–11.

Blum, John Morton. *The Republican Roosevelt.* Cambridge, Mass.: Harvard University Press, 1954.

Bryan, James W. "The Railroad Bill and the Commerce Court," *American Political Science Review* 4, 4 (November 1910), 546–54.

Buck, Solon. *The Granger Movement: A Study of Agricultural Organization and Its Political, Economic and Social Manifestations, 1870–1880.* Cambridge, Mass.: Harvard University Press, 1913.

Campbell, E. G. *The Reorganization of the American Railroad System 1893–1900.* New York: Columbia University Press, 1938.

Carson, Robert B. *Main Line to Oblivion: The Disintegration of the New York Railroads in the Twentieth Century.* Port Washington, N.Y.: Kennikat Press, 1971.

   "Railroads and Regulation Revisited: A Note on Problems of Historiography and Ideology," *The Historian* 34, 3 (May 1972), 437–46.

Coats, A. W. "Henry Carter Adams: A Case Study in the Emergence of the Social Sciences in the United States, 1850–1900," *Journal of American Studies* 2, 2 (October 1968), 177–97.

Cochran, Thomas C. *Railroad Leaders, 1845–1890.* Cambridge, Mass.: Harvard University Press, 1953.

Cunningham, William J. *American Railroads: Government Control and Reconstruction Politics.* Chicago: A. W. Shaw, 1922.

Cushman, Robert. *The Independent Regulatory Commissions.* London: Oxford University Press, 1941.

Dix, George E. "The Death of the Commerce Court: A Study in Institutional Weakness," *Journal of American Legal History* 8, 2 (July 1964), 238–60.

Dixon, Frank H. "The Interstate Commerce Act as Amended in 1906," *The Quarterly Journal of Economics* 21 (November 1906), 535–48.

   "The Mann–Elkins Act: Amending the Act to Regulate Commerce," *The Quarterly Journal of Economics* 24, 4 (August 1910), 593–633.

   Railroads and Government: Their Relations in the United States, 1910–1921. New York: Scribners, 1922.

Dorfman, Joseph, ed. *Two Essays by Henry Carter Adams.* New York: Columbia University Press, 1954.

Dorfman, Joseph. *The Economic Mind in American Civilization.* 5 vols. New York: Viking Press, 1959.

Fellmeth, Robert C. *The Interstate Commerce Commission: The Public Interest and the ICC.* New York: Grossman, 1970.

Grodinsky, Julius. *Transcontinental Railway Strategy: A Study of Businessmen.* Philadelphia: University of Pennsylvania Press, 1962.

Hadley, Arthur T. *Railroad Transportation: Its History and Laws.* New York: Putnam, 1885.

"Railroad Business under the Interstate Commerce Act," *The Quarterly Journal of Economics* 3 (January 1889), 170–87.

Hammond, M. B. "Railway Rate Theories of the Interstate Commerce Commission," *The Quarterly Journal of Economics* 25 (November 1910), pp. 1–66; 25 (February 1911), pp. 279–336; 25 (May 1911), pp. 471–538.

Haney, Lewis Henry. *A Congressional History of the Railways in the United States, 1850–1887.* Bulletin of the University of Wisconsin, no. 342. Madison, 1910.

Harbeson, Robert W. "Railroads and Regulation, 1877–1916: Conspiracy or Public Interest?" *Journal of Economic History* 27 (June 1967), 218–39.

"Transport Regulation: A Centennial Evaluation," *ICC Practitioners Journal* 39, 5 (July–August 1972), 628–36.

Hilton, George W. "The Consistency of the Interstate Commerce Act," *Journal of Law and Economics* 19 (October 1966), 87–113.

Hines, Walker D. *War History of American Railroads.* New Haven, Conn.: Yale University Press, 1928.

Hoogenboom, Ari and Olive. *A History of the ICC: From Panacea to Palliative.* New York: Norton, 1976.

Hudson, James F. *The Railways and the Republic.* New York: Harper & Brothers, 1886.

Huntington, Samuel P. "The Marasmus of the ICC: The Commission, The Railroads and the Public Interest," *Yale Law Journal* 61 (April 1952), 467–509.

The Interstate Commerce Commission Fiftieth Anniversary. The George Washington Law Review, 5, 3 (March 1937).

Jones, Alan. "Thomas M. Cooley and the Interstate Commerce Commission: Continuity and Change in the Doctrine of Equal Rights," *Political Science Quarterly* 81, 4 (December 1966), 610–69.

"Thomas M. Cooley and 'Laissez Faire Constitutionalism': A Reconsideration," *Journal of American History* 53, 4 (March 1967), 751–77.

Kerr, K. Austin. *American Railroad Politics, 1914–1920: Rates, Wages and Efficiency.* University of Pittsburgh Press, 1965.

Kirkland, Edward Chase. *Business in the Gilded Age: The Conservative's Balance Sheet.* Madison: University of Wisconsin Press, 1952.

Charles Francis Adams, Jr., 1835–1915: The Patrician at Bay. Cambridge, Mass.: Harvard University Press, 1965.

Kolko, Gabriel. *Railroads and Regulation, 1877–1916.* New York: Norton, 1965.

Kraines, Oscar. "Brandeis' Philosophy of Scientific Management," *Western Political Quarterly* 13, 1 (March 1960), 191–201.

MacAvoy, Paul W. *The Economic Effects of Regulation: The Trunk Line Car-*

tels and the Interstate Commerce Commission Before 1900. Cambridge, Mass.: MIT Press, 1965.

McCain, C. C., ed. *A Compendium of Transportation Theories.* Washington, D.C.: Kensington, 1893.

McFarland, Carl. *Judicial Control of the Federal Trade Commission and the Interstate Commerce Commission, 1920–1930.* Cambridge, Mass.: Harvard University Press, 1933.

Martin, Albro. *Enterprise Denied: Origins of the Decline of American Railroads.* New York: Columbia University Press, 1971.

"The Troubled Subject of Railroad Regulation in the Gilded Age – A Reappraisal," *Journal of American History* 61 (September 1974), 339–71.

Meyer, Hugo Richard. *Government Regulation of Railway Rates.* New York: Macmillan, 1905.

Miller, George. *Railroads and the Granger Laws.* Madison: University of Wisconsin Press, 1971.

Nash, Gerald D. "The Reformer Reformed: John H. Reagan and Railroad Regulation," *Business History Review* 29, 2 (June 1955), 189–97.

"Origins of the Interstate Commerce Act of 1887," *Pennsylvania History* 24 (July 1957), 181–90.

Purcell, Edward, Jr. "Ideas and Interests: Business and the Interstate Commerce Act," *Journal of American History* 54 (December 1967), 561–78.

Reynolds, George G. *The Distribution of Power to Regulate Interstate Carriers Between the Nation and the States.* New York: Columbia University Press, 1928.

Ripley, William Z. "Present Problems in Railway Regulation," *Political Science Quarterly* 27, 3 (September 1912), 428–53.

Railroads: Rates and Regulation. New York: Longmans, Green, 1912.

Railroads: Finance and Organization. New York: Longmans, Green, 1915.

Seligman, R. A. "Railway Tariffs and the Interstate Commerce Law," *Political Science Quarterly* 2 (June 1887), 223–64.

Sharfman, I. L. *The American Railroad Problem: A Study in War and Reconstruction.* New York: Century, 1921.

The Interstate Commerce Commission: A Study in Administrative Law and Procedure. 4 vols. New York: Commonwealth Fund, 1931–1937.

Smalley, Harrison Standish. "Railroad Rate Control," *Publications of the American Economic Association,* third series, 7, 2 (May 1906), 1–145.

Tollefson, A. M. "Judicial Review of the Decisions of the Interstate Commerce Commission," *Minnesota Law Review* 2, 5 (April 1927), 385–421.

Volin, Tazar. "Henry Carter Adams, Critic of Laissez Faire," *Journal of Social Philosophy* 3, 3 (April 1938), 235–56.

Weeks, O. Douglas. "Some Political Ideas of Thomas McIntyre Cooley," *Southwestern Political Science Quarterly* 6, 1 (June 1925), 30–9.

Withers, John L. "The Administrative Theories and Practices of William Howard Taft." Ph.D. diss., University of Chicago, 1956.

Index